Expanding Philosophical Horizons

An Anthology of Nontraditional Writings

Max O. Hallman

Merced College

D1361557

 Wadsworth Publishing Company

I(T)P™ An International Thomson Publishing Company

Belmont . Albany . Bonn . Boston . Cincinnati . Detroit . London . Madrid . Melbourne
Mexico City . New York . Paris . San Francisco . Singapore . Tokyo . Toronto . Washington

Philosophy Editor: *Tammy Goldfeld*
Editorial Assistant: *Kelly Zavislak*
Production Editor: *Karen Garrison*
Managing Designer: *Stephen Rapley*
Print Buyer: *Barbara Britton*
Permissions Editor: *Robert Kauser*
Cover: *Harry Voigt*
Compositor: *Wadsworth Digital Productions*
Printer: *Malloy Lithographing*
Signing Representative: *Joanne Terhaar*

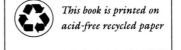

*This book is printed on
acid-free recycled paper*

For more information, contact Wadsworth Publishing Company:

Wadsworth Publishing Company
10 Davis Drive
Belmont, California 94002, USA

International Thomson Publishing Europe
Berkshire House 168-173
High Holborn
London, WC1V 7AA, England

Thomas Nelson Australia
102 Dodds Street
South Melbourne 3205
Victoria, Australia

Nelson Canada
1120 Birchmount Road
Scarborough, Ontario
Canada M1K 5G4

International Thomson Editores
Campos Eliseos 385, Piso 7
Col. Polanco
11560 México D.F. México

International Thomson Publishing GmbH
Königswinterer Strasse 418
53227 Bonn, Germany

International Thomson Publishing Asia
221 Henderson Road
#05-10 Henderson Building
Singapore 0315

International Thomson Publishing Japan
Hirakawacho Kyowa Building, 3F
2-2-1 Hirakawacho
Chiyoda-ku, Tokyo 102, Japan

Library of Congress Cataloging-in-Publication Data
Hallman, Max O.,
    Expanding philosophical horizons : an anthology of nontraditional
writings / Max O. Hallman
        p.   cm.
    Includes bibliographical references
    ISBN 0-534-25308-3
    1. Philosophy—Introductions.   2. Multiculturalism.   I. Title
BD21.H226   1995
100—dc20   94-35096

EXPANDING PHILOSOPHICAL HORIZONS
An Anthology of Nontraditional Writings

For Bobbie, my S.S.S.W.,
who continues to expand my horizons in countless directions,
and for Hannah, Dylan, and Aliena,
whose playfulness and joy protect me from the spirit of gravity.

Contents

Chapter 3: *Knowledge and Truth* 92

Chapter 4: *Ethics* 131

Chapter 5: *Politics*

Chapter 6: *Religion*

Preface

Today in the hallowed halls of higher education, there is a raging dispute over the content of the curriculum. Many scholars, including some from the area of philosophy, are attempting to define and defend a core traditional curriculum, the content of which is determined by appealing to preeminence or some such criterion. In most cases this traditional canon, to use a word that has intentional theological overtones, is decidedly Western, decidedly white, and decidedly male.

Other scholars, also including some from the area of philosophy, have launched an all-out attack on this traditional canon. They not only point out the somewhat arbitrary and subjective criteria that are often used to determine the exact content of the canon, but they also argue that the political import of the canon is to devalue and exclude voices that are non-Western, nonwhite, and nonmale. This critique is accompanied by a call for the rejection (or at least the decentralization) of the traditional canon, along with a subsequent diversification of the curriculum.

As the title of this collection of writings clearly indicates, my own sympathies lie with those scholars who have called for an expansion of the philosophical canon. A large part of my reasoning for believing that expansion is necessary, however, has nothing to do with theoretical concerns or political positions. Rather, my own classes are becoming more and more culturally diverse, and I believe that an expanded philosophical canon will better serve the needs and interests of my students. Yet, this does not mean that the traditional canon must be entirely abandoned. Indeed, as I have found in my own excursions outside the domain of the canon, noncanonical writings can be used to enrich the teaching and discussion of canonical material.

It is with this discovery in mind that I have chosen and organized the selections contained in the present volume. While this anthology could no doubt serve as the primary text (or one of the primary texts) for a class in nontraditional philosophy, it can also be used to complement classes that continue to include study and discussion of writings found in the traditional canon. Indeed, I believe that you will discover what I did—in having students read these selections along with canonical writings, their understanding of traditional texts will be enhanced, and class discussion will be greatly enlivened.

Organization

My goal in this anthology is to present provocative and philosophically significant writings from nontraditional sources. The texts have been selected from many different cultures and perspectives, and they have been taken from ancient as well as modern sources. However, to make the text easier to integrate into existing courses, I have grouped these writings according to traditional philosophical categories, such as self-identity, ethics, and religion. Of course, many of these writings cut across such categories, and my arrangement is certainly not the only possible arrangement of the writings. As with any text, you are free to reorder or reclassify the writings to fit your curricular needs.

Within each chapter I have arranged the selections in what seemed, at least to me, the most logical order. For example in the chapter on self-identity, I begin with three selections that deal with the existence or nonexistence of a substantial self or soul, followed by one selection that discusses the universal nature of being human. I then include three selections dealing with more "particular" aspects of self-identity—gender identity, bodily identity, and racial identity. Selections in the other chapters are also arranged in an order that will facilitate comparisons and contrasts with preceding or succeeding selections.

Features

Since the authors and selections found in this anthology have not generally been included in the traditional canon, it is likely that some of them will not be familiar to those of you who choose to adopt this text. Indeed, one of the main difficulties that often stands in the way of curriculum diversification is that philosophy graduate schools have not usually provided students with a multicultural education. To help remedy this deficiency, and to situate the readings for students using the text, I have included brief biographical or historical sketches before each selection. Also, since many of the selections contain terminology that is not part of the standard Western philosophical vocabulary, I have included an extensive glossary of non-Western and technical terms at the end of the text.

Moreover, to help students better understand what they are reading, I have included introductory summaries for each selection, as well as a set of questions for thought. Some of the questions for thought are intended to help students focus on the more important parts of the text that they are reading; others are intended to stimulate them to think about their own unique experiences in light of the reading. All of these questions should prove useful for class discussion sessions if you include such sessions in your syllabus.

In addition to chapter introductions, I have provided a general introduction to the text. This introduction consists of several short sections that will help orient students to the study of philosophy. One section gives students an account of my own first experiences in a philosophy class. Another section attempts to define philosophy, while a further section provides information on how to get the most out of this text.

Finally, since most philosophy classes require writing, I have included an appendix on how to write philosophically. My goal in this appendix is to offer students useful information on the various stages of successful philosophical writing, from choosing a topic and literary form to editing and proofreading.

Acknowledgments

The publication of this text would not have been possible without the help and encouragement of many people, and I would like to thank everyone who offered advice and support.

Beginning at the beginning, I would like to thank Professor Harold French of the University of South Carolina for first introducing me to non-Western thinking. In the same vein, I would like to thank Professor Michael Zimmerman of Tulane University for opening up my horizons to other nontraditional philosophical sources.

I would also like to offer gratitude to Dr. Rosalie Otero of the University of New Mexico and Dr. Susan Kilgore of Washington State University for their work as co-chairs of the National Collegiate Honors Council Committee on Women and Minorities, and for their positive feedback on this project. Similarly, I would like to thank Professor Bill Moldrup of Merced College for his positive feedback and for his valuable insights into the intricacies of textbook publishing.

Gratitude is also due to Billy Wilson at Phi Theta Kappa for putting together a wonderful summer institute devoted to unity and diversity issues, and to Billy, Mike Watson, and Rod Risley for allowing me to serve as seminar leader at this institute.

Thanks also to Dr. Gregory Rienzo, past president of Merced Justice and Peace, for introducing me to the philosophical theology of Gustavo Gutierrez, and to Professor Robert McAfee Brown for suggesting the Gutierrez selection included in this volume.

This text could not have been completed in a timely fashion without the aid of the library staff at Merced College. Special thanks go to Susan Walsh, library director, and to Ed Brush and Dee Near, research librarians. Their help in tracking down texts and biographical information was invaluable.

At Wadsworth, I am especially grateful to Joanne Terhaar, who first suggested that I submit the proposal for this text and who provided continuous support during the review and publication process, and to Tammy Goldfeld, who no doubt represents the ideal editor—enthusiastic, knowledgeable, and persistent. I would also like to thank Bob Kauser and Kelly Zavislak, for cheerfully and promptly providing me with information and forms whenever I called, and Karen Garrison for flawlessly guiding the text through the various phases of production.

In addition, I am indebted to the following reviewers for their insightful comments and helpful suggestions: Raymond A. Belliotti, SUNY, Fredonia; Michael McMahon, College of the Canyons; Shelley M. Park, University of Central Florida; and Sheila Ruth, Southern Illinois University.

Lastly, I would like to thank my students for making the teaching of philosophy a joyous experience, and Jodi Frade for teaching me that musical-poetical-bodily dialogue is not just an empty concept.

Introduction

Beginning in Philosophy

How does one begin an introductory book in philosophy? Perhaps an appropriate way to begin is by telling you a little about my first experiences in a philosophy class. On the first day of class, I remember the professor telling us that philosophy begins in wonder. Although initially I wasn't too sure what he meant, after being in the class for a week I decided that the statement was a perfect description of philosophy. Indeed, at that point not only did I wonder what the heck was going on, but I also wondered why in the world I had signed up for the class in the first place. In high school I had studied math, biology, and English, and thus I pretty much knew what to expect in those classes. But philosophy was entirely new—new questions, new terminology, a new way of thinking. So, as with any other new environment, it took me a few weeks to orient myself to my surroundings.

One of the problems was that even defining philosophy seemed difficult. The professor told us that the word *philosophy* was derived from two Greek words, *philein* and *sophia*, which translate as "love" and "wisdom," respectively. He also told us that the ancient Greek philosopher Pythagoras first used the term. When asked whether he was a wise man, Pythagoras reportedly replied that he was a "lover of wisdom." Being a typical nineteen-year-old, I had no problem with the idea of being a lover, but I wasn't so certain about the wisdom part. I knew that I loved my mother, my girlfriend, and even my car, but I wasn't sure that wisdom was something that one could love.

Another problem was that the philosophers we were reading had a major difficulty—they didn't seem to be able to agree on anything. And given the large and obscure words that they often used, I could easily understand why. How can

1

you agree with someone if you aren't exactly sure of what he or she is saying? So, there I was in my first philosophy class—confused, confused, and more confused.

Given this initial reaction, you may wonder why I stayed in the class. You may be even more bewildered by the fact that I decided to devote my life to teaching this perplexing stuff to others. Why exactly does one become a philosopher, a lover of wisdom? I believe that the answer to this question, at least in my own case, is the same as the answer that Joseph Campbell gave to Bill Moyers in an episode of the wonderful PBS series "The Power of Myth." When Moyers asked Campbell why he had devoted his life to the study of mythology, Campbell replied that he didn't believe in studying anything just because people said that it ought to be studied. Campbell said that, on the contrary, you ought to study mythology or anything else only if it "catches you." Well, in that beginning philosophy class many years ago, I was caught. For although philosophy was definitely confusing, I noticed that it dealt with those crucial questions of human existence that most intrigued me: Who am I? What can I know? What is truth? What is real? How ought I to act? What is justice? Am I truly free? Does God exist? What happens to me when I die?

In this book, which will introduce many of you to philosophy, I have gathered together a varied assortment of nontraditional writings that deal with many of these important questions of human existence. Although you may not (indeed cannot) agree with all of the authors' viewpoints, I believe that you will find each of these selections to be thought provoking and personally significant. Of course, some of the selections will no doubt prove to be challenging reading, and you may initially find yourself as confused as I was when I first began studying philosophy. But as you read the selections carefully and discuss them in class, I believe that this initial confusion will dissipate. For some of you the confusion may suddenly disappear; for others the process will be more like an early-morning fog that is gradually burned away by the sun. Once your initial confusion dissipates, you may find yourself caught by the study of philosophy—as I was years ago, and as I still am today.

Toward a Definition of Philosophy

In the preceding section, I mentioned that one of my first impressions of philosophy was that philosophers seemed to disagree about everything. What may surprise you, however, is that philosophers can't even agree on an exact definition of philosophy. While we can trace the origin of the term to the Greek words that translate as the "love of wisdom," it seems that this definition has been interpreted in many different ways throughout the history of philosophy. Some philosophers believe that wisdom is best loved or attained through the use of reason; others tell us that reason is useless for loving or attaining wisdom. Some philosophers see philosophy as being akin to religion or morality or even art; others see it as being more akin to science. Some philosophers believe that philosophy is (and ought to be) purely speculative, that is, divorced from everyday or practical concerns; others tell us that philosophy is the most practical of studies.

Fortunately, one does not need to have a precise definition of philosophy to begin studying it. However, since I am writing a book that will acquaint many of you with philosophy for the first time, I believe that I owe you at least an attempt at a definition. Of course, given the controversial nature of this task, my definition is certainly not the only way of defining philosophy; nor does it necessarily cover all of the ways in which philosophy has been practiced.

In my own classes, after telling students about the honorific definition of philosophy derived from the ancient Greeks (*philein* + *sophia*), I offer the three following statements in an attempt to arrive at a definition:

1. Philosophy is a distinctive way of thinking.
2. Philosophy is a kind of conversation.
3. Philosophy, if taken seriously, is an agent of change.

Of course, each of these statements requires further discussion and thought. What kind of thinking is philosophy, and how does it differ from other types of thinking? What do I mean by saying that philosophy is a "kind of conversation"? Finally, in what ways does philosophy serve as an agent of change?

Let us begin with the first statement. One can distinguish types of thinking in at least two ways: One can claim that the content of one kind of thinking differs from the content of another, or one can claim that the actual process of thinking differs in the one case from other cases. The following concrete examples should make this distinction clearer. Much of our thinking is devoted to resolving simple practical problems in life, problems such as what we're going to have for lunch. In this kind of thinking, we look at several factors, weigh them, and come to a decision. If the problem is what to have for lunch, we might consider how hungry we are, how much time we have, how much money we have, and the locations of potential sources of food. At other times, however, we may be called on to solve some rather abstract algebraic problem (for many of us, this occurs only when we are enrolled in an algebra class). It should be obvious that the content of our thinking in this case differs greatly from the content in the first case (we are thinking about algebraic equations and not food). It should also be clear that the kind of thinking required to do an abstract algebraic equation differs from the kind of thinking required to solve simple, practical problems of everyday life. One way of stating this difference is to say that solving algebra problems requires thinking at a higher level of abstraction than does solving simple, practical problems of everyday life.

In claiming that philosophy is a distinctive kind of thinking, what I am saying is that philosophical thinking often differs from other kinds of thinking in both content and process. As you read the articles in this text, you will no doubt see that philosophical thinking deals with things that many types of thinking never touch. Unlike most other disciplines, philosophy deals with those large but extremely significant problems of human life—problems such as the nature of self-identity and the nature of ultimate reality.

This difference in content is not the only difference between philosophical thinking and other ways of thinking. The way in which philosophers approach these problems seems to differ from other ways of dealing with problems. The German philosopher Martin Heidegger says that the difference is that philosophers concern themselves with meditative thinking (or at least they ought to), whereas other types of problems require the use of calculative thinking. The difference between these two types of thinking is that calculative thinking is devoted to computing possibilities, to dealing with questions that begin with the word *how*, while meditative thinking is devoted to contemplating meaning, to dealing with questions that begin with the word *why*. Although not all philosophers would accept Heidegger's distinction between meditative thinking and calculative thinking, or agree with him that the task of philosophy is to think meditatively, most would agree that philosophical thinking differs from other types of thinking in process as well as content.

The second statement offered above, namely that philosophy is a kind of conversation, gives us another way of attempting to define philosophy. By saying that philosophy is a kind of conversation, I mean that philosophy provides us with a language that allows us to converse with others about many of the really important topics in our lives. Thus in one sense, this is just another way of distinguishing the content of philosophical thinking from the content of most other types of thinking. However, by identifying philosophy as a kind of conversation, the emphasis is placed on communicating with others. Whereas you could think philosophically while alone in your room, a genuine conversation requires more than one participant. What philosophy provides is a vocabulary and various strategies of meaningful dialogue that will allow you to communicate with others on levels that may not now be possible. The study of philosophy not only should provide you with a new set of terms, it also should help you to clarify your ideas and to express them in a more coherent fashion.

Finally, turning to the third statement above, that philosophy, if taken seriously, is an agent of change, what I mean to suggest is that the study of philosophy ought to make a difference in your life. Some of you may recall the remark that the musician Sting made about music at the Live Aid concert: "The purpose of music is not merely to entertain; the purpose of music is to change the world" (rough paraphrase). Of course, if you had been familiar with the history of philosophy when you heard this remark, you would have recognized that this statement was very similar to a statement that Karl Marx made about philosophy in the nineteenth century: "The philosophers have only *interpreted* the world differently; the point is, however, to *change* it." What Sting is saying about music and what Marx is saying about philosophy is that music and philosophy should not be mere pastimes but should help to change the world, it is hoped for the better.

Of course, at least in the case of philosophy, some of you may be doubtful about the accuracy of this claim. This would be especially true if you were familiar with some of the typical stereotypes about philosophers and philosophical thinking. One of the enduring stereotypes of philosophers, which can be traced back at least to the ancient Greek comedian Aristophanes, is that philosophers have their heads in the clouds and thus get nothing done. A recent example of this stereotype used for comic purposes was the Monty Python skit depicting Greek and German philosophers playing against one another in a soccer game. All of the philosophers stand around rubbing their chins and contemplating who knows what while the soccer ball rests in the middle of the field. Finally, one of the Greek philosophers (I believe it was Socrates) comes to the conclusion that he should kick the ball. After reaching this decision, he scores easily while the German philosophers continue to rub their chins.

While this stereotype is humorous (even philosophers with a sense of humor find it to be so), it does not accurately reflect the true nature of philosophy. Philosophers have almost always been interested in helping to initiate social or individual change. In the West, philosophers often defend themselves against this stereotype by pointing to the fact that Aristotle was the tutor of Alexander the Great, or to the fact that modern philosophers such as Simone de Beauvoir, Bertrand Russell, and Jean-Paul Sartre (among others) worked for social change by taking to the streets and participating in protests and demonstrations. Outside the Western tradition, we have the equally important examples of the Chinese philosophers, such as Confucius and Mencius, who attempted to implement their political theories by becoming active in court life. Even the Buddha, who was more interested in personal or individual change than in social change, spent a large portion of his life traveling throughout India, delivering his message of self-transformation.

Of course, when I say that philosophy is an agent of change, I am not claiming that the study of philosophy will radically transform the course of history, or even that it will necessarily effect wide-ranging changes in the course of your life. What I am claiming, however, is that if you take the study of philosophy seriously, if you carefully read and think about the selections in this text, the you that emerges from this class should be somewhat different from the you that entered it.

How to Get the Most Out of This Text

I have written this text with you, the student, in mind. Two of my main criteria for selecting writings were readability and the probable level of student response. That is, I wanted to find writings that raised issues of importance to you and that were not extremely difficult to read. As I suggested in the preceding section, philosophical writings often use unfamiliar terminology (an unflattering word for this is *jargon*), but I have tried to find writings that minimize the use of such terminology. However, since several of the selections in this book are taken from non-Western sources, it is inevitable that some of the terms will be "foreign" to you. For this reason, I have included a glossary at the back of the text that contains definitions of the important non-Western and technical terms found in the selections.

I have also provided general introductions for each chapter, as well as introductions for each selection. The chapter introductions orient you to the topic covered by the chapter and identify the principal questions discussed in the chapter. The selection introductions give you biographical information about the authors, as well as historical information for some of the more ancient writings. These introductions also contain a summary of the following selection, and several questions for thought related to it. I suggest that you quickly read the questions for thought prior to reading the selection, and that you read and think about them more carefully immediately after reading the selection. As you will see, some of these questions deal with the content of the reading, but many more of them are intended to help you relate the reading to your own experience. Finally, I have included an appendix on writing philosophically that should help you with the paper or papers that you may have been assigned. This appendix is arranged sequentially, and it is intended to provide you with tips on many different components of successful philosophical writing.

Self-Identity

1

How many times in your life have you been told to "just be yourself"? Or perhaps you've heard someone say, "I'm not myself today." Most of the time we take these statements at face value without giving them much thought. I am about to go to a job interview, and my mother tells me to be myself. Translation: "Act naturally and don't be pretentious." Or my best friend, who is normally a whiz at basketball, can't even hit the rim. When I ask her what's wrong, she says, "I'm just not myself today." Translation: "She's feeling ill, or she's worried about the philosophy exam she just took." I don't give her statement much more thought unless, of course, I'm choosing up sides for a game.

However, at some point in your life—perhaps because you're not *yourself* that day—you may pause and think about those statements. What does it mean to "just be *yourself*"? And how can you not be yourself today, or any other day for that matter? When this occurs, you've entered the strange and sometimes frustrating land of philosophical reflection. More specifically, in raising these particular questions, you have journeyed to an especially desolate path in the land of philosophical reflection, a path known as the search for self-identity.

At this point I know that some of you are saying, "Is this guy for real? The land of philosophical reflection? The path of the search for self-identity? I've never been there, and I have absolutely no desire to go. Besides, there's a new episode of my favorite show on the tube, a new kill-all-the-aliens-with-karate-chops-and-nuclear-weapons video game at the arcade, a rock concert at the arena, and a new action movie at the theater. So who has time for the land of philosophical reflection or the path of the search for self-identity?"

What can I say to all that? I can tell you, as I do my own students, that you ought to think about these things because some day you might be kidnapped by a mad philosopher who will tie you to a chair and refuse to let you go until you satisfactorily answer his or her questions about the true nature of your self-identity. More seriously, I can tell you that, as a human being with the capacity for thought, you are destined to enter the land of philosophical reflection and to travel down the path of the search for self-identity, whether you like it or not. In fact, even cartoon characters (consider Popeye's oft-repeated line, "I yam what I yam") and gods (consider Yahweh's response to Moses' question about his name, "I AM; that is who I am") are not immune from reflecting on their identities.

Fortunately, given the desolate nature of the path of the search for self-identity, we are not forced to walk this path alone. The history of philosophy is filled with characters who have undertaken this journey before us. In Western philosophy, we have the wonderful example of Socrates who, being guided by the oracular saying "Know thyself," devoted much of his life to philosophical reflection. In fact, we are told that when given the choice of renouncing his philosophical principles or dying, Socrates chose death. In Eastern philosophy, we have the equally wonderful example of Siddhartha. Siddhartha, being of royal blood, was born into a life of luxury, filled with political power, great wealth, and hundreds of dancing girls. However, he renounced all this in the quest for self-knowledge, a quest that eventually led him to the Bo tree and the attainment of Nirvana (blessedness). From this moment on, he became known as the Buddha (the Enlightened One).

In addition to the stories of these and other philosophical "heroes," we have available to us a tremendous range of writings that deal with various aspects of the question of self-identity. Indeed, as you begin your own journey down the path of the search for self-identity, you will find, as others have before you, that the main path, which is marked by the general question "Who am I?" quickly divides into many other paths marked by many other questions. These other questions include, Do I have an enduring self or soul? If so, what is the nature of this enduring self or soul? Is there such a thing as a universal or basic human nature? Or does the nature of being human change with time and place? How important is my body in determining my self-identity? How important is my gender or race in determining my self-identity? To what extent is my identity determined by others, and to what extent is it self-created?

In this chapter, I have gathered several writings, from various times and cultures, that deal with some of these questions concerning self-identity. The first two, which are taken from the sacred writings of ancient India, deal mainly with the question of whether we have an enduring self or soul. As you will see from your reading, the answer given to this question in one of the writings differs greatly from the answer given in the other. The third selection, written by the modern Argentinian author Jorge Luis Borges, consists of two playful "parables" that question the possibility of achieving a unified self-identity. Put another way, Borges suggests that if someone tells you to "Be yourself," he or she doesn't really understand the nature of human existence. The fourth selection, which was written in ancient China, deals with the universal nature of being human. Mencius, the author, gives us one possible picture—a very positive one at that—of what it is to be human.

While the first four selections deal principally with the broader or more general questions of whether there is an enduring self or soul, or whether there is a universal human nature, the final three writings deal with the narrower or more specific questions of gender, bodily, and racial identity. (In philosophy, saying that a question is narrower or more specific does not necessarily mean that it is less important, or even that it will be easier to answer.) Simone de Beauvoir, a modern French philosopher, raises the question of what it is to be a woman as opposed to a man, while arguing that women have usually been portrayed as being inferior to men in traditional Western philosophy, psychology, and religion. Elizabeth Spelman, a modern North American philosopher, looks at the way the body has often been devalued in Western culture, and argues that this devaluation of the body has important social and political consequences. Finally, Naomi Zack, who currently teaches philosophy at the State University of New York, questions the concept of race and asks what it means to be of mixed race—from a personal as well as a cultural perspective.

Taken together, these selections will raise many of the questions that have been associated with the philosophical problem of self-identity. They will also show you how a small number of thoughtful people have attempted to answer them. But, as I have already suggested in the Introduction, the goal of studying philosophy is not merely to learn what others have had to say on some issue of philosophical importance. Rather, one of the principal goals of studying philosophy is to develop and clarify your own beliefs about the issue in question. When you are reading these various writings that deal with the nature of self-identity, ask yourself the following questions: What is the author telling me about who I am? Does what the author says agree with what I already believe about my own self-identity? If not, does the author give me any good reasons for changing my views? In raising such questions as you read the selections, you will discover that the path of the search for self-identity may be desolate, but it is nevertheless personally fulfilling. You may also discover, as I have, that at times reflecting on the nature of your self-identity can be even more entertaining than a television show, a rock concert, or the latest action film, and even more exciting than zapping all the aliens with karate chops and nuclear weapons.

A Dialogue with Death   1.1

FROM THE UPANISHADS

The Upanishads make up the fourth section of each of the Vedas, the most sacred writings of the religion of Hinduism. According to scholars, the origins of Hinduism can be traced to the period between 1750 and 1200 B.C.E., when Aryans migrated into the Indus valley. While there is some dispute as to the dates of the composition of the Vedas, it is generally agreed that there was a time span of several hundred years between the writing of the most ancient part of the Vedas, the hymns or *mantras*, and the writing of the Upanishads. The latter, which consist of a collection of philosophical reflections from the classical period of Hinduism, were perhaps begun as early as 900 B.C.E. Like the selection from the *Katha Upanishad*, which is reprinted below, many of these philosophical reflections are written in dialogue form.

Whereas earlier Hindu writings had assumed the existence of many gods, the Upanishads generally affirm the existence of one supreme god and reality, namely, *Brahman*. Also, whereas earlier writings had emphasized religious ritual and sacrifice as the principal way of relating to the gods, the Upanishads suggest that a type of philosophical reflection or meditation (*Yoga*) is the most appropriate spiritual or religious path. Indeed, one of the main themes of the Upanishads, which is stated in the selection that follows, is that through the practice of Yoga you will eventually discover your enduring, eternal self, your *Atman*, and realize that your Atman is really identical to Brahman. In other words, this selection suggests that each of us has an eternal self that is one with the divine nature, and that it is only illusion or false knowledge (*maya*) that prevents us from recognizing the truth of this sameness or identity. Of course, one of the assumptions of this writing, as of Hindu writings in general, is that it will take you many lifetimes to move beyond false knowledge and illusion, and thus your Atman will be reincarnated many times into diverse physical forms. However, this writing promises that once you truly discover your Atman and recognize its sameness with Brahman, you will escape this cycle of birth, life, death, and rebirth, and you will become "immortal and pure."

Questions for Thought

1. What are the two paths described by the writer, and what does each of them offer?
2. What does the writer mean by Atman? How does the concept of Atman compare with and/or differ from your own views concerning your self-identity?
3. What does the writer mean by Brahman? Is the notion of Brahman compatible with your own thoughts about God or divinity? Why or why not?
4. Do you think that you have lived an earthly life before this one or that you will live an earthly life after this one? Would you like to be reborn into another physical form?
5. What do you think of the effectiveness of structuring this writing as a dialogue with death?

Nachiketas: When a man dies, this doubt arises: some say "he is" and some say "he is not." Teach me the truth.

Death: Even the gods had this doubt in times of old; for mysterious is the law of life and death. Ask for another boon. Release me from this.

Nachiketas: This doubt indeed arose even to the gods, and you say, O Death, that it is difficult to understand; but no greater teacher than you can explain it, and there is no other boon so great as this.

Death: Take horses and gold and cattle and elephants; choose sons and grandsons that shall

From *The Upanishads*, translated by Juan Mascaró. © 1965 Juan Mascaró.
Reprinted by permission of Penguin Books Ltd.

live a hundred years. Have vast expanses of land, and live as many years as you desire.

Or choose another gift that you think equal to this, and enjoy it with wealth and long life. Be a ruler of this vast earth. I will grant you all your desires.

Ask for any wishes in the world of mortals, however hard to obtain. To attend on you I will give you fair maidens with chariots and musical instruments. But ask me not, Nachiketas, the secrets of death.

Nachiketas: All these pleasures pass away, O End of all! They weaken the power of life. And indeed how short is all life! Keep thy horses and dancing and singing.

Man cannot be satisfied with wealth. Shall we enjoy wealth with you in sight? Shall we live whilst you are in power? I can only ask for the boon I have asked.

When a mortal here on earth has felt his own immortality, could he wish for a long life of pleasures, for the lust of deceitful beauty?

Solve then the doubt as to the great beyond. Grant me the gift that unveils the mystery. This is the only gift Nachiketas can ask.

Death: There is the path of joy, and there is the path of pleasure. Both attract the soul. Who follows the first comes to good; who follows pleasure reaches not the End.

The two paths lie in front of man. Pondering on them, the wise man chooses the path of joy; the fool takes the path of pleasure.

You have pondered, Nachiketas, on pleasures and you have rejected them. You have not accepted that chain of possessions wherewith men bind themselves and beneath which they sink.

There is the path of wisdom and the path of ignorance. They are far apart and lead to different ends. You are, Nachiketas, a follower of the path of wisdom: many pleasures tempt you not.

Abiding in the midst of ignorance, thinking themselves wise and learned, fools go aimlessly hither and thither, like blind led by the blind.

What lies beyond life shines not to those who are childish, or careless, or deluded by wealth. "This is the only world: there is no other," they say; and thus they go from death to death.

Not many hear of him; and of those not many reach him. Wonderful is he who can teach about him; and wise is he who can be taught. Wonderful is he who knows him when taught.

He cannot be taught by one who has not reached him; and he cannot be reached by much thinking. The way to him is through a Teacher who has seen him: He is higher than the highest thoughts, in truth above all thought.

This sacred knowledge is not attained by reasoning; but it can be given by a true Teacher. As your purpose is steady you have found him. May I find another pupil like you!

I know that treasures pass away and that the Eternal is not reached by the transient. I have thus laid the fire of sacrifice of Nachiketas, and by burning in it the transient I have reached the Eternal.

Before your eyes have been spread, Nachiketas, the fulfillment of desire, the dominion of the world, the eternal reward of ritual, the shore where there is no fear, the greatness of fame and boundless spaces. With strength and wisdom you have renounced them all.

When the wise rests his mind in contemplation on our God beyond time, who invisibly dwells in the mystery of things and in the heart of man, then he rises above pleasures and sorrow.

When a man has heard and has understood and, finding the essence, reaches the Inmost, then he finds joy in the Source of joy. Nachiketas is a house open for thy Atman, thy God.

Nachiketas: Tell me what you see beyond right and wrong, beyond what is done or not done, beyond past and future.

Death: I will tell you the Word that all the Vedas glorify, all self-sacrifice expresses, all sacred studies and holy life seek. That Word is OM.

That Word is the everlasting Brahman: that Word is the highest End. When that great Word is known, one is great in the heaven of Brahman.

Atman, the Spirit of vision, is never born and never dies. Before him there was nothing, and he is ONE for evermore. Never-born and eternal, beyond times gone or to come, he does not die when the body dies.

If the slayer thinks that he kills, and if the slain thinks that he dies, neither knows the ways of truth. The Eternal in man cannot kill: the Eternal in man cannot die.

Concealed in the heart of all beings is the Atman, the Spirit, the Self; smaller than the smallest atom, greater than the vast spaces. The man who surrenders his human will leaves sorrows behind, and beholds the glory of the Atman by the grace of the Creator.

Resting, he wanders afar; sleeping, he goes everywhere. Who else but my Self can know that God of joy and of sorrows?

When the wise realize the omnipresent Spirit, who rests invisible in the visible and permanent in the impermanent, then they go beyond sorrow.

Not through much learning is the Atman reached, not through the intellect and sacred teaching. It is reached by the chosen of him—because they choose him. To his chosen the Atman reveals his glory.

Not even through deep knowledge can the Atman be reached, unless evil ways are abandoned, and there is rest in the senses, concentration in the mind and peace in one's heart.

Who knows in truth where he is? The majesty of his power carries away priests and warriors, and death itself is carried away.

In the secret high place of the heart there are two beings who drink the wine of life in the world of truth. Those who know Brahman, those who keep the five sacred fires and those who light the three-fold fire of Nachiketas call them "light" and "shade."

May we light the sacred fire of Nachiketas, the bridge to cross to the other shore where there is no fear, the supreme everlasting Spirit!

Know the Atman as Lord of a chariot; and the body as the chariot itself. Know that reason is the charioteer; and the mind indeed is the reins.

The horses, they say, are the senses; and the paths are the objects of sense. When the soul becomes one with the mind and the senses he is called "one who has joys and sorrows."

He who has not right understanding and whose mind is never steady is not the ruler of his life, like a bad driver with wild horses.

But he who has right understanding and whose mind is ever steady is the ruler of his life, like a good driver with well-trained horses.

He who has not right understanding, is careless and never pure, reaches not the End of the journey; but wanders on from death to death.

But he who has understanding, is careful and ever pure, reaches the End of the journey, from which he never returns.

The man whose chariot is driven by reason, who watches and holds the reins of his mind, reaches the End of the journey, the supreme everlasting Spirit.

Beyond the senses are their objects, and beyond the objects is the mind. Beyond the mind is pure reason, and beyond reason is the Spirit in man.

Beyond the Spirit in man is the Spirit of the universe, and beyond is Purusha, the Spirit Supreme. Nothing is beyond Purusha: He is the End of the path.

The light of the Atman, the Spirit, is invisible, concealed in all beings. It is seen by the seers of the subtle, when their vision is keen and is clear.

The wise should surrender speech in mind, mind in the knowing self, the knowing self in the Spirit of the universe, and the Spirit of the universe in the Spirit of peace.

Awake, arise! Strive for the Highest, and be in the Light! Sages say the path is narrow and difficult to tread, narrow as the edge of a razor.

The Atman is beyond sound and form, without touch and taste and perfume. It is eternal, unchangeable, and without beginning or end: indeed, above reasoning. When consciousness of the Atman manifests itself, man becomes free from the jaws of death. . . .

I will now speak to you of the mystery of the eternal Brahman; and of what happens to the soul after death.

The soul may go to the womb of a mother and thus obtain a new body. It even may go into trees or plants, according to its previous wisdom and work. There is a Spirit who is awake in our sleep and creates the wonder of dreams. He is Brahman, the Spirit of Light, who in truth is called the Immortal. All the worlds rest on that Spirit and beyond him no one can go. . . .

The whole universe comes from him and his life burns through the whole universe. In his power is the majesty of thunder. Those who know him have found immortality.

From fear of him fire burns, and from fear of him the sun shines. From fear of him the clouds and the winds, and death itself, move on their way.

If one sees him in this life before the body passes away, one is free from bondage; but if not, one is born and dies again in new worlds and new creations.

Brahman is seen in a pure soul as in a mirror clear, and also in the Creator's heaven as clear as light; but in the land of shades as remembrance of dreams, and in the world of spirits as reflections in trembling waters.

When the wise man knows that the material senses come not from the Spirit, and that their waking and sleeping belong to their own nature, then he grieves no more.

Beyond the senses is the mind, and beyond mind is reason, its essence. Beyond reason is the Spirit in man, and beyond this is the Spirit of the universe, the evolver of all.

And beyond is Purusha, all-pervading, beyond definitions. When a mortal knows him, he attains liberation and reaches immortality.

His form is not in the field of vision: no one sees him with mortal eyes. He is seen by a pure heart and by a mind and thoughts that are pure. Those who know him attain life immortal.

When the five senses and the mind are still, and reason itself rests in silence, then begins the Path supreme.

This calm steadiness of the senses is called Yoga. Then one should become watchful, because Yoga comes and goes.

Words and thoughts cannot reach him and he cannot be seen by the eye. How can he then be perceived except by him who says "He is"?

In the faith of "He is" his existence must be perceived, and he must be perceived in his essence. When he is perceived as "He is," then shines forth the revelation of his essence.

When all desires that cling to the heart are surrendered, then a mortal becomes immortal, and even in this world he is one with Brahman.

When all the ties that bind the heart are unloosened, then a mortal becomes immortal. This is the sacred teaching.

One hundred and one subtle ways come from the heart. One of them rises to the crown of the head. This is the way that leads to immortality; the others lead to different ends.

Always dwelling within all beings is the Atman, the Purusha, the Self, a little flame in the heart. Let one with steadiness withdraw him from the body even as an inner stem is withdrawn from its sheath. Know this pure immortal light; know in truth this pure immortal light.

Epilogue: And Nachiketas learnt the supreme wisdom taught by the god of after-life, and he learnt the whole teaching of inner-union, of Yoga. Then he reached Brahman, the Spirit Supreme, and became immortal and pure. So in truth will anyone who knows his Atman, his higher Self.

The Questions of King Milinda on the Self

FROM THE BUDDHIST SCRIPTURES

The religion of Buddhism was founded in North India in the sixth century B.C.E. According to Buddhist teaching, the founder of this religion was a man named Siddhartha of the Gautama clan, the son of a minor raja or ruler of ancient India. Although he reportedly was raised amid splendor and luxury, Siddhartha became dissatisfied with his life when he discovered the pain and suffering that seemed to essentially characterize human existence. After becoming aware of sickness, old age, and death, Siddhartha renounced his worldly goods, left his family, and embarked on a journey in search of spiritual enlightenment. He first sought enlightenment through the study of traditional Hindu texts, and then by practicing an extreme form of asceticism. Finding both of these avenues to be fruitless, Siddhartha reportedly sat under the Bo tree for forty days and forty nights. During this time, he engaged in intense meditation and finally attained enlightenment. From that time forward, Siddhartha became known as the Buddha, the Awakened or Enlightened One. After attaining enlightenment, the Buddha spent the remaining years of his life teaching his religious insights to others.

The Buddha's followers organized themselves into a monastic order, or *Sangha*, and the monks continued to disseminate and expand on the Buddha's teachings. The following selection is taken from one of the many Buddhist sacred scriptures. It is written in the form of a dialogue between the Buddhist monk Nagasena and the half-Greek king Milinda.

Although the literary form of this selection is similar to that of the preceding one, the basic philosophical claims differ greatly. Whereas Death told Nachiketas that his identity consisted of an enduring, eternal self or Atman, the Buddhist monk Nagasena tells King Milinda that he has no enduring self at all. This Buddhist doctrine is appropriately labeled *anatman*, for the term *anatman* literally means being without an Atman or soul. As you might expect, King Milinda is astounded at this suggestion. However, Nagasena uses various means, including an analogy with a chariot, to eventually convince the king of the truth of this doctrine. The main conclusion of the dialogue is that human existence consists of constant change or continuous process, which excludes any possibility of fixed identity.

Given that Buddhists deny the existence of an Atman or enduring self, it might seem to you that they would also have to renounce the Hindu doctrine of reincarnation. This, however, is not the case. In fact, Nagasena uses several other analogies to suggest that there is a causal connection that ties one incarnation to the next. This causal connection, according to Nagasena and Buddhists in general, is sufficient to explain the possibility of reincarnation, even though there is no soul or fixed identity passed from one incarnation into the next.

Questions for Thought

1. Would you agree with Nagasena that you have no enduring self or soul? Why or why not?
2. Assuming that you do not have an enduring self or soul, what makes your identity different from that of your best friend?
3. What is the point of the chariot analogy? Do you think that this analogy works?
4. Do you think that you are the same person now as you were when you were a child? Why or why not?
5. Do you agree with Nagasena's claim that the doctrine of reincarnation makes sense even without the assumption of an enduring self or soul? Are Nagasena's analogies adequate to convince you of this point?
6. If you were required to write a philosophy paper, would you write it in dialogue form? Why or why not?

Book II, Chapter 1, Section 1

NOW MILINDA THE KING WENT UP TO WHERE the venerable Nagasena was, and addressed him with the greetings and compliments of friendship and courtesy, and took his seat respectfully apart. And Nagasena reciprocated his courtesy, so that the heart of the king was propitiated.

And Milinda began by asking, "How is your Reverence known, and what, Sir, is your name?"

"I am known as Nagasena, O king, and it is by that name that my brethren in the faith address me. But although parents, O king, give such a name as Nagasena . . . , yet this, Sire . . . is only a generally understood term, a designation in common use. For there is no permanent individuality (no soul) involved in the matter."

Then Milinda called upon the Yonakas and the brethren to witness: "This Nagasena says there is no permanent individuality (no soul) implied in his name. Is it now even possible to approve him in that?" And turning to Nagasena, he said: "If . . . there be no permanent individuality (no soul) involved in the matter, who is it, pray, who gives to you members of the Order your robes and food and lodging and necessaries for the sick? Who is it who enjoys such things when given? Who is it who lives a life of righteousness? Who is it who devotes himself to meditation? Who is it who attains the goal of the Excellent Way, to the Nirvana of Arahatship? And who is it who destroys living creatures? Who is it who takes what is not his own? Who is it who lives an evil life of worldly lusts, who speaks lies, who drinks strong drink, who (in a word) commits any one of the five sins which work out their bitter fruit even in this life? If that be so there is neither merit nor demerit; there is neither doer nor causer of good or evil deeds; there is neither fruit nor result of good or evil Karma.—If, most reverend Nagasena, we are to think that were a man to kill you there would be no murder, then it follows that there are no real masters or teachers in your Order, and that your ordinations are void.—You tell me that your brethren in the Order are in the habit of addressing you as Nagasena. Now what is that Nagasena? Do you mean to say that the hair is Nagasena?"

"I don't say that, great king."

"Or the hairs on the body, perhaps?"

"Certainly not."

"Or is it the nails, the teeth, the skin, the flesh, the nerves, the bones, the marrow, the kidneys, the heart, the liver, the abdomen, the spleen, the lungs, the larger intestines, the lower intestines, the stomach, the feces, the bile, the phlegm, the pus, the blood, the sweat, the fat, the tears, the serum, the saliva, the mucus, the oil that lubricates the joints, the urine, or the brain, or any or all of these, that is Nagasena?"

And to each of these he answered no.

"Is it the outward form then that is Nagasena, or the sensations, or the ideas, or . . . the constituent elements of character, or the consciousness, that is Nagasena?"

And to each of these also he answered no.

"Then is it all these Skandhas combined that are Nagasena?"

"No! great king."

"But is there anything outside the five Skandhas that is Nagasena?"

And still he answered no.

"Then thus, ask as I may, I can discover no Nagasena. Nagasena is a mere empty sound. Who then is the Nagasena that we see before us? It is a falsehood that your reverence has spoken, an untruth!'"

And the venerable Nagasena said to Milinda the king: "You, Sire, have been brought up in great luxury, as beseems your noble birth. If you were to walk this dry weather on the hot and sandy ground, trampling under foot the gritty, gravelly grains of the hard sand, your feet would hurt you. And as your body would be in pain, your mind would be disturbed, and you would experience a sense of bodily suffering. How then did you come, on foot, or in a chariot?"

"I did not come, Sir, on foot. I came in a carriage."

"Then if you came, Sire, in a carriage, explain to me what that is. Is it the pole that is the chariot?"

"I did not say that."

"Is it the axle that is the chariot?"

"Certainly not."

"Is it the wheels, or the framework, or the ropes, or the yoke, or the spokes of the wheels, or the goad, that are the chariot?"

And to all these he still answered no.

"Then is it all these parts of it that are the chariot?"

"No, Sir."

"But is there anything outside them that is the chariot?"

And still he answered no.

"Then thus, ask as I may, I can discover no chariot. Chariot is a mere empty sound. What then is the chariot you say you came in? It is a falsehood that your Majesty has spoken, an untruth! There is no such thing as a chariot!"

When he had thus spoken the five hundred Yonakas shouted their applause, and said to the king: "Now let your Majesty get out of that if you can."

And Milinda the king replied to Nagasena, and said: "I have spoken no untruth, reverend Sir. It is on account of its having all these things—the pole, and the axle, the wheels, and the framework, the ropes, the yoke, the spokes, and the goad—that it comes under the generally understood term, the designation in common use, of 'chariot.'"

"Very good! Your Majesty has rightly grasped the meaning of 'chariot.' And just even so it is on account of all those things you questioned me about—the thirty-two kinds of organic matter in a human body, and the five constituent elements of being—that I come under the generally understood term, the designation in common use, of 'Nagasena.' For it was said, Sire, by our Sister Vagira in the presence of the Blessed One: 'Just as it is by the condition precedent of the co-existence of its various parts that the word "chariot" is used, just so is it that when the Skandhas are there we talk of a "being."'"

"Most wonderful, Nagasena, and most strange. Well has the puzzle put to you, most difficult though it was, been solved. Were the Buddha himself here he would approve your answer. Well done, well done, Nagasena!"

Book II, Chapter 2, Section 1

The king said: "He who is born, Nagasena, does he remain the same or become another?"

"Neither the same nor another."

"Give me an illustration."

"Now what do you think, O king? You were once a baby, a tender thing, and small in size, lying flat on your back. Was that the same as you who are now grown up?"

"No. That child was one, I am another."

"If you are not that child, it will follow that you have had neither mother nor father, no! nor teacher. You cannot have been taught either learning, or behaviour, or wisdom. What great king! is the mother of the embryo in the first stage different from the mother of the embryo in the second stage, or the third, or the fourth? Is the mother of the baby a different person from the mother of the grown-up man? Is the person who goes to school one, and the same when he has finished his schooling another? Is it one who commits a crime, another who is punished by having his hands or feet cut off?"

"Certainly not. But what would you, Sir, say to that?"

The Elder replied: "I should say that I am the same person, now that I am grown up, as I was when I was a tender tiny baby, flat on my back. For all these states are included in one by means of this body."

"Give me an illustration."

"Suppose a man, O king, were to light a lamp, would it burn the night through?"

"Yes, it might do so."

"Now, is it the same flame that burns in the first watch of the night, Sir, and in the second?"

"No."

"Or the same that burns in the second watch and in the third?"

"No."

"Then is there one lamp in the first watch, and another in the second, and another in the third?"

"No. The light comes from the same lamp all the night through."

"Just so, O king, is the continuity of a person or thing maintained. One comes into being, another passes away; and the rebirth is, as it were, simultaneous. Thus neither as the same nor as another does a man go on to the last phase of his self-consciousness."

"Give me a further illustration."

"It is like milk, which when once taken from the cow, turns, after a lapse of time, first to curds, and then from curds to butter, and then from butter to ghee. Now would it be right to say that the milk was the same thing as the curds, or the butter, or the ghee?"

"Certainly not; but they are produced out of it."

"Just so, O king, is the continuity of a person or thing maintained. One comes into being, another passes away; and the rebirth is, as it were, simultaneous. Thus neither as the same nor as another does a man go on to the last phase of his self-consciousness."

"Well put, Nagasena."

Book II, Chapter 3, Section 6

The king said: "Is there, Nagasena, such a thing as the soul?"

"What is this, O king, the soul (Vedagu)?"

"The living principle within, which sees forms through the eye, hears sounds through the ear, experiences tastes through the tongue, smells odors through the nose, feels touch through the body, and discerns things through the mind—just as we, sitting here in the palace, can look out of any window out of which we wish to look, the east window or the west, or the north or the south."

The Elder replied: "I will tell you about the five doors, great king. Listen, and give heed attentively. If the living principle within sees forms through the eye in the manner that you mention, choosing its window as it likes, can it not then see forms not only through the eye, but also through each of the other five organs of sense? And in like manner can it not then as well hear sounds, and experience taste, and smell odors, and feel touch, and discern conditions through each of the other five organs of sense, besides the one you have in each case specified?"

"No, Sir."

"Then these powers are not united one to another indiscriminately, the latter sense to the former organ, and so on. Now we, as we are seated here in the palace, with these windows all thrown open, and in full daylight, if we only stretch forth our heads, see all kinds of objects plainly. Can the living principle do the same when the doors of the eyes are thrown open? When the doors of the ear are thrown open, can it do so? Can it then not only hear sounds, but see sights, experience tastes, smell odors, feel touch, and discern conditions? And so with each of its windows?"

"No, Sir."

"Then these powers are not united one to another indiscriminately. Now again, great king, if Dinna here were to go outside and stand in the gateway, would you be aware that he had done so?"

"Yes, I should know it."

"And if the same Dinna were to come back again, and stand before you, would you be aware of his having done so?"

"Yes, I should know it."

"Well, great king, would the living principle within discern, in like manner, if anything possessing flavor were laid upon the tongue, its sourness, or its saltness, or its acidity, or its pungency, or its astringency, or its sweetness?"

"Yes, it would know it."

"But when the flavor had passed into the stomach would it still discern these things?"

"Certainly not."

"Then these powers are not united one to the other indiscriminately. Now suppose, O king, a man were to have a hundred vessels of honey brought and poured into one trough, and then, having had another man's mouth closed over and tied up, were to have him cast into the trough full of honey. Would he know whether that into which he had been thrown was sweet or whether it was not?"

"No, Sir."

"But why not?"

"Because the honey could not get into his mouth."

"Then, great king, these powers are not united one to another indiscriminately."[1]

"I am not capable of discussing with such a reasoner. Be pleased, Sir, to explain to me how the matter stands."

Then the Elder convinced Milinda the king with discourse drawn from the Abhidhamma, saying: "It is by reason, O king, of the eye and of forms that sight arises, and those other conditions—contact, sensation, idea, thought, abstraction, sense of vitality, and attention—arise each simultaneously with its predecessor. And a similar succession of cause and effect arises when each of the other five organs of sense is brought into play. And so herein there is no such thing as soul (Vedagu)."

NOTES

1. That is: "Your 'living principle within' cannot make use of whichever of its windows it pleases. And the simile of a man inside a house does not hold good of the soul." —TRANS.

Parables on the Self

JORGE LUIS BORGES

Jorge Luis Borges (1899–1986), who won the Nobel Prize for literature, was born in Argentina. Although most of his major writings were published before 1952, he did not become internationally known until French translations of his works were "discovered" in the late 1950s. While Borges is better known in literary than in philosophical circles, his poetry, short stories, essays, and "parables" are deeply philosophical in nature. The following two parables are taken from a collection of Borges's writings, *Labyrinths*, which was first published in English in 1962.

The first parable, "Everything and Nothing," is written as a first-person narrative in which Shakespeare ponders the nature of his identity (or rather his lack of identity). As an actor Shakespeare plays many parts, but he realizes, like the Buddhist monk in the preceding selection, that behind these numerous masks there is nothing substantial to be found. In the second parable, "Borges and I," which is also written in first-person form, the author does discover an identity, but he finds that this identity is gradually displaced or overwhelmed by his public persona, the persona of Borges. By the end of the parable, this displacement is so complete that the author does not know who has composed what has been written. Taken together, these parables might be described as postmodern reflections on the loss of self-identity.

Questions for Thought

1. Think about the various roles that you play in life. What, if anything, distinguishes you from the roles you play?
2. What do you think Shakespeare's statement to God (found near the end of the first parable) means? What is the significance of God's reply?
3. Have you ever tried to be someone else? Do you think you could become someone else if you tried?
4. How effective is the ending of the second parable? Do you believe that the statement should be taken literally? Why or why not?
5. In what ways are Borges's views similar to the views of the Buddhist monk in the preceding selection? In what ways are they different?

Everything and Nothing

THERE WAS NO ONE IN HIM; BEHIND HIS FACE (which even through the bad paintings of those times resembles no other) and his words, which were copious, fantastic and stormy, there was only a bit of coldness, a dream dreamt by no one. At first he thought that all people were like him, but the astonishment of a friend to whom he had begun to speak of this emptiness showed him his error and made him feel always that an individual should not differ in outward appearance. Once he thought that in books he would find a cure for his ill and thus he learned the small Latin and less Greek a contemporary would speak of; later he considered that what he sought might well be found in an elemental rite of humanity, and let himself be initiated by Anne Hathaway one long June afternoon. At the age of twenty-odd years he went to London. Instinctively he had already become proficient in the habit of simulating that he was someone, so that others would not discover his condition as no one; in London he found the profession to which he was predestined, that of the actor, who on a stage plays at being another before a gathering of people who play at taking him for that other person. His histrionic tasks brought him a singular satisfaction, perhaps the first he had ever known; but once the last verse had been acclaimed and the last dead man withdrawn from the stage, the hated flavor of unreality returned to him. He ceased to be Ferrex or Tamerlane and became no one again. Thus hounded, he took to imagining other heroes and other tragic fables. And so, while his flesh fulfilled its destiny as flesh in the taverns and brothels of London, the soul that inhabited him was Caesar, who disregards the augur's admonition, and Juliet, who abhors the lark, and Macbeth, who converses on the plain with the witches who are also Fates. No one has ever been so many men as this man, who like the Egyptian Proteus could exhaust all the guises of reality. At times he would leave a confession hidden away in some corner of his work, certain that it would not be deciphered; Richard affirms that in his person he plays the part of many and Iago claims with curious words "I am not what I am." The fundamental identity of existing, dreaming and acting inspired famous passages of his.

For twenty years he persisted in that controlled hallucination, but one morning he was suddenly gripped by the tedium and the terror of being so many kings who die by the sword and so many suffering lovers who converge, diverge and melodiously expire. That very day he arranged to sell his theater. Within a week he had returned to his native village, where he recovered the trees and rivers of his childhood and did not relate them to the others his muse had celebrated, illustrious with mythological allusions and Latin terms. He had to be someone; he was a retired impresario who had made his fortune and concerned himself with loans, lawsuits and petty usury. It was in this character that he dictated the arid will and testament known to us, from which he deliberately excluded all traces of pathos or literature. His friends from London would visit his retreat and for them he would take up again his role as poet.

History adds that before or after dying he found himself in the presence of God and told Him: "I who have been so many men in vain want to be one and myself." The voice of the Lord answered from a whirlwind: "Neither am I anyone; I have dreamt the world as you dreamt your work, my Shakespeare, and among the forms in my dream are you, who like myself are many and no one."

Borges and I

The other one, the one called Borges, is the one things happen to. I walk through the streets of Buenos Aires and stop for a moment, perhaps mechanically now, to look at the arch of an entrance hall and the grillwork on the gate; I know of Borges from the mail and see his name on a list of professors or in a biographical dictionary. I like hourglasses, maps, eighteenth-century topography, the taste of coffee and the prose of Stevenson; he shares these preferences, but in a vain way that turns them into the attributes of an actor. It would be an exaggeration to say that ours is a hostile relationship; I live, let myself go on living, so that Borges may contrive his literature, and this literature justifies me. It is no effort for me to confess that he has achieved some valid pages, but those pages cannot save me, perhaps because what is good belongs to no one, not even to him, but rather to the language and to tradition. Besides, I am destined to perish, definitively, and only some instant of myself can survive in him. Little by little, I am giving over everything to him, though I am quite aware of his perverse custom of falsifying and magnifying things. Spinoza knew that all things long to persist in their being; the stone eternally wants to be a stone and the tiger a tiger. I shall remain in Borges, not in myself (if it is true that I am someone), but I recognize myself less in his books than in many others or in the laborious strumming of a guitar. Years ago I tried to free myself from him and went from the mythologies of the suburbs to the games with time and infinity, but those games belong to Borges now and I shall have to imagine other things. Thus my life is a flight and I lose everything and everything belongs to oblivion, or to him.

I do not know which of us has written this page.

Reflections on Human Nature   1.4

MENCIUS

Mencius (372–289 B.C.E) was Confucius' most famous disciple. Like Confucius, Mencius was reportedly the only child of a poor widow who had to work very hard to support and educate him. Other traditions say that Mencius studied under the disciples of Tzu Ssu, the grandson of Confucius, and that, like Confucius, Mencius became a political adviser to some of the rulers of his time. His views on human nature are often contrasted with the views of Hsün Tzu, another of the disciples of Confucius, who claimed that human nature was basically evil. However, it was in his arguments with Kao Tzu, about whom little is known, that Mencius' views on human nature were stated in greatest detail.

In the following sections from the Book of Mencius, a collection of dialogues and sayings probably compiled by Mencius' pupils after his death, Mencius argues against two of Kao Tzu's closely related claims: (1) the claim that at birth human beings are neither good nor evil, and (2) the claim that a person becomes good or just because of external input. In opposition to Kao Tzu, Mencius insists that all humans are endowed with certain natural qualities—a sense of pity, of shame, of respect, and of right and wrong. Because of these natural qualities, the source of goodness or justice lies within. In other words, unless a person's development is perverted by some external force, that person will naturally become good and just. As in many other Chinese writings, the principal arguments of both Kao Tzu and Mencius take the form of analogies or comparisons, in this case analogies or comparisons between human nature and the nature of other things such as wood and water.

Questions for Thought

1. Do you believe that there is an essential human nature? Why or why not?
2. Are human beings really born with a propensity for goodness as Mencius claims?
3. Assuming that Mencius is correct, why is there so much violence and injustice in the world today?
4. Can you think of Western philosophical or religious views that are similar to the views of Mencius? Can you think of views that contradict or oppose Mencius' position?
5. How effective do you think Mencius' analogies or comparisons are in supporting his claims?
6. Can you think of a different analogy or comparison that would also support Mencius' position? Can you think of one that would weaken his position?

Book Six, Part I

6A:1

KAO TZU SAID: "THE NATURE OF MAN IS COMPArable to the nature of the wood of the willow tree. Such things as Justice and Humanity are comparable to cups and bowls carved in willow wood. To make man's nature Humane or Just is comparable to making cups and bowls from willow wood."

Mencius replied: "But when the wood is carved into a bowl, is its nature left unscarred? No! It becomes a bowl only at the price of suffering damage to its original nature. If that is so, then must a man suffer damage to his original nature in order to become Humane and Just? In such a view, to make men Humane and Just is to violate their nature. From what you say, one would be forced to such a conclusion."

6A:2

Kao Tzu said: "The nature of man is comparable to water trapped in a whirlpool. Open a channel for it on the east side and it will flow away to the east. Open a channel for it on the west side and it will flow away to the west. This is because man's nature is neither inherently good nor bad, just as it is not inherently in the nature of water to flow to the east or to the west."

Mencius replied: "It is assuredly not in the nature of water to flow to the east or to the west, but can one say that it is not in the nature of water to flow upwards or downwards? Man's nature is inherently good, just as it is the nature of water to flow downwards. As there is no water that flows upwards, so there are no men whose natures inherently are bad. Now you may strike forcefully upon water, and it will splash above your head. With a series of dams, you may force it uphill. But this is surely nothing to do with the nature of water; it happens only after the intrusion of some exterior force. A man can be made to do evil, but this is nothing to do with his nature. It happens only after the intrusion of some exterior force."

6A:3

Kao Tzu said: "What I mean by nature is the thing that gives life."

Mencius asked: "Do you mean that in the sense that you would say that whiteness is the thing that whitens?"

Kao Tzu said: "Yes, certainly!"

Mencius continued: "Then it would follow that the whiteness of a white feather and the whiteness of white snow are comparable, and similarly that the whiteness of white snow and the whiteness of white jade are comparable?"

Reprinted by permission of Toronto University Press.

Kao Tzu said: "Yes, certainly."

Mencius replied: "With that line of reasoning would you not have to say that the nature of a dog and the nature of an ox are comparable, and so the nature of an ox and the nature of a man are comparable?"

6A:4

Kao Tzu said: "What I mean by nature is food and color (the taste and senses). I regard Humanity as pertaining to these senses and not external to them. Justice, on the other hand, is something external; it does not pertain to the senses."

Mencius said: "How can you say that the one is inherent and the other external?"

Kao Tzu said: "To a man who is my senior I pay, in Justice, the deference due to his seniority. This is not because paying such deference is an intrinsic part of *me*; I react to the stimulus of his seniority just as I see a white thing as white, since I am actuated by its whiteness, which is external to myself. It is for this reason that I say such things are external."

Mencius said: "If in speaking of the whiteness of a white horse, we say that it differs in no way from the whiteness of a white man, I suppose we must say that the 'seniority' (old age) of an old horse differs in no way from the 'seniority' of an old man. In which case, in what does Justice repose? In 'seniority' itself or in him who responds to seniority as he, in Justice, should?"

Kao Tzu said: "I feel love for my younger brother, but I feel no love for the younger brother of a man of Ch'in. My brother provokes a feeling of pleasure within me, and so I say it is inherent. To a man from Ch'u who is my senior I pay the deference due to his seniority, just as I would pay deference to a senior of my own family. My doing so provokes a feeling of pleasure within my seniors. So accordingly I say that Justice is an external thing."

Mencius said: "My enjoyment of a dish cooked by a man of Ch'in differs in no way from my enjoyment of a similar dish cooked by my own people. This is true of a number of similar material things. Since it is so, would you still assert that the enjoyment of food is something external?"[1]

6A: 6

Kung-tu Tzu said: "Kao Tzu says, 'Man's nature is neither good nor bad.' Others say man's nature may tend in either direction. They say in the reigns of the good kings Wen and Wu[2] the people were disposed to do good. In the reigns of the bad kings Yu and Li[3] the people were disposed to do evil. Still others say some men's natures are good while others are bad. These say that, under a good sovereign like Yao,[4] a bad man like Hsiang appeared, and that, to a bad father like Ku-sou, a good son Shun[5] was born. . . . Now, Sir, you say, 'Man's nature is good.' I suppose that these others are wrong?"

Mencius said: "It is of the essence of man's nature that he do good. That is what I mean by good. If a man does what is evil he is guilty of the sin of denying his natural endowment. Every man has a sense of pity, a sense of shame, a sense of respect, a sense of right and wrong. From his sense of pity comes *jen* (Humanity); from his sense of shame comes *yi* (Justice); from his sense of respect, *li* (the observance of rites); from his sense of right and wrong *chih* (wisdom). *Jen, yi, li,* and *chih* do not soak in from without; we have them within ourselves. It is simply that we are not always consciously thinking about them. So I say, 'Seek them and you have them. Disregard them and you lose them.' Men differ, some by twice, some by five times, and some by an incalculable amount, in their inability to exploit this endowment. The *Book of Songs*[6] says,

> Heaven gave birth to all mankind
> Gave them life and gave them laws.
> In holding to them
> They lean towards the virtue of excellence.

Confucius said, 'This poet really understood the Way.' Thus, to possess life is to possess laws. These are to be laid hold upon by the people, and thus they will love the virtue of excellence."

6A: 7

Mencius said: "When the harvest is good, the younger people are for the most part amenable, but when the harvest is lean, they are obstreperous. Their reacting differently under these differing circumstances is not due to the nature with which Heaven has endowed them but to those who create these overwhelming conditions. Sow the barley and cover it with soil. Providing that the ground is uniform and the barley is sown at one time, it will spring to life, and in due time all the barley will ripen. However, differing circumstances do arise; some ground is rich, some is poor; some well watered, some not; not all is equally well-tended. Even so, things of a kind resemble each other. And can we doubt that human beings are any different? The Sages and we ourselves are things of a kind. Lung Tzu[7] said, 'The sandal-maker may not know beforehand the size of his customer's feet, but we can be sure that he will not make the sandals the size of baskets.' Sandals resemble each other; men's feet are things of a kind. All men relish flavorings in their food. But it took an Yi Ya[8] first to discover those flavorings. Suppose Yi Ya's nature differed in kind from those of other men, just as the nature of horses and hounds differs from that of a man. How could it have happened that, whatever flavorings humans like, all derive from Yi Ya? As far as flavorings are concerned, the world is indebted to Yi Ya, but this could only happen because all men's palates are similar.

"This, too, is true of the ear. For music, the world is indebted to K'uang the Music Master.[9] But this could only happen because all men's ears are similar. This, too, is true of the eyes. No one would deny that Tzu-tu[10] was handsome, unless he was blind.

"Therefore, the human mouth enjoys its flavorings, the ear its music, the eye its beauty. These things are all alike. And is this not true of the things of the heart? What are those things that all hearts have in common? I say, 'the underlying principle, the essential Justice.'

"The Sages (differ from us only) in being the first to discover those things which all hearts have in common. The underlying principle and the essential Justice evoke joy in our hearts just as rich meat delights our palate."

NOTES

1. The dialogue between Mencius and Kao Tzu ends at this point. The remaining subsections record dialogues between Mencius and his disciples.
2. The first two rulers of the Chou dynasty, who are often cited as ideal examples of wise and beneficent rule.
3. Kings who ruled in the eighth and ninth centuries B.C.E., and who often serve as examples of wicked rulers.
4. Mythical sage–emperor who supposedly ruled in the third millennium B.C.E. According to tradition, he lived the simple life of a common farmer.
5. The mythical sage–emperor who supposedly succeeded Yao.
6. An anthology of early Chinese poetry.
7. An ancient wise man.
8. Chef of Duke Huan of Ch'i.
9. Concert master for Duke P'ing of Chin.
10. An ancient person who was known for his handsome features.

SIMONE DE BEAUVOIR

Simone de Beauvoir (1908–1986) attended the Sorbonne where, to the dismay of her parents, she studied philosophy. After teaching philosophy at several institutions in the 1930s, she became very active in the existentialist movement that was growing in Paris during and after World War II. De Beauvoir expressed her ideas in philosophical writings such as *The Second Sex* (1949–1950) and in literary writings as well. Perhaps the best known of her literary writings is the lengthy novel *The Mandarins*, which was published in 1955. She was also co-founder (with Jean-Paul Sartre and Maurice Merleau-Ponty) of *Les Temps modernes*, a journal devoted to the analysis of political and literary questions from an existentialist perspective. Like many of the existentialists, de Beauvoir was socially committed and participated in the various protest movements of her time. Despite her many accomplishments and writings, she was not the subject of a separate article in *The Encyclopedia of Philosophy*, although she was mentioned in the article devoted to Sartre, her frequent companion.

In the following selection, which is excerpted from the Introduction to *The Second Sex*, de Beauvoir raises the question of what it means to be a woman. While observing that the answer to this question is often linked to the notion of femininity, she denies that femininity represents a fixed concept or essence. Indeed, in opposition to Mencius, she denies the existence of any universal human essence, and claims that the concept of femininity, like the concept of humanity, is socially and historically determined.

Adopting the standpoint of existentialist ethics, de Beauvoir argues that human beings have the capacity to freely determine their own destinies. In other words, she claims that human existence is characterized by transcendence, that is, by the possibility of choosing one's own goals and projects. However, she believes that realizing one's transcendence is limited by both internal and external obstacles. Internally, there is a tendency to absolve ourselves of responsibility and the difficulty of decision by allowing others to control our lives. And externally, there are others who, in pursuing their own transcendence, willingly dominate and oppress us.

While all human beings encounter these obstacles to realizing their transcendence, de Beauvoir argues that women have been especially limited by external obstacles and their internalization. Indeed, using many examples from philosophy, theology, and literature, she claims that women have been relegated to the position of the Other or the inessential in Western society. As such, woman's transcendence has been blocked not only by the existential obstacles faced by all human beings, but by a wide range of legal, social, theological, and scientific barricades as well.

Questions for Thought

1. What does de Beauvoir mean by the term *femininity*? What do you think the term means?
2. Do you agree with de Beauvoir's claim that women have traditionally been subordinated to men in Western culture? Do you believe that this is still true today?
3. De Beauvoir claims that males and females are conditioned to be different from birth on. Do you think that this is still true?
4. Why does de Beauvoir believe that the story of creation found in Genesis makes women subordinate to men? Do you agree with her interpretation of this story?
5. Why, according to de Beauvoir, has the subordination of women been so hard to overcome? Do you agree with her claim that women have been partially responsible for this continued subordination?
6. De Beauvoir raises the following questions: "What opportunities precisely have been given to us [women] and what withheld? What fate awaits our younger sisters, and what directions should they take?" How would you answer these questions?

Introduction

FOR A LONG TIME I HAVE HESITATED TO WRITE A book on woman. The subject is irritating, especially to women; and it is not new. Enough ink has been spilled in the quarreling over feminism, now practically over, and perhaps we should say no more about it. It is still talked about, however, for the voluminous nonsense uttered during the last century seems to have done little to illuminate the problem. After all, is there a problem? And if so, what is it? Are there women, really? Most assuredly the theory of the eternal feminine still has its adherents who will whisper in your ear: "Even in Russia women still are *women*"; and other erudite persons—sometimes the very same—say with a sigh: "Woman is losing her way, woman is lost." One wonders if women still exist, if they will always exist, whether or not it is desirable that they should, what place they occupy in this world, what their place should be. "What has become of women?" was asked recently in an ephemeral magazine.

But first we must ask: what is woman? "*Tota mulier in utero*," says one, "woman is a womb." But in speaking of certain women, connoisseurs declare that they are not women, although they are equipped with a uterus like the rest. All agree in recognizing the fact that females exist in the human species; today as always they make up about one half of humanity. And yet we are told that femininity is in danger; we are exhorted to be women, remain women, become women. It would appear, then, that every female human being is not necessarily a woman; to be so considered she must share in that mysterious and threatened reality known as femininity. Is this attribute something secreted by the ovaries? Or is it a Platonic essence, a product of the philosophic imagination? Is a rustling petticoat enough to bring it down to earth? Although some women try zealously to incarnate this essence, it is hardly patentable. It is frequently described in vague and dazzling terms that seem to have been borrowed from the vocabulary of the seers, and indeed in the times of St. Thomas it was considered an essence as certainly defined as the somniferous virtue of the poppy.

But conceptualism has lost ground. The biological and social sciences no longer admit the existence of unchangeably fixed entities that determine given characteristics, such as those ascribed to woman, the Jew, or the Negro. Science regards any characteristic as a reaction dependent in part upon a *situation*. If today femininity no longer exists, then it never existed. But does the word *woman*, then, have no specific content? This is stoutly affirmed by those who hold to the philosophy of the enlightenment, of rationalism, of nominalism; women, to them, are merely the human beings arbitrarily designated by the word *woman*. Many American women particularly are prepared to think that there is no longer any place for woman as such; if a backward individual still takes herself for a woman, her friends advise her to be psychoanalyzed and thus get rid of this obsession. In regard to a work, *Modern Woman: The Lost Sex*, which in other respects has its irritating features, Dorothy Parker has written: "I cannot be just to books which treat of woman as woman. . . . My idea is that all of us, men as well as women, should be regarded as human beings." But nominalism is a rather inadequate doctrine, and the antifeminists have had no trouble in showing that women simply *are not* men. Surely woman is, like man, a human being; but such a declaration is abstract. The fact is that every concrete human being is always a singular, separate individual. To decline to accept such notions as the eternal feminine, the black soul, the Jewish character, is not to deny that Jews, Negroes, women exist today—this denial does not represent a liberation for those concerned, but rather a flight from reality. Some years ago a well-known woman writer refused to permit her portrait to appear in a series of photographs especially devoted to women writers; she wished to be counted among the men. But in order to gain this privilege she made use of her husband's influence! Women who assert that they are men lay claim none the less to masculine considera-

tion and respect. I recall also a young Trotskyite standing on a platform at a boisterous meeting and getting ready to use her fists, in spite of her evident fragility. She was denying her feminine weakness; but it was for love of a militant male whose equal she wished to be. The attitude of defiance of many American women proves that they are haunted by a sense of their femininity. In truth, to go for a walk with one's eyes open is enough to demonstrate that humanity is divided into two classes of individuals whose clothes, faces, bodies, smiles, gaits, interests, and occupations are manifestly different. Perhaps these differences are superficial, perhaps they are destined to disappear. What is certain is that right now they do most obviously exist.

If her functioning as a female is not enough to define woman, if we decline also to explain her through "the eternal feminine," and if nevertheless we admit, provisionally, that women do exist, then we must face the question: what is a woman?

To state the question is, to me, to suggest, at once, a preliminary answer. The fact that I ask it is in itself significant. A man would never get the notion of writing a book on the peculiar situation of the human male. But if I wish to define myself, I must first of all say: "I am a woman"; on this truth must be based all further discussion. A man never begins by presenting himself as an individual of a certain sex; it goes without saying that he is a man. The terms *masculine* and *feminine* are used symmetrically only as a matter of form, as on legal papers. In actuality the relation of the two sexes is not quite like that of two electrical poles, for man represents both the positive and the neutral, as is indicated by the common use of *man* to designate human beings in general; whereas woman represents only the negative, defined by limiting criteria, without reciprocity. In the midst of an abstract discussion it is vexing to hear a man say: "you think thus and so because you are a woman"; but I know that my only defense is to reply: "I think thus and so because it is true," thereby removing my subjective self from the argument. It would be out of the question to reply: "And you think the contrary because you are a man," for it is understood that the fact of being a man is no peculiarity.[1] A man is in the right in being a man; it is the woman who is in the wrong. It amounts to this: just as for the ancients there was an absolute vertical with reference to which the oblique was defined, so there is an absolute human type, the masculine. Woman has ovaries, a uterus; these peculiarities imprison her in her subjectivity, circumscribe her within the limits of her own nature. It is often said that she thinks with her glands. Man superbly ignores the fact that his anatomy also includes glands, such as the testicles, and that they secrete hormones. He thinks of his body as a direct and normal connection with the world, which he believes he apprehends objectively, whereas he regards the body of woman as a hindrance, a prison, weighed down by everything peculiar to it. "The female is a female by virtue of a certain *lack* of qualities," said Aristotle; "we should regard the female nature as afflicted with a natural defectiveness." And St. Thomas for his part pronounced woman to be an "imperfect man," an "incidental" being. This is symbolized in Genesis where Eve is depicted as made from what Bossuet called "a supernumerary bone" of Adam.

Thus humanity is male and man defines woman not in herself but as relative to him; she is not regarded as an autonomous being. Michelet writes: "Woman, the relative being. . . ." And Benda is most positive in his *Rapport d'Uriel*: "The body of man makes sense in itself quite apart from that of woman, whereas the latter seems wanting in significance by itself. . . . Man can think of himself without woman. She cannot think of herself without man." And she is simply what man decrees; thus she is called "the sex," by which is meant that she appears essentially to the male as a sexual being. For him she is sex—absolute sex, no less. She is defined and differentiated with reference to man and not he with reference to her; she is the incidental, the inessential as opposed to the essential. He is the Subject, he is the Absolute—she is the Other. . . .

Now, woman has always been man's dependent, if not his slave; the two sexes have never shared the world in equality. And even today woman is heavily handicapped, though her situation is beginning to change. Although nowhere is her legal status the same as man's,[2] and frequently it is much to her disadvantage. Even when her rights are legally recognized in the abstract, long-standing custom prevents their full expression in the mores. In the economic sphere men and women can almost be said to make up two castes; other things being equal, the former hold the better jobs, get higher wages, and have more opportunity for success than their new competitors. In industry and politics men have a great many more positions and they monopolize the most important posts. In addition to all this, they enjoy a traditional prestige that the education of children tends in every way to support, for the present enshrines the past—and in the past all history has been made by men. At the present time, when women are beginning to take part in the affairs of the world, it is still a world that belongs to men—they have no doubt of it at all and women have scarcely any. To decline to be the Other, to refuse to be a party to the deal—this would be for women to renounce all the advantages conferred upon them by their alliance with the superior caste. Man-the-sovereign will provide woman-the-liege with material protection and will undertake the moral justification of her existence; thus she can evade at once both economic risk and the metaphysical risk of a liberty in which ends and aims must be contrived without assistance. Indeed, along with the ethical urge of each individual to affirm his subjective existence, there is also the temptation to forgo liberty and become a thing. This is an inauspicious road, for he who takes it—passive, lost, ruined—becomes henceforth the creature of another's will, frustrated in his transcendence and deprived of every value. But it is an easy road; on it one avoids the strain involved in undertaking an authentic existence. When man makes of woman the *Other*, he may, then, expect her to manifest deep-seated tendencies toward complicity. Thus, woman may fail to lay claim to the status of subject because she lacks definite resources, because she feels the necessary bond that ties her to man regardless of reciprocity, and because she is often very well pleased with her role as the *Other*.

But it will be asked at once: how did all this begin? It is easy to see that the duality of the sexes, like any duality, gives rise to conflict. And doubtless the winner will assume the status of absolute. But why should man have won from the start? It seems possible that women could have won the victory; or that the outcome of the conflict might never have been decided. How is it that this world has always belonged to the men and that things have begun to change only recently? Is this change a good thing? Will it bring about an equal sharing of the world between men and women?

These questions are not new, and they have often been answered. But the fact that woman *is the Other* tends to cast suspicion upon all the justifications that men have ever been able to provide for it. These have all too evidently been dictated by men's interest. A little-known feminist of the seventeenth century, Poulain de la Barre, put it this way: "All that has been written about women by men should be suspect, for the men are at once judge and party to the lawsuit." Everywhere, at all times, the males have displayed their satisfaction in feeling that they are lords of creation. "Blessed be God . . . that He did not make me a woman," say the Jews in their morning prayers, while their wives pray on a note of resignation: "Blessed be the Lord, who created me according to His will." The first among blessings for which Plato thanked the gods was that he had been created free, not enslaved; the second, a man, not a woman. But the males could not enjoy this privilege fully unless they believed it to be founded on the absolute and the eternal; they sought to make the fact of their supremacy into a right. "Being men, those who have made and compiled the laws have favored their own sex, and jurists have elevated these laws into prin-

ciples," to quote Poulain de la Barre once more.

Legislators, priests, philosophers, writers, and scientists have striven to show that the subordinate position of woman is willed in heaven and advantageous on earth. The religions invented by men reflect this wish for domination. In the legends of Eve and Pandora men have taken up arms against women. They have made use of philosophy and theology, as the quotations from Aristotle and St. Thomas have shown. . . .

In proving woman's inferiority, the antifeminists . . . began to draw not only upon religion, philosophy, and theology, . . . but also upon science—biology, experimental psychology, etc. At most they were willing to grant "equality in difference" to the *other* sex. That profitable formula is most significant; it is precisely like the "equal but separate" formula of the Jim Crow laws aimed at the North American Negroes. As is well known, this so-called equalitarian segregation has resulted only in the most extreme discrimination. The similarity just noted is in no way due to chance, for whether it is a race, a caste, a class, or a sex that is reduced to a position of inferiority, the methods of justification are the same. "The eternal feminine" corresponds to "the black soul" and to "the Jewish character." True, the Jewish problem is on the whole very different from the other two—to the anti-Semite the Jew is not so much an inferior as he is an enemy for whom there is to be granted no place on earth, for whom annihilation is the fate desired. But there are deep similarities between the situation of woman and that of the Negro. Both are being emancipated today from a like paternalism, and the former master class wishes to "keep them in their place"—that is, the place chosen for them. In both cases the former masters lavish more or less sincere eulogies, either on the virtues of "the good Negro" with his dormant, childish, merry soul—the submissive Negro—or on the merits of the woman who is "truly feminine"—that is, frivolous, infantile, irresponsible—the submissive woman. In both cases the dominant class bases its argument on a state of affairs that it has itself created.

As George Bernard Shaw puts it, in substance, "The American white relegates the black to the rank of shoeshine boy; and he concludes from this that the black is good for nothing but shining shoes." This vicious circle is met with in all analogous circumstances; when an individual (or a group of individuals) is kept in a situation of inferiority, the fact is that he *is* inferior. But the significance of the verb *to be* must be rightly understood here; it is in bad faith to give it a static value when it really has the dynamic Hegelian sense of "to have become." Yes, women on the whole *are* today inferior to men; that is, their situation affords them fewer possibilities. The question is: should that state of affairs continue?

Many men hope that it will continue; not all have given up the battle. The conservative bourgeoisie still see in the emancipation of women a menace to their morality and their interests. Some men dread feminine competition. Recently a male student wrote in the *Hedbo-Latin*: "Every woman student who goes into medicine or law robs us of a job." He never questioned his rights in this world. And economic interests are not the only ones concerned. One of the benefits that oppression confers upon the oppressors is that the most humble among them is made to *feel* superior; thus, a "poor white" in the South can console himself with the thought that he is not a "dirty nigger"—and the more prosperous whites cleverly exploit this pride. . . .

We should consider the arguments of the feminists with no less suspicion, however, for very often their controversial aim deprives them of all real value.

If the "woman question" seems trivial, it is because masculine arrogance has made of it a "quarrel"; and when quarreling one no longer reasons well. People have tirelessly sought to prove that woman is superior, inferior, or equal to man. Some say that, having been created after Adam, she is evidently a secondary being; others say on the contrary that Adam was only a rough draft and that God succeeded in producing the human being in perfection when He created Eve. Woman's brain is smaller; yes, but it is

relatively larger. Christ was made a man; yes, but perhaps for his greater humility. Each argument at once suggests its opposite, and both are often fallacious. If we are to gain understanding, we must get out of these ruts; we must discard the vague notions of superiority, inferiority, equality which have hitherto corrupted every discussion of the subject and start afresh.

Very well, but just how shall we pose the question? And, to begin with, who are we to propound it at all? Man is at once judge and party to the case; but so is woman. What we need is an angel—neither man nor woman—but where shall we find one? Still, the angel would be poorly qualified to speak, for an angel is ignorant of all the basic facts involved in the problem. With a hermaphrodite we should be no better off, for here the situation is most peculiar; the hermaphrodite is not really the combination of a whole man and a whole woman, but consists of parts of each and thus is neither. It looks to me as if there are, after all, certain women who are best qualified to elucidate the situation of woman. Let us not be misled by the sophism that because Epimenides was a Cretan he was necessarily a liar; it is not a mysterious essence that compels men and women to act in good or in bad faith, it is their situation that inclines them more or less toward the search for truth. Many of today's women, fortunate in the restoration of all the privileges pertaining to the estate of the human being, can afford the luxury of impartiality—we even recognize its necessity. We are no longer like our partisan elders; by and large we have won the game. In recent debates on the status of women the United Nations has persistently maintained that the quality of the sexes is now becoming a reality, and already some of us have never had to sense in our femininity an inconvenience or an obstacle. Many problems appear to us to be more pressing than those which concern us in particular, and this detachment even allows us to hope that our attitude will be objective. Still, we know the feminine world more intimately than do the men because we have our roots in it, we grasp more immediately than do men what it means to a human being to be feminine; and we are more concerned with such knowledge. I have said that there are more pressing problems, but this does not prevent us from seeing some importance in asking how the fact of being women will affect our lives. What opportunities precisely have been given us and what withheld? What fate awaits our younger sisters, and what directions should they take? . . .

But it is doubtless impossible to approach any human problem with a mind free from bias. The way in which questions are put, the points of view assumed, presuppose a relativity of interest; all characteristics imply values, and every objective description, so called, implies an ethical background. Rather than attempt to conceal principles more or less definitely implied, it is better to state them openly at the beginning. This will make it unnecessary to specify on every page in just what sense one uses such words as *superior, inferior, better, worse, progress, reaction,* and the like. If we survey some of the works on woman, we note that one of the points of view most frequently adopted is that of the public good, the general interest; and one always means by this the benefit of society as one wishes it to be maintained or established. For our part, we hold that the only public good is that which assures the private good of the citizens; we shall pass judgment on institutions according to their effectiveness in giving concrete opportunities to individuals. But we do not confuse the idea of private interest with that of happiness, although that is another common point of view. Are not women of the harem more happy than women voters? Is not the housekeeper happier than the working-woman? It is not too clear just what the word *happy* really means and still less what true values it may mask. There is no possibility of measuring the happiness of others, and it is always easy to describe as happy the situation in which one wishes to place them.

In particular those who are condemned to stagnation are often pronounced happy on the pretext that happiness consists in being at rest.

This notion we reject, for our perspective is that of existentialist ethics. Every subject plays his part as such specifically through exploits or projects that serve as a mode of transcendence; he achieves liberty only through a continual reaching out toward other liberties. There is no justification for present existence other than its expansion into an indefinitely open future. Every time transcendence falls back into immanence, stagnation, there is a degradation of existence into the "en-soi"—the brutish life of subjection to given conditions—and of liberty into constraint and contingence. This downfall represents a moral fault if the subject consents to it; if it is inflicted upon him, it spells frustration and oppression. In both cases it is an absolute evil. Every individual concerned to justify his existence feels that his existence involves an undefined need to transcend himself, to engage in freely chosen projects.

Now, what peculiarly signalizes the situation of woman is that she—a free and autonomous being like all human creatures—nevertheless finds herself living in a world where men compel her to assume the status of the Other. They propose to stabilize her as object and to doom her to immanence since her trancendence is to be overshadowed and forever transcended by another ego (*conscience*) which is essential and sovereign. The drama of woman lies in this conflict between the fundamental aspirations of every subject (ego)—who always regards the self as the essential—and the compulsions of a situation in which she is the inessential.

NOTES

1. It is especially interesting to read this in light of the remarks that Georges de Beauvoir, Simone's father, often made about her: "Simone has a man's brain. She thinks like a man; she is a man." —ED.

2. A translator's note, which was written in the early 1950s, reads: "At the moment an 'equal rights' amendment to the Constitution of the United States is before Congress." Of course, forty years later, that equal rights amendment has still not been approved. —ED.

1.6 Woman as Body: Ancient and Contemporary Views

ELIZABETH V. SPELMAN

Elizabeth V. Spelman (b. 1945) teaches philosophy at Smith College in Northampton, Massachusetts, where her specialties include ethics, feminist theory, race theory, and metaphysics. She has also been interested in examining the philosophical foundations of feminist theory. Spelman has written several journal articles that critique the traditional philosophical distinction between mind and body, as well as a book, *Inessential Woman*, which was published by Beacon Press in 1988. She presently is at work on a book entitled *Unworthy Subjects: Suffering and the Economy of Attention*.

In the following selection, which originally appeared in the journal *Feminist Studies*, Spelman looks at the implications of the mind/body distinction in the writings of one ancient philosopher (Plato) and four contemporary feminist writers (Simone de Beauvoir, Betty Friedan, Shulamith Firestone, and Mary Daly). She notes that in the writings of each of these authors the distinction between mind and body has been accompanied by a hierarchical ordering in which the mind has been considered to be much more important to our self-identity than has our body. She further notes that this hierarchical ordering of mind over body has been used as the basis for creating social and political hierarchies in which some humans (those who are more "mental" in nature) assume rule over other humans (those who are more "bodily" in nature). For this reason, she argues that if we are truly interested in eliminating sexism and racism, we must carefully re-examine the distinction between mind and body, as well as the hierarchical ordering that has traditionally accompanied it.

While Spelman does a good job of summarizing the philosophical thinking of Plato, the Greek philosopher who lived in Athens from 427 to 347 B.C.E, you will no doubt find Plato's views easier to understand once you recognize the many similarities between his views and the Hindu views found in the first selection in this chapter. In that earlier selection from the Upanishads, a distinction was made between the mental or spiritual aspect of human existence (the Atman) and the bodily aspect. You were told that the spiritual aspect, the Atman, was much more important to your self-identity than was the bodily aspect. Indeed, the writers of the Upanishads told you that your Atman or soul will be incarnated in many different bodies, and that you will attain liberation or salvation only when you are able to resist the pleasures of the body and discover the truly spiritual nature of your identity. As you will see from Spelman's description, Plato's views on the nature of the mind and body are almost identical to these views found in the Upanishads. You may also find it interesting to note that, like Plato's views, those found in the Upanishads have been used in conjunction with social and political hierarchies in which women and certain other humans have been subjugated to others. Traditional Hindu society was not only divided into four basic groups or castes—with the highest (the Brahmins or priests) being the most "mental" and the lowest (the Shudras or servants) being the most "bodily"—women were expected to stay in the home and to remain totally dependent on the chief male of the household.

Questions for Thought

1. How important is your body in determining who you are?
2. Can we really distinguish our spiritual or mental aspect from our bodily aspect as Plato and the writers of the Upanishads have tried to do? Why or why not?
3. Do you believe that people who distinguish the mind or soul from the body generally place more significance on the mind or soul?
4. Assuming that people who make this distinction do place more significance on the mind or soul, why do you think this happens?
5. How, according to Spelman, are sexism and racism philosophically connected? Do you agree with her analysis?
6. What are Spelman's main points of contention with the four feminists that she criticizes? Why does she believe that the views of Adrienne Rich are much more acceptable than the views of the other feminists?
7. Assume for the moment that getting more in touch with your body (or becoming more "embodied" to use Spelman's word) is important. What are some of the ways in which you might accomplish this?

WHAT PHILOSOPHERS HAVE HAD TO SAY ABOUT women typically has been nasty, brutish, and short. A page or two of quotations from those considered among the great philosophers (Aristotle, Hume, and Nietzsche, for example) constitutes a veritable litany of contempt. Because philosophers have not said much about women,[1] and, when they have, it has usually been in short essays or chatty addenda which have not been considered to be part of the central body of their work, it is tempting to regard their expressed views about women as asystemic: their remarks on women are unofficial asides which are unrelated to the heart of their philosophical doctrines. After all, it might be thought, how could one's views about something as unimportant as women have anything to do with one's views about something as important as the nature of knowledge, truth, reality, freedom? Moreover—and this is the philosopher's move par excellence—wouldn't it be charitable to consider those opinions about women as coming merely from the *heart*, which all too easily responds to the tenor of the times, while philosophy "proper" comes from the *mind*, which resonates not with the times but with the truth?

Part of the intellectual legacy from philosophy "proper," that is, the issues that philosophers have addressed which are thought to be the serious province of philosophy, is the soul/body or mind/body distinction (differences among the various formulations are not crucial to this essay). However, this part of philosophy might have not merely accidental connections to attitudes about women. For when one recalls that the Western philosophical tradition has not been noted for its celebration of the body, and that women's nature and women's lives have long been associated with the body and bodily functions, then a question is suggested. What connection might there be between attitudes toward the body and attitudes toward women?

This article is reprinted in part from *Feminist Studies*, Vol. 8, No. 1 (Spring 1982): 109–131, by permission of the publisher, Feminist Studies, Inc., c/o Women's Studies Program, University of Maryland, College Park, MD 20742.

If one begins to reread philosophers with an eye to exploring in detail just how they made the mind/body distinction, it soon becomes apparent that in many cases the distinction reverberates throughout the philosopher's work. How a philosopher conceives of the distinction and relation between soul (or mind) and body has essential ties to how that philosopher talks about the nature of knowledge, the accessibility of reality, the possibility of freedom. This is perhaps what one would expect—systematic connections among the "proper" philosophical issues addressed by a given philosopher. But there is also clear evidence in the philosophical texts of the relationship between the mind/body distinction, on the one hand, and the scattered official and unofficial utterances about the nature of women, on the other.

In this article, I shall refer to the conceptual connections between a philosopher's views about women and his expressed metaphysical, political, and ethical views. That is, I shall refer to conceptual relations internal to the texts themselves, and not to relations between the texts and their political and historical contexts. . . .

My focus below is on the works of Plato, to discover what connections there are between his views about women and his views about the philosophical issues for which he is regarded with such respect. . . . What I hope to show is why it is important to see the connections between what Plato says about women and other aspects of his philosophical positions. For as I shall explain in the latter part of this essay, feminist theorists frequently have wanted to reject the kinds of descriptions of woman's nature found in Plato and other philosophers, and yet at the same time have in their own theorizing continued to accept uncritically other aspects of the tradition that informs those ideas about "woman's nature." In particular, by looking at the example of Plato, I want to suggest why it is important for feminists not only to question what these philosophers have said about women, but also what philosophers have had to say about the mind/body distinction.

Plato's Lessons About the Soul and the Body

Plato's dialogues are filled with lessons about knowledge, reality, and goodness, and most of the lessons carry with them strong praise for the soul and strong indictments against the body. According to Plato, the body, with its deceptive senses, keeps us from real knowledge; it rivets us in a world of material things which is far removed from the world of reality; and it tempts us away from the virtuous life. It is in and through the soul, if at all, that we shall have knowledge, be in touch with reality, and lead a life of virtue. Only the soul can truly know, for only the soul can ascend to the real world, the world of the Forms or Ideas. That world is the perfect model to which imperfect, particular things, we find in matter merely approximate. It is a world which, like the soul, is invisible, unchanging, not subject to decay, eternal. To be good, one's soul must know the Good, that is, the Form of Goodness, and this is impossible while one is dragged down by the demands and temptations of bodily life. Hence, bodily death is nothing to be feared: immortality of the soul not only is possible, but greatly to be desired, because when one is released from the body one finally can get down to the real business of life, for this real business of life is the business of the soul. Indeed, Socrates describes his own commitment, while still on earth, to encouraging his fellow Athenians to pay attention to the real business of life:

> [I have spent] all my time going about trying to persuade you, young and old, to make your first and chief concern not for your bodies nor for your possessions, but for the highest welfare of your souls. [*Apology* 30a–b]

Plato also tells us about the nature of beauty. Beauty has nothing essentially to do with the body or with the world of material things. *Real* beauty cannot "take the form of a face, or of hands, or of anything that is of the flesh" (*Symposium* 221a). Yes, there are beautiful things, but they only are entitled to be described that way because they "partake in" the form of Beauty, which itself is not found in the material world. Real beauty has characteristics which merely beautiful *things* cannot have; real beauty

> is an everlasting loveliness which neither comes nor goes, which neither flowers nor fades, for such beauty is the same on every hand, the same then as now, here as there, this way as that way, the same to every worshiper as it is to every other. [*Symposium* 221a]

Because it is only the soul that can know the Forms, those eternal and unchanging denizens of Reality, only the soul can know real Beauty; our changing, decaying bodies can only put us in touch with changing, decaying pieces of the material world.

Plato also examines love. His famous discussion of love in the *Symposium* ends up being a celebration of the soul over the body. Attraction to and appreciation for the beauty of another's body is but a vulgar fixation unless one can use such appreciation as a stepping stone to understanding Beauty itself. One can begin to learn about Beauty, while one is still embodied, when one notices that this body is beautiful, that that body is beautiful, and so on, and then one begins to realize that Beauty itself is something beyond any particular beautiful body or thing. The kind of love between people that is to be valued is not the attraction of one body for another, but the attraction of one soul for another. There is procreation of the spirit as well as of the flesh (*Symposium* 209a). All that bodies in unison can create are more bodies—the children women bear—which are mortal, subject to change and decay. But souls in unison can create "something lovelier and less mortal than human seed," for spiritual lovers "conceive and bear the things of the spirit," that is, "wisdom and all her sister virtues" (*Symposium* 209c). Hence, spiritual love between men is preferable to physical love between men and women. . . .

So, then, one has no hope of understanding the nature of knowledge, reality, goodness, love, or beauty unless one recognizes the distinction between soul and body; and one has no hope of attaining any of these unless one works hard on freeing the soul from the lazy, vulgar, beguiling body. A philosopher is someone who is committed to doing just that, and that is why philosophers go willingly unto death; it is, after all, only the death of their bodies, and finally, once their souls are released from their bodies, these philosophical desiderata are within reach.

The offices and attributes of the body vis-à-vis the soul are on the whole interchangeable, in Plato's work, with the offices and attributes of one part of the soul vis-à-vis another part. The tug-of-war between soul and body has the same dynamics, and the same stakes, as the tug-of-war between "higher" and "lower" parts of the soul. For example, sometimes Plato speaks as if the soul should resist the desires not of the body, but of part of its very self (*Gorgias* 505b). Sometimes he describes internal conflict as the struggle between soul and body, and sometimes as the battle among the rational, the spirited, and the appetitive parts of the soul. The spirited part of the soul is supposed to help out the rational part in its constant attempt to "preside over the appetitive part which is the mass of the soul in each of us and the most insatiate by nature"; unless it is watched, the appetitive part can get "filled and infected with the so-called pleasures associated with the body" (*Republic* 442a–b).

The division among parts of the soul is intimately tied to one other central and famous aspect of Plato's philosophy that hasn't been mentioned so far: Plato's political views. His discussion of the parts of the soul and their proper relation to one another is integral to his view about the best way to set up a state. The rational part of the soul ought to rule the soul and ought to be attended by the spirited part in keeping watch over the unruly appetitive part; just so, there ought to be rulers of the state (the small minority in whom reason is dominant), who, with the aid of high-spirited guardians of order, watch over the multitudes (whose appetites need to be kept under control).

What we learn from Plato, then, about knowledge, reality, goodness, beauty, love, and statehood, is phrased in terms of a distinction between soul and body, or alternatively and roughly equivalently, in terms of a distinction between the rational and irrational. And the body, or the irrational part of the soul, is seen as an enormous and annoying obstacle to the possession of these desiderata. If the body gets the upper hand (!) over the soul, or if the irrational part of the soul overpowers the rational part, one can't have knowledge, one can't see beauty, one will be far from the highest form of love, and the state will be in utter chaos. So the soul/body distinction, or the distinction between the rational and irrational parts of the soul, is a highly charged distinction. An inquiry into the distinction is no mild metaphysical musing. It is quite clear that the distinction is heavily value-laden. Even if Plato hadn't told us outright that the soul is more valuable than the body, and the rational part of the soul is more important than the irrational part, that message rings out in page after page of his dialogues. The soul/body distinction, then, is integral to the rest of Plato's views, and the higher worth of the soul is integral to that distinction.

Plato's View of the Soul and Body, and His Attitude Toward Women

Plato, and anyone else who conceives of the soul as something unobservable, cannot of course speak as if we could point to the soul, or hold it up for direct observation. At one point, Plato says no mere mortal can really understand the nature of the soul, but one perhaps could tell what it resembles (*Phaedrus* 246a). So it is not surprising to find Plato using many metaphors and analogies to describe what the soul is *like*, in order to describe relations between the soul and the body or relations between parts of the soul. For example, thinking, a function of the soul, is described by analogy to talking (*Theaetetus* 190a; *Sophist* 263e). The parts of the soul are

likened to a team of harnessed, winged horses and their charioteer (*Phaedrus* 246a). The body's relation to the soul is such that we are to think of the body vis-à-vis the soul as a tomb (*Gorgias* 493a), as a grave or prison (*Cratylus* 400c), or as barnacles or rocks holding down the soul (*Republic* 611e–612a). Plato compares the lowest or bodylike part of the soul to a brood of beasts (*Republic* 590c).

But Plato's task is not only to tell us what the soul is like, not only to provide us with ways of getting a fix on the differences between souls and bodies, or differences between parts of the soul. As we've seen, he also wants to convince us that the soul is much more important than the body, and that it is to our peril that we let ourselves be beckoned by the rumblings of the body at the expense of harkening to the call of the soul. And he means to convince us of this by holding up for our inspection the silly and sordid lives of those who pay too much attention to their bodies and do not care enough for their souls; he wants to remind us of how unruly, how without direction, are the lives of those in whom the lower part of the soul holds sway over the higher part. Because he can't *point* to an adulterated soul, he points instead to those embodied beings whose lives are in such bad shape that we can be sure that their souls are adulterated. And whose lives exemplify the proper soul/body relationship gone haywire? The lives of women (or sometimes the lives of children, slaves, and brutes).

For example, how are we to know when the body has the upper hand over the soul, or when the lower part of the soul has managed to smother the higher part? We presumably can't see such conflict, so what do such conflicts translate into, in terms of actual human lives? Well, says Plato, look at the lives of women.[2] It is women who get hysterical at the thought of death (*Phaedo* 60a, 112d; *Apology* 35b); obviously, their emotions have overpowered their reason, and they can't control themselves. The worst possible model for young men could be "a woman, young or old or wrangling with her husband, defying heaven, loudly boasting, fortunate in her own conceit, or involved in misfortune or possessed by grief and lamentation—still less a woman that is sick, in love, or in labor" (*Republic* 395d–e). He continues:

> When in our own lives some affliction comes to us you are aware that we plume ourselves . . . on our ability to remain calm and endure, in the belief that this is the conduct of a man, and [giving in to grief] that of a woman [*Republic* 605c–d].

To have more concern for your body than your soul is to act just like a woman; hence, the most proper penalty for a soldier who surrenders to save his body, when he should be willing to die out of the courage of his soul, is for the soldier to be turned into a woman (*Laws* 944e). Plato believed that souls can go through many different embodied life-times. There will be certain indications, in one's life, of the kind of life one is leading now; and unless a man lives righteously now, he will as his next incarnation "pass into a woman" and if he doesn't behave then, he'll become a brute! (*Timaeus* 42b–c, 76e, 91a).

Moreover, Plato on many occasions points to women to illustrate the improper way to pursue the things for which philosophers are constantly to be searching. For example, Plato wants to explain how important and also how difficult the attainment of real knowledge is. He wants us to realize that not just anyone can have knowledge, there is a vital distinction between those who really have knowledge and those who merely think they do. Think, for example, about the question of health. If we don't make a distinction between those who know what health is, and those who merely have unfounded and confused opinions about what health is, then "in the matter of good or bad health . . . any woman or child—or animal, for that matter—knows what is wholesome for it and is capable of curing itself" (*Theaetetus* 171c). The implication is clear: if any

old opinion were to count as real knowledge, then we'd have to say that women, children, and maybe even animals have knowledge. But surely *they* don't have knowledge! And why not? For one thing, because they don't recognize the difference between the material, changing world of appearance, and the invisible, eternal world of Reality. In matters of beauty, for example, they are so taken by the physical aspects of things that they assume that they can see and touch what is beautiful; they don't realize that what one knows when one has knowledge of real Beauty cannot be something that is seen or touched. Plato offers us, then, as an example of the failure to distinguish between Beauty itself, on the one hand, and beautiful things, on the other, "boys and women when they see bright-colored things" (*Republic* 557c). They don't realize that it is not through one's senses that one knows about beauty or anything else, for real beauty is eternal and unchangeable and can only be known through the soul.

So the message is that in matters of knowledge, reality, and beauty, don't follow the example of women. They are mistaken about those things. In matters of love, women's lives serve as negative examples also. Those men who are drawn by "vulgar" love, that is, love of body for body, "turn to women as the object of their love, and raise a family" (*Symposium* 208e); those men drawn by a more "heavenly" kind of love, that is, love of soul for soul, turn to other men. But there are strong sanctions against physical love between men: such physical unions, especially between older and younger men, are "unmanly." The older man isn't strong enough to resist his lust (as in woman, the irrational part of the soul has overtaken the rational part), and the younger man, "the impersonator of the female," is reproached for this "likeness to the model" (*Laws* 836e). The problem with physical love between men, then, is that men are acting like women. . . .

To anyone at all familiar with Plato's official and oft-reported views about women, the above recitation of misogynistic remarks may be quite surprising. Accounts of Plato's views about women usually are based on what he says in book 5 of the *Republic*. In that dialogue, Plato startled his contemporaries, when as part of his proposal for the constitution of an ideal state, he suggested that

> there is no pursuit of the administrators of a state that belongs to woman because she is a woman or to a man because he is a man. But the natural capacities are distributed alike among both creatures, and women naturally share in all pursuits and men in all [*Republic* 455d–e].

The only difference between men and women, Plato says at this point, is that women have weaker bodies than men, but this is no sign that something is amiss with their souls. . . .

Well now, what are we to make of this apparent double message in Plato about women? What are we to do with the fact that on the one hand, when Plato explicitly confronts the question of women's nature, in the *Republic*, he seems to affirm the equality of men and women; while on the other hand, the dialogues are riddled with misogynistic remarks? I think that understanding the centrality and importance of the soul/body distinction in Plato's work helps us to understand this contradiction in his views about women. As we've seen, Plato insists, over and over again in a variety of ways, that our souls are the most important part of us. Not only is it through our souls that we shall have access to knowledge, reality, goodness, beauty; but also, in effect we *are* our souls; when our bodies die and decay, we, that is our souls, shall live on. Our bodies are not essential to our identity; in their most benign aspect, our bodies are incidental appendages; in their most malignant aspect, they are obstacles to the smooth functioning of our souls. If we *are* our souls, and our bodies are not essential to who we are, then it doesn't make any difference, ultimately, whether we have a woman's body or a man's body. When one thinks about this emphasis in Plato's thought,

his views about the equality of women and men seem integral to the rest of his views. If the only difference between women and men is that they have different bodies, and if bodies are merely incidental attachments to what constitutes one's real identity, then there is no important difference between men and women.

But as we have also seen, Plato seems to want to make very firm his insistence on the destructiveness of the body to the soul. In doing so, he holds up for our ridicule and scorn those lives devoted to bodily pursuits. Over and over again, women's lives are depicted as being such lives. His misogyny, then, is part of his somatophobia: the body is seen as the source of all the undesirable traits a human being could have, and women's lives are spent manifesting those traits.

So the contradictory sides of Plato's views about women are tied to the distinction he makes between soul and body and the lessons he hopes to teach his readers about their relative value. When preaching about the overwhelming importance of the soul, he can't but regard the kind of body one has as of no final significance, so there is no way for him to assess differentially the lives of women and men; but when making gloomy pronouncements about the worth of the body, he points an accusing finger at a class of people with a certain kind of body—women—because he regards them, as a class, as embodying (!) the very traits he wishes no one to have. In this way, women constitute a deviant class in Plato's philosophy, in the sense that he points to their lives as the kinds of lives that are not acceptable philosophically: they are just the kinds of lives no one, especially philosophers, ought to live. It is true that Plato chastises certain kinds of men: sophists, tyrants, and cowards, for example. But he frequently puts them in their place by comparing them to women! . . .

In summary, Plato does not merely embrace a distinction between soul and body; for all the good and hopeful and desirable possibilities for human life (now and in an afterlife) are aligned with the soul, while the rather seedy and undesirable liabilities of human life are aligned with the body (alternatively, the alignment is with the higher or lower parts of the soul). There is a highly polished moral gloss to the soul/body distinction in Plato. One of his favorite devices for bringing this moral gloss to a high luster is holding up, for our contempt and ridicule, the lives of women. This is one of the ways he tries to make clear that it makes no small difference whether you lead a soul-directed or a bodily directed life.

Feminism and "Somatophobia"

There are a number of reasons why feminists should be aware of the legacy of the soul/body distinction. It is not just that the distinction has been wound up with the depreciation and degradation of women, although, as has just been shown, examining a philosopher's views of the distinction may give us a direct route to his views about women.

First of all, as the soul or mind or reason is extolled, and the body or passion is denounced by comparison, it is not just women who are both relegated to the bodily or passionate sphere of existence and then chastised for belonging to that sphere. Slaves, free laborers, children, and animals are put in "their place" on almost the same grounds as women are. The images of women, slaves, laborers, children, and animals are almost interchangeable. For example, we find Plato holding that the best born and best educated should have control over "children, women and slaves . . . and the base rabble of those who are free in name," because it is in these groups that we find "the mob of motley appetites and pleasures and pains" (*Republic* 431b–c). As we saw above, Plato lumps together women, children, and animals as ignoramuses. . . . A common way of denigrating a member of any one of these groups is to compare that member to a member of one of the other groups—women are

thought to have slavish or childish appetites, slaves are said to be brutish. Recall too, that Plato's way of ridiculing male homosexuals was to say that they imitated women. It is no wonder that the images and insults are almost interchangeable, for there is a central descriptive thread holding together the images of all these groups. The members of these groups lack, for all intents and purposes, mind or the power of reason; even the humans among them are not considered fully human.

It is important for feminists to see to what extent the images and arguments used to denigrate women are similar to those used to denigrate one group of men vis-à-vis another, children vis-à-vis adults, animals vis-à-vis humans, and even—though I have not discussed it here—the natural world vis-à-vis man's will (yes, man's will). For to see this is part of understanding how the oppression of women occurs in the context of, and is related to, other forms of oppression or exploitation.

There is a second reason why feminists should be aware of the legacy of the soul/body distinction. Some feminists have quite happily adopted both the soul/body distinction and relative value attached to soul and to body. But in doing so, they may be adopting a position inimical to what on a more conscious level they are arguing for.

For all her magisterial insight into the way in which the image of woman as body has been foisted upon and used against us, Simone de Beauvoir can't resist the temptation to say that woman's emancipation will come when woman, like man, is freed from this association with—according to the male wisdom of centuries—the less important aspect of human existence. According to *The Second Sex*, women's demand is "not that they be exalted in their femininity; they wish that in themselves, as in humanity in general, transcendence may prevail over immanence."[3] But in de Beauvoir's own terms, for "transcendence" to prevail over "immanence" is for spirit or mind to prevail over matter or body, for reason to prevail over passion and desire. This means not only that the old images of women as mired in the world of "immanence"—the world of nature and physical existence—will go away. It will also happen that women won't lead lives given over mainly to their "natural" functions: "the pain of childbirth is on the way out"; "artificial insemination is on the way in."[4] Although de Beauvoir doesn't explicitly say it, her directions for women are to find means of leaving the world of immanence and joining the men in the realm of transcendence. Men have said, de Beauvoir reminds us, that to be human is to have mind prevail over body; and no matter what disagreements she has elsewhere with men's perceptions and priorities, de Beauvoir here seems to agree with them. Explicitly de Beauvoir tells us not to be the people men have dreamt us up to be; but implicitly, she tells us to be the people men have dreamt themselves up to be.

I'm not insisting that de Beauvoir should have told us to stay where we are. The burden of her book is to describe the mixture of fear, awe, and disgust in men's attitudes toward the physical world, the body, the woman. Men have purchased one-way tickets to Transcendence in their attempt to deny, or conquer and control, the raging Immanence they see in themselves and project onto women. De Beauvoir says that this attitude toward corporeality has informed men's oppression of women, and yet her directions for women seem to be informed by just the same attitude. But can we as a species sustain negative attitudes and negative ideologies about the bodily aspects of our existence and yet keep those attitudes and ideologies from working in behalf of one group of people as it attempts to oppress other groups? Let me cite some examples to show how unlikely it is that such entrenched values can linger without doing some harm.

The first example comes from Plato. The contradiction we saw in Plato's views about women comes precisely from the source we have just been talking about. For it is just insofar as Plato continues to regard our bodily existence as cause for disappointment, embarrassment, and evil, that he finds the lives of women (and others) the occasion for scorn and ridicule—and this despite his insistence elsewhere in his writings on the equality of women and men.

A second example comes from Betty Friedan. She may seem too easy a target, but I think that something closely connected to what I'm going to point out about her thought can also be found in feminists considered much more radical than she is. Very early in *The Feminine Mystique*,[5] Friedan remarks on the absence, in women's lives, of "the world of thought and ideas, the life of the mind and spirit."[6] She wants women to be "culturally" as well as "biologically" creative—she wants us to think about spending our lives "mastering the secrets of the atoms, or the stars, composing symphonies, pioneering a new concept in government or society."[7] And she associates "mental activity" with the "professions of highest value to society."[8] Friedan thus seems to believe that men have done the more important things, the mental things; women have been relegated in the past to the less important human tasks involving bodily functions, and their liberation will come when they are allowed and encouraged to do the more important things in life.

Friedan's analysis relies on our old friend, the mind/body distinction, and Friedan, no less than Plato or de Beauvoir, quite happily assumes that mental activities are more valuable than bodily ones. Her solution to what she referred to as the "problem that has no name" is for women to leave (though not entirely) woman's sphere and "ascend" into man's. Certainly there is much pleasure and value in the "mental activities" she extols. But we can see the residue of her own negative attitude about tasks associated with the body: the bodily aspects of our existence must be attended to, but the "liberated" woman, who is on the ascendant, can't be bothered with them. There is yet another group of people to whom these tasks will devolve: servants. Woman's liberation—and of course it is no secret that by "woman," Friedan could only have meant middle-class white women—seems to require woman's dissociation and separation from those who will perform the bodily tasks which the liberated woman has left behind in pursuit of "higher," mental activity. . . .

I mentioned that feminists considered more radical than Friedan share something very close to her attitudes about the body: Shulamith Firestone is a case in point. In *The Dialectic of Sex*, Firestone traces the oppression of women to what she calls a "fundamental inequality" produced by nature: "half the human race must bear and rear the children of all of them."[9] Apart from the fact that we need some explanation of how Nature dictated that women should *rear* children, we also need to understand what it is about bearing children that Firestone finds oppressive. According to Firestone, the fact of their childbearing capacity has been used to justify the oppression of women. But it is not just this that concerns and bothers her. She also thinks that in and of itself childbearing is dreadful; the way in which she describes pregnancy and childbirth tells us that she would find them oppressive even in the absence of oppressive institutions set up around them. She calls pregnancy "barbaric"; and says that "childbirth *hurts*."[10] Curiously, Firestone elsewhere is angered at the male image of what women ought to look like—"Women everywhere rush to squeeze into the glass slipper, forcing and mutilating their bodies with diets and beauty programs";[11] and in fact she reminds her readers that, contrary to male myths, human beauty allows for "growth and flux and decay."[12] Yet she doesn't hesitate to describe pregnancy as a "deformation" of the body.[13] The disgust and fear she expressed reminds one of de Beauvoir's many descriptions of male attitudes toward specifically female and specifically physical functions. As Adrienne Rich has pointed out, "Firestone sees childbearing . . . as purely and simply

the victimizing experience it has often been under patriarchy."[14]

Undoubtedly, woman's body has been part of the source of our oppression in several senses. First, pregnancy and childbirth have in fact made women vulnerable, for a long time in the history of the species, and even for a short time in the history of the most economically privileged of women. Second, woman has been portrayed as essentially a bodily being, and this image has been used to deny her full status as a human being wherever and whenever mental activity as over against bodily activity has been thought to be the most human activity of all. But is the way to avoid oppression to radically change the experience of childbirth through technology, as Firestone suggested, and insist that woman *not* be seen as connected to her body at all, that is, to insist that woman's "essential self," just as man's, lies in her mind, and not in her body? If so, then we are admitting tacitly that the men—from Plato on down—have been right all along, in insisting on a distinction between mind or soul and body, and insisting that mind is to be valued more than body. They've only been wrong in ungenerously denying woman a place up there with them, among the other minds. Woman's liberation, on this view, is just a much belated version of the men's liberation that took place centuries ago, when men figured out ways both to dissociate themselves from, and/or conquer, the natural world and that part of them—their bodies—which reminds them of their place in that natural world. And one would think, reading feminists as different as de Beauvoir, Friedan, and Firestone, that indeed what woman's liberation ultimately means is liberation from our bodies—both in fact, and in definition. . . .

There is of course much more to be said about de Beauvoir, Friedan, and Firestone than my brief remarks here. And of course there is much more to feminist theory than what they have said, although their theories have been influential for different segments of the women's movement, and their works constitute important landmarks in the development of feminist theory. Even in the recent work of Mary Daly, who knows the ways of the Church "Fathers" too well to describe women's liberation simply in terms of a spirituality divorced from embodiment, it is difficult to see in any detail what women free from the shackles of patriarchy will be like: "Spinsters" appear to have none of the characteristics of personal identity which are related to embodiment: color, culture, specific histories. In her insistence on all women overcoming the barriers that have been used to divide us, Daly ends up with a general notion of woman that seems to be abstracted from any of the particular facts about us which make us different from one another. As Judith Plaskow has remarked, Daly offers "a vision of wild and ecstatic, but essentially contentless and disembodied, freedom."[15]

What I have tried to do here is bring attention to the fact that various versions of women's liberation may themselves rest on the very same assumptions that have informed the deprecation and degradation of women, and other groups, in the past. Those assumptions are that we must distinguish between soul and body, and that the physical part of our existence is to be devalued in comparison to the mental. Of course, these two assumptions alone don't mean that women or other groups have to be degraded; it's these two assumptions, along with the further assumption that woman is body, or is bound to her body, or is meant to take care of the bodily aspects of life, that have so deeply contributed to the degradation and oppression of women. And so perhaps feminists would like to keep the first two assumptions (about the difference between mind and body, and the relative worth of each of them) and somehow get rid of the last— in fact, that is what most of the feminists previously discussed have tried to do. Nothing that has been said so far has amounted to an argument against those first two assumptions: it hasn't been shown that there is no foundation for

the assumptions that the mind and body are distinct and that the body is to be valued less than the mind.

There is a feminist thinker, however, who has taken it upon herself to chip away directly at the second assumption and to a certain extent at the first. Both in her poetry, and explicitly in her recent book, *Of Woman Born*, Adrienne Rich has begun to show us why use of the mind/body distinction does not give us appropriate descriptions of human experience; and she has begun to remind us of the distance we keep from ourselves when we try to keep a distance from our bodies.[16] She does this in the process of trying to redefine the dimensions of the experience of childbirth, as she tries to show us why childbirth and motherhood need not mean what they have meant under patriarchy.

We are reminded by Rich that it is possible to be alienated from our bodies not only by pretending or wishing they weren't there, but also by being "incarcerated" in them.[17] The institution of motherhood has done the latter in its insistence on seeing woman only or mainly as a reproductive machine. Defined as flesh by flesh-loathers, woman enters the most "fleshly" of her experiences with that same attitude of flesh-loathing—surely "physical self-hatred and suspicion of one's own body is scarcely a favorable emotion with which to enter an intense physical experience."[18]

But Rich insists that we don't have to experience it as a "torture rack";[19] but neither do we have to mystify it as a "peak experience." The experience of childbirth can be viewed as a way of recognizing the integrity of our experience, because pain itself is not usefully catalogued as something just our minds or just our bodies experience. Giving birth is painful, indeed; but painkillers are not necessarily the appropriate way to deal with pain, for we are no less estranged from our bodies, no less put at men's disposal, when "rescued" from our pain by drugs. The point of "natural childbirth" should be thought of not as enduring pain, but as having an active physical experience—a distinction we recognize as crucial for understanding, for example, the pleasure in athletics.

Rich recognizes that feminists have not wanted to accept patriarchal versions of female biology, of what having a female body means. It has seemed to feminists, she implies, that we must either accept that view of being female, which is, essentially, to be a body, or deny that view and insist that we are "disembodied spirits."[20] It perhaps is natural to see our alternatives that way:

> We have been perceived for too many centuries as pure Nature, exploited and raped like the earth and the solar system; small wonder if we not try to become Culture: pure spirit, mind.[21]

But we don't *have* to do that, Rich reminds us; we can appeal to the physical without denying what is called "mind." We can come to regard our physicality as "resource, rather than a destiny":

> In order to live a fully human life we require not only *control* of our bodies (though control is a prerequisite); we must touch the unity and resonance of our physicality, our bond with the natural order, the corporeal ground of our intelligence.[22]

Rich doesn't deny that we will have to start thinking about our lives in new ways; she even implies that we'll have to start thinking about thinking in new ways. Maybe it will give such a project a small boost to point out that philosophers for their part still squabble about mind/body dualism; the legacy of dualism is strong, but not unchallenged by any means. And in any event, as I have noted earlier, one can hardly put the blame for sexism (or any other form of oppression) on dualism itself. Indeed, the mind/body distinction can be put to progressive political ends, for example, to assert equality between human beings in the face of physical differences between them. There is nothing intrinsically sexist or otherwise oppres-

sive about dualism, that is, about the belief that there are minds and there are bodies and that they are distinct kinds of things. But historically, the story dualists tell often ends up being a highly politicized one: although the story may be different at different historical moments, often it is said not only that there are minds (or souls) and bodies, but also that one is meant to rule and control the other. And the stage is thereby set for the soul/body distinction, now highly politicized and hierarchically ordered, to be used in a variety of ways in connection with repressive theories of the self, as well as oppressive theories of social and political relations. Among the tasks facing feminists is to think about the criteria for an adequate theory of self. Part of the value of Rich's work is that it points to the necessity of such an undertaking, and it is no criticism of her to say that she does no more than remind us of some of the questions that need to be raised.

A Final Note About the Significance of Somatophobia in Feminist Theory

In the history of political philosophy, the grounds given for the inferiority of women to men often are quite similar to those given for the inferiority of slaves to masters, children to fathers, animals to humans. In Plato, for example, all such subordinate groups are guilty by association with one another and each group is guilty by association with the bodily. In their eagerness to end the stereotypical association of woman and body, feminists such as de Beauvoir, Friedan, Firestone, and Daly have overlooked the significance of the connections—in theory and practice—between the derogation and oppression of women on the basis of our sexual identity and the derogation and oppression of other groups on the basis of, for example, skin color or class membership. It is as if in their eagerness to assign women a new place in the scheme of things, these feminist theorists have by implication wanted to dissociate women from other subordinate groups. One problem with this, of course, is that those other subordinate groups include women.

What is especially significant about Rich's recent work is that, in contrast to these other theorists, she both challenges the received tradition about the insignificance and indignity of bodily life and bodily tasks and explicitly focuses on racism as well as sexism as essential factors in women's oppression. I believe that it is not merely a coincidence that someone who attends to the first also attends to the second. Rich pauses not just to recognize the significance attached to the female body, but also to re-examine that significance. "Flesh-loathing" is loathing of flesh by some particular group under some particular circumstances—the loathing of women's flesh by men, but also the loathing of black flesh by whites. . . . After all, bodies are always particular bodies—they are male or female bodies (our deep confusion when we can't categorize a body in either way supports and does not belie the general point); but they are black or brown or biscuit or yellow or red bodies as well. We cannot seriously attend to the social significance attached to embodiment without recognizing this. I believe that it is Rich's recognition of this that distinguishes her work in crucial ways from that of most other major white feminists. Although the topic of feminism, sexism, and racism deserves a much fuller treatment,[23] it is important to point out in the context of the present paper that not only does Rich challenge an assumption about the nature of the bodily that has been used to oppress women, but unlike other feminists who do not challenge this assumption, she takes on the question of the ways in which sexism and racism interlock. Somatophobia historically has been symptomatic not only of sexism, but also of racism, so it is perhaps not surprising that someone who has examined that connection between flesh-loathing and sexism would undertake an examination of racism.

Feminists may find it fruitful to examine the extent to which attitudes toward and ideologies about the body have played a role not only in sexist institutions and analyses, but also in the analyses feminists themselves are developing in response to such institutions and theories. A theory of embodiment, which must include a theory of the social significance of embodiment, is part of the needed feminist theory of self referred to earlier. Such a theory might reveal some deep connections among sexism, racism, and classism. It might also help expose some of the relations between homophobia and racism, insofar as both historically have such strong connections to fear of sexuality. We also need to ask what theories of embodiment are presupposed by feminist analyses of women's health. All these examinations are part of our refusal to pay homage to a long tradition of somatophobia—a tradition it has been hard for us to shake.

NOTES

1. There is no reason to think philosophers used "man" or its equivalent in other languages generically. For example, in discussing the conditions of happiness for "man," Aristotle raises the question of whether a "man's" being self-sufficient is compatible with his having a wife (*Nicomachean Ethics* 1097b11).

All references to Plato are from *Collected Dialogues of Plato*, ed. Edith Hamilton and Huntington Cairns (New York: Pantheon, 1963), and are supplied in parentheses in the text.

2. Although Plato objects to certain types of men—sophists, tyrants, and so forth—his disdain for women is always expressed as disdain for women in general and not for any subgroup of women. Moreover, one of the ways he shows his disdain for certain types of men is to compare them to women.

3. Simone de Beauvoir, *The Second Sex* (New York: Knopf, 1952), p. 123.

4. *Ibid.*, p. 111.

5. Betty Friedan, *The Feminine Mystique* (New York: Norton, 1963).

6. *Ibid.*, p. 36.

7. *Ibid.*, p. 247.

8. *Ibid.*, p. 277.

9. Shulamith Firestone, *The Dialectic of Sex* (New York: Bantam, 1970), p. 205.

10. *Ibid.*, p. 198.

11. *Ibid.*, p. 152.

12. *Ibid.*, p. 155.

13. *Ibid.*, p. 198.

14. Adrienne Rich, *Of Woman Born* (New York: Norton, 1976), p. 174.

15. Judith Plaskow, from a lecture entitled "Woman as Body: The History of an Idea," Oberlin College, Oberlin, Ohio, April 1979. I learned about this lecture long after I first entitled this essay.

16. Rich, *Of Woman Born*.

17. *Ibid.*, p. 13.

18. *Ibid.*, p. 163.

19. *Ibid.*, p. 157.

20. *Ibid.*, p. 40.

21. *Ibid.*, p. 285.

22. *Ibid.*, p. 39.

23. This topic is more fully covered in some of the selections in Chapter 5 of this text, especially in bell hooks's "Racism and Feminism." —Ed.

An Autobiographical View of Mixed Race and Deracination   1.7

NAOMI ZACK

Naomi Zack (b. 1944) now teaches philosophy at the State University of New York at Albany. However, after receiving her Ph.D. from Columbia University in 1970, she began a twenty-year odyssey outside the domain of academia. During this time, she made films, ran a small business, and did free-lance writing. She also gained the depth of experience on issues of race and race relations that is reflected in the following article. This same depth of experience is evident in her recently published book, *Race and Mixed Race* (Temple University Press, 1993).

Zack begins the article below by noting that in American society racial categories are disjunctive; that is, one must be of one race or another (in this case either black or white), but not both. However, as de Beauvoir noted concerning the relationship of male to female, the two disjunctive categories are not reciprocal. As Zack notes in several places in her article, in American society being white has traditionally been viewed as being preferable to being black. Moreover, one was considered white only if one had all white ancestors; anyone with even one nonwhite ancestor was considered nonwhite and therefore nondesirable. Such a schema or system of racial designation, according to Zack, is obviously both racist and unjust. It is also scientifically indefensible, for Zack points out that this system of racial classification lacks any basis in physiology or biology. Rather, as de Beauvoir suggested concerning the concept of femininity, Zack claims that the concept of race is socially and historically determined. Since it is both racist and unjust and since it has no defensible theoretical basis, Zack suggests that the concept of race ought to be rejected, a move that she calls "deracination."

One of the remarkable things about Zack's article is that she combines this rather theoretical analysis of the concept of race (an analysis that she refers to as the problematization of race) with personal reflections on her own self-identity. Being of mixed race, in her case having a black father and a Jewish mother, Zack finds that the traditional schema of racial classification, especially given its disjunctive nature, interferes with her own self-development or self-emancipation. While she notes that self-development or self-emancipation begins with self-respect, she does not believe that it can be fully attained in isolation. On the contrary, Zack believes that an essential component of self-development or self-emancipation depends on what others think about us—our self-respect must be complemented by the respect of others. However, given the traditional schema of racial classification found in American society, Zack believes that a person of mixed race is not likely to receive this respect from others. Thus, her call for deracination, her refusal to have anything to do with the concept of race, has personal as well as theoretical implications.

Questions for Thought

1. What does Zack mean by the concept of race? What do you think the concept of race means?
2. To what extent, if any, does your race determine your self-identity?
3. Do you agree with Zack's claim that self-development or self-emancipation depends on the valuation of others? Why or why not?
4. Why do you think that sexual relations between black and white people have been taboo in American society? Can you think of any justification whatsoever that would support this taboo?
5. What does Zack mean by "deracination"? Do you agree with her that deracination is desirable? Would you consider yourself to be deracinated?
6. I have pointed out a couple of similarities between Zack's views and those of de Beauvoir. Can you think of other similarities?

The Subject

AMERICAN RACIAL CATEGORIES ARE EXCLUSIVELY disjunctive: Thou shalt have a race, and, thy race must be black or white, but not both! As a result of this imperative disjunction, the person of mixed black and white race may pose a problem for others. The mixed-race person may also encounter contradictory identities in her view of herself. These contradictory identities do not admit of any easeful resolution.

In racial matters self-emancipation may be a last recourse. But self-emancipation can lead the person of mixed race to conclusions which are jarring in their ahistoricality, and unacceptable to people whose racial identities are not self-contradictory. I will call the awareness of the problem of mixed race, by a person of mixed race, the problematization of mixed race. And I will call the solution of the problematization of mixed race, deracination. Deracination is a problem for people with black or white racial identities. An awareness of the problem of deracination by a deracinated person could be called the problematization of deracination. These distinctions between problems and problematizations are merely a preliminary way of demarcating racial existence, which includes experience, values and ideology, from racial theory. Problematization is on the side of theory.

The First Person

I am going to begin by describing some facts about myself which it has taken me many years

This article appeared in an American Philosophical Association Newsletter on Philosophy and the Black Experience (Issue no. 91:1, Spring 1992). © 1992, The American Philosophical Association. Reprinted by permission of the author.

to be able to describe evenly. It has taken me a long time to be able to even describe these facts, publicly, because of warps in my psychology, warps which I do not consider it irresponsible to insist are the effects of warps in external social reality.

My mother was a Jew whose parents came to this country from Lithuania, in 1903. My father was an African-American whose father was born a slave and whose mother claimed Sioux (Native American) descent. My parents were never married to each other and only my mother raised me. My mother was ashamed of her relationship with my father and she encouraged me to deny my black ancestry. She was not an observant Jew and neither am I. But she saw the world through (what I take to be) Jewish eyes and felt the world with (what I take to be) Jewish fears, and I have never been able to avoid (what I take to be) the same apperceptions. In other words, I believe I "identify" with my mother.

My mother knew herself to be a Jew, totally. Many Jews believe that if one's mother is a Jew, then one is a Jew oneself and it does not matter what one's father is. In American society, Jews are classified as white racially. For these reasons, I have usually been designated as white on official documents, especially those documents which do not have a category of undesignated "other."

I do not like to explicitly say that I am white because that is a lie—in American society, if one has a black parent, then one is black. I am black.

There are known to be blacks in the USA who have become Jews by religious conversion, but there is no widely recognized category of hereditary Jews who are racially black. Until recently, the American Jews I have known, have, with varying degrees of (slight) skepticism, accepted me as a Jew, with the understanding that my father was not a Jew—they have not been specially concerned with how he was not a Jew.[1] But my husbands and the close friends of my adult life have been white gentiles, for the most part. After I have told them that my father was black, a veil has often dropped over any understanding they had about how one inherits a Jewish identity. They have often made the judgment that I have been passing (for white), and that I cannot be a Jew because my father was black. This judgment has been echoed by some blacks I have known. In a way that I intuitively understand, the judgment by blacks that I have been passing (for white) has sometimes been accompanied by resentment and implied moral condemnation.

I am a Jew and therefore I am white. I am black and therefore I am not white. This contradiction is very difficult to think about without momentum from self-emancipation. Self-emancipation is a movement of values.

Self-Emancipation and Valuation

What am I? The racial and ethnic answers to this question can have a direct bearing on how I feel and whether my life, in general, is bearable to me. This question, What am I? as a question about racial and ethnic identity, divides into three categories: what I think I am; what others think I am; what I want others to think I am. The answers have value-neutral, value-positive and value-negative, first-, second- and third-person aspects. The goal of self-emancipation is to unite a value-positive answer to the question What do I think I am? with a value-positive answer to the question What do others think I am? This movement from a value-positive, first-person description of myself, to a value-positive, second- and third-person description of me, is contained in how I *want* others to value me. Thus, first I aim to feel good about myself and then I aim to get others to have good feelings toward me; although at stake is something more stringent than feelings, more than a matter of being liked, something which at least involves respect. Self-emancipation is thereby a social activity which begins with positive self-valuation. Oppression is also a social activity, although it need not begin in value-negative, third-person judgments; oppression may begin with self-interest, for example.

Self-emancipation is difficult to get started because the self which needs to be positively revalued in order to overcome oppression has already been identified by negative valuations from others. Every step up in value will be resisted by those who not only devalue me but consider it their right to do so. Solitary acts of self-revaluation may at the outset be indistinguishable from delusions of grandeur and other alienated and isolated anti-social expressions of inner life, which have little to do with freedom. Positive self-valuation about race and ethnicity requires that negative valuations which express racism and ethnocentricity be somehow overcome. There are few forms of negative valuation in the USA which are more oppressive than racial designations. American racial designations are based on a kinship schema of black and white racial inheritance. A person of mixed race must begin with this schema in order to answer the question, What am I?

The Kinship Schema of Black and White Racial Inheritance

There is a strong asymmetry between black and white racial inheritance. If a person has a black parent, a black grand-parent or black great "n" grand-parents (where n is indeterminate, in principle), then that person is considered black. But if a person has a white parent, or three white grand-parents, or X white great "n" grand-parents (where X is any odd number and n is still indeterminate, in principle), then that person is not thereby considered white. This is a kinship schema and it means that whiteness is nothing more than the absence of any black forebears, and blackness is nothing more than the presence of one black forebear. Apart from this cultural schema, there is no natural black or white racial substratum or essence which anyone can identify in physiological terms. Nevertheless, the kinship schema of racial inheritance is so widely accepted that it is assumed to have a physiological basis. It is assumed that if one refers to a person's race according to this schema, then one is referring to some objective and universal-to-that-race characteristic of the person.

As a social entity, the black race in America is perceived to have an ethnic cohesion based on family affiliation; the recognition of black people by white people and other black people; the general negative value of being black; and the shared cultural practices, preferences, aspirations and experiences of black people. This entire social situation contributes to black ethnicity or black identity.[2] Given the false identification of race with a physiological substratum, an analogy could be drawn between race and ethnicity, and sex and gender. But the analogy breaks down insofar as there is now less tolerance of critiques of ethnicity than critiques of gender.

In contrast to black ethnic identity, white ethnic identity in the USA is usually based on differences in the national origins of the forebears of white people. Thus, while black ethnic identity is believed to be racial, white ethnic identity refers to foreign nationality. Two exceptions to this rule come to mind, however: White supremacists appear to base their ethnicity solely on the absence of non-white forebears in their heredity. And some white ethnic groups, such as Jews, and perhaps Roman Catholics, seem to base their ethnic identity primarily on their religion.

The above sketch of the schema of black and white racial inheritance and the description of racial ethnicity in the USA is not new and neither does it contradict the common sense racial and ethnic categorizations which most American people make. If one adds the negative valuation of blacks in comparison to whites, to the strong asymmetry in the schema of black and white racial inheritance, it is impossible to escape the conclusion that the schema is both racist in favor of whites and unjust. The schema is racist in favor of whites because it automatically excludes some people, who have white ancestors, from member-ship in the white race, while others with white ancestry are not thereby excluded. This exclusionary force of the schema reinforces social beliefs about the superiority of whites in comparison to blacks. The schema is unjust because it denies individuals with black forebears the right to claim anything of positive racial value on the basis of having white forebears. Thus, the schema discriminates against people with black forebears, with respect to their having white forebears, solely because they have black forebears.

The Problemization of Mixed Race

I mean to distinguish between the problem of mixed race and the problematization of mixed race. The problem of mixed race is a problem for white people, mainly, because historically sexual relations between white people and black people were socially taboo—they were also illegal for long periods of American history. The existence of an individual of mixed race was, and still is, proof that these taboos had been violated, and it was proof which many proponents of the prohibitions valued negatively in social and moral spheres. The problematization of mixed race is formulated by a person of mixed race when she thinks about the schema of racial inheritance and the prevailing attitudes about race and ethnicity. Except in cases of extreme despair, the person of mixed race does not have a problem with mixed race because she does not have a problem with the bare fact of her own existence.

The first part of the problematization of mixed race is in the designation of the term "mixed race" for someone who has both black and white forebears. Strictly speaking, the designation should never be made and fails to make sense. According to the accepted schema of racial inheritance, everyone with at least one black forebear is black and everyone with all white forebears is white. Therefore everyone is either black or white. There are no people of mixed race.

Black people are likely to perceive the person who is culturally and ethnically white, but racially black, as an inauthentic black person, someone who is disloyal to other black people or who evades or denies racial discrimination by attempting to pass (for white). From a black ethnic perspective it is not plausible that someone who is designated as of mixed race in white contexts might have spent so much of her life in white contexts that she does not have a black ethnic identity. The (authentic) racial and ethnic black person will hold the person of mixed race responsible for not having had the courage (and good faith) to acquire a black ethnic identity, as soon as she became aware of the injustice of racism and racial discrimination against black people. There is a moral injunction here that one ought not to benefit from a loophole in what one knows to be an unjust situation. The black person, who functions as a white person in white contexts, under the honorarium of a mixed race designation, has an obligation, supererogatory though it may be, to insist that her skills be recognized by white people as the skills of a black person. If this person of mixed race does not do that, then it can only be because she agrees with the negative valuation of black people by white people. This, then, is how I understand the implied moral argument.

I think that the argument is persuasive up to a point. The argument is only persuasive as long as one accepts the strongly asymmetrical kinship schema of racial designation. The argument ceases to be persuasive when one's racial existence does not support this schema. If one spent one's formative years with white people and failed to realign one's ethnic identity in adolescence, when it may still have been possible, then the moral argument may not so much be a spur to action as the cause of bad conscience. My bad conscience is not assuaged by claims of Jewish ethnic identity because the difficulty of the Jewish experience is not immediate in contemporary American society. While I do not think that it can be conclusively argued that in a conflict between two allegiances, morality is always on the side of the claim which represents the greater present suffering, if present action is called for, one is obligated to respond to the present situation. Any bad conscience can be a spur to an intellectual and moral position which has merits in spite of its origins. The bad conscience which has grown out of my problematization of mixed race has at times led me to a position of deracination. But regardless of my conscience, the position of deracination has strong merits.

Deracination

This is the position of deracination: The schema of racial inheritance in the USA is racist and unjust. As a rational woman with both black and white forebears, I do not accept this schema. I refuse to be pressured into denying the existence of black forebears to please whites, and I refuse to be pressured into denying my white ethnicity and my white forebears, to please blacks. There is no biological foundation of the concept of race. The concept of race is an oppressive cultural invention and convention, and I refuse to have anything to do with it. I refuse to be reasonable in order to placate either blacks or whites who retain non-empirical and irrational categorizations. Therefore, I have no racial affiliation and will accept no racial designations. If more people joined me in refusing to play the unfair game of race, fewer injustices based on the concept of race would be perpetrated.

The literal meaning of the term "deracination" is "to be plucked up by the roots." What is it in me that is supposed to have roots? What is the "soil" in which these "roots" have a natural and not-to-be-disturbed location? Affiliations with others in the present, mental reconstructions of the past and plans for the future based on my "roots," and their "soil," especially plans which I would have to impose on my children, are all active, deliberate doings, which require choices and expenditures of energy in the present and future. There is no automatic "claim" exerted by "roots." I am not a

fish out of water, a cat up a tree, or any kind of plant. If I cannot follow the imperative disjunction, Thou shalt have a race, and, thy race shall be black or white!, then perhaps I can construct a racial identity of mixed race. Failing that construction, perhaps there are some shreds of benign universalism with which I can cover my deracinated self, or maybe there is still some humanistic soil in which an aracial self can be "implanted."

Even if I had a black ethnic identity from childhood or had developed one as an adult, any attempt to synthesize black and white ethnic identities would be doomed to fail as soon as I confronted the racial antagonisms and tensions in wider social reality. Any attempt to base my identity on membership in both black and white races could only take place on a level not subject to racial tensions and antagonisms. The level on which I could be both black and white would be culturally isolated.[3] If racial identity is based on wider group membership, then a black and white racial identity would be but another form of deracination, and perhaps a needlessly complicated one.

The new use of the term "of color" may represent an effort to by-pass some of the contradictions and bitterness in racial categorization. Anyone who is not white is a person of color. But to say that I am a person of color is merely to say what I am not racially, i.e., not white. This categorization glides over my diverse ethnic experiences and cannot even begin to describe the ways in which I am not white. Using the term "of color" in effect deracinates non-whites within the category of non-white. It is but another instance of the tendency of whites to assign race itself to non-whites, perhaps analogously to the way in which men assign sex itself to members of the female gender. What is needed is a term which will deracinate people who are white, as well as non-white, some racial analogue to the designation "no religious affiliation."

The position of deracination could lead to conflicts at the intersection of racial identity and family membership. If a person is deracinated because she has both black and white forebears, her relatives may not have the same racial heredity, or if they do, they may not share her position of deracination. But the insistence on racial uniformity within a family is no more or less worthy of fulfillment than other forms of family uniformity, such as political or religious sameness, for example. If people who are biologically related have divisive differences, then those differences ought to be addressed on their own merits (as they often are during times of rapid social change).

The Problematization of Deracination

Again, I want to distinguish between the problem and the problematization. Deracination is a problem for people who belong to races and wish to categorize everyone else in racial terms as well. The problematization of deracination, as I have proposed it, has to do with the viewpoint of a deracinated person.

In ordinary, walking-around reality, the deracinated person will not have solved anything. People will still insist on categorizing her racially and her explicit refusal to participate in their (racializing) attempts will only add to their scorn and dislike of her. In her own mind she will be relieved from many contentious dialogues and ambivalent impulses. But as soon as she puts her position into plain language, she will have a problem with others.

Intellectually, deracination is not in harmony with the spirit of the times. For the past two or three decades, there has been an intensification of ethnicity and in expressions of pride in the culture of forebears, among different groups in America. This has its correlative in the critiques by feminists and other marginal spokespersons of the perceived white, upper class, heterosexist, male tradition in Philosophy. Continental Philosophy, since Martin Heidegger, as well as deconstructionist literary theory, has been increasingly preoccupied with the limitations

imposed on thought by different European languages, and with the question of whether translation is even possible. In Philosophy of Science, the idea that competing theories may be incommensurable has unsettled much contemporary discussion. Politically, nationalism has probably never been as insistent a theme in any other period of world peace as it has in recent years. These generalities about diversities, as well as practical considerations, make it unlikely that a case for universalism of any kind can be formulated in a convincing manner at this time. But this is not to say that the case cannot be formulated at all—a philosophic analysis of American concepts of race might leave no rational alternative.

With deracination, one may come full circle to an old ideal of universalism within the refuge of abstract thought. This is a treacherous place because the universalism may once more conceal a bias in favor of certain groups. In this new universalism the bias would be in favor of raceless races—it would be a bias of anti-race. But unlike racism, which is an asymmetrical privileging of race, anti-race would be a theoretical move that blocks the privileging of race by undermining racial designations. Furthermore, the risk of this anti-race bias may be outweighed by the gains of self-emancipation. In self-emancipation, it may be necessary to deracinate oneself in order to understand the problems and problematizations of race and ethnicity, and to address them evenly. It may also be necessary to remove everything concerning race from oneself, in order to feel good about being the self who is obliged to ask and answer the question, What am I?

NOTES

1. American concepts of race and ethnic identity are not stable over time. In recent years, I have noticed that some American Jews have become more insistent on their racial whiteness. Furthermore, it is by no means a foregone conclusion that a majority of

Jews accept someone who does not have two Jewish parents, as a Jew.

2. It is important to remember that these generalizations only hold true in American society. In European society there is a longer history of the identification of race with ethnicity, especially by anti-Semites. The French anti-Semite, for example, bases both his own racial identity and his ethnic pride on the fact that his forebears originated in the same place where he lives. See Jean-Paul Sartre's analysis in *Anti-Semite and Jew* (New York: Schocken Books, 1948), especially pp. 7–30.

3. There have always been isolated individuals and small groups without voices of authority who have refused to be pressured into identities of black or white racial designations. See for example, *Interrace*, a magazine which features interracial heterosexual relationships and persons of mixed-race in the entertainment industry.

Creation and Reality 2

In the introduction to the last chapter, I asked you how many times someone had told you to "just be yourself," and whether you had ever heard someone say, "I'm not myself today." These questions led us to the path of the search for self-identity, a path marked by the more general question "Who am I?" However, in journeying down this path, you may have noticed the signposts for several other paths marked by different questions. For example, in thinking about who you were, you may have been led to the question of how you got here. And in thinking about how you got here, you may have wondered how other things got here as well. Or to take another example, in thinking about the nature of your identity, you may have been led to questions about the identity of other persons or things. Put somewhat differently, in thinking about your own existence, you may have been led to consider the existence or nonexistence of other things as well.

If you were led to any of these other questions, then you were on the verge of another philosophical journey, the journey down the path of reflecting on creation and reality (otherwise known as the path of metaphysical thinking). Even if none of these questions occurred to you in reading the last chapter, I am sure that you have encountered this path before. For just as people have told you to be yourself, they have probably also told you to "be real." Of course, you might initially think that this is just another way of telling you to be yourself. But is this all that is involved? If we think about this statement philosophically, we might ask ourselves what it means to be "real." Does this statement imply that I'm somehow being "unreal," and that the person is telling me to come more fully into reality? Assuming that this is what the statement means, you might wonder how you can bring about this movement from unreality to reality. If you're not already fully real, how can you make yourself more real?

But even if no one has ever told you to be real, even if you have never thought about the nature of reality and unreality, you have still probably been on the verge of the path of metaphysical thinking. I'm certain that you have heard the following question, or some version of it, used as a way of proving the existence of God: "If God doesn't exist, how did we get here?" Of course, by bringing up God, this question could point us to another philosophical path that we will examine later, the path of religious thinking. But it can also direct us toward questions about creation and reality. Indeed, when you unpack this question, you will discover that it is actually making several claims about the nature of creation and reality. First, it is obviously suggesting that God exists, that is, that God is real. Second, it is claiming that the existence or reality of God explains our own existence or reality. Or put in terms of creation rather than existence and reality, this question is implying that we are here because we were created by God.

Of course not all of you believe in God. And even if you believe in God, it does not necessarily follow that you believe you were created by such a being. Still, as a thinking human being, it is very likely that you have, at some point in your life, raised the two principal questions of this chapter: (1) What is real? and (2) How did what is real come into being (assuming, of course, that it didn't always exist)? Indeed, some people raise these or similar questions quite early in life. My wife, who teaches kindergarten, told me the following story about a kindergarten pupil in another class at her school. The pupil had been absent for a couple of days. When he returned, his teacher asked him if he missed being at school. The pupil replied with a question of his own—"What is being?" There he was, at age five, already beginning his journey down the path of reflecting on creation and reality.

In this chapter, as in the last one, I have collected several articles from various cultures that will help you on your own journey down this path. The first four selections consist of creation stories with which you are probably not familiar. Each of these stories represents an attempt by a certain group of people (two of the stories are African, one is Native American, and the other is from India) to mythically explain how they and the universe came into being. The next two selections attempt to explain the true nature of reality. In one of them you are told that ultimate reality consists of the *Tao*, an unnamable and mysterious "force" that is the source of all life and all movement. In the other, you are told that what is ultimately real are materialistic fluids that come together to produce everything that exists. The final two writings critique one of the fundamental notions of Western metaphysics, the notion of a fixed, objective reality that exists independently of the knowing subject. The first of the two suggests that this notion results from a distortion of what the author calls "immediate reality" or "pure experience." The second of the two claims that our conception of reality results from a process of mythmaking and symbolizing, a process labeled "psychic activism." This last selection also suggests that traditional Western myths and symbols, that is, traditional Western ways of constructing reality, have resulted in a society that is "woman/body/earth hating."

FROM THE SACRED STORYTELLING OF AFRICA

The following creation story comes to us from the Boshongo, one of the Bantu peoples of central and south Africa. Like most African myths, this story was originally told in oral form, and it is impossible to determine exactly when the story originated.

For those of you familiar with other creation stories, especially the story found in Genesis, this myth may seem a bit shocking. But the story does answer one question that the story in Genesis fails to address—it provides a reason why the creator god began creation. According to this African story, the process of creation began when Bumba, the first creator god, became sick and started vomiting. The sun, the moon, the stars, and the first living creatures were Bumba's throw up. The first humans were also produced in this manner (a beginning far removed from the claim made in Genesis that humans were created in the "image" of God). Interestingly, once he gets over his initial sickness, Bumba turns the act of creating over to others. The first living creatures produced all the other creatures, except for the white ants and the kite, which were produced by Bumba's sons. Another of Bumba's sons created the first plant, from which all other plants evolved. This creation story ends with a theme found in many other African myths, the theme of the brotherhood of humans and other animals.

Questions for Thought

1. How does this story compare with/differ from other creation myths with which you are familiar?
2. Why do you think Bumba turns the process of creation over to his sons?
3. What is the role of Tsetse in the story? What do you make of the fact that Tsetse is the only creature in the story identified as female?
4. Do you agree with the claim found at the end of the story that humans and animals are brothers? Why or why not?
5. If you were to create a myth explaining the coming into being of the universe, how would you begin?

IN THE BEGINNING, IN THE DARK, THERE WAS nothing but water, and Bumba was alone.

One day Bumba was in terrible pain. He retched and strained and vomited up the sun. After that light spread over everything. The heat of the sun dried up the water until the black edges of the world began to show. Black sandbanks and reefs could be seen. But there were no living things.

Excerpt from *The Beginning: Creation Myths Around the World* by Maria Leach and Jane Bell Fairservis, illustrator. © 1956 by Harper & Row, Publishers, Inc. Reprinted by permission of HarperCollins Publishers, Inc.

Bumba vomited up the moon and then the stars, and after that the night had its light also.

Still Bumba was in pain. He strained again and nine living creatures came forth; the leopard named Koy Bumba, and Pongo Bumba the crested eagle, the crocodile, Ganda Bumba, and one little fish named Yo; next, old Kono Bumba, the tortoise, and Tsetse, the lightning, swift, deadly, beautiful like the leopard, then the white heron, Nyanyi Bumba, also one beetle, and the goat named Budi.

Last of all came forth men. There were many men, but only one was white like Bumba. His name was Loko Yima.

The creatures themselves then created all the creatures. The heron created all the birds of the air except the kite. He did not make the kite. The crocodile made serpents and the iguana. The goat produced every beast with horns. Yo, the small fish, brought forth all the fish of all the seas and waters. The beetle created insects.

Then the serpents in their turn made grasshoppers, and the iguana made the creatures without horns.

Then the three sons of Bumba said they would finish the world. The first, Nyonye Ngana, made the white ants; but he was not equal to the task, and died of it. The ants, however, thankful for life and being, went searching for black earth in the depths of the world and covered the barren sands to bury and honor their creator.

Chonganda, the second son, brought forth a marvelous living plant from which all trees and grasses and flowers and plants in the world have sprung. The third son, Chedi Bumba, wanted something different, but for all his trying made only a bird called the kite.

Of all the creatures, Tsetse, lightning, was the only troublemaker. She stirred up so much trouble that Bumba chased her into the sky. Then mankind was without fire until Bumba showed the people how to draw fire out of trees. "There is fire in every tree," he told them, and showed them how to make the fire drill and liberate it. Sometimes today Tsetse still leaps down and strikes the earth and causes damage.

When at last the work of creation was finished, Bumba walked through the peaceful villages and said to the people, "Behold these wonders. They belong to you." Thus from Bumba, the Creator, the First Ancestor, came forth all the wonders that we see and hold and use, and all the brotherhood of beasts and man.

2.2   The Descent from the Sky

FROM THE SACRED STORYTELLING OF AFRICA   ·

The following creation story, like the preceding one, comes from the oral traditions of Africa. The Yoruba people, the source of this story, are centered in the southwestern corner of Nigeria and in the republic of Benin. The Yoruba culture is an ancient one, perhaps dating back as early as the first millennium B.C.E. When Portuguese explorers first made contact with the Yoruba in the fifteenth century, they lived in well-organized urban centers, such as Ife and Benin, which were surrounded by farmland. Artistically, the Yoruba are known for their poetry, sculpture, and dance, which are intimately linked to a sophisticated system of religious beliefs and practices. They are also known for a method of divination that involves the casting of palm nut kernels on a special divination tray. As the following myth indicates, the Yoruba associate this method of divination with Orunmila, one of the orisha or deities who dwells in the sky.

Unlike the preceding creation myth, the Yoruba myth posits the existence of two types of divine beings: the male sky orisha led by Olorun and the female orisha, Olokun, who inhabits the dark waters below. Creation of the world as we know it begins when one of the sky orisha, Obatala, judges the realm of Olokun to be one of "great wet monotony." Obatala convinces Olorun to allow him to create land amid the dark waters, and to eventually populate it with living beings. After consulting Orunmila (the diviner orisha) about how to proceed, Obatala follows Orunmila's instructions and creates land. He then builds a house and plants a palm nut, and Olorun creates the sun. Next, Obatala fashions human figures from clay, pausing in the midst of his work to make palm wine. When Obatala has finished making the figures, some of which are misshapen because Obatala has drunk too much palm wine, he calls on Olorun to breath life into the figures. Eventually, other orisha descend from the sky to help the humans, and the sky orisha, led by Olorun, resist Olokun's attempts to destroy the land and the humans who populate it.

Questions for Thought

1. What are the basic differences between this creation myth and the preceding one?
2. What are the explanatory advantages, if any, of having two types of divine beings?
3. What does this myth tell you about the relationship of men to women in Yoruba culture?
4. What is the significance of the palm wine episode? What is it intended to explain? Do you think this explanation makes sense?
5. On the basis of this reading, how would you define an orisha? In what ways, if any, does it differ from your own conception of divinity?
6. If you were to write a creation myth, how would you explain the creation of humans?

IN ANCIENT DAYS, AT THE BEGINNING OF TIME, there was no solid land here where people now dwell. There was only outer space and the sky, and, far below, an endless stretch of water and wild marshes. Supreme in the domain of the sky was the orisha, or god, called Olorun, also known as Olodumare and designated by many praise names. Also living in that place were numerous other orishas, each having attributes of his own, but none of whom had knowledge or powers equal to those of Olorun. Among them was Orunmila, also called Ifa, the eldest son of Olorun. To this orisha Olorun had given the power to read the future, to understand the secret of existence and to divine the processes of fate. There was the orisha Obatala, King of the White Cloth, whom Olorun trusted as though he also were a son. There was the orisha Eshu, whose character was neither good nor bad. He was compounded out of the elements of chance and accident, and his nature was unpredictability. He understood the principles of speech and

Reprinted by permission of Harold Courlander.

language, and because of this gift he was Olorun's linguist. These and the other orishas living in the domain of the sky acknowledged Olorun as the owner of everything and as the highest authority in all matters. Also living there was Agemo, the chameleon, who served Olorun as a trusted servant.

Down below, it was the female deity Olokun who ruled over the vast expanses of water and wild marshes, a grey region with no living things in it, either creatures of the bush or vegetation. This is the way it was, Olorun's living sky above and Olokun's domain of water below. Neither kingdom troubled the other. They were separate and apart. The orishas of the sky lived on, hardly noticing what lay below them.

All except Obatala, King of the White Cloth. He alone looked down on the domain of Olokun and pondered on it, saying to himself, "Everything down there is a great wet monotony. It does not have the mark of any inspiration or living thing." And at last he went to Olorun and said, "The place ruled by Olokun is nothing but sea, marsh and mist. If there were solid land in that domain, fields and forests, hills and valleys, surely it could be populated by orishas and other living things."

Olorun answered, "Yes, it would be a good thing to cover the water with land. But it is an ambitious enterprise. Who is to do the work? And how should it be done?"

Obatala said, "I will undertake it. I will do whatever is required."

He left Olorun and went to the house of Orunmila, who understood the secrets of existence, and said to him, "Your father has instructed me to go down below and make land where now there is nothing but marsh and sea, so that living beings will have a place to build their towns and grow their crops. You, Orunmila, who can divine the meanings of all things, instruct me further. How may this work be begun?"

Orunmila brought out his divining tray and cast sixteen palm nuts on it. He read their meanings by the way they fell. He gathered them up and cast again, again reading their meanings. And when he had cast many times he added meanings to meanings, and said, "These are the things you must do: Descend to the watery wastes on a chain of gold, taking with you a snail shell full of sand, a white hen to disperse the sand, a black cat to be your companion, and a palm nut. That is what the divining figures tell us."

Obatala went next to the goldsmith and asked for a chain of gold long enough to reach from the sky to the surface of the water.

The goldsmith asked, "Is there enough gold in the sky to make such a chain?"

Obatala answered, "Yes, begin your work. I will gather the gold." Departing from the forge of the goldsmith, Obatala went to Orunmila, Eshu and the other orishas, asking each of them for gold. They gave him whatever they had. Some gave gold dust, some gave rings, bracelets or pendants. Obatala collected gold from everywhere and took it to the goldsmith.

The goldsmith said, "More gold is needed."

So Obatala continued seeking gold, and after that he again returned to the goldsmith, saying, "Here is more metal for your chain."

The goldsmith said, "Still more is needed."

Obatala said, "There is no more gold in the sky."

The goldsmith said, "The chain will not reach to the water."

Obatala answered, "Nevertheless, make the chain. We shall see."

The goldsmith went to work. When the chain was finished he took it to Obatala. Obatala said, "It must have a hook at the end."

"There is no gold remaining," the goldsmith said.

Obatala replied, "Take some of the links and melt them down."

The goldsmith removed some of the links, and out of them he fashioned a hook for the chain. It was finished. He took the chain to Obatala.

Obatala said, "Now I am ready." He fastened the hook on the edge of the sky and lowered the chain. Orunmila gave him the things that were needed—a snail shell of sand, a white hen, a black cat, and a palm nut. Then Obatala gripped the chain with his hands and feet and began the descent. The chain was very long. When he had descended only half its length Obatala saw that he was leaving the realm of light and entering the region of greyness. A time came when he heard the wash of waves and felt the damp mists rising from Olokun's domain. He reached the end of the golden chain, but he was not yet at the bottom, and he clung there, thinking, "If I let go I will fall into the sea."

While he remained at the chain's end thinking such things, he heard Orunmila's voice from above, saying, "The sand."

So Obatala took the snail shell from the knapsack at his side and poured out the sand.

Again he heard Orunmila call to him, saying this time, "The hen."

Obatala dropped the hen where he had poured the sand. The hen began at once to scratch at the sand and scatter it in all directions. Wherever the sand was scattered it became dry land. Because it was scattered unevenly the sand formed hills and valleys. When this was accomplished, Obatala let go of the chain and came down and walked on the solid earth that had been created. The land extended in all directions, but still it was barren of life.

Obatala named the place where he had come down Ife. He built a house there. He planted his palm nut and a palm tree sprang out of the earth. It matured and dropped its palm seeds. More palm trees came into being. Thus there was vegetation at Ife. Obatala lived on, with only his black cat as a companion.

After some time had passed, Olorun the Sky God wanted to know how Obatala's expedition was progressing. He instructed Agemo the chameleon to descend the golden chain. Agemo went down. He found Obatala living in his house at Ife. He said, "Olorun instructed me

this way: He said, 'Go down, discover for me how things are with Obatala.' That is why I am here."

Obatala answered, "As you can see, the land has been created, and palm groves are plentiful. But there is too much greyness. The land should be illuminated."

Agemo returned to the sky and reported to Olorun what he had seen and heard. Olorun agreed that there should be light down below. So he made the sun and set it moving. After that there was warmth and light in what had once been Olokun's exclusive domain.

Obatala lived on, with only his black cat for a companion. He thought, "Surely it would be better if many people were living here." He decided to create people. He dug clay from the ground, and out of the clay he shaped human figures which he then laid out to dry in the sun. He worked without resting. He became tired and thirsty. He said to himself, "There should be palm wine in this place to help a person go on working." So he put aside the making of humans and went to the palm trees to draw their inner fluid, out of which he made palm wine. When it was fermented he drank. He drank for a long while. When he felt everything around him softening he put aside his gourd cup and went back to modeling human figures. But because Obatala had drunk so much wine his fingers grew clumsy, and some of the figures were misshapen. Some had crooked backs or crooked legs, or arms that were too short. Some did not have enough fingers, some were bent instead of being straight. Because of the palm wine inside him, Obatala did not notice these things. And when he had made enough figures to begin the populating of Ife he called out to Olorun the Sky God, saying, "I have made human beings to live with me here in Ife, but only you can give them the breath of life." Olorun heard Obatala's request, and he put breath in the clay figures. They were no longer clay, but people of blood, sinews and flesh. They arose and began to do the things that humans do. They built houses for themselves near Obatala's house, and in this way the place Obatala named Ife became the city of Ife.

But when the effects of the palm wine had worn off Obatala saw that some of the humans he had made were misshapen, and remorse filled his heart. He said, "Never again will I drink palm wine. From this time on I will be the special protector of all humans who have deformed limbs or who have otherwise been created imperfectly." Because of Obatala's pledge, humans who later came to serve him also avoided palm wine, and the lame, the blind, and those who had no pigment in their skin invoked his help when they were in need.

Now that humans were living on the earth, Obatala gave people the tools they needed to perform their work. As yet there was no iron in the world, and so each man received a wooden hoe and a copper bush knife. The people planted and began the growing of millet and yams, and, like the palm tree, they procreated. Ife became a growing city and Obatala ruled as its Oba or Paramount Chief. But a time came when Obatala grew lonesome for the sky. He ascended by the golden chain, and there was a festival on the occasion of his return. The orishas heard him describe the land that had been created below, and many of them decided to go down and live among the newly created human beings. Thus many orishas departed from the sky, but not before Olorun instructed them on their obligations. "When you settle on the earth," he said, "never forget your duties to humans. Whenever you are supplicated for help, listen to what is being asked of you. You are the protectors of the human race. Obatala, who first descended the chain and dried up the waters, he is my deputy in earthly affairs. But each of you will have a special responsibility to fulfill down below." As for Obatala, he rested in the sky for some time. After that, whenever he wanted to know how things were going at Ife, he returned for a visit. The city of Ife lived on.

But Olokun, the orisha of the sea on whose domain land had been created, was angry and humiliated. And so one time when Obatala was resting in the sky Olokun decided to destroy the land and replace it again with water. She sent great waves rushing against the shores and flooded the low ground everywhere, causing marshes to reappear on every side. She inundated the fields where humans were growing their crops and drowned many of the people of Ife. All that Obatala had created was disappearing, and mankind was suffering. The people called for help from Obatala, but he did not hear them. So they went to the orisha Eshu, who now lived on earth, and begged him to carry to Obatala word of the disaster that was overwhelming them.

Eshu said to them, "Where is the sacrifice that should accompany the message?"

They brought a goat and sacrificed it, saying, "This is the food for Obatala."

But Eshu did not move. He said, "Where is the rest?"

The people said, "We do not understand you. Have we not brought a sacrifice for Obatala?"

Eshu answered, "You ask me to make a great journey. You ask me to be your linguist. Does not a person make a gift to the lowliest of messengers? Give me my part, then I will go."

So the people gave a sacrifice to Eshu, after which he left them and went up to the sky to tell Obatala what was happening to the land and the people over which he ruled.

Obatala was troubled. He was not certain how to deal with Olokun. He went to the orisha Orunmila to ask for advice. Orunmila consulted his divining nuts, and at last he said to Obatala, "Wait here in the sky. Rest yourself. I will go down this time. I will turn back the water and make the land rise again." So it was Orunmila instead of Obatala who went down to Ife. As Orunmila was the oldest son of Olorun, he had the knowledge of medicine, and he had many other powers as well. He used his powers in Ife, causing Olokun's waves to weaken and the marshes to dry up. The waters of the sea were turned back, and at last Olokun's attempt to reclaim her territory came to an end.

Having accomplished all this, Orunmila prepared to return to the sky. But the people came to him and asked him to stay because of his knowledge. Orunmila did not wish to stay in Ife forever. So he taught certain orishas and men the arts of controlling unseen forces, and he also taught others the art of divining the future, which is to say the knowledge of how to ascertain the wishes and intentions of the Sky God, Olorun. Some men he taught to divine through the casting of palm nuts. Others he taught to foretell the future by the casting of cowry shells or sand or chains. Afterwards, Orunmila went back to the sky and, like Obatala, he frequently made visits to the earth to see how things were going among human beings. What Orunmila taught men about divining was never lost. It was passed on by one generation of babalawos, or diviners, to another.

Earthly order—the understanding of relationships between people and the physical world, and between people and the orishas—was beginning to take shape. But all was not yet settled between Olokun, the orisha of the sea, and the supreme orisha Olorun. Olokun considered ways in which she might humiliate or outwit the Sky God. The powers of the sky deities had proved to be greater than her own. But Olokun had the knowledge of weaving and dying cloth, and she had clothes of delicate textures and brilliant colors. She believed that in this respect she excelled all other orishas, including Olorun himself. So one day she sent a message to Olorun, challenging him to a contest to show which had the greater knowledge of cloth-making.

Olorun received the challenge. He thought, "Olokun seeks to humiliate me. Nevertheless, she has unequaled knowledge about the making of cloth. Yet, how can I ignore the challenge?" He thought about the matter. Then he sent for Agemo, the chameleon. He instructed Agemo to carry a message to Olokun. Agemo went down from the sky to the place where Olokun lived. Agemo said to Olokun, "The Owner of the Sky, Olorun, greets you. He says that if your cloth is as magnificent as you claim, he will enter the contest. Therefore he asks that you show me some of your most radiant weaving so that I may report to him on the matter."

Because Olokun was vain she could not refrain from showing her cloths to Agemo. She put on a skirt cloth of brilliant green and displayed it to the chameleon. As Agemo looked at it his skin turned the exact color of the skirt. Olokun then put on an orange-hued cloth, and Agemo's skin turned orange. When Olokun brought out a red shirt cloth, Agemo's skin turned red. Olokun was perturbed. She tried a cloth of several colors and saw the chameleon's skin reproduce it perfectly. Olokun thought, "This person is only a messenger, nothing more. Yet in an instant he can duplicate the exact color of my finest cloth. What, then, can the great Olorun do?"

Seeing the futility of competing with Olorun, the orisha of the sea said to Agemo, "Give my greetings to the Owner of the Sky. Tell him that Olokun acknowledges his greatness."

Thus Olokun withdrew her challenge to the Sky God, and Olorun remained supreme in all things.

How the World Was Made and The Origin of Disease and Medicine

FROM THE SACRED
STORYTELLING OF THE CHEROKEE

The Cherokee or Yûñ'wiyă' (literally "real people") are a Native American people of Iroquoian lineage. Once inhabitants of the Great Lakes region, they moved to the Southern Allegheny and Great Smokey Mountains region prior to the arrival of European immigrants. It has been estimated that in 1650 about 22,500 Cherokee lived in this area that covered part of eight states. Prior to the early 1700s, the Cherokee lived in small, autonomous villages that were ruled by two political entities—a White organization that ruled in times of peace, and a Red organization that ruled in times of conflict or war. However, in the early 1700s the Cherokee formed a tribal state, which eventually became known as the Cherokee Nation.

During the 1700s, a series of treaties deprived the Cherokee of much of their land, and there were numerous skirmishes with the European settlers. But by the early 1800s, the Cherokee were rapidly assimilating European culture. They modeled their government after that of the United States, and adopted European methods of agriculture, weaving, and house building. After developing a syllabic alphabet, the Cherokee began publishing the first Native American newspaper in 1828. However, in this same year gold was discovered on Cherokee land in Georgia, a discovery that had ominous implications for the Cherokee Nation. After several years of land grabbing by European immigrants, the state of Georgia negotiated the Treaty of New Echota, which was signed by seventy-nine Cherokee in 1835. This treaty gave up all land east of the Mississippi River. Although almost 16,000 Cherokee signed a letter rejecting the treaty and the treaty was subsequently invalidated by the Supreme Court, the state of Georgia ignored the court decision. After President Andrew Jackson refused to enforce the court decision, troops were sent to force the Cherokee (numbering more than 17,000) to undertake a 116-day march to Indian Territory in what is now Oklahoma. During this march, which became known as the "Trail of Tears," the Cherokee were provided with inadequate clothing, food, and medical attention. As a result, about 4,000 people died during the harsh journey.

The Cherokee who made it to Indian Territory set up their government in what is today Tahlequah, Oklahoma. In 1984, Wilma Mankiller became the first female principal chief of this group, which is known as the Western Band. Today the Western Band has over 50,000 members. Sixty families who refused to move were later joined by about 1,200 Cherokee who escaped during the forced march. They formed the Eastern Band, and eventually reaquired 56,000 acres of the 7,000,000 acres fraudulently seized from them. Today the Eastern Band numbers about 9,000, and many of them live in or near Cherokee, North Carolina. The following stories were told by members of the Eastern Band during the late nineteenth century.

The first story, "How the World Was Made," contains a common creation motif about the earth being originally covered with water. However, unlike similar stories from other cultures, the creation of land is not the work of a god or gods, but the work of animals. The Water-beetle brings mud to the surface, and the Great Buzzard creates mountains and valleys. The animal conjurers then set the sun in its place in the sky. The first two humans, a brother and a sister, arrive on the scene after the plants and animals.

The second story, as the title indicates, is an account of how disease and medicine came into the world. Like certain African stories, this story takes a dim view of humans. Whereas humans were originally few in number and peaceful, they eventually overpopulate the earth and begin to kill animals. The various animals meet to decide how to defend themselves against the humans, and they create a number of diseases that can kill humans. Only the intervention of the Plants, who side with the humans and offer themselves as medicines, prevents the extermination of the human species.

Questions for Thought

1. How many levels of existence are described in the first story? What is the explanatory function of each level?
2. In what ways, if any, is the Cherokee account of the origin of the earth similar to modern scientific accounts?
3. What do these stories tell you about the relationship between the Cherokee and the animals? How does this compare with/differ from traditional European attitudes toward animals?
4. Do you find the Cherokee account of the origin of disease believable? If not, how would you explain the existence of disease?
5. Do you agree with the Cherokee belief about the standing of the human species in the natural world? Why or why not?

How the World Was Made

THE EARTH IS A GREAT ISLAND FLOATING IN A SEA of water, and suspended at each of the four cardinal points by a cord hanging down from the sky vault, which is of solid rock. When the world grows old and worn out, the people will die and the cords will break and let the earth sink down into the ocean, and all will be water again. . . .

When all was water, the animals were above in Gălûñ'lătĭ, beyond the arch; but it was very much crowded, and they were wanting more room. They wondered what was below the water, and at last Dâyuni'sĭ, "Beaver's Grandchild," the little Water-beetle, offered to go and see if it could learn. It darted in every direction over the surface of the water, but could find no firm place to rest. Then it dived to the bottom and came up with some soft mud, which began to grow and spread on every side until it became the island which we call the earth. It was afterward fastened to the sky with four cords, but no one remembers who did this.

At first the earth was flat and very soft and wet. The animals were anxious to get down, and sent out different birds to see if it was yet dry, but they found no place to alight and came back again to Gălûñ'lătĭ. At last it seemed to be time, and they sent out the Buzzard and told him to go and make ready for them. This was the Great

Buzzard, the father of all the buzzards we see now. He flew all over the earth, low down near the ground, and it was still soft. When he reached the Cherokee country, he was very tired, and his wings began to flap and strike the ground, and wherever they struck the earth there was a valley, and where they turned up again there was a mountain. When the animals above saw this, they were afraid that the whole world would be mountains, so they called him back, but the Cherokee country remains full of mountains to this day.

When the earth was dry and the animals came down, it was still dark, so they got the sun and set it in a track to go every day across the island from east to west, just overhead. It was too hot this way, and Tsiska'gĭlĭ', the Red Crawfish, had his shell scorched a bright red, so that his meat was spoiled; and the Cherokee do not eat it. The conjurers put the sun another handbreadth higher in the air, but it was still too hot. They raised it another time, and another, until it was seven handbreadths high and just under the arch. Then it was right, and they left it so. This is why the conjurers call the highest place Gûlkwâ'gine Di'gălûñ'lătiyûñ', "the seventh height," because it is seven handbreadths above the earth. Every day the sun goes along under this arch, and returns at night on the upper side to the starting place.

There is another world under this, and it is like ours in everything—animals, plants, and people—save that the seasons are different. The streams that come down from the mountains are the trails by which we reach this underworld, and the springs at their heads are the doorways by which we enter it, but to do this one must fast and go to water and have one of the underground people for a guide. We know that the seasons in the underworld are different from ours, because the water in the springs is always warmer in winter and cooler in summer than the outer air.

When the animals and plants were first made—we do not know by whom—they were told to watch and keep awake for seven nights, just as young men now fast and keep awake when they pray to their medicine. They tried to do this, and nearly all were awake through the first night, but the next night several dropped off to sleep, and the third night others were asleep, and then others, until, on the seventh night, of all the animals only the owl, the panther, and one or two more were still awake. To these were given the power to see and to go about in the dark, and to make prey of the birds and animals which must sleep at night. Of the trees only the cedar, the pine, the spruce, the holly, and the laurel were awake to the end, and to them it was given to be always green and to be greatest for medicine, but to others it was said: "Because you have not endured to the end you shall lose your hair every winter."

Men came after the animals and plants. At first there were only a brother and sister until he struck her with a fish and told her to multiply, and so it was. In seven days a child was born to her, and thereafter every seven days another, and they increased very fast until there was danger that the world could not keep them. Then it was made that a woman should have only one child in a year, and it has been so ever since. . . .

The Origin of Disease and Medicine

In the old days the beasts, birds, fishes, insects, and plants could all talk, and they and the people lived together in peace and friendship. But as time went on the people increased so rapidly that their settlements spread over the whole earth, and the poor animals found themselves beginning to be cramped for room. This was bad enough, but to make it worse Man invented bows, knives, blowguns, spears, and hooks, and began to slaughter the larger animals, birds, and fishes for their flesh or their skins, while the smaller creatures, such as the frogs and worms, were crushed and trodden upon without thought, out of pure carelessness or contempt. So the animals resolved to consult upon measures for their common safety.

The Bears were the first to meet in council in their townhouse under Kuwâ'hǐ mountain, the "Mulberry Place," and the old White Bear chief presided. After each in turn had complained of the way in which Man killed their friends, ate their flesh, and used their skins for his own purposes, it was decided to begin war at once against him. Someone asked what weapons Man used to destroy them. "Bows and arrows, of course," cried all the Bears in chorus. "And what are they made of?" was the next question. "The bow of wood, and the string of our entrails," replied one of the Bears. It was then proposed that they make a bow and some arrows and see if they could not use the same weapons against Man himself. So one Bear got a nice piece of locust wood and another sacrificed himself for the good of the rest in order to furnish a piece of his entrails for the string. But when everything was ready and the first Bear stepped up to make the trial, it was found that in letting the arrow fly after drawing back the bow, his long claws caught the string and spoiled the shot. This was annoying, but someone suggested that they might trim his claws, which was accordingly done, and on a second trial it was found that the arrow went straight to the mark. But here the chief, the old White Bear, objected, saying it was necessary that they should have long claws in order to be able to climb trees. "One of us has already died to furnish the bowstring, and if we now cut off our claws we must all starve together. It is better to trust to the teeth and claws that nature gave us, for it is plain that Man's weapons were not intended for us."

No one could think of any better plan, so the old chief dismissed the council and the Bears dispersed to the woods and thickets without having concerted any way to prevent the increase of the human race. Had the result of the council been otherwise, we should now be at war with the Bears, but as it is, the hunter does not even ask the Bear's pardon when he kills one.

The Deer next held a council under their chief, the Little Deer, and after some talk decided to send rheumatism to every hunter who should kill one of them unless he took care to ask their pardon for the offense. They sent notice of their decision to the nearest settlement of humans and told them at the same time what to do when necessity forced them to kill one of the Deer tribe. Now, whenever the hunter shoots a Deer, the Little Deer, who is swift as the wind and cannot be wounded, runs quickly up to the spot and, bending over the bloodstains, asks the spirit of the Deer if it has heard the prayer of the hunter for pardon. If the reply be "Yes," all is well, and the Little Deer goes on his way; but if the reply be "No," he follows on the trail of the hunter, guided by the drops of blood on the ground, until he arrives at his cabin in the settlement, when the Little Deer enters invisibly and strikes the hunter with rheumatism, so that he becomes at once a helpless cripple. No hunter who has regard for his health ever fails to ask pardon of the Deer for killing it, although some hunters who have not learned the prayer may try to turn aside the Little Deer from his pursuit by building a fire behind them in the trail.

Next came the Fishes and Reptiles, who had their own complaints against Man. They held their council together and determined to make their victims dream of snakes twining about them in slimy folds and blowing foul breath in their faces, or to make them dream of eating raw or decaying fish, so that they would lose appetite, sicken, and die. This is why people dream about snakes and fish.

Finally the Birds, Insects, and smaller animals came together for the same purpose, and the Grubworm was chief of the council. It was decided that each in turn should give an opinion, and then they would vote on the question as to whether or not Man was guilty. Seven votes should be enough to condemn him. One after another denounced Man's cruelty and injustice toward the other animals and voted in favor of his death. The Frog spoke first, saying: "We must do something to check the increase of the race, or people will become so numerous that we shall be crowded from off the earth. See how they have kicked me about because I'm ugly, as they say, until my back is covered with sores"; and here he showed the spots on his skin. Next came the Bird—no one remembers now which one it was—who condemned Man "because he burns my feet off," meaning the way in which the hunter barbecues birds by impaling them on a stick set over the fire, so that their feathers and tender feet are singed off. Others followed in the same strain. The Ground-squirrel alone ventured to say a good word for Man, who seldom hurt him because he was so small, but this made the others so angry that they fell upon the Ground-squirrel and tore him with their claws, and the stripes are on his back to this day.

They began to devise and name so many new diseases, one after another, that had not their invention at last failed them, no one of the human race would have been able to survive. The Grubworm grew constantly more pleased as the name of each disease was called off, until at last they reached the end of the list, when someone proposed to make menstruation some-times fatal to women. On this he rose up in his place and cried: "Wadâñ'! [Thanks] I'm glad some more of them will die, for they are getting so thick that they tread on me." The thought fairly made him shake with joy, so that he fell over backward and could not get on his feet again, but had to wriggle off on his back, as the Grubworm has done ever since.

When the Plants, who were friendly to Man, heard what had been done by the animals, they determined to defeat the latter's evil designs. Each Tree, Shrub, and Herb, down even to the Grasses and Mosses, agreed to furnish a cure for some one of the diseases named, and each said: "I shall appear to help Man when he calls upon me in his need." Thus came medicine; and the plants, every one of which has its use if we only knew it, furnish the remedy to counteract the evil wrought by the revengeful animals. Even weeds were made for some good purpose, which we must find out ourselves. When the doctor does not know what medicine to use for a sick man the spirit of the plant tells him.

2.4   Creation of the World from the Self

FROM THE UPANISHADS

As mentioned in the introduction to the first selection in Chapter 1, the Upanishads make up the fourth section of the Vedas, the most sacred writings of the religion of Hinduism. It is generally believed that the earliest of the Upanishads was written around 900 B.C.E., but most of them were written hundreds of years later. Whereas the first three sections of the Vedas were written in the form of hymns and ritual chants, the Upanishads take the form of philosophical dialogues and myth. For these stylistic reasons, as well as for the many similarities in content, the Upanishads can be fruitfully compared with the writings of Plato. The following creation story is from the *Brhad-āranyaka-Upanishad*, which many scholars view as the most important of the Upanishads.

In this creation myth, unlike the first three, there is only one being prior to creation—the self in the form of a person. Fear arises within this self, but the self realizes that this fear is unfounded since there is nothing outside of itself that could possibly harm it. However, in coming to this realization, the self discovers its aloneness. To overcome this aloneness, the self expands and splits into male and female. The two halves unite and human beings are born. However, the female half is bothered by the semi-incestuous nature of the relationship ("How can he unite with me after having produced me from himself?"), and she takes many female animal forms as disguises. But the male half takes the corresponding male form in each case and mates with her. The various types of animals are produced in this manner. The creator self then produces fire, food, the gods, and all of the separate forms found within the universe. Once this creation is complete, the self enters into everything that exists. The selection ends by identifying this creative self with Brahman, and by saying that the goal of knowledge is to discover the ultimate identity between one's own self and Brahman.

Questions for Thought

1. What do you think of the claim that the original being who created the universe was a self in the form of a person? Is this claim compatible with your own views about the origin of the universe?
2. How does the writer of this myth account for the origin of humans? Do you find this explanation satisfactory? Why or why not?
3. Do you think the female half of the self was justified in trying to avoid the male half? What is this motif intended to explain?
4. The last sentence of section 5 ("He who knows this as such comes to be in that creation of his") has been taken as a statement of humanity's place in the universe. What do you think this statement means?
5. Do you agree that Brahman or the creative force of the universe is to be found in everything that exists? Why or why not?
6. What seems to be the role of the gods in this myth? What is the relation of humans to the gods?
7. If you were to write a creation myth, how would it end?

1. IN THE BEGINNING THIS (WORLD) WAS ONLY the self, in the shape of a person. Looking around he saw nothing else than the self. He first said, "I am." Therefore arose the name of I. Therefore, even to this day when one is addressed he says first "This is I" and then speaks whatever other name he may have. Because before all this, he burnt all evils, therefore he is a person. He who knows this, verily, burns up him who wishes to be before him.

2. He was afraid. Therefore one who is alone is afraid. This one then thought to himself, "Since there is nothing else than myself, of what am I afraid?" Thereupon his fear, verily, passed away, for, of what

should he have been afraid? Assuredly it is from a second that fear arises.

3. He, verily, had no delight. Therefore he who is alone has no delight. He desired a second. He became as large as a woman and a man in close embrace. He caused that self to fall into two parts. From that arose husband and wife. Therefore, as Yājñavalkya used to say, this (body) is one half of oneself, like one of the two halves of a split pea. Therefore this space is filled by a wife. He became united with her. From that human beings were produced.[1]

4. She thought, "How can he unite with me after having produced me from himself?" Well, let me hide myself. She became a cow, the other became a bull and was united with her and from that cows were born. The one became a mare, the other a stallion. The one became a she-ass, the other a he-ass and was united with her; and from that one-hoofed animals were born. The one became a she-goat, the other a he-goat, the one became a ewe, the other became a ram and was united with her and from that goats and sheep were born. Thus, indeed, he produced everything whatever exists in pairs, down to the ants.

5. He knew, I indeed am this creation for I produced all this. Therefore he became the creation. He who knows this as such comes to be in that creation of his.

6. Then he rubbed back and forth and produced fire from its source, the mouth and the hands. Both these (mouth and the hands) are hairless on the inside for the source is hairless on the inside. When they (the people) say "sacrifice to him," "sacrifice to the other one," all this is his creation indeed and he himself is all the gods. And now whatever is moist, that he produced from semen, and that is Soma.

This whole (world) is just food and the eater of food. Soma is food and fire is the eater of food. This is the highest creation of *Brahma*, namely, that he created the gods who are superior to him. He, although mortal himself, created the immortals. Therefore it is the highest creation. Verily, he who knows this becomes (a creator) in this highest creation.

7. At that time this (universe) was undifferentiated. It became differentiated by name and form (so that it is said) he has such a name, such a shape.[2] Therefore even today this (universe) is differentiated by name and shape (so that it is said) he has such a name, such a shape. He (the self) entered in here even to the tips of the nails, as a razor is (hidden) in the razor-case, or as fire in the fire-source. Him they see not for (as seen) he is incomplete, when breathing he is called the vital force, when speaking voice, when seeing the eye, when hearing the ear, when thinking the mind. These are merely the names of his acts. He who meditates on one or another of them (aspects) does not know, for he is incomplete, with one or another of these (characteristics). The self is to be meditated upon for in it all these become one. This self is the foot-trace of all this, for by it one knows all this, just as one can find again by footprints (what was lost). He who knows this finds fame and praise.

8. That self is dearer than a son, is dearer than wealth, is dearer than everything else and is innermost. If one were to say to a person who speaks of anything else than the Self as dear that he will lose what he holds dear, he would very likely do so. One should meditate on the Self alone as dear. He who meditates on the Self alone as dear, what he holds dear, verily, will not perish.

9. They say, since men think that, by the knowledge of *Brahman*, they become all, what, pray, was it that *Brahman* knew by which he became all?

10. *Brahman*, indeed, was this in the beginning. It knew itself only as "I am *Brahman*." Therefore it became all. Whoever among the gods became awakened to this, he, indeed, became that. It is the same in the case of seers, the same in the case of men. Seeing this, indeed, the seer Vāmadeva knew, "I was Manu and the Sun, too."[3] This is so even now. Whoever knows thus, "I am *Brahman*," becomes this all. Even the gods cannot prevent his becoming thus, for he becomes their self. So whoever worships another divinity (than his self) thinking that he is one and (*Brahman*) another, he knows not. He is like an animal to the gods. As many animals serve a man so does each man serve the gods. Even if one animal is taken away, it causes displeasure, what should one say of many (animals)? Therefore it is

not pleasing to those (gods) that man should know this.[4]

NOTES

1. This bears comparison with the myth of the hermaphrodites from the Moon that is found in Plato's *Symposium* (189e–191e).

2. *Nāma-rūpa*: name and shape which together make the individual. The *nāma* is not the name but the idea, the archetype, the essential character, and the *rūpa* is the existential context, the visible embodiment of the idea. In every object there are these two elements, the principle which is grasped by the intellect and the envelope which is apprehended by the senses. While *nāma* is the inner power, *rūpa* is its sensible manifestation. If we take the world as a whole, we have the one *nāma* or all-consciousness informing the one *rūpa*, the concrete universe. The different *nāma-rūpas* are the differentiated conditions of the one *nāma*, the world consciousness.

3. Vāma-deva is the seer of the fourth book of the *Rig Veda*.

4. The gods are not pleased that men should know the ultimate truth, for then they would know the subordinate place the gods hold and give up making them offerings.

The Way of Nature   2.5

LAO-TZU

Lao-tzu (ca. 551–479 B.C.E.) is traditionally identified as the author of the *Tao Te Ching* and thus as the founder of Taoism. Although there is very little in the way of historical knowledge about the life of Lao-tzu, frequently repeated legends suggest that he was the keeper of the royal archives during the time when the Chou Dynasty was disintegrating. Dissatisfied with his job and court life, Lao-tzu reportedly left his post for the life of a mountain hermit. Before heading off into anonymity, he was stopped by the guard at a mountain pass and coerced into writing down his views on the nature of the universe, human existence, and government. The resulting text was the *Tao Te Ching*. The following selections are taken from Stephen Mitchell's excellent translation of this nearly "untranslatable" classic.

The principal concept in the *Tao Te Ching* is the Tao, a term that is often translated as the "Way." However, as the following excerpts clearly show, the Tao, which is the ultimate source of all life, cannot be adequately described or even named. Its mystery can only be approached by metaphor and paradox. By analogy, it is like a well that never dries up, like the "mother of the universe," like an electron that "contains uncountable galaxies." Elsewhere in the *Tao Te Ching*, it is likened to water, which is ever-flowing, ever-changing. Paradoxically, it is "hidden but always present," the primordial form that is no form. But one message in the Tao Te Ching does come across clearly—human happiness is only attainable if one harmonizes one's life with the movement of the Tao. As the words of section 14 tell us: "You can't know it, but you can be it, at ease in your own life."

Questions for Thought

1. What do you think the author means by the Tao? Can you think of other analogies that might be used to represent it?
2. In section 4, it is said that the Tao is "older than God." Does it make sense to say that something is older than God? Why or why not?
3. How, according to the author, can one gain an awareness of the Tao?
4. Why do you think the author considers it important to harmonize one's life with the movement of the Tao? Do you think your life is in harmony with the Tao?
5. One might say that the Tao represents the ultimate nature of reality. How would you describe the ultimate nature of reality?

1
The tao that can be told
is not the eternal Tao.
The name that can be named
is not the eternal Name.

The unnamable is the eternally real.
Naming is the origin
of all particular things.

Free from desire, you realize the mystery.
Caught in desire, you see only the manifestations.

Yet mystery and manifestations
arise from the same source.
This source is called darkness

Darkness within darkness.
The gateway to all understanding.
. . .

4

The Tao is like a well:
used but never used up.
It is like the eternal void:
filled with infinite possibilities.

It is hidden but always present.
I don't know who gave birth to it.
It is older than God.
. . .

Excerpts from *Tao Te Ching* by Stephen Mitchell. © 1988 by Stephen Mitchell.
Reprinted by permission of HarperCollins Publishers, Inc.

14
Look, and it can't be seen.
Listen, and it can't be heard.
Reach, and it can't be grasped.
Above, it isn't bright.

Below, it isn't dark.
Seamless, unnamable,
it returns to the realm of nothing.
Form that includes all forms,
image without an image,
subtle, beyond all conception.

Approach it and there is no beginning;
follow it and there is no end.
You can't know it, but you can be it,
at ease in your own life.
Just realize where you come from:
this is the essence of wisdom.
. . .

25
There was something formless and perfect
before the universe was born.
It is serene. Empty.
Solitary. Unchanging.
Infinite. Eternally present.
It is the mother of the universe.
For lack of a better name,
I call it the Tao.

It flows through all things,
inside and outside, and returns
to the origin of all things.

The Tao is great.
The universe is great.
Earth is great.
Man is great.
These are the four great powers.

Man follows the earth.
Earth follows the universe.
The universe follows the Tao.
The Tao follows only itself.
. . .

32
The Tao can't be perceived.

Smaller than an electron,
it contains uncountable galaxies.
If powerful men and women
could remain centered in the Tao,
all things would be in harmony.
The world would become a paradise.
All people would be at peace,
and the law would be written in their hearts.

When you have names and forms,
know that they are provisional.
When you have institutions,
know where their functions should end.
Knowing when to stop,
you can avoid any danger.

All things end in the Tao
as rivers flow into the sea.
. . .

40
Returning is the movement of the Tao.
Yielding is the way of the Tao.

All things are born of being.
Being is born of non-being.
. . .

51
Every being in the universe
is an expression of the Tao.
It springs into existence,
unconscious, perfect, free,
takes on a physical body,
lets circumstances complete it.
That is why every being
spontaneously honors the Tao.

The Tao gives birth to all beings,
nourishes them, maintains them,
cares for them, comforts them, protects them,
takes them back to itself,
creating without possessing,
acting without expecting,
guiding without interfering.
That is why love of the Tao
is in the very nature of things.

The Nature of Things

WANG CHUNG

Wang Chung (ca. 27–97 C.E.) studied at the Imperial College at Loyang, where he was reportedly an avid reader. After completing his studies, he lived a life of relative poverty and obscurity as a teacher and minor government official. However, he did write several books on a wide variety of topics: ethics, macrobiotics, metaphysics, and government. Only his, *Lun-Hêng*, from which the following selection was taken, has survived. His translator, Alfred Forke, refers to Wang Chung as a heterodox philosopher, a materialist, and an eclectic, "whose views do not agree with the current ideas of either Confucianists or Taoists."

Wang Chung's materialism is evident in the following selection, which is excerpted from chapters entitled "Spontaneity" and "The Nature of Things." Throughout this selection, it is claimed that everything in the universe is produced from the spontaneous mixture of "the fluids of Heaven and Earth." The materialistic nature of these fluids is demonstrated by the example used to explain how the creative process works—the mixture of male and female fluids to produce a child. Another aspect of Wang's materialism that is emphasized in this selection is his rejection of purpose in the workings of nature. In contrast to the traditional Chinese claim that everything happens because of the design of Heaven (or according to God's will, to use a more Western phrasing), Wang claims that the spontaneous movement of nature is devoid of intention. As he bluntly says, "Heaven does not act and thus it does not speak." Rather, borrowing the Taoist concept of *wu wei*, Wang says that the way of nature is the way of "inactive action" or actionless activity. The final aspect of Wang's materialism that comes across in this selection is his identification of human actions with the processes of nature. Virtue or righteousness is not determined by good intentions, but by the amount of heavenly fluid one possesses. And the way of the wise man, like the way of nature, is the way of inactive action, the way of spontaneous creation.

Questions for Thought

1. What does the author mean by spontaneous action? Do you agree that spontaneity characterizes the way of the universe?
2. Do you think that Wang's example of sexual reproduction is useful in explaining his position? Why or why not?
3. What does Wang mean by saying the righteousness is determined by the amount of heavenly fluid one possesses? Do you agree with his analysis of righteousness?
4. Does the concept of "inactive action" make sense to you? How does Wang try to explain it?
5. Do you consider yourself to be a spontaneous person? If not, would you like to be? Why or why not?

BY THE FUSION OF THE FLUIDS OF HEAVEN AND Earth all things of the world are produced spontaneously, just as by the mixture of the fluids of husband and wife children are born spontaneously. Among the things thus produced, creatures with blood in their veins are sensitive of hunger and cold. Seeing that grain can be eaten, they use it as food, and discovering that silk and hemp can be worn, they take it as raiment. Some people are of the opinion that Heaven produces grain for the purpose of feeding mankind, and silk and hemp to cloth them. That would be tantamount to making Heaven the farmer of man or his mulberry girl;[1] it would not be in accordance with spontaneity. Therefore this opinion is very questionable and unacceptable.

Reasoning on Taoist principles we find that Heaven emits its fluid everywhere. Among the many things of this world grain dispels hunger, and silk and hemp protect from cold. For that reason man eats grain, and wears silk and hemp. That Heaven does not produce grain, silk, and hemp purposely, in order to feed and cloth mankind, follows from the fact that by calamitous changes it does not intend to reprove man. Things are produced spontaneously, and man wears and eats them; the fluid changes spontaneously, and man is frightened by it, for the usual theory is disheartening. Where would be spontaneity, if the heavenly signs were intentional, and where inaction?[2]

Why must we assume that Heaven acts spontaneously? Because it has neither mouth nor eyes. Activity is connected with the mouth and the eyes: the mouth wishes to eat, and the eyes to see. These desires within manifest themselves without. That the mouth and the eyes are craving for something, which is considered an advantage, is due to those desires. Now, provided that the mouth and the eyes do not affect things, there is nothing which they might long for, why should there be activity then?

How do we know that Heaven possesses neither mouth nor eyes? From Earth. The body of the Earth is formed of earth, and earth has neither mouth nor eyes. Heaven and Earth are like husband and wife. Since the body of the Earth is not provided with a mouth or eyes, we know that Heaven has no mouth or eyes either. Supposing that Heaven has a body, then it must be like that of the Earth, and should it be air only, this air would be like clouds and fog. How can a cloudy or nebular substance have a mouth or an eye?

Some one might argue that every movement is originally inaction. There is desire provoking the movement, and, as soon as there is motion, there is action. The movements of Heaven are similar to those of man, how could they be inactive? I reply that, when Heaven moves, it emits its fluid. Its body moves, the fluid comes forth, and things are produced. When man moves his fluid, his body moves, his fluid then comes forth, and a child is produced. Man emitting his fluid does not intend to beget a child, yet the fluid being emitted, the child is born of itself. When Heaven is moving, it does not desire to produce things thereby, but things are produced of their own accord. That is spontaneity. Letting out its fluid it does not desire to create things, but things are created of themselves. That is inaction.

But how is the fluid of Heaven, which we credit with spontaneity and inaction? It is placid, tranquil, desireless, inactive, and unbusied. . . .

In the State of Sung a man carved a mulberry-leaf of wood, and it took him three years to complete it. Confucius said, "If the Earth required three years to complete one leaf, few plants would have leaves." According to this dictum of Confucius the leaves of plants grow spontaneously, and for that reason they can grow simultaneously. If Heaven made them, their growth would be as much delayed as the carving of the mulberry-leaf by the man of the Sung State.

Let us look at the hair and feathers of animals and birds, and their various colors. Can they all have been made? If so, animals and birds would never be quite finished. In spring we see the plants growing, and in autumn we see them full-grown. Can Heaven and Earth have done this, or do things grow spontaneously? If we may say that Heaven and Earth have done it, they must have used hands for the purpose. Do Heaven and Earth possess many thousand or many ten thousand hands to produce thousands and ten thousands of things at the same time?

The things between Heaven and Earth are like a child in his mother's womb. After ten months pregnancy the mother gives birth to the child. Are his nose, his mouth, his ears, his hair, his eyes, his skin with down, the arteries, the fat, the bones, the joints, the nails, and the teeth grown of themselves in the womb, or has the mother made them?

Why is a dummy never called a man? Because it has a nose, a mouth, ears, and eyes, but not a spontaneous nature. Wu Ti was very fond of his consort Wang. When she had died, he pondered whether he could not see her figure again. The Taoists made an artificial figure of the lady.[3] When it was ready, it passed through the palace gate. Wu Ti, greatly alarmed, rose to meet her, but, all of a sudden, she was not seen any more. Since it was not a real, spontaneous being, but a semblance, artificially made by jugglers, it became diffuse at first sight, dispersed, and vanished. Everything that has been made does not last long, like the image of the empress, which appeared only for a short while.

The Taoist school argues on spontaneity, but it does not know how to substantiate its cause by evidence. Therefore their theory of spontaneity has not yet found credence. However, in spite of spontaneity there may be activity for a while in support of it. Ploughing, tilling, weeding, and sowing in spring are human actions. But as soon as the grain has entered the soil, it begins growing by day and night. Man can do nothing for it, or if he does, he spoils the thing.

A man of Sung was sorry that his sprouts were not high enough; therefore he pulled them out. But, on the following day, they were dry, and died. He who wishes to do what is spontaneous, is on a par with this man of Sung.

The following question may be raised: "Man is born from Heaven and Earth. Since Heaven and Earth are inactive, man, who has received the fluid of Heaven, ought to be inactive likewise. Why does he act nevertheless?"

For the following reason. A man with the highest, purest, and fullest virtue has been endowed with a large quantity of the heavenly fluid; therefore he can follow the example of Heaven, and be spontaneous and inactive like it. He who has received but a small quota of the fluid, does not live in accordance with righteousness and virtue, and does not resemble Heaven and Earth. Hence he is called unlike, which means that he does not resemble Heaven and Earth. Not resembling Heaven and Earth, he cannot be accounted a wise man or a sage. Therefore he is active.

Heaven and Earth are the furnace, and the creating is the melting process. How can all be wise, since the fluid of which they are formed is not the same? Huang and Lao were truly wise. Huang is Huang Ti and Lao is Lao-tzu. Huang and Lao's conduct was such, that their bodies were in a state of quietude and indifference. Their government consisted in inaction. They took care of their persons, and behaved with reverence, hence *Yin* and *Yang* were in harmony. They did not long for action, and things were produced of themselves; they did not think of creating anything, and things were completed spontaneously. . . .

The principle of Heaven is inaction. Accordingly in spring it does not do the germinating, in summer the growing, in autumn the ripening, or in winter the hiding of the seeds. When the *Yang* fluid comes forth spontaneously, plants will germinate and grow of themselves, and, when the *Yin* fluid rises, they ripen and disappear of their own accord.

When we irrigate garden land with water drawn from wells or drained from ponds, plants germinate and grow also, but, when showers of rain come down, the stalks, leaves, and roots are all abundantly soaked. Natural moisture is much more copious than artificial irrigation from wells and ponds. Thus inactive action brings the greatest results. By not seeking it, merit is acquired, and by not affecting it, fame is obtained. Rain-showers, merit, and fame are something great, yet Heaven and Earth do not work for them. When the fluid harmonizes, rain gathers spontaneously. . . .

Heaven expands above, and Earth below. When the fluid from below rises, and the fluid on high descends, all things are created in the middle. While they are growing, it is not necessary that Heaven should still care for them, just as the father does not know the embryo, after it is in the mother's womb. Things grow spontaneously, and the child is formed of itself. Heaven and Earth, and father and mother, can take no further cognizance of it. But after birth, the way of man is instruction and teaching, the way of Heaven, inaction and yielding to nature. Therefore Heaven allows the fish to swim in the rivers, and the wild beasts to roam in the mountains, following their natural propensities. It does not drive the fish up the hills, or the wild beasts into the water. Why? Because that would be an outrage upon their nature, and a complete disregard of what suits them. The people resemble fish and beasts. High virtue governs them as easily, as one fries small fish, and as Heaven and Earth would act. . . .

Those who believe in reprimands, refer to human ways as a proof. Among men a sovereign reprimands his minister, and high Heaven reprimands the sovereign. It does so by means of calamitous events, they say. However, among men it also happens that the minister remonstrates with his sovereign. When Heaven reprimands an emperor by visiting him with calamities, and the latter wishes at the same time to remonstrate with high Heaven,

how can he do it? If they say that Heaven's virtue is so perfect, that man cannot remonstrate with it, then Heaven possessed of such virtue, ought likewise to keep quiet, and ought not to reprimand. When the sovereign of Wan Shih did wrong, the latter did not say a word, but at table he did not eat, which showed his perfection. An excellent man can remain silent, and august Heaven with his sublime virtue should reprimand? Heaven does not act, therefore it does not speak. The disasters, which so frequently occur, are the work of the spontaneous fluid.

Heaven and Earth cannot act, nor do they possess any knowledge. When there is a cold in the stomach, it aches. This is not caused by man, but the spontaneous working of the fluid. The space between Heaven and Earth is like that between the back and the stomach.[4]

If Heaven is regarded as the author of every calamity, are all abnormalities, great and small, complicated and simple, caused by Heaven also? A cow may give birth to a horse, and on a cherry-tree a plum may grow. Does, according to the theory under discussion, the spirit of Heaven enter the belly of the cow to create the horse, or stick a plum upon a cherry-tree?

Lao[5] said, "The Master said, 'Having no official employment, I acquired many arts,' and he said, 'When I was young, my condition was low, and therefore I acquired my ability in many things, but they were mean matters.'" What is low in people, such as ability and skillfulness, is not practiced by the great ones. How could Heaven, which is so majestic and sublime, choose to bring about catastrophes with a view to reprimanding people?

Moreover, auspicious and inauspicious events are like the flushed color appearing on the face. Man cannot produce it, the color comes out of itself. Heaven and Earth are like the human body, the transformation of their fluid, like the flushed color. How can Heaven and Earth cause the sudden change of their fluid, since man cannot produce the flushed color? The change of the fluid is spontaneous, it appears of itself, as the color comes out of itself. . . .

The literati declare that Heaven and Earth produce man on purpose. This assertion is preposterous, for, when Heaven and Earth mix up their fluids, man is born as a matter of course unintentionally. In just the same manner a child is produced spontaneously, when the essences of husband and wife are harmoniously blended. At the time of such an intercourse, the couple does not intend to beget a child. Their passionate love being roused, they unite, and out of this union a child is born. From the fact that husband and wife do not purposely beget a child one may infer that Heaven and Earth do not produce man on purpose either.

However, man is produced by Heaven and Earth just as fish in a pond, or lice on man. They grow in response to a peculiar force, each species reproducing itself. This holds good for all the things which come into being between Heaven and Earth.

NOTES

1. Who feeds the silkworms.
2. Inaction does not mean motionlessness, but spontaneous action without any aim or purpose. It is more or less mechanical, and not inspired by a conscious spirit.
3. The apparition of the lady was evoked by the court magician Shao Wêng in 121 B.C.E.
4. And it is likewise filled with the fluid.
5. One of Confucius' disciples, not Lao-tzu.

2.7   The True Features of Reality

KITARŌ NISHIDA

Kitarō Nishida (1875–1945) taught at Kanazawa Higher School and then at Kyoto University as a professor of philosophy. On retiring from Kyoto University, he devoted much of his time to writing. Among his many published works are *Ippansha no jikakuteki taikei* (*The Self-Conscious System of the Universal*, 1930), *Mu no jikakuteki gentei* (*The Self-Conscious Determination of Nothingness*, 1932), *Tetsugaku no konponmondai* (*The Fundamental Problems of Philosophy*, 1933–1934), and *Tetsugaku ronbunshū* (*A Collection of Philosophical Essays*, seven volumes, 1935–1946).

Nishida is perhaps best known as a philosophical precursor of the Kyoto school of philosophy, a group of Japanese scholars who attempted to fuse Eastern and Western concepts into a world philosophy. Nishida's contribution to this movement has been described by Masao Abe as follows: "Realizing the uniqueness of the Eastern way of thinking, Nishida took absolute nothingness as ultimate reality and tried to give it a logical foundation through his confrontation with Western philosophy. Forming his synthesis on the basis of historical life innate in human existence, which is neither Eastern nor Western, he neither established a new Eastern philosophy nor reconstructed Western philosophy but created a new world philosophy."

In this selection from a short work entitled *An Inquiry into the Good*, Nishida critiques traditional conceptions of reality and knowledge. His main criticism is that in traditional philosophy, reality and knowledge are often divorced from the practical demands of life. In this divorce, knowledge is portrayed as the objective description of a fixed reality that exists independently of the knowing subject. It is also traditionally claimed that science is the vehicle best suited for discovering such knowledge.

In opposition to this traditional conception of knowledge and reality, Nishida describes what he calls immediate reality or pure experience. In immediate reality or pure experience, there is no opposition between subject and object, and no separation of knowledge, feeling, and volition. As his example of the listener who is enraptured by exquisite music is intended to show, immediate reality or pure experience is a unified activity. In such a state we are one with the music, or more accurately, the separation between listener and music does not yet exist. All separation (including the separation between subject and object, and the separation between knowing, feeling, and willing) represents a movement away from and distortion of immediate reality. Nishida says that separation results in abstract concepts, which are the subject matter of scholars and scientists. However, immediate reality, which is undivided and includes feeling and willing as well as knowing, is the proper domain of art, religion, and philosophy. As Nishida says, "A scientist's way of explanation is slanted toward just one aspect of knowledge, whereas in a complete explanation of reality we must satisfy intellectual demands as well as the demands of feeling and the will."

Questions for Thought

1. What does Nishida mean by immediate reality? Do you believe you have access to immediate reality?
2. Do you agree with Nishida's claim that knowledge must not be divorced from feeling and will? Why or why not?
3. How effective is Nishida's example of the person enraptured by music in illustrating his claim that immediate reality exists? Can you think of other examples that might support the existence of immediate reality?
4. Nishida claims that scientific descriptions of reality are not as satisfying as artistic descriptions. On what basis does he make this claim? Do you agree with him on this point?
5. What would you consider to be an adequate description of a flower? What would you consider to be an adequate description of love?

The Starting Point of the Inquiry

PHILOSOPHICAL VIEWS OF THE WORLD AND OF human life relate closely to the practical demands of morality and religion, which dictate how people should act and where they can find peace of mind. People are never satisfied with intellectual convictions and practical demands that contradict each other. Those with high spiritual demands fail to find satisfaction in materialism, and those who believe in materialism come to harbor doubts about spiritual demands. Fundamentally, truth is singular. Intellectual truth and practical truth must be one and the same. Those who think deeply or are genuinely serious inevitably seek congruence between knowledge

From Kitarō Nishida, *An Inquiry Into the Good* (1990), pp. 37, 38, 47–50.
Reprinted by permission of Yale University Press.

and the practical realm of feeling and willing. We must now investigate what we ought to do and where we ought to find peace of mind, but this calls first for clarification of the nature of the universe, human life, and true reality.

The Indian religio-philosophical tradition, which provides the most highly developed congruence of philosophy and religion, holds that knowledge is good and delusion is evil. The fundamental reality of the universe is Brahman, which is our soul, our Atman. Knowledge of this identity of Brahman and Atman is the culmination of Indian philosophy and religion. Christianity was entirely practical at its inception, but because the human mind insistently demands intellectual satisfaction, Christian philosophy was developed in the Middle Ages. In the Chinese tradition, the system of morality at first lacked philosophical elaboration, but since the Sung period this dimension has predominated. Such historical trends in the Indian, Christian, and Chinese traditions attest to the basic human demand for congruence between our knowledge and our feeling and will.

In classical Western philosophy beginning with Socrates and Plato, didactic goals were central, whereas in modern times knowledge has assumed a prominent position, making the unity of the intellectual and the emotional-volitional aspects more difficult. In fact, the two dimensions now tend to diverge, and this in no way satisfies the fundamental demands of the human mind.

To understand true reality and to know the true nature of the universe and human life, we must discard all artificial assumptions, doubt whatever can be doubted, and proceed on the basis of direct and indubitable knowledge. From the perspective of common sense, we think that things exist in the external world apart from consciousness and that in the back of consciousness there is something called the mind, which performs various functions. Our assumption that mind and matter exist independently constitutes the basis of our conduct and is itself based on the demands posed by our thinking. This assumption leaves much room for doubt. Science, which does not take the most profound explanation of reality as its goal, is constructed on such hypothetical knowledge. But insufficiently critical thinking is also found in philosophy, which does take that explanation as its goal. Many philosophers base their thinking on existing assumptions and hence fail to engage in penetrating doubt. . . .

The True Features of Reality

What is immediate reality before we have added the fabrications of thinking? In other words, what is a fact of truly pure experience? At the time of pure experience, there is still no opposition between subject and object and no separation of knowledge, feeling, and volition; there is only an independent, self-sufficient, pure activity.

Intellectualist psychologists regard sensations and ideas as the requisite elements of mental phenomena and hold that all mental phenomena are constituted by their union. From this perspective, they construe a fact of pure experience to be the most passive state of consciousness, namely, sensation. But this approach confuses the results of academic analysis with the facts of direct experience. In facts of direct experience, there is no pure sensation. What we term pure sensation is already a simple perception, but no matter how simple, perception is not at all passive: it necessarily includes active—constructive—elements. (This is obvious when we consider examples of spatial perception.)

The characterization of pure experience as active becomes clearer when we examine such complex cognitive activities as association and thinking. Though association is usually deemed passive, the direction of the linkage of ideas in association is determined not only by circumstances in the external world, but also by the internal qualities of consciousness. Association and thinking thus differ only in degree. Moreover, people divide the phenomena of consciousness into knowledge, but in actuality we do not find these three types of phenomena. In fact, each and every phenomenon of consciousness possesses all three aspects. (For instance, although academic research is considered a purely intellectual activity, it can never exist apart from feeling and the will.) Of these three aspects the will is the most fundamental form of consciousness. As voluntarist psychologists assert, our consciousness is always active: it begins with an impulse and ends with the will. However simple, the most direct phenomena of consciousness take the form of the will—that is, the will is a fact of pure experience. . . .

In pure experience, our thinking, feeling, and willing are still undivided; there is a single activity, with no opposition between subject and object. Such opposition arises from the demands of thinking, so it is not a fact of direct experience. In direct experience there is only an independent, self-sufficient event, with neither a subject that sees nor an object that is seen. Just like when we become enraptured by exquisite music, forget ourselves and everything around us, and experience the universe as one melodious sound, true reality presents itself in the moment of direct experience. Should the thought arise that the music is the vibration of air or that one is listening to music, at that point one has already separated oneself from true reality because that thought derives from reflection and thinking divorced from the true state of the reality of the music.

It is usually thought that subject and object are realities that can exist independently of each other and that phenomena of consciousness arise through their activity, which leads to the idea that there are two realities: mind and matter. This is a total mistake. The notions of subject and object derive from two different ways of looking at a single fact, as does the distinction between mind and matter. But these dichotomies are not inherent in the fact itself. As a concrete fact, a flower is not at all like the purely material flower of scientists; it is pleasing, with a beauty of color, shape, and scent. Heine gazed at the stars in a quiet night sky and called them golden tacks in the azure.[1] Though astronomers would laugh at his words as the folly of a poet, the true nature of stars may very well be expressed in his phrase.

In the independent, self-sufficient true reality prior to the separation of subject and object, our knowledge, feeling, and volition are one. Contrary to popular belief, true reality is not the subject matter of dispassionate knowledge; it is established through our feeling and willing. It is not simply an existence but something with meaning. If we were to remove our feelings and the will from this world of actuality, it would no longer be a concrete fact—it would become an abstract concept. The world described by physicists, like a line without width and a plane without thickness, is not something that actually exists. In this respect, it is the artist, not the scholar, who arrives at the true nature of reality. Each and every thing we see or hear contains our individuality. Though we might speak of identical consciousness, our consciousnesses are not truly the same. When viewing a cow, for example, farmers, zoologists, and artists have different mental images. Depending on one's feeling at the moment, the same scenery can appear resplendently beautiful or depressingly gloomy. Buddhist thought holds that according to one's mood the world becomes either heaven or hell. Thus our world is constructed upon our feeling and volition. However much we talk about the objective world as the subject matter of pure knowledge, it cannot escape its relation to our feelings.

People think that the world seen scientifically is most objective in that it exists independently of our feeling and volition. But it is in no way divorced from the demands of feeling and the will because scientific inquiry derives from actual demands in our struggle for survival. As especially Jerusalem has said, the idea that a power in the external world performs various activities—this idea being the fundamental principle of the scientific world view—is generated by analogical inference from one's will.[2] Ancient explanations of things in the universe were anthropomorphic, and they are the springboard from which contemporary scientific explanations developed.

Taking the distinction between subject and object as fundamental, some think that objective elements are included only in knowledge and that idiosyncratic, subjective events constitute feeling and volition. This view is mistaken in its basic assumptions. If we argue that phenomena arise by means of the mutual activity of subject and object, then even such content of knowledge as color or form can be seen as subjective or individual. If we argue further that there is a quality in the external world that gives rise to feeling and volition, then they come to possess an objective base, and it is therefore an error to say they are totally individual. Our feeling and volition allow for communication and sympathy between individuals; they have a trans-individual element.

Because we think that such emotional and volitional entities as joy, anger, love, and desire arise in individual people, we also think that feeling and the will are purely individual. Yet it is not that the individual possesses feeling and the will, but rather that feeling and the will create the individual. Feeling and the will are facts of direct experience.

The anthropomorphic explanation of the myriad things in the universe is the way of explanation used by ancient people and naive children in all eras. Although scientists might laugh it away—indeed, it is infantile—from a certain perspective this is the true way of explaining reality. A scientist's way of explanation is slanted toward just one aspect of knowledge, whereas in a complete explanation of reality we must satisfy intellectual demands as well as the demands of feeling and the will.

To the Greeks, all of nature was alive. Thunder and lightning were the wrath of Zeus on Mount Olympus, the voice of the cuckoo was Philamela's lament of the past.[3] To the natural eye of a Greek, the true meaning of the present appeared just as it was. Contemporary art, religion, and philosophy all strive to express this true meaning.

NOTES

1. Heinrich Heine (1797–1856) was a German poet and critic who was heavily influenced by German romanticism.

2. K. W. Jerusalem, *Einleitung in die Philosophie*, 6, Aufl. 27.

3. Friedrich Schiller, *Die Götter Griechenlands*. An English translation of Schiller's poem, "The Gods of Greece," can be found in J. G. Fischer, ed., *Schiller's Works*, vol. 1 (Philadelphia: George Barrie, 1883), p. 36.

2.8   On Psychic Activism: Feminist Mythmaking

JANE CAPUTI

Jane Caputi (b. 1953) is an associate professor of American Studies at the University of New Mexico, Albuquerque. She is the author of *The Age of the Sex Crime*, a feminist analysis of the atrocity of sexual murder, and co-author (with Mary Daly) of *Webster's First New Intergalactic Wickedary of the English Language*. Her most recent work, which was creatively titled *Gossips, Gorgons, and Crones: The Fates of the Earth*, was published by Bear and Company in 1993.

In the essay reprinted below, Caputi discusses the way in which reality is created through the use of symbols and myth, a process that she terms "psychic activism." After claiming that our current mythology is decidedly phallocentric, she discusses the various ways in which contemporary women are smashing such phallocentric myths and symbols, and subsequently "reconceptualizing reality and changing the world." Caputi briefly summarizes the work of several psychic activists, including Mary Daly, Audre Lorde, Paula Gunn Allen, and Gloria Anzaldúa. She also describes several of the woman-identified products of their mythmaking—from the revitalization of assorted goddess imagery to the creation of other symbols of empowerment, such as the Gorgon, the Crone, and the *mestiza*. Caputi claims that psychic activists and their re-creations are needed to displace the male-created myths and symbols of domination and oppression, myths and symbols that have supported a "woman/body/earth hating society."

Questions for Thought

1. What does Caputi mean by psychic activism? Have you ever engaged in this activity?
2. Do you agree with Caputi's claim that traditional Western myths and symbols have been patriarchally biased? Why or why not?
3. What is the difference between a Gorgon and a Crone? Do you believe that these symbols empower women?
4. What myth or symbol do you find most empowering?
5. What are the common assumptions of the psychic activists discussed by Caputi? What are some of the areas of disagreement between them?
6. Do you agree with Caputi that our society is "woman/body/earth hating"? Why or why not?

Gyn/Ecology . . . involves the dispelling of the mind/spirit/body pollution that is produced out of man-made myths . . . it also . . . involves speaking forth the New Words.[1]

I hold to the traditional Indian views on language, that words have power, that words become entities. When I write I keep in mind that it is a form of power and salvation that is for the planet. If it is good and enters the world, perhaps it will counteract the destruction that seems to be getting so close to us. I think of

language and poems, even fictions, as prayers and small ceremonies.[2]

By creating a new mythos—this is, a change in the way we perceive reality, the way we see ourselves, and the ways we behave—*la mestiza* creates a new consciousness.[3]

IN *SEXUAL POLITICS*, KATE MILLETT WROTE THAT "under patriarchy the female did not herself develop the symbols by which she is described."[4] Mary Daly, in *Beyond God the Father*, declared

From "On Psychic Activism: Feminist Mythmaking," in *The Feminist Companion to Mythology*, Jane Caputi; Carolyne Larrington (ed.). Reprinted by permission of HarperCollins Publishers, London.

that "women have had the power of naming stolen from us."[5] One of the most significant developments to emerge out of the contemporary feminist movement is the quest to reclaim that symbolizing/naming power, to refigure the female self from a gynocentric perspective, to discover, revitalize and create a female oral and visual mythic tradition and use it, ultimately, to change the world.

Throughout this century, feminist thinkers have continued to expose the patriarchal bias of mythographers (past and present) and the ways that these entrenched mythic symbols and paradigms construct and maintain phallocentric reality. . . . Simultaneously, . . . feminist thinkers actively reinterpret ancient myth, focusing attention on female divinities, supernaturals and powers that have been repressed and silenced. And this is no mere academic pursuit. Rather, feminist use of myth stems from an understanding of myth to be a "language construct that contains the power to transform something (or someone) from one state or condition to another . . . it is at base a vehicle, a means of transmitting paranormal power."[6] Thus, with varying degrees of self-consciousness, women as "witches" call mythic themes and personae into present time as a way to "cast spells . . . to promote changes of consciousness. . . . To respell the world means to redefine the root of our being. It means to redefine us and therefore change us."[7]

Carol P. Christ writes that one of the most basic feminist symbols—the Goddess—positively values female *will*: "In ritual magic, the energy raised is directed by willpower. Women who celebrate in Goddess circles believe they can achieve their wills in the world."[8] Such rituals need not be overtly sacred ceremonies to a Goddess, but can take the forms of writings, demonstrations, speeches, informal gatherings. Whenever feminists engage in energy-raising mythic/symbolic thought and image-making, capable of reconceptualizing reality and changing the world, this is what I call *psychic activism*.

In the gynocentric tradition of the Keres people (Pueblo Indians of what is now New Mexico), the creatrix is Ts'its'tsi'nako, Thought-Woman, also known as Thinking Woman or Spider Grandmother. Pueblo writer Leslie Marmon Silko narrates their creation myth:

> Ts'its'tsi'nako, Thought-Woman,
> is sitting in her room
> and whatever she thinks about
> appears.
> She thought of her sisters,
> Nau'ts'ity'i and I'tcts'ity'i,
> and together they created the Universe
> this world
> and the four worlds below.
> Thought-Woman, the spider,
> named things and
> as she named them
> they appeared.[9]

Thought-Woman creates the world by thinking and speaking it into being, by telling its story. As another Pueblo Indian writer, Paula Gunn Allen, observes: "The thought for which Grandmother Spider is known is the kind that results in physical manifestation of phenomena: mountains, lakes, creatures, or philosophical–sociological systems."[10] Phallocentric thought/myth results in the physical manifestation of phenomena such as social inequality, toxic waste, nuclear weapons, genocide, gynocide. When women refuse and refute these thoughts/myths and instead foray into the realm traditionally forbidden to our sex—the realm of the sacred storytellers, symbol and myth-makers—we participate in the creative powers of Thought Women, employing thinking, naming and willing as forms of power exercised consciously and/or intuitively in the creation of the world(s) we inhabit. . . .

Dreaming in Female

I came into the movement [Black Power], trying to be the perfect African woman. In the process I find out there used to be a cult of women in Africa who were warriors . . . who cut a man's penis and stuck it in his mouth as a mark that they had done this. . . . I learn that the lightning bolt originally belonged to a female deity. I started learning things that whisper of very strong women. . . . I had to confront, finally, the "men's room" . . . I mean a room in this collective spiritual household where women were not allowed to go, because according to the males we would be struck by lightning if we went in there. So one day I just on my own decided I'm going to walk in there and . . . *smash a myth.*[11]

I am an old woman with a deck of cards
A witch, an Amazon, a Gorgon
A seer, a clairvoyant, a poet.
I have visions of becoming and
I dream in female.[12]

The journey engaged in by many contemporary feminists is twofold: one involving both patriarchal myth-smashing and woman-identified myth-making. Beginning in the late 1960s, innumerable feminists began to reject patriarchal myth and to dream openly in female, conjuring up diversely named Goddesses, Amazons, Warriors, Witches, Two-Headed Women (psychics or mediums in African-American traditions) . . . , Mermaids, Gorgons, Sibyls and Crones as metaphors of cosmic/female power. A lesbian-feminist journal, *Amazon Quarterly*, appeared; the Artemis Café opened in San Francisco; a lesbian-feminist collective in Washington D.C. named itself "The Furies"; and a New York radical feminist group dubbed itself W.I.T.C.H. (Women's International Conspiracy from Hell).

These namings are rarely arbitrary; they deliberately recall a specific mythic power from the past into the present. For example, a radical feminist nurses group named itself *Cassandra*, because "We are all too actively aware of the fact that nursing's voice is not heard, and more basically that women's voices are not heard in the world. But we know that although myths are very powerful, we do re-create myths."[13] This re-creation of myth is what Emily Culpepper, in

her superb study of the use of symbols in the women's movement, calls "gynergetic symbolization." As she observes: "Breaking out of the bondage of being Woman/The Other/Symbol, women become Self-Conscious subjects, primary symbolizers who weave our own view of the Self and cosmos."[14]

The drive to become a psychic activist, to smash phallocentric myth while creating women-identified words, symbols and myths is a major force behind the extensive philosophical writings of Mary Daly. In *Beyond God the Father* (1973), *Gyn/Ecology* (1978), *Pure Lust* (1984), and *Webster's First New Intergalactic Wickedary of the English Language* (Daly with Caputi, 1987), this self-described "Revolting Hag" critiques patriarchal myth while inventing an astonishing variety of mythic identities for women and names for female power. *Muses, Fates, Gorgons, Furies, Harpies, Amazons,* and *Dragons* are some of the more familiar personae she presents as preferred female role models. Simultaneously, she takes words such as *Spinsters, Witches, Hags, Crones, Nags, Scolds, Prudes,* and *Shrews*—all with negative associations in phallocentric contexts—and redefines them as shimmering metaphors for female strengths. . . .

Psychic activism is at the root of Daly's philosophy. In *Pure Lust* she writes: "Symbols . . . participate in that to which they point. They open up levels of reality otherwise closed to us and they unlock dimensions and elements of our souls which correspond to these hidden dimensions and elements of reality."[15] Most frequently, Daly refers to her new words and images as *metaphors*, because metaphor, while it includes the power of symbols, also evokes "action, movement. . . . Metaphors function to Name change, and therefore they elicit change. . . . [metaphor] is associated with transforming action."[16] Such metaphors work to change not only the self, but also the world. Daly continues, "The word *reality* is nothing less than an Ontological Battleground. The risks are ultimate."[17] She calls upon women to fight fire with

Fire, to become metapatterning, metapatriarchal "Artists"—shape-shifting and spinning gynocentric metaphors to Name and hence elicit transmutations, both personal and social, to move out of patriarchal reality and into what she calls "Metamorphospheres."[18]

Daly has been one of the most prolific generators of gynergetic symbolization; her new words and symbols have been widely welcomed and extremely influential. Yet *Gyn/Ecology* has been subjected to some criticism for ethnocentrism.

In 1979, poet Audre Lorde wrote a personal letter to Daly, asking why the Goddess images Daly used in *Gyn/Ecology* were "only white, western-european, judeo-christian? Where was Afrekete, Yemanje, Oyo and Mawulisa? . . . because so little material on non-white female power and symbol exists in white women's words from a radical feminist perspective, to exclude this aspect of connection from even comment in your work is to deny the fountain of non-european female strength and power that nurtures each of our visions. . . ."[19]

In *The Black Unicorn*, Lorde herself provides a valuable glossary of African Goddesses and traditions. Understanding as well that individual names have been lost, in a later poem, "Call," Lorde cries out to "Aido Hwedo: The Rainbow Serpent; also a representation of all ancient divinities who must be worshipped but whose names and faces have been lost in time."[20] Lorde commingles evocations of Aido Hwedo with names of African Goddesses as well as historical and contemporary women: Rosa Parks, Fannie Lou Hamer, Assata Shakur, Yaa Asantewa. Ancestor reverence is intrinsic to African religions, and it remains so to much of contemporary African-American feminist symbolizations. Luisah Teish declares: "The veneration of our foremothers is essential to our self respect. . . ."[21]

Clearly, not only mythic personae change among different cultures, but also mythic sources and emphases. Paula Gunn Allen writes: "The [American] Indian collective unconscious . . . encompasses much more than goddesses, gods, and geometric symbols. More important than its characters are narrative strands, historical trauma, and other sorts of information that lend significance and pattern to individual and communal life."[22] Luisah Teish invokes the tradition of European witchcraft, but reminds us that feminists also must reclaim the two-headed woman, the root worker (herbalist) and the matrifocal tradition of *Voudou*. Poet and essayist Marilou Awiakta uses Amazons as a metaphor in her essay on the power of her Cherokee ancestresses, but rejects the image presented in Greek mythology. Moreover, she ties the story of her own menstrual coming of age among the elders at the menstrual lodge with the story of Nanyehi, the last "Beloved Women" (head of the Women's Council of the Cherokee Nation) and the events leading up to the historical trauma of the Cherokee removal:

> These women are not the Amazons of the Greek fable. While they are independent and self-defined, they do not hate men and use them only at random for procreation. . . . But did the Greek patriarchs tell the truth? . . . I'm wary of the Greeks bearing fables. Although there is little proof that they described the Amazons accurately, ample evidence suggests that they encountered—and resented—strong women like my Grandmothers and characterized them as heinous in order to justify destroying them (a strategy modern patriarchs still use). . . . [W]hy should I bother with distant Greeks and their nebulous fables when I have the spirits of the Grandmothers, whose roots are struck deep in my native soil and whose strength is as tangible and tenacious as the amber-pitched pine at my back.[23]

Like Awiakta's Amazons/Grandmothers, radical, feminist evocations of Goddesses must be just so tangible, tenacious and rooted in the world. Women, as Christ argued, certainly do need the Goddess in order to acknowledge "the legitimacy of female power as a beneficent and independent power."[24] But that Goddess cannot be imagined as always white, heterosexual, maternal or ethereal, for, as Sjöö and Mor remind us:

> . . . the Goddess [does not] "live" solely in elite separatist retreats, dancing naked in the piney woods under a white and well-fed moon. The Goddess at this moment is starving to death in refugee camps, with a skeletal child clutched to her dry nipples. . . . The Goddess is on welfare, raising her children in a ghetto next to a freeway interchange that fills their blood cells and neurons with lead. The Goddess is an eight-year-old girl being used for the special sexual thrills of visiting businessmen in a Brazilian brothel. The Goddess is patrolling with a rifle . . . trying to save a revolution in Nicaragua. The Goddess is Winnie Mandela in South Africa, saying "Don't push me." I.e., the Goddess IS the world—the Goddess is *in* the world. And *nobody* can escape the world.[25]

Along with the widespread resurgence of Goddess imagery, radical feminist psychic activists conjure specific powers and symbols in response to particular social crises. Next I will turn to several examples of this: the Gorgon as a force inspiring resistance to sexual violence and the multifarious symbolizations wrought by the anti-nuclear and ecofeminist movements.

Repulsive to Men

Since the early 1970s, the Medusa, the Greek Gorgon with hair of snakes who was able to turn men to stone merely by gazing upon them, has been a power symbol for feminists. Like much of Greek myth, the story of the Medusa is rooted in African, gynocentric elements.

In a stirring article, Culpepper analyzes not only the significance of the Gorgon face as a symbol of contemporary women's rage, but also the ways that "feminists are *living* the knowledge gained from tapping deep and ancient symbolic/mythic power to change our lives."[26] She relates an incident which occurred one night in 1980 as she sat alone in her house working. Someone knocked at the door and, after looking out and thinking it was someone

she knew, she opened the door. A stranger came in and immediately attacked her. Culpepper, at first off guard, gathered herself and fought back, throwing out the would-be attacker. She includes a selection from her journal recalling the incident: "I am staring him out, pushing with my eyes too. My face is bursting, contorting with terrible teeth, flaming breath, erupting into ridges and contortions of rage, hair hissing. It is over in a flash. I can still see his eyes, stunned, wide and staring, almost as if *I* am acting strange, as if *I* were acting wrong!"[27] Afterwards, she realized that she "needed to look at the terrible face that had erupted and sprung forth from within" during her fight:

> As I felt my face twist again into the fighting frenzy, I turned to the mirror and looked. What I saw in the mirror was a Gorgon, a Medusa, if *ever* there was one. This face was my own and yet I knew I had seen it before and I knew the name to utter. "Gorgon! Gorgon!" reverberated in my mind. I knew then why the attacker had become so suddenly petrified.[28]

In this world where men daily perpetrate outrages upon women, as Culpepper notes, it is imperative that women "learn how to manifest a visage that will repel men when necessary. . . . The Gorgon has much vital, literally life-saving information to teach women about anger, rage, power and the release of the determined aggressiveness sometimes needed for survival."[29]

Gorgons do not live only in the imaginary/past world of myth and story. Rather, they/we live today. Robin Morgan writes, "We are the myths. We are the Amazons, the Furies, the Witches. We have never not been here, this exact sliver of time, this precise place."[30] Deeply realizing this truth, as Culpepper demonstrates, can be literally life-saving.

Spinning at the Gate

On 20 March, 1980, The Spinsters, "an affinity group of women-identified women," performed a myth-based protest at a nuclear power plant in

Vermont USA, by weaving intricate designs of colored yarn between the trees of the entrance to the plant. Their accompanying leaflet read in part: "We, as life-givers, will not support any life-threatening force. Nuclear madness imminently endangers our children, their future and the earth. On Monday, March 31, women will be reweaving the web of life into the site of Vermont Yankee."[31] This practice, repeated in countless feminist anti-nuclear demonstrations, deliberately invokes the metaphoric web of Spider Woman; indeed, the web symbol (pointing to the interconnection and interdependency of all life) has become primary to the language and philosophic underpinnings of the ecofeminist movement.

Other symbols also are evoked in anti-nuclear theory and activism. Since both phallo-sexual and nuclear violations are rooted in the same ethic of masculinist domination, it makes sense that the Gorgon also intuitively would be invoked as an anti-nuclear symbol. From Freud on, the Medusa has signified castration and the Gorgon does signify women's capacity to emasculate what Diana Russell calls "nuclear phallacies."[32] In another vein, Barbara Deming writes: This is a song for gorgons—

Whose dreaded glances in fact can bless.
The men who would be gods we turn
Not to stone but to mortal flesh and blood
    and bone.
If we could stare them into accepting this,
The world could live at peace."[33]

Moreover, as Daly and I suggest in *The Wickedary*, the Gorgon is she whose "*face can stop a clock*." Since 1947, the *Bulletin of the Atomic Scientists* has published a "doomsday clock" which depicts how many minutes there are to "midnight," that is, how close the world is to nuclear holocaust:

Spinsters Spinning about-face the fact that clockocracy's clocks are elementary moons. . . . Lusty women, in tune with the Moon, pose the poignant Question: Is the Moon's Face the

Face that can stop the doomsday clock? . . . [W]omen as Gorgons look toward the madmen and turn them to stone—the doomsday men with their doomsday clocks.[34]

Another mythic figure of female power, that of the ancient woman, the ancestor or Crone, also manifests as an anti-nuclear metaphor. As feminist mythographer Barbara Walker relates, the Crone is the general designation of the third of the Triple Goddess's aspects (embodied in figures such as Hecate and Kali) and one associated with old age, death, the waning moon, winter and rebirth. As a harbinger of rebirth, the Crone's appearance signals a call to profound transformation and healing. Nor Hall writes that the function of the old wise woman "is to be of assistance in times of difficult passage. As midwife to the psyche she is constellated in 'emergency' situations where a spirit, a song, an alternative, a new being is emerging."[35]

In the face of a global ecological emergency, Barbara Walker calls for the reinstitution of the Crone, not as some "deity actually existing 'out there,'" but as a chosen metaphor:

Most of all the Crone can represent precisely the kind of power women so desperately need today, and do not have: the power to force men to do what is right, for the benefit of future generations and of the earth itself. . . . Metaphors like these take on practical meaning in women's capacity to see through men's pretenses and to reject men's self-serving images. Men feared the judgmental eye of the wise-woman even when she was socially powerless. This, then, is the chink in the armor of patriarchal establishments. When many women together say no and mean it, the whole structure can collapse. . . . She had better do it soon, for he is already counting down to doomsday.[36]

Ecofeminism

The planet, our mother, Grandmother Earth, is physical and therefore a spiritual, mental, and emotional being. Planets are alive, as are all their by-products or expressions, such as animals, vegetables, minerals, climactic and meteorological phenomena. Believing that our mother, the beloved Earth, is inert matter is destructive to yourself.[37]

The area of feminist activism that most overtly politicizes symbolization and spirituality is the ecofeminist movement. Caroline Merchant has demonstrated that in western thought women and nature consistently have been associated and jointly devalued, and that the modern metaphor of the Earth as machine has been used to further patriarchal domination. To counter these toxic beliefs and metaphors, "Radical feminism . . . celebrates the relationship between women and nature through the revival of ancient rituals centered on Goddess worship, the moon, animals, and the female reproductive system. . . . Spirituality is seen as a source of both personal and social change. Goddess worship rituals . . . lectures, concerts, art exhibitions, street and theater products, and direct political action . . . all are examples of the re-visioning of nature and women as powerful forces."[38]

Merchant cautions, however, that ecofeminism runs "the risk of perpetuating the very hierarchies it seeks to overthrow" by stressing biological femaleness and the identification of women with nature. "Any analysis that makes women's essence and qualities special ties them to a biological destiny that thwarts the possibility of liberation."[39] I agree that ecofeminists must beware adopting a dualistic worldview. Yet when we acknowledge such aspects of "biological destiny" as the capacity to give birth, menstruation, menopause, aging and death, and place positive valuations on these, this actually is a profoundly revolutionary act in a women/body/earth hating society, dedicated to denying these bodies/destinies. Merchant continues: "A politics grounded in women's culture, experience, and values can be seen as reactionary";[40] here she alludes to a widespread critique (proffered mainly by socialist and postmodern feminists) deriding as "essentialist" (based in a belief

in differing female and male natures) and "totalizing" (ignoring vast historical and cultural differences) those philosophical approaches that celebrate women's culture or experiences. For example Mary Lydon writes: "To claim essential womanhood, to assert oneself as subject, to demand the freedom to write 'like a woman,' to reclaim women's history, to speak their sexuality is a powerful temptation. Yet it must be resisted, I would argue, taking a leaf from Foucault's book.'"[41]

To my mind, however, this postmodern approach is seriously flawed and functions, as Susan Bordo maintains, "to harness and tame the visionary and creative energy of feminism as a movement of cultural resistance and transformation."[42] Essentially, it profoundly disempowers women by submitting to masculinist authority and forbidding feminist bonding, mythmaking and the invocation of what, at least at this historical moment, many of us conceptualize as gynocentric values. Imagining an open-ended gynocentric culture does not require the erasure of women's diversity or the worship of a fixed female essence—quite the opposite. Of course, as many thinkers have observed, if what is promoted as "women's culture" is actually middle-class, Euro-American women's culture, this would be genuinely reactionary. Still, female bonding and myth-making can occur based not on some illusory all-embracing female culture, but on women's common "Otherness" to patriarchy.[43]

Elinor Gadon and Gloria Orenstein have explored in their works on feminist sacred art, the ways that ecofeminist beliefs can assume visual forms as artists root their works in archaic (Earth) Goddess imagery. Gadon calls such artists "the visionaries, the seers of our time" and avers that those artists "who are reclaiming the sacred iconography of the Goddess are creating a new social reality."[44] Artists who incorporate Earth-based spirituality and Goddess imagery in their works include Ana Mendieta, Judith Anderson, Betty LaDuke, Betsy Damon, Helene Aylon and Vijali.

A central part of ecofeminist spirituality is the concept, rooted in the African, Native American and pre-industrial European traditions, that Earth (understood as female) and everything on it is alive, that everything, as Alice Walker declares, "is a human being."[45] Carol Lee Sanchez, a Laguna Pueblo (New Mexico) thinker, poet and artist, extends this concept to include even inanimate objects. Pointing to "an ever-widening gulf between 'daily life' and 'spirituality'" in technological culture, she avers: "I believe Euro-Americans waste the resources and destroy the environment in the Americas because they are not spiritually connected to this land base, because they have no ancient mythos or legendary origins rooted to this land."[46] She deplores the modern western schism between the sacred and the profane and contrasts it to the Tribal tradition that recognizes "all things in the known universe to be equally sacred." Sanchez believes that not only must all non-Tribal Americans acknowledge and become thoroughly familiar with the indigenous spiritual frameworks of this hemisphere, but that we must rethink our culture's social and technological processes and philosophies and compare them with Tribal principles, philosophies and social structures, working ultimately toward the creation of "a non-Indian Tribal community." Such a community formally acknowledges the sacredness of everyday life through songs and ceremonies. It also would reverence the realities of the modern world, for:

> I believe it is time to create new songs of acknowledgment as well as ceremonies that include metals, petrochemicals, and fossil fuels, electricity, modern solar power systems, and water power systems. I also believe it is very important to make sacred, to acknowledge the new ways and elements in our lives—from nuclear power . . . to plastics to computers. It is time now, again, for the entire world to honor these Spirits, these new molecular forms in order to restore harmony and balance to our out-of-control systems and, in particular, to our modern technologies.[47]

Sanchez is *not* proposing that non-Indians somehow become Indians. Rather, she is suggesting that non-Indians learn from and synthesize Tribal philosophies and practices into daily practice and technological realities, thus becoming members of a never-before-seen new world Tribal community.

New Mythic Identities

THUS FAR, I HAVE EXAMINED A NUMBER OF mythic models and metaphors cast into being by feminist thinkers. In this last section, I briefly will examine three others to show further the range of contemporary imaginings: the griot-historian, the *mestiza* and the cyborg.

Barbara Omolade invokes and reshapes a multiplicity of symbols in her conception of the Black feminist scholar as a "griot-historian," including the "griot" (an African court personage, usually a man, whose function was to praise royal lineage) and the African *orisha*, Oshun (goddess of love and rivers):

> A "griot historian" is a scholar in any discipline who connects, uses, and understands the methods and insights of both Western and African world-views and historical perspectives to further develop a synthesis—an African American woman's social science with a unique methodology, sensibility, and language. . . . She carves out new lands of the mind while reaching back to her spiritual and cultural sources, the major one of course being African, with its rivers and memories. One river named for the African orisha, Oshun, a symbol of female power and sensuality, is a guiding power for the griot-historian's quest.

Omolade invokes the ancestor and enacts the pattern of both myth-smashing and myth-making:

The griot-historian must "break de chains" of Western thought . . . be baptized by some force outside the tradition of Western civilization and become submerged in the waters of Black women's pain, power, and potential. . . . [T]he griot-historian . . . must overcome her fear of the stigma of being the daughter of Aunt Jemima, the granddaughter of "negra wenches" . . . the great granddaughter of Africans called "primitive and animal-like." Seeing the woman beyond the shame affirms the use of historical truths to sing praise songs which resurrect the lives and experiences of the orisha, the warrior, and the "drylongso" Black woman.[48]

Chicana thinker and poet Gloria Anzaldúa proposes yet another identity grounded in her unique position as a woman who has grown up "between two cultures, the Mexican (with a heavy Indian influence) and the Anglo (as a member of a colonized people in our own territory)."[49] A *mestiza*, of course, is a woman who borders races, but in Anzaldúa's conception, includes one who straddles psychological, sexual and spiritual boundaries. Thus accustomed to transcending dividing lines:

> . . . she can't hold concepts or ideas in rigid boundaries. [B]y remaining flexible [she is] . . . able to stretch the psyche horizontally and vertically. . . . The new *mestiza* copes by developing a tolerance for contradictions, a tolerance for ambiguity. . . . She learns to juggle cultures. She has a plural personality. . . . The work of *mestiza* consciousness is to break down the subject–object duality that keeps her a prisoner and to show . . . how duality is transcended. The answer to the problem between the white race and the colored, between males and females, lies in healing the split that originates in the very foundation of our lives, our culture, our languages, our thoughts. A massive uprooting of dualistic thinking in the individual and collective consciousness is the beginning of a long struggle, but one that could . . . bring us to the end of rape, of violence, of war.[50]

Omolade and Anzaldúa's mythic identities spring from a racial and, in Anzaldúa's case, a sexual (Lesbian) background. Another feminist identity, that of Donna Haraway's "cyborg," is located in what many other feminists would consider to be prime patriarchal reality—science and technology.

In Haraway's view, "the boundary between science fiction and social reality is an optical illusion."[51] The cyborg is a fictional creature, "a hybrid of machine and organism," but, as Haraway argues, in social reality we now *are* cyborgs, living in ways that break down the borders between animal, human and machine. In her schema, the cyborg betokens a "world without gender, which is perhaps a world without genesis, but maybe also a world without end."[52] Haraway refuses the worldviews of such feminists as Susan Griffin, Audre Lorde and Adrienne Rich who "insist on the organic, opposing it to the technological."[53] Taking a postmodernist stance, she aims to deconstruct those premises which she deems to have contributed so heavily to the structure of the "Western self," distinctions ordered in the Adam and Eve myth which presupposes a state of "original unity . . . with nature"[54] and innocence. "Cyborg writing is about the power to survive, not on the basis of original innocence, but on the basis of seizing the tools to mark the world that marked them as other."[55] Haraway urges that feminists see technology and science not only as agents of "complex dominations," but as "possible means of great human satisfaction."[56] She concludes: "Though both are bound in the spiral dance, I would rather be a cyborg than a goddess."[57]

Intriguingly, all three of these rousingly imaginative identities are based upon synthesis; all seek ways to break from western paradigms and to transcend dualism. While Omolade and Anzaldúa imagine identities formed as a result of and in opposition to colonialism, Haraway's cyborg results from technology. It remains to be seen if Haraway's cyborg is truly oppositional or if "seizing tools to mark the world" merely continues a long-established pattern of phallo-technological domination/manipulation. Moreover, is innocence a thoroughly bankrupt concept? Can't we point to some states which signify if not "innocence" then integrity, e.g. the body of the girl before incest, Native American societies before colonization and genocide? While feminist symbolizers must suspect those old patriarchal images, we, equally, must be wary of the shiny new ones. As Haraway herself acknowledges, the cyborg is the "offspring of militarism and patriarchal capitalism."[58] She simultaneously deems it an "illegitimate offspring," thus possessing radical potential; still, the cyborg's complicity in constructing the patriarchal present (and future) must continue to be explored.

Whether by naming ourselves Cyborgs or Goddesses, Two-Headed Women, *Mestizas* or Crones, it is clear that feminists, as Mary Daly prophesied in the early 1970s, are laying claim to the power of Naming and hence realizing (making real) ourselves and the world we invoke. This multifaceted and gynergetic foray into language, myth, symbol and image is one of the most elemental feminist strategies in our quest to change—and then change again—the world.

NOTES

1. Mary Daly, *Gyn/Ecology: The Metaethics of Radical Feminism* (Boston: Beacon Press, 1978), p. 315.
2. Linda Hogan, "Daughters, I Love You," in P. McAllister, ed., *Reweaving the Web of Life: Feminism and Nonviolence* (Philadelphia: New Society Publishers, 1982), p. 352.
3. Gloria Anzaldúa, *Borderlands/La Frontera: The New Mestiza* (San Francisco: Spinsters/Aunt Lute Book Company, 1987), p. 80.
4. Kate Millet, *Sexual Politics* (New York: Doubleday and Company, 1969, 1970), pp. 64–65.
5. Mary Daly, *Beyond God the Father: Toward a Philosophy of Women's Liberation* (Boston: Beacon Press, 1973), p. 8.

6. Paula Gunn Allen, *The Sacred Hoop: Recovering the Feminine in American Indian Traditions* (Boston: Beacon Press, 1986), p. 103.
7. M. Sjöö and B. Mor, *The Great Cosmic Mother: Rediscovering the Religion of the Earth* (San Francisco: Harper & Row, 1987), p. 425.
8. Carol P. Christ, "Why Women Need the Goddess," in C. Christ and J. Plaskow, eds., *Womanspirit Rising: A Feminist Reader in Religion* (San Francisco: Harper & Row, 1979), p. 284.
9. Leslie Marmon Silko, *Ceremony* (New York: Signet Books, New American Library, 1977), p. 1.
10. Paula Gunn Allen, *The Sacred Hoop*, p. 122.
11. Luisah Teish, "O.K. Momma, Who the Hell Am I?: An Interview with Luisah Teish," in C. Moraga and G. Anzaldúa, eds., *This Bridge Called My Back: Writings by Radical Women of Color* (New York: Kitchen Table/Women of Color Press, 1981, 1983), p. 231.
12. Barbara Starrett, "I Dream in Female: The Metaphors of Evolution," in *Amazon Quarterly*, vol. 3, no. 1, p. 26.
13. Quoted in Emily Culpepper, "Philosophia in a New Key: The Revolt of the Symbols," Ph.D. Thesis, Harvard University (1983), p. 343.
14. *Ibid.*, p. 161.
15. Mary Daly, *Pure Lust: Elemental Feminist Philosophy* (Boston: Beacon Press, 1984), p. 25.
16. *Ibid.*
17. *Ibid.*, p. 394.
18. *Ibid.*, p. 408.
19. Audre Lorde, "An Open Letter to Mary Daly," in *This Bridge Called My Back*, pp. 94–95.
20. Audre Lorde, *Our Dead Behind Us* (New York: W. W. Norton, 1986), pp. 73–75.
21. Luisah Teish, "Woman's Spirituality: A Household Act," in B. Smith, ed., *Home Girls: A Black Feminist Anthology* (New York: Kitchen Table/Women of Color Press, 1983), p. 333.
22. Paula Gunn Allen, ed., *Spider Woman's Granddaughters: Traditional Tales and Contemporary Writing by Native American Women* (New York: Fawcett Columbine, 1989), pp. 23–24.
23. Marilou Awiakta, "Amazons in Appalachia," in B. Brandt, ed., *A Gathering of Spirit: A Collection of North American Indian Women* (Ithaca: Firebrand Books, 1988), pp. 129–130.
24. Carol P. Christ, "Why Women Need the Goddess," p. 277.
25. M. Sjöö and B. Mor, *The Great Cosmic Mother*, pp. 417–418.
26. Emily Culpepper, "Gorgons: A Face for Con-

temporary Women's Rage," in *Woman of Power*, issue 3, Winter/Spring 1986, p. 23.

27. *Ibid.*, p. 24.

28. *Ibid.*

29. *Ibid.*

30. Robin Morgan, *Going Too Far: The Personal Chronicle of a Feminist* (New York: Random House, 1977), p. 142.

31. C. Reid, "Reweaving the Web of Life," in *Reweaving the Web of Life*, p. 290.

32. Diana Russell, ed., *Exposing Nuclear Phallacies* (New York: Pergamon Press, The Athene Series, 1989).

33. Barbara Deming, "A Song for Gorgons," in *Reweaving the Web of Life*, p. 43.

34. Mary Daly with Jane Caputi, *Webster's First New Intergalactic Wickedary of the English Language* (Boston: Beacon Press, 1987), pp. 281–282.

35. Nor Hall, *The Moon and the Virgin: Reflections on the Archetypal Feminine* (New York: Harper & Row, 1980), p. 197.

36. Barbara Walker, *The Crone: Woman of Age, Wisdom and Power* (San Francisco: Harper & Row, 1986), pp. 175–178.

37. Paula Gunn Allen, "The Woman I Love Is a Planet; The Planet I Love Is a Tree," in I. Diamond and G. F. Orenstein, eds., *Reweaving the World: The Emergence of Ecofeminism* (San Francisco: Sierra Club Books, 1990), p. 52.

38. Caroline Merchant, "Ecofeminism and Feminist Theory," in *Reweaving the World*, p. 101.

39. *Ibid.*, p. 102.

40. *Ibid.*

41. Mary Lydon, "Foucault and Feminism: A Romance of Many Dimensions," in I. Diamond and L. Quinby, eds., *Feminism and Foucault: Reflections on Resistance* (Boston: Northeastern University Press, 1988), p. 138.

42. Susan Bordo, "Feminism, Postmodernism, and Gender-Scepticism," in L. J. Nicholson, ed., *Feminism/Postmodernism* (New York and London: Routledge, 1990), p. 136.

43. Mary Daly, *Pure Lust*, pp. 394–395.

44. Elinor Gadon, *The Once and Future Goddess: A Symbol for Our Time* (San Francisco: Harper & Row, 1989), p 256. See also G. F. Orenstein, *The Reflowering of the Goddess* (New York: Pergamon, The Athene Series, 1990).

45. Alice Walker, *Living by the Word* (San Diego: Harcourt Brace Jovanovich, 1988), p. 139.

46. Carol Lee Sanchez, "New World Tribal Communities: An Alternative Approach for Recreating Egalitarian Societies," in J. Plaskow and C. Christ, eds., *Weaving the Visions: New Patterns in Feminist Spirituality* (San Francisco: Harper & Row, 1989), p. 345.

47. *Ibid.*, pp. 352–353.

48. Barbara Omolade, "The Silence and the Song: Toward a Black Woman's History through a Language of Her Own," in J. M. Braxton and A. N. McLaughlin, eds., *Wild Women in the Whirlwind: Afra-American Culture and the Contemporary Literary Renaissance* (New Brunswick: Rutgers University Press, 1990), p. 285.

49. Gloria Anzaldúa, *Borderlands/La Frontera*, preface, unpaged.

50. *Ibid.*, pp. 79–80.

51. Donna Haraway, "A Manifesto for Cyborgs," in *Socialist Review*, no. 80, March–April, 1985, p. 66.

52. *Ibid.*, pp. 66–67.

53. *Ibid.*, p. 92.

54. *Ibid.*, p. 67.

55. *Ibid.*, pp. 93–94.

56. *Ibid.*, p. 100.

57. *Ibid.*, p. 101.

58. *Ibid.*, p. 68.

3 Knowledge and Truth

In reading the selections in the last chapter, you may have wondered how the authors knew what they claimed to know, and whether some of their claims were true. Did Bumba really vomit up the sun and moon? Is this statement to be taken literally? If it is, how did the creator of this myth know that Bumba threw up the sun and moon? More basically, how did the creator of this myth even know that Bumba existed? In a later selection, you were told that originally there was only the one self in the form of a person, and that human beings were created when this one self split in two and mated with itself. One does not have to be an extreme skeptic to wonder whether these statements are true. Even if we believe that they are true, we still might wonder how the author came to know them.

If any of these questions occurred to you as you were reading earlier selections, then you were, like it or not, on the verge of traversing yet another philosophical path. We can call this the path of reflecting on knowledge and truth, known in Western philosophy as the path of epistemological thinking. Indeed, in traditional Western philosophy, especially during the seventeenth and eighteenth centuries, this was a favorite path of philosophers. Reacting against the metaphysical claims that were commonly heard during his day, the British philosopher John Locke reportedly commented to one of his friends, "You and I have had enough of this kind of fiddling." Even though Locke's *An Essay Concerning Human Understanding* contains some metaphysical fiddling itself, his principal purpose in the book was to examine human mental faculties and to establish the boundaries and limitations of human knowledge. Of course, Locke was just one of many traditional Western philosophers who traveled down the path of epistemology.

The quest to define and understand the nature of truth has an equally long history in the West. While earlier Greek philosophers, including Plato and Aristotle, had already addressed this problem, it was a Roman government official named Pontius Pilate who gave voice to one of the simplest and best-known formulations of the question itself. During his examination of Jesus of Nazareth, Pilate reportedly asked, "What is truth?"

In the nontraditional selections contained in this chapter, as in many traditional Western writings, questions relating to the nature of knowledge and the nature of truth are often interwoven. Also, several of the selections, like their traditional Western counterparts, are concerned with establishing the limitations of human knowledge. Indeed, the first two selections, as well as the final one, can be read as attempts to circumscribe epistemological boundaries. However, in contrast to Locke and many of his contemporaries, most of the writers below do not limit the quest for knowledge and truth to the domain of understanding or reason. Indeed, one of the common themes of these writings is that the traditional Western emphasis on understanding and reason too narrowly restricts the search for knowledge and truth. While this claim can be gleaned from all of the writings in this chapter, it is the central focus of the selections by Benally, Chang, and Vasconcelos.

Reading these selections can help you on your own journey down the path of epistemological thinking, but they cannot serve as substitutes for your own reflections. You will find this chapter much more meaningful if you compare and contrast your beliefs with those of the authors. In other words, the most important questions are What do you believe to be true? And how do you know that what you believe to be true is indeed true?

Two Dialogues on Dogmatism and Truth   3.1

FROM THE BUDDHIST SCRIPTURES

As stated in the introduction to the Buddhist selection in Chapter 1, Buddhism arose in Northern India in the sixth century B.C.E. Its founder, Siddhartha of the Gautama clan, reportedly left a life of great luxury—which he considered to be a life of illusion—to seek the true meaning of human existence. This act in itself clearly illustrates that Siddhartha, who was later to be known as the Buddha, had recognized one of the basic epistemological distinctions, the distinction between truth and illusion.

After trying to attain the true meaning of human existence by studying the traditional Hindu teachings, and then by practicing extreme asceticism, Siddhartha achieved enlightenment by intensely meditating for forty days. On achieving enlightenment, he became a wandering teacher, an enlightened figure, who attempted to impart what he had learned and accomplished to others. No doubt because of his own failure to attain enlightenment through the study of theological teachings and dogmas, the Buddha is often portrayed in Buddhist literature as warning his disciples to avoid dogmatic statements and metaphysical speculations. This is one of the dominant themes in these two brief selections. The first selection is from the *Sutta-Nipata*. The second selection, the well-known "Parable of the Arrow," is from the *Majjhima-nikāya*. Like many other Buddhist writings, the first selection is written in the form of a dialogue between the Buddha and one of his followers. The second selection is written in parable form, that is, in the form of a story that illustrates a religious or philosophical point.

In the first selection, the Buddha (the Lord) says that dogmatic assertions can lead only to dissension and not to truth. True knowledge or wisdom can be attained only by freeing oneself from earthly worries and disputes. In the second selection, the Buddha tells the story of a man who has been shot by a poisoned arrow. In typical scholarly fashion, the man seeks to know the nature of the arrow and the bow used to shoot it, the name of the man who shot it, and the kind of poison used. In seeking such knowledge, however, the man overlooks the obvious—if he does not remove the arrow, he will die. The point again is that we should not waste precious time seeking to know useless theories and dogmas. Rather, we should set about doing what is really important in life; namely, we should actively attempt to expunge the poison that is killing us. In Buddhist philosophy, this poison is *tanha* or desire.

Questions for Thought

1. What are the Buddha's principal reasons for rejecting dogmatism? Do you agree with the Buddha's analysis?
2. Can you think of any of your own beliefs that might be characterized as dogmatic?
3. How effective is the parable of the arrow in illustrating the Buddha's point?
4. Are you familiar with other religious or philosophical parables? If so, how do they compare with or differ from the parable of the arrow?
5. Can you create a brief parable of your own that could be used to illustrate something that you believe to be true?

Truth Is Above Sectarian Dogmatism[1]

The Enquirer: Fixed in their pet beliefs, these divers wranglers bawl—"Hold this, and truth is yours"; "Reject it, and you're lost." Thus they contend, and dub opponents "dolts" and "fools." Which of the lot is right, when all as experts pose?

The Lord: Well, if dissent denotes a "fool" and stupid "dolt," then all are fools and dolts—since each has his own view. Or, if each rival creed proves lore and brains and wit, no "dolts" exist—since all alike are on a par. I count not that as true which those affirm, who call each other "fools." They call each other so, because each deems his own view "Truth."

The Enquirer: What some style "truth," the rest call empty lies; strife reigns. Pray why do anchorites (religious hermits) not speak in unison?

The Lord: There's one sole "Truth" (not two), to know which bars men's strife. But such a motley crowd of "truths" have they evolved, that anchorites, perforce, speak not in full accord.

The Enquirer: What makes these "experts" preach "truths" so diverse? Is each inherited? Or just a view they've framed themselves?

The Lord: Apart from consciousness, no diverse truths exist. Mere sophistry declares this [view] "true," and that view "false." The senses' evidence, and works, inspire such scorn for others, and such smug conviction *he* is right, that all rivals rank as "sorry, brainless fools." When he admits himself to "expert's" rank and style, this fires his scorn anew and off he starts again. Chock-full of error, drunk with pride and arrogance, he consecrates himself a "sage"—so grand in his perfected "view." . . . Delight in their dear views makes sectaries assert that all who disagree "miss Purity and err." These divers sectaries—these sturdy advocates of private paths to bliss—claim Purity as theirs alone, not found elsewhere. Whom should the sturdiest venture to call a "fool," when this invites the like retort upon himself? Stubborn in theories which they themselves devised, these wrangle on through life. Leave then dogmatic views and their attendant strife!

The Enquirer: Take those who dogmatize and lay sole claim to Truth. Is blame their constant fate? Are they not praised as well?

The Lord: Yes, though a trifling thing is all of this . . . and it does not lead to Peace. Wherefore one should shun strife and aim at Peace, which knows no strife. No vulgar theories engage the wise. Why should the free seek bondage, when phenomena of sense appeal to them no more? They that place practice first, deeming that regimen wins Purity, take vows to practice only what their "master taught as pure"—experts self-styled who cling to mere phenomena! . . .

The Enquirer: The doctrine some vaunt "best," others term "low." Which states the fact? . . .

The Lord: Ah! It is her own dear creed which each proclaims as "rare." His rival's creed is "low." And so they squabble on, each claiming truth as *his*! If other's criticisms could make a doctrine "low," then none is excellent. For all unite to damn all doctrines, save their own. As they extol their "Way," so they revere their creeds. Their tune is still the same: "Our purity" is its theme.

The true Brahmin adopts nothing from others, owes nothing to others' views; immune from strife, he deems no theory "the Truth." . . . No true Brahmin attains the goal by mere research; no partisan is he, nor brother-sectary; all vulgar theories—which others toil to learn—he knows, but heeds them not. From earthly trammels freed, aloof from party broils, at peace where peace has fled, the unheeding sage ignores what others toil to learn. From whilom cankers purged, with no fresh growths afoot, from lusts and dogmas free, quit too of theories, he goes his stainless way, devoid of self-reproach.

The Parable of the Arrow

Thus I have heard: The Lord was once dwelling near Sāvatthi, at Jetavana in the park of Anāthapindika. Now the elder Mālunkyāputta had retired from the world, and as he meditated the thought arose: "These theories have been left unexplained by the Lord, set aside, and rejected, whether the world is eternal or not eternal, whether the world is finite or not, whether the soul (life) is the same as the body, or whether the soul is one thing and the body another, whether a Buddha (Tathāgāta) exists after death or does not exist after death, and whether a Buddha both exists and does not exist after death, and whether a Buddha is non-existent and not non-existent after death—these things the Lord does not explain to me, and that he does not explain them to me does not please me; it does not suit me. I will approach the Lord, and ask about this matter. . . . If the Lord does not explain to me, I will give up the training, and return to a worldly life." [When Mālunkyāputta had approached and put his questions the Lord replied:] "Now did I, Mālunkyāputta, ever say to you, 'Come Mālunkyāputta, lead a religious life with me, and I will explain to you whether the world is eternal or not eternal, whether the world is finite or not, whether the soul is the same as the body, or whether the soul is one thing and the body another, whether a Buddha exists after death or does not exist after death, and whether a Buddha both exists and does not exist after death, and whether a Buddha is non-existent and not non-existent after death?'"

"You did not, reverend sir."

"Anyone, Mālunkyāputta, who should say 'I will not lead a religious life with the Lord, until the Lord explains to me whether the world is eternal or not eternal, whether the world is finite or not, whether the soul is the same as the body, or whether the soul is one thing and the body another, whether a Buddha exists after death or does not exist after death, and whether a Buddha both exists and does not exist after death, and whether a Buddha is non-existent and not non-existent after death' that person would die, Mālunkyāputta, without its being explained. It is as if a man had been wounded by an arrow thickly smeared with poison, and his friends, companions, relatives, and kinsmen were to get a surgeon to heal him, and he were to say, 'I will not have this arrow pulled out, until I know by what man I was wounded, whether he is of the warrior caste, or a brahmin, or the agricultural, or the lowest caste.' Or if he were to say, 'I will not have this arrow pulled out until I know of what name or family the man is . . . or whether he is tall, or short, or of middle height . . . or whether he is black, or dark, or yellowish . . . or whether he comes from such and such a village, or town, or city . . . or until I know whether the bow with which I was wounded was a chāpa or a kondanda, or until I know whether the bow-string was of swallow-wort, or bamboo-fiber, or sinew, or hemp, or of milk-sap tree, or until I know whether the shaft was from a wild or cultivated plant . . . or whether it was feathered from a vulture's wing or a heron's, or a hawk's, or a peacock's, or a sithilahanu-bird's . . . or whether it was wrapped round with the sinew of an ox, or of a buffalo,

or of a ruru-deer, or of a monkey . . . or until I know whether it was an ordinary arrow, or a razor arrow, or a vekanda, or an iron arrow, or a calf-tooth arrow, or one of karavīra leaf.' That man would die, Mālunkyāputta, without knowing all this."

"It is not on the view that the world is eternal, Mālunkyāputta, that a religious life depends; it is not on the view that the world is not eternal that a religious life depends. Whether the view is held that the world is eternal, or that the world is not eternal, there is still re-birth, there is old age, there is death, and grief, lamentation, suffering, sorrow, and despair, the destruction of which even in this life I announce. It is not on the view that the world is finite. . . . It is not on the view that a Tathāgata exists after death. . . . Therefore, Mālunkyāputta, consider as unexplained what I have not explained, and consider as explained what I have explained. And what, Mālunkyāputta, have I not explained? Whether the world is eternal I have not explained, whether the world is not eternal . . . whether a Tathāgata is born non-existent and not non-existent after death I have not explained. And why Mālunkyāputta, have I not explained this? Because this, Mālunkyāputta, is not useful; it is not concerned with the principle of a religious life, does not conduce to aversion, absence of passion, cessation, tranquillity, supernatural faculty, perfect knowledge, Nirvana, and therefore I have not explained it."

"And what, Mālunkyāputta, have I explained? Suffering have I explained, the cause of suffering, the destruction of suffering, and the path that leads to the destruction of suffering have I explained. For this, Mālunkyāputta, is useful; this is concerned with the principle of a religious life; this conduces to aversion, absence of passion, cessation, tranquillity, supernatural faculty, perfect knowledge, Nirvana; and thus have I explained it. Therefore, Mālunkyāputta, consider as unexplained what I have not explained, and consider as explained what I have explained."

Thus spoke the Lord and with joy the elder Mālunkyāputta applauded the words of the Lord.

NOTES

1. Although this selection appears in verse form in Chalmers's translation, I am rendering it into prose to enhance its clarity.—ED.

The Sorting Which Evens Things Out   3.2

CHUANG-TZU

Chuang-tzu (b. 369 B.C.E.) was a follower of Lao-tzu, a semilegendary figure of the sixth century B.C.E. in China. Lao-tzu is credited with having written the *Tao Te Ching*, the book that contains the philosophical foundation of Taoism. Chuang-tzu spread the teachings of Lao-tzu and urged the Chinese rulers and people to accept Lao-tzu as their master teacher. As is the case with Lao-tzu, very little is known about Chuang-tzu's life, except that he once served as a minor government official and later refused a more prominent government position (the position of prime minister of the province of Ch'u) in order to maintain his political and philosophical independence. Although the *Chuang-tzu*, from which the following selection is taken, is credited solely to Chuang-tzu, most scholars agree that it consists of a collection of Taoist writings from various authors.

Like the preceding Buddhist selections, this Taoist selection begins by commenting on the doctrinal differences among humans. Chuang-tzu compares these differences to the tubes of pan-pipes, each making its own discordant sound. He notes that the disciples of the various philosophers use language to refute the doctrines of their opponents, but that their opponents do the same. The result is continuous disputation without the possibility of agreement or solution. Unlike these scholars, the sage refuses to argue; that is, the sage refuses to use language to discriminate or divide what is into this reality or that. Rather, the sage realizes that what is (the Way or Tao) cannot be reached by division or discrimination. As Chuang-tzu bluntly puts it, "The Way never had borders." Near the end of this selection, Chuang-tzu says that accepting our ignorance is perhaps the highest knowledge that we can attain in this life. He compares life to a dream and says that the sage realizes that this life is a only dream. However, one who is not a sage mistakenly believes that he or she can clearly distinguish between waking experience and dreamed experience.

Questions for Thought

1. Why does Chuang-tzu believe that disputation or argument is useless? Do you agree with him on this point?

2. Does Chuang-tzu believe that it is possible for humans to know the true nature of reality? Do you think anyone knows the true nature of reality?
3. What does Chuang-tzu mean by the Way (Tao)? How does he know that the Way exists?
4. How is the sage described in this selection? How would you describe a sage or wise person?
5. Why does Chuang-tzu think he might be a butterfly? How do you know that your present experience is not a dream?

1

TZU-CH'I OF NAN-KUO RECLINED HIS ELBOW ON an armrest, looked up at the sky and exhaled, in a trance as though he had lost the counterpart of himself. Yen-ch'eng Tzu-yu stood in waiting before him.

"What is this?" he said. "Can the frame really be made to be like withered wood, the heart like dead ashes? The reclining man here now is not the reclining man of yesterday."

"You do well to ask that, Tzu-yu! This time I had lost my own self, did you know it? You hear the pipes of men, don't you, but not yet the pipes of earth, the pipes of earth, but not yet the pipes of Heaven?"

"I venture to ask the secret of it."

"That hugest of clumps of soil blows out breath, by the name the 'wind.' Better if it were never to start up, for whenever it does, ten thousand hollow places burst out howling. Don't tell me you have never heard how the hubbub swells! The recesses in mountain forests, the hollows that pit great trees a hundred spans round, are like nostrils, like mouths, like ears, like sockets, like bowls, like mortars, like pools, like puddles. Hooting, hissing, sniffing, sucking, mumbling, moaning, whistling, wailing, the winds ahead sing out AAH!, the winds behind answer EEEH! Breezes strike up a tiny chorus, the whirlwind a mighty chorus. When the gale has passed, all the hollows empty; and don't tell me you have never seen how the quivering slows and settles!"

"The pipes of earth, these are the various hollows; the pipes of men, these are rows of tubes. Let me ask about the pipes of Heaven."

"Who is it that puffs out the myriads which are never the same, who in their self-ending is sealing them up, in their self-choosing is impelling the force into them?"[1] . . .

2

Once we have received the completed body we are aware of it all the time we await extinction. Is it not sad how we and other things go on stroking or jostling each other, in a race ahead like a gallop which nothing can stop? How can we fail to regret that we labor all our lives without seeing success, wear ourselves out with toil in ignorance of where we shall end? Is man's life really as stupid as this? Or is it that I am the only stupid one, and there are others not so stupid? But if you go by the completed heart and take it as your authority, who is without such an authority?[2] The fool has one just as he has. For there to be "That's it, that's not" before they are formed in the heart would be to "go to Yüeh today and have arrived yesterday."[3] This would be crediting with existence what has not existence; and if you do that, even the daemonic Yu could not understand you, and how can you expect to be understood by me?

From *The Seven Inner Chapters and Other Writings from the Book Chuang-tzu*, translated by A. C. Graham. Reprinted by permission of Allen & Unwin.

3

Saying is not blowing breath, saying says something; the only trouble is that what it says is never fixed. Do we really say something? Or have we never said anything? If you think it different from the twitter of fledglings, is there proof of the distinction? Or isn't there any proof? By what is the Way hidden, that there should be a genuine or a false? By what is saying darkened, that sometimes "That's it" and sometimes "That's not?" Wherever we walk, how can the Way be absent? Whatever the standpoint, how can saying be unallowable? The Way is hidden by formation of the lesser, saying is darkened by its foliage and flowers. And so we have the "That's it, that's not" of Confucians and Mohists, by which what is *it* for one of them is not for the other, what is *not* for one of them is for the other. If you wish to affirm what they deny and deny what they affirm, the best means is Illumination.

No thing is not "other," no thing is not "it." If you treat yourself too as "other" they do not appear, if you know of yourself you know of them. Hence it is said: "'Other' comes out from 'it,' 'it' likewise goes by 'other'"—the opinion is that "it" and "other" are born simultaneously. However, "simultaneously with being alive one dies," and simultaneously with dying one is alive, simultaneously with being allowable something becomes unallowable and simultaneously with being unallowable it becomes allowable. If going by circumstance that's it, then going by circumstance that's not; if going by circumstance that's not, then going by circumstance that's it. This is why the sage does not take this course, but opens things up to the light of Heaven; his too is a "That's it" which goes by circumstance. . . .[4]

4

The men of old, their knowledge had arrived at something: at what had it arrived? There were some who thought there had not yet begun to be things—the utmost, the exhaustive, there is no more to add. The next thought there were things, but there had not yet begun to be borders. The next thought there were borders to them, but there had not yet begun to be "That's it, that's not." The lighting up of "That's it, that's not" is the reason why the Way is flawed. The reason why the Way is flawed is the reason why love becomes complete. Is anything really complete or flawed? Or is nothing really complete or flawed? To recognize as complete or flawed is to have as model the Chao when they play the zither; to recognize as neither complete nor flawed is to have as model the Chao when they don't play the zither. Chao Wen strumming on the zither, Music-master K'uang propped on his stick, Hui Shih leaning on the sterculia, had the three men's knowledge much farther to go? They were all men in whom it reached a culmination, and therefore was carried on to too late a time. It was only in being preferred by them that what they knew about differed from an Other; because they preferred it they wished to illumine it, but they illumined it without the Other being illumined, and so the end of it all was the darkness of chop logic. And his own son too ended with only Chao Wen's zither string, and to the end of his life his musicianship was never completed. May men like this be said to be complete? Then so am I. Or may they not be said to be complete? Then neither am I, nor is anything else.

Therefore the glitter of glib implausibilities is despised by the sage. The "That's it" which deems, he does not use, but finds for things lodging-places in the usual. It is this that is meant by "using Illumination."[5] . . .

5

The Way has never had borders, saying has never had norms. It is by a "That's it" which deems that a boundary is marked. Let me say something about the marking of boundaries. You can locate as there and enclose by a line, sort out and assess, divide up and discriminate between alternatives, compete over and fight over: these I call our Eight Powers. What is outside the cosmos the sage locates as there but does not sort out. What is within the cosmos the sage sorts out but does not assess. The records of the former kings in the successive reigns in the Annals the sage assesses, but he does not argue over alternatives.

To "divide," then, is to leave something undivided; to "discriminate between alternatives" is to leave something which is neither alternative. "What?" you ask. The sage keeps it in his breast, common men argue over alternatives to show it to each other. Hence I say: "To 'discriminate between alternatives' is to fail to see something."

6

The greatest Way is not cited as an authority,
The greatest discrimination is unspoken,
The greatest goodwill is cruel,
The greatest honesty does not make itself
    awkward,
The greatest courage does not spoil for a fight.

When the Way is lit it does not guide,
When speech discriminates it fails to get there,
Goodwill too constant is at someone's expense,
Honesty too clean is not to be trusted,
Courage that spoils for a fight is immature.

These five in having their corners rounded off come close to pointing the direction. Hence to know how to stay within the sphere of our ignorance is to attain the highest. Who knows an unspoken discrimination, an untold Way? It is this, if any is able to know it, which is called the Treasury of Heaven. Pour into it and it does not fill, bale out from it and it is not drained, and you do not know from what source it comes. . . .

7

How do I know that to take pleasure in life is not a delusion? How do I know that we who hate death are not exiles since childhood who have forgotten the way home? Lady Li was the daughter of a frontier guard at Ai. When the kingdom of Chin first took her the tears stained her dress; only when she came to the palace and shared the King's square couch and ate the flesh of hay-fed and grain-fed beasts did she begin to regret her tears. How do I know that the dead do not regret that ever they had an urge to life? Who banquets in a dream at dawn wails and weeps, who wails and weeps in a dream at dawn goes out to hunt. While we dream we do not know that we are dreaming, and in the middle of a dream interpret a dream within it; not until we wake do we know that we were dreaming. Only at the ultimate awakening shall we know that this is the ultimate dream. Yet fools think they are awake, so confident that they know what they are, princes, herdsmen, incorrigible! You and Confucius are both dreams, and I who call you a dream am also a dream. . . .

8

Last night Chuang Chou[6] dreamed he was a butterfly; spirits soaring he was a butterfly, . . . and he did not know about Chou. When all of a sudden he awoke, he was Chou with all his wits about him. He does not know whether he is Chou who dreams he is a butterfly or a butterfly who dreams he is Chou. Between Chou and the butterfly there was necessarily a dividing; just this is what is meant by the transformations of things.

NOTES

1. Chuang-tzu's parable of the wind compares the conflicting utterances of philosophers to the different notes blown by the same breath in the long and short tubes of the pan-pipes, and the noises made by the wind in hollows of different shapes. It is natural for differently constituted persons to think differently; don't try to decide between their opinions, listen to Heaven who breathes through them.

2. In Chuang-tzu's physiology, as in much of the ancient world, the heart was believed to be the seat of thinking.—ED.

3. "I go to Yüeh today but come yesterday" is a paradox of the Sophist Hui Shih, . . . here mentioned only for its absurdity.

4. In (Chinese) disputation if an object fits the name "ox" one affirms with the demonstrative word *shih* "(That) is it"; if it is something other than an ox one denies with a *fei* "(That) is not." Here Chuang-tzu tries to discredit disputation by the objection that at any moment of change both alternatives will be admissible. . . . Chuang-tzu sees it as the lesson of disputation that one is entitled to affirm or deny anything of anything. He thinks of Confucians and Mohists who stick rigidly to their affirmations and denials as lighting up little areas of life and leaving the rest in darkness; the Illumination of the sage is a vision which brings everything to light.

5. Systems of knowledge are partial and temporary like styles on the zither, which in forming sacrifice some of the potentialities of music, and by their very excellence make schools fossilize in decline. Take as model Chao Wen *not* playing the zither, not yet committed, with all his potentialities intact.

6. Chuang-tzu's private name was Chou.—ED.

Navajo Ways of Knowing   3.3

HERBERT JOHN BENALLY

Herbert John Benally (b. 1944) lives in Sweetwater, Arizona, on the Navajo Reservation. While many members of his family have sought to preserve native traditions by following the path of the medicine man, he has attempted to achieve the same goal through teaching and curriculum reform. Currently, he teaches courses in Navajo history, culture, and philosophy at Navajo Community College in Shiprock, New Mexico. In addition, his writings on Navajo ways of learning have been used as the basis for curriculum reform at Navajo Community College and in several of the K–12 schools on the reservation. They have also provided the philosophical foundation for a program to combat substance abuse among students in grades K–12. Benally has presented his views on educational reform in workshops at several national and international conferences, including a recent meeting of the Global Alliance for the Transformation of Education.

In the following selection, which was originally titled "Spiritual Knowledge for a Secular Society," Benally discusses the intimate connection between spirituality and knowledge in Navajo thinking. He describes four types of sacred knowledge ("that which gives direction to life," "sustenance," "the gathering of family," and "rest, contentment and respect for creation"), and explains why each of these types of sacred knowledge was traditionally associated with a part of the day and with one of the four cardinal directions. Benally argues that to achieve a harmonious life, we must focus on each of these four areas of knowledge and maintain a balance among them. In doing so, we not only will achieve harmony within the family and the human community, but will also find harmony between the human and the natural world. On the other hand, failure to recognize the importance of each type of knowledge or to maintain a balance between them will produce dire consequences. As Benally says, "When we are not taught in this way, drawing on all four areas of knowledge, we become spiritually, emotionally, socially, physically and environmentally impoverished."

Questions for Thought

1. What are the four types of knowledge found in traditional Navajo thinking? Why are each of them associated with a specific part of the day?
2. What is the purpose of prayer in Navajo life? What is the purpose of prayer, if any, in your own life?
3. How does Benally view the relationship of competition and community? In what ways, if any, does this differ from the way in which you view the relationship of competition and community?
4. What are the basic features of the traditional Navajo family system? How does this compare with or differ from the characteristics of your own family system?
5. How is the natural world viewed in Navajo thinking? How do you view the natural world?
6. If you were to categorize the types of human knowledge, how many categories would you list, and what would these categories be?

TRADITIONAL NAVAJO WISDOM RECOGNIZES SPIRituality as the foundation of all knowledge necessary for achieving harmony, or *hózhǫ́*, the Beauty Way of Life. This foundation is as relevant today as it ever was, and could serve as the basis of an approach to teaching which avoids the separation of secular and spiritual knowledge that characterizes Western society. The connection between that separation and the problems of contemporary life is apparent, and calls for a close re-examination of this traditional wisdom. The Navajo organized their knowledge, as well as their life activities, around the parts of the day and the four cardinal directions. This system of organization was placed by the Holy People in the primordial era. At that time the gods laid the foundation of this world with grandfathers and grandmothers fire, water, air, and soil. Around that foundation they placed the four different lights and four forms of sacred knowledge which would regulate man and all life's activities. With the dawn they placed "that which gives direction to life" (*bik'ehgo da'i-ináanii*) and with the blue twilight they placed "sustenance" (*nihigáál*). "The gathering of family" (*aha'áná'oo'nííł*) was placed with the yellow evening twilight and "rest, contentment and respect for creation" (*háá'áyį́íh, sihasin dóó hodílzin*) was placed with the darkness. "All of these things placed will direct all lives from here on," it was said.

I. Bik'ehgo Da'ináanii

The first area of knowledge, "that which gives direction to life," emphasizes character development, particularly excellence of heart and mind. This encompasses all knowledge which enables the individual to make intelligent decisions whenever a choice involving values is to be made. Just as dawn brings light, this area of knowledge brings clarity and perspective to the mind, permeating all aspects of one's life. This area of learning includes beliefs, self-discipline, and values that provide standards of behavior and give meaning to life.

The Navajo believe that the gods pass over the country at dawn. If an individual is up and about he will be blessed by them with health and prosperity. Corn pollen is usually offered to these gods and a petition extended to them at this time. It was believed that the things which they petitioned for became part of one's thoughts, planning, teaching and life. In time the petitioner

Reprinted by permission of Tribal College.

becomes one with his prayer. It was important to pray. It helped one to organize the priorities in his life and to clarify his thinking. His spirituality was recognized as the source of both his strength and his enlightenment.

It was also believed that one should get up at dawn and run. To the elders this was not just a physical exercise but an activity that brought about physical, mental and spiritual well-being. By running at dawn one disciplines and strengthens his mind in order to be in control in all situations. With a well-developed constitution he can overcome any adversity that may arise.

Another way of establishing a strong foundation is by listening to the wisdom of the elders and keeping their words close to one's heart. "If things are to be it's up to you," "remember the young and the old and those yet to be born," and "stability comes from a clear purpose for being" are some of the teachings that have survived. This wisdom has been passed from generation to generation and finds roots in one's being, becoming the source of strength throughout one's life.

The dawn provides the blueprint for building a good life. It is the source of fortitude, sound teaching, standards of conduct and appreciation for life. Without the guiding principles provided by the dawn there would be no standards by which people could evaluate the effectiveness of their thoughts and actions. They would be unable to fully experience life or to develop a genuine appreciation for themselves, others and nature. They would run the risk of falling into great disharmony, hunger, illness, poverty and other social ills which are so prevalent today.

II. Nihigáál

The second area of knowledge, associated with the blue twilight, is sustenance. This area focuses on obtaining self-reliance, providing for the family and being a contributing member of the community. To achieve these goals one must recognize work in all its dimensions including the ethical, vocational, social and environmental. All of these areas are connected and interdependent. For instance, traditional Navajo wisdom views objects of material wealth as having spirit and personality. There is a Navajo saying, "*Yódí dóó nitl'iz soosáadoo*," "May the spirit of all good things show favor upon me." Attracting these good spirits requires a certain attitude and personality. They come to the person who exercises prudence, order, industry, patience and kindness, and most importantly, to one who is prayerful. These qualities are all founded on the principle of receiving and giving. Sharing promotes happiness, while excessiveness inclines one toward evil. Conversely, when one sleeps late he attracts the being of poverty and his cousins—hunger, shame, apathy, disorder and ignorance. The good spirits will avoid a house that is disorganized, where vulgar and abusive language is used and where there is idleness.

Another aspect of sustenance involves learning how to work and becoming responsible. Children learn specific skills "on the job" well before they are able to understand the nature of the work or the responsibility involved. It was said that the livestock teach the child dependability, resourcefulness and responsibility. For example, when a sheep is lost the child is sent back to find it. The job was not considered complete until every sheep was accounted for. This might sometimes be a hard lesson but was absolutely necessary for adult life. Elders would advise parents to "Teach the children while they are yet tender and when their minds can still be bent and shaped like a young willow" and remind them that "It is harder when their minds have formed. Instill in them appropriate habits and they will discover reasons for their behavior when they come of age."

Cooperation was the basis of Navajo communal existence. On the other hand, competition was never foreign to the Navajo—in fact, it was the basis of their traditional games. However, making competition a part of one's life was frowned upon because it led to pride, which was considered an evil. Everyone was expected to come to the aid of their neighbors in time of need. "My people are my insurance" was how one woman put it when describing the events surrounding the loss of a loved one. Her people had come from miles around to console her and to help her with the substantial expenses with which she was faced. Helping in Navajo society was an opportunity to show the person being helped respect and regard.

The elders watch the stars, particularly Pleiades, the . . . "seeds of all kinds." They were instructed to watch this constellation in order to know when to start planting. The community performs a blessing on the seeds when . . . the "seeds of all kinds" set in the west. During the seed blessing ceremony, offerings are made at sacred places to the gods for moisture and for a good harvest. The seeds which had been blessed are then planted. Everyone worked together as a single unit to plant and harvest. When the harvest and winter storage were completed a special ceremony of thanksgiving was made to the gods.

Work, which is central to the blue twilight, is a life-sustaining principle. It is essential for obtaining and preserving one's dignity. Dignity and respectability are not possible unless a person is able to provide for his family and help those that need assistance. The worker understands that material possessions are based upon the principles of giving and receiving, and of industry and integrity. He is a skilled provider who understands the forces of nature and is able to use them to his benefit. He understands that cooperation within the community is the key to assuring the general welfare of the community. In order to maintain prosperity he continues to offer prayers for blessings and thanksgiving to the creators, who are the source of sustenance. A person who is ignorant or neglectful of these principles invites poverty, apathy, health problems and discord in the family and community.

III. Aha'ánaá'oo'níít

The third category of knowledge is associated with the yellow evening twilight. It focuses on *k'é*, a term which encompasses emotional ties and relationships associated with the family, extended family, community, nation as a whole, and the natural environment. The term *k'é* in Navajo conveys love, cherishing, caring, esteem, as well as the simple acknowledgment of the inherent value of others.

This learning begins at home. One of the teachings within our tribe centers on the relationship between husband and wife. A primary source for this teaching comes from the relationship between Father Sky and Mother Earth. When the plants, animals, seasons and constellations were completed and ready to be put into motion, Mother Earth is said to have asked, "Who will be responsible for all of these creations and their movements?" The Holy People replied that this responsibility will be placed in the hands of Sky Father. He will awake and put all things in motion. In the spring he will awaken you with thunder from your rest and with his help you will make all things grow and mature. In the fall he will once again sound the thunder, his scepter of leadership, at which time your work will be completed and you will rest. Father Sky then covers Mother Earth with a white blanket for the winter months. His primary work begins and woe to those who have been lazy and unprepared. Cold and hunger will find them and teach them the value of industry and preparation.

Mother Earth, the prototypical mother, is gentle and kind—no one who truly understands the nature of things must suffer from cold or hunger during the summer months. She nurtures and strengthens all living things and prepares them for the future. She follows the lead of her husband Father Sky. Father Sky exemplifies fatherhood, which includes unwavering leadership, tenderness toward Mother Earth, sternness in teaching, and gentleness to those of his children who are industrious and prepared.

Our elders taught that a man carries his shield on his left arm, protecting his family, his beliefs, his land and his freedom. The mother carries her cooking utensils in her right hand to represent her shield against hunger, illness and other adversities. Between the two parents a great deal of security is provided to the children from which they can achieve maturity. It is the weak, undisciplined and immature parent who does not understand what is required in the role of a parent who leaves the children in darkness, hunger, cold, to be ravaged by all manner of afflictions.

Appreciation for all that is included in the concept of *k'é* originates within the home where kinship terms, rather than names, are generally used to address family members. It is very difficult to translate the expression of endearment that these terms convey into another tongue. Kinship relationship terms communicate and reinforce an acceptance and a sense of belonging and caring to the person to whom they are directed. For example, the word that the mother uses with her children is *shee'awee shiyazhi*, my dear little one. Notice in these kinship expressions the word "my": my child, my sister, my mother, my grandfather, etc. The kinship terms are not just empty expressions, but living words that lie at the foundation of self-esteem. When terms of endearment are absent a gray area of doubt emerges in the mind of the young person regarding acceptance and belonging. The loneliness, alienation and rejection felt by the young person may become contributing factors in the young person trying to seek acceptance in negative ways.

The use of appropriate kinship terms between siblings and other family members defines their respective roles and encourages positive family ties. I have personally observed that children in a family that uses kinship terms to address each other tend to get along much better than children in families where personal names are used.

The Navajo family system employs a hierarchical structure in which people are recognized according to their age. With maturity comes the responsibility to care, to teach and to set an example for those that are younger. The younger were obligated to respect and obey those that were older. It reflected very poorly on both the older and younger sibling when they argued. This system of relating remained with the individual throughout his life. One is not necessarily respected simply on the basis of how much he may have or what he can do. Respect is primarily based on age. When we use personal names we become equals, and being at the same level seems to encourage competition and bickering. The two systems can be compared by observing that one encourages respect and cooperation and the other conflict and competition.

A child's identity is based on his immediate family and clan membership. He represents his family wherever he goes, and in whatever he does. A person is never alone; he carries with him his family's reputation and their expectations. Any behavior contrary to that expected behavior reflects negatively both on that individual and his family. An individual can never divorce himself from his family. As long as parents and grandparents are living, it is expected that their positions in the family hierarchy will be honored.

Another major element involved in establishing relations among Navajos is the clan system. One is born *into* the mother's clan and is born *for* the father's clan. The maternal and paternal grandfathers usually are of different clans. One addresses a member of his clan as brother and sister. Members of the father's clan are addressed as paternal aunts and uncles and are thought of as the father's relatives. Individuals who are members of one's maternal or paternal grandfather's clans are thought of as that grandfather's relative and treated accordingly. The Navajo people function like one large extended family according to the clan system. The knowledge and use of the clan system in our tribe is therefore very important. It is the basis for holding each other in high regard and for dealing with each other as family. The interpersonal relationships learned in the home are thus lived out in the community. Family relationships are the foundation of all social interaction on the reservation.

Our elders are constantly reminding us to question the aims of schools and churches operating on the reservation. What is the point of having schools and churches if they do not teach compassion for the elders and for those who are less fortunate? We see on the reservation senior citizens alone during the winter without anyone to take care of them, to take them to the hospital or to the store to buy food. Frequently, their children had been educated or baptized and moved away, leaving their families behind. "Where is the compassion, concern, and kindness that we thought were being taught in the classroom and in the churches?" they often inquire. The old way was to care for the elders who occupied positions of honor in the community. We are losing respect for this great source of moral support as well as a vital link with our heritage. Learning must be sought which will increase our level of concern for the welfare of our children, youth and elders.

IV. Háá'áyįįh, Sihasin Dóó Hodílzin

The fourth area of knowledge is associated with darkness. The focus in this area is on reverence and respect for nature. The Navajo sees the world full of life and intelligence. He learns to interact with the intelligence around him with appropriate respect and dignity. There is a great natural order to the universe of which man is an integral part. Man is endowed with the ability to observe and imitate this order. For example, the Navajo have found that certain birds mate for life and have become symbols of fidelity in marriage. Proper interaction with this order requires knowledge of one's position and moving from there with reverence or, as a Navajo would put it, with k'é.

There is tremendous power in the natural order. We move with this power interdependently. We follow a course that is followed by all intelligence, or creation—a world of order and prosperity. As one recognizes his being as a part of a great circle manifested in the seasons, including birth and old age and the movement of the celestial bodies, he finds renewing power and strength. To the Navajo people all creation is endowed with great powers and the ability to bestow blessings in each of their respective seasons.

To understand this power we must return to the time of the placement of all things. The mountains, for example, were endowed with thinking, planning, prayer, teaching and material things. They were placed and dressed in that way for our benefit. As the clouds rest upon the mountains and the rains fall, the water begins to flow, taking with it the blessings of the mountains. When we utilize this water it unfolds the gifts of prayer, thinking, planning, teaching, and prosperity that it carries from the mountains. We may either use this blessing that was provided by the Holy People for our benefit, or destroy it through improper or disrespectful use.

All creation is connected and interdependent. If any part of the system is upset, the whole system is affected, creating an imbalance. The contemporary threats of pollution, toxicity and destruction of our ozone attest to this connection and interdependence. I believe we are only now finally beginning to understand this circle of connection.

Gratitude is at the very heart of respect and reverence for nature. Gratitude is directed to the water, the trees, plants and animals that nourish and shelter, and especially to the creators, that their blessings would never diminish. In this way the great law of receiving and giving is recognized.

In the Navajo world spiritual understanding is that which gives vitality and meaning to all life. The Western educational system requires us to separate the religious from the secular. Native Americans prefer to maintain their spiritually holistic perspective. When they are forced to put holism aside they find their lives and the values that give them meaning disintegrating or diminishing, and replaced with a fragmented and incoherent philosophy that leads into the mire of social disintegration.

Finding a Balance

The essence of the Navajo philosophy is holism and the goal it sets for life is peace and harmony. By balancing the four cardinal areas of Navajo knowledge the individual will develop sound beliefs and values and be prepared to make responsible decisions. He will develop knowledge and skills so that he will be able to provide for his family, demonstrate good leadership within the family and community, and retain a sense of reverence for all things, both those on the earth and in the heavens. There is a great central focus where all forms of knowledge converge. In Navajo, this point of convergence is the synthesis of knowledge obtained from the cardinal points that find expression in appreciation, reverence, and love for harmony.

The Navajo organized their lives according to these four areas of knowledge. It seems that if we were all educated in this way we would find balance. This "balançe" is similar to the way a nutritionist would speak about a balanced diet. If a person does not eat properly he will not have vitality and general good health. When we are not taught in this way, drawing on all four areas of knowledge, we become spiritually, emotionally, socially, physically and environmentally impoverished. We become narrow in our views and cannot see the connection between all knowledge. We wind up perpetuating the imbalance within and between ourselves, other people and the natural world.

This traditional wisdom is not only relevant today, but is even necessary to restore the balance which many of us have lost along with our most cherished traditions. Understanding and practicing the essence of the principles placed in each of the four directions will give us a strong foundation to make wise decisions for ourselves, our families and our communities. The internalization of these principles immunizes us from many of the adversities of life. When we recognize and become one with the divine power of the circle of creation we experience the Beauty Way of Life, or *hózhǫ.*

What the West Can Learn from Oriental Thought   3.4

CHIA-SEN CHANG, TANG CHUN-I,
MOU TSUNG-SAN, HSU FO-KUAN

Chia-sen (Carsun) Chang (1886–1969) is best known in the West for his two-volume work on neo-Confucianism, *The Development of Neo-Confucian Thought*, which was published in 1962. He also published a book on the sixteenth-century idealist philosopher Wang Yang-ming. The selection below, which was published on New Year's Day in 1958, is taken from a manifesto written by Chang and several of his colleagues.

In this part of the manifesto, the authors discuss the advantages and disadvantages of Western civilization. They note that while Western civilization represents the attainment of a very high level of technological knowledge that has benefited all humanity, it is also plagued by numerous problems and crises. The authors then argue that dire consequences can be avoided only if some of the lessons of Eastern thinking inform the West. One of these lessons is accepting the value of the present moment, rather than blindly pursuing unlimited progress. Another lesson that the East can teach the West is the philosophical inadequacy of viewing all knowledge in terms of abstract universal concepts. As in the preceding article by Benally, Chang and his colleagues stress the importance of seeking wisdom, that is, seeking an all-embracing knowing that breaks down conceptual barriers and dogmatic differences. Finally, the authors emphasize the necessity of complementing love with respect in our relationships with other human beings and with the universe. Whereas they claim that love is compatible with the will to dominate or possess, respect expunges this will to dominate or possess by transforming love into compassion. Compassion allows us to overcome nationalistic differences and other forms of provincialism, and to view "the whole world like one family."

Questions for Thought

1. What are the authors' principal criticisms of Western civilization? Do you think that their criticisms are valid? Why or why not?
2. In what ways are the criticisms of traditional Western thinking found in this selection similar to the criticisms found in the Benally article? In what ways are they different?
3. What do Chang and his colleagues mean by valuing the present moment? Do you value the present moment?
4. What do the authors say about the Western conception of God? Do you think they are accurate in what they say?
5. Why do the authors believe that love is an inadequate foundation for establishing human relationships? Do you agree? In what ways does love differ from respect?
6. The authors claim that Eastern thinking encourages the attitude that "the whole world is like one family." How do they support this claim? Do you think that this attitude should be encouraged? If so, what steps should be taken to encourage it?

THE DEVELOPMENT OF WESTERN CIVILIZATION IS outlined by innumerable flashes of brilliancy as well as many crises. Such crises have their origin in man's inability to control his cultural products and inventions. Thus, perhaps the highest achievement of modern scientific technology is nuclear fission, and yet the biggest world problem now is precisely due to the fact that Western civilization is unable to control this nuclear fission. We cannot, of course, assert that oriental cultures can surmount such difficulties, but it is clear that the formation of a world civilization is contingent upon co-operation on a high plane among the various cultures of the world. What the Orient, in particular China, needs in preparation for this has been delineated [elsewhere]. What, in our opinion, the West should learn from the East will now be set forth.

In the first place, the West needs the spirit and capacity of sensing the presence of what *is* at

From *The World Treasury of Modern Religious Thought*, edited by Jaroslav Pelikan, Little, Brown and Company, 1990.

every particular moment (*Tang-hsia-chi-shih*), and of giving up everything that can be had (*I-ch'ieh-fang-hsia*). The strength of the West's cultural spirit lies in its ability to push ahead indefinitely. However, there is no secure foundation underlying this feverish pursuit of progress. Along with this pursuit of progress there is a feeling of discontentment and of emptiness. In order to fill this emptiness, the individual and the nation constantly find new ways for progress and expansion. At the same time external obstructions and an internal exhaustion of energy cause the collapse of the individual and the nation. This is why the most powerful ancient Western nations collapsed and never did recover from their downfall. Chinese culture traces all values to "hsin-hsin," and in so doing achieves the capacity to "accept what is self-sufficient at the moment." Chinese thought has always regarded "retreat" as more fundamental than "advance." Complementing the characteristically Western push for progress, this will provide a solid and secure foundation for Western civilization.

Moreover, as the West builds its culture on the activities of the intellect it is principally concerned with the formation of concepts. In thus attributing the essence of life to intellectual processes, it tends unwittingly to value human life in proportion to its conceptual content. Such a criterion is not without merit, but it overlooks the fact that concepts as such are separate and distinct from life. When human life is committed to certain clear-cut concepts, it can no longer enjoy and adapt itself. This is the prime cause of the West's difficulty in achieving communion with the East. Authentic communication is possible only if the participant parties present an "empty mind" ready to identify with one another. While concepts can be a means of communicating between those mutually sympathetic, they can also be the most obstinate obstacle to genuine communication. As such, they—consisting of premeditated plans and objectives, abstract ideals of human relations and values, forming our prejudices, passions, habit-

ual notions, etc.—must all be suppressed. In Indian thought this is known as the "wisdom of emptiness" or "wisdom of liberation from worldliness." In Taoism it is called the wisdom of the "void" or "nothingness"; and in Chinese Buddhism it is known as the wisdom of "emptiness," "freedom from pre-conceptions, pre-determinations, obstinacy, or egoism," and "broad-mindedness." With such wisdom, everything is seen through as if transparent, so that though one still possesses concepts and ideals of thought one can readily disentangle oneself from them and not be limited and confined by them.

The second element the West can learn from the East is all-round and all-embracing understanding or wisdom. This Chuang-tzu called "spiritual understanding" or "meeting the object with the spirit." In Western science or philosophy, principles and universals are attained by intellect and are sharply enunciated and defined. They are abstract and cannot be applied to what is concrete, because the characteristics which are peculiar to each class, and which are inexhaustible, have been eliminated. Wisdom is needed to comprehend and to deal with all the unprecedented changes of life. This wisdom does not operate by adhering to universals, but by submerging universals in order to observe the changing conditions and peculiarities. To a large extent universals are determined by particular classes of objects. Universals which are related to these objects can be stored in the mind and called upon to function when the case applies. On the other hand one needs to submerge universals in order to rise to a higher plane of comprehension. In this way one's mind and wisdom which are all embracing achieve what Chuang-tzu calls "spiritual understanding." Meng-tzu said: "What has passed is merged; what has been preserved goes to the spirit and revolves with the universe." The term "spiritual" in Chinese means "stretchability." In applying universals to the physical world, certain universals correspond to certain physical objects. In the event that there is no correspondence between universals and objects the mind feels frustrated. Should one possess an all-embracing wisdom, he would not feel thwarted.

This wisdom is similar to the dialectical method and to Bergson's "intuition." The dialectical method employs a new kind of universal to explain a concrete reality, e.g., Hegel's philosophy of history. Nonetheless, the method is limited in its scope. The characteristic of the all-embracing wisdom of the Chinese, on the other hand, is a comprehensive understanding of reality. Bergson's "intuition" is similar to this, but his "intuition" is merely a fundamental tenet of his philosophical theory and does not penetrate his entire outlook on reality. In the Chinese view of life this wisdom goes into its literature, art, philosophy, Ch'an Buddhism, and the dialogues of the Sung Confucianists; it also shapes the attitudes of the scholars in their daily lives. This is why the Chinese can feel a unity with the universe. They can adapt themselves to different changes without feeling frustration. The Western world is in great need of this wisdom if she intends to understand the nature of different cultures and to have an authentic communication with them. In addition to their knowledge, technology, ideals, and God, they must above all search deeper for the source of life, the depth of personality and the common origin of human culture in order to arrive at a true unity with mankind.

The third point that the West can learn from the East is a feeling of mildness and compassion. The Westerner's loyalty to ideals, his spirit of social service, and his warmth and love for others are indeed precious virtues, to which oriental counterparts cannot measure up. However, the highest affection between men is not zeal or love, for with these emotions is often mingled the will to power and its acquisitive instinct. To forestall such an adulteration, Western civilization principally relies on its religious emphasis on personal humility and on all merits ultimately coming from God. However, the name of God can be borrowed as a back-prop in the conviction that one's actions bear His sanction; or else one may even selfishly wish to possess Him, such

as during a war to pray for victory. It is for this reason that Christianity also teaches forgiveness. But extreme forgiveness tends to become complete renunciation of the world. To avoid such a fault zeal and love must again be emphasized, thus forming a logical circle and leaving the intermingling of love and the will to dominate or to possess still an unresolved difficulty. The resolution lies in eradicating this will to dominate or possess, and this is possible only if love is accompanied by respect. In that case, if I feel that the source of my love for others is God's infinite love, then my respect for others is likewise boundless. As the Chinese put it, the good man "serves his parents like Heaven" and "employment of people is as important as sacrificial services." Genuine respect for others is possible only if man is without qualifications considered as an end in himself; but with such a respect love expresses itself though *li* (etiquette), thereby becoming courteous and mild. In this way love is transformed into compassion. This is precisely the Buddhist doctrine of "the great compassion." Its difference from ordinary love lies in the fact that in ordinary love the lover's spiritual feeling flows towards others in the manner of "regarding others as oneself," and this may frequently be mingled with the desire to possess others. Compassion, on the other hand, is the sympathetic consonance between the life-spirit of one's own and another's authentic being. Here, there is also natural interflowing of true sympathy, which is partly directed outwards and partly inwards. The emotional flowback makes it possible to purge any desire to dominate or possess. In other words, to effect such a transformation of Western love, God must be identified with man's heart of hearts, manifesting Himself through our bodies as the direct communication between the life-spirits of all authentic being, not merely as a transcendental being, the object of man's prayers.

Fourthly, the West can obtain from the East the wisdom of how to perpetuate its culture. Contemporary Western culture is, it is true, at its height of brilliance, yet many observers have been concerned with its future, whether it will perish like ancient Greece and Rome. Culture is the expression of a people's spiritual life, and by the laws of nature all expression drains the energy of life. If this energy is exhausted, perishing is inevitable. To preserve his spiritual life, man needs a depth formed by an historical awareness which reaches both into the past and into the future, and this depth connects with the life-giving source of the cosmos. In the West, this life-giving source is called God. In their religious life, Westerners could have more or less come into contact with the source were it not that they relied on prayer and faith. As it is, God is an external transcendental being and man can only reflect on His eternity. Besides, through prayer and faith what approaches God is man's spirit in adoration, not his authentic being. Painstaking labor is needed to make possible an authentic being's contact with the life-giving source. Man must begin by seeing to it that all his external acts do not merely follow a natural course, but rather go against this natural course to return to the cosmic life-giving source, and only then to fulfill nature. By such exertions against the natural course, energy is diverted into communication with the cosmic life-giving source. From this point of view, the West's chief concern with speed and efficiency constitutes a great problem. While the former easygoing attitude of the Chinese is not a suitable remedy in many respects, yet the maximum rate of progress with which the West leads the world is not conducive to durability. There will come the day when the West will realize that without lasting history and culture, though there be an eternal God, man cannot live peacefully. The West needs to develop an historical awareness with which to tap the live-giving source. It will then come to appreciate the value of conservation of life-energy and the meaning of filial piety, and learn to fulfill the ancestral will in order to preserve and prolong its culture.

The fifth point the West can learn from the East is the attitude that "the whole world is like one family." Though there are many nations now, mankind will eventually become one and undivided. Chinese thought has emphasized this attitude. Thus Motians advocate all-embracing love; Taoists urge forgetting the differences; Buddhists advise commiseration and love for all things; and Confucians teach universal kindness (*jen*). The Christian doctrine of love has much in common with the Confucian doctrine of universal kindness. However, Christianity insists that man is tainted by original sin and that salvation comes from God, from above. Confucians, on the other hand, generally believe that human nature is good and that man can attain sagehood and thence harmony in virtue with Heaven by his own efforts. We think it better to rely on both rather than just Christianity in working towards world union. This is because Christianity is an organized religion, with numerous sects which are difficult to harmonize. Furthermore, it has its doctrines of heaven and hell, so that Christian love really comes with a proviso, namely that "you accept my religion." The Confucian view, however, is that all men can achieve sagehood. It has no organization, and does not require worship of Confucius since any man can potentially become like him. Consequently, Confucianism does not conflict with any religion. It has a concept of Heaven and Earth, but has no hell for those of differing views. If indeed the world is to be united, the Confucian spirit certainly deserves emulation. The same attitude can be found in Buddhism and Brahmanism, which also deserve close study.

Our list is, of course, by no means exhaustive. What we have pointed out is that the West must also learn from the East if it is to carry out its task as the world's cultural leader. These things are certainly not entirely alien to Western culture. However, we would like to see their seeds bloom into full blossom.

JOSÉ VASCONCELOS

José Vasconcelos (1882–1959) was born in Oaxaca, Mexico. During his very active life, he participated in the Mexican Revolution, was instrumental in Mexican educational reform, and ran unsuccessfully for the presidency in 1929. In addition to serving as rector of the National University of Mexico, he also served as visiting professor at the University of Chicago and as director of the Biblioteca Nacional de México. Despite his preoccupation with political and educational reform, Vasconcelos still managed to find time to develop a sophisticated philosophical system, a system he named "aesthetic monism." Unfortunately, most of his writings have not been translated into English.

In the following selection from his *Tratado de metafísica*, Vasconcelos discusses the nature and types of knowledge. He argues that although each discipline has its own form of knowledge with a distinct methodology and subject matter, these varied forms of knowledge are linked to each other by a common connection or movement—the movement toward liberation or transcendence. However, he notes that traditional Western thinking has often overlooked this common connection for two reasons: (1) it has taken thought to be synonymous with knowledge, and (2) in so doing, it has excluded emotions and aesthetic experience as possible sources of knowledge. The result is that the search for knowledge has emphasized reason or analytical judgment to the exclusion of art.

While Vasconcelos does not totally reject the value of reason and analytical judgment, he argues that by making them the sole source of knowledge, Western thinking has become fixated on rigid concepts, on abstract logical formulas that do not allow for creative transformation. In opposition to such rigid concepts, Vasconcelos praises the fluidity of aesthetic judgments, especially the judgments of music and poetry. As he so poetically says, such judgments are "an open sesame that elevates us, with soul rejuvenated, to an improved and transcendental creation." Despite his praise for such judgments, Vasconcelos warns us that we must be careful not to allow ourselves to move so far in the direction of emotional and aesthetic experience that we deny the importance of reason and analytical judgment. The goal of philosophy is to combine all of the varied forms of knowledge, to "interlace" reason and passion, analytical judgment and aesthetic judgment. Only by achieving this balance in our own lives can we become the creative, harmonious beings that we are capable of becoming.

Questions for Thought

1. What, according to Vasconcelos, can aesthetic judgments and emotions reveal to us that analytical judgments cannot? What, if anything, have you learned from your emotions?
2. What does Vasconcelos mean when he says that "reason is to the soul what body is to the spirit"? Do you think this is an appropriate analogy?

3. How does Vasconcelos conceive art and the artist? Do you agree with his conception?
4. How important is art in your life? Do you consider yourself to be a creative individual?
5. What, according to Vasconcelos, is the proper nature of philosophy? How would you define philosophy?

IT IS OF SPECIAL INTEREST TO NOTE THAT EACH series of particular disciplines is made up of common elements, and that the only thing distinguishing one from another is an intrinsic distinctive characteristic in the orientation of movement. In the areas of reality, from the atom to grace, there is a series of broad and concentrated fields, but there is always a substantial unity, a community of existence, and the possibility of their concurrence in the final goal of redemption.

The sensible world, the intelligible, and transcendental reversion, here are the three fundamental categories; the methodological problem is to determine the common connection that allows them to coexist without conflict and, moreover, to concur in a common direction toward liberation. To define the relationship and the manner of transition among the diverse manifestations of existence is one of the purposes of the philosophy sketched in these pages, and our method, as well, must be in accord with this purpose. To show, at the same time, that not only the soul but also nature suffers and rejoices because of this eagerness to transcend itself, is another of the fundamental goals of our doctrine.

Necessary agreement between method and subject matter can only result from the comparison of the reality which is being dealt with and the system which interprets it and orders it. We have already stated that aesthetics gives us a type of dialectic exclusively its own; its aim is to create suprasensible realities and at the same time transmute its external energy. Whether it derives an image from reality or whether it envelopes the object itself in an aura of beauty, aesthetic emotion imposes upon existence its own order and logic, which has always been recognized in old sayings as "logic of the heart," "the heart has its reasons that reason does not understand," etc.

Its standards—alogical logic, free rhythm, the passion of becoming—go beyond the objective law but without being alien to it, without ceasing to move it and modify it in a fundamental fashion; on the contrary, beauty frequently transfigures the object and raises it to the plane of emotion. According to aesthetic standards, the object enters the realm of the spirit, by dint of the combined witchery of beauty's image, the affinity, and the pathos. At this point, analytical judgment and the image itself become fused in a dynamism of the emotions, which is creative of beauty, just as structure becomes one with energy and maintains it in the atom, and as the body maintains and nourishes conscious life. Reason is to the soul what the body is to the spirit, a framework of fixed movements; we must go beyond it in order to delve into its infinite profundities.

For example, with music the judgment plunges itself into the abyss, where it is dissolved; I am referring to logical judgment; but on the other hand, another model makes its appearance which is, as it were, a sort of more flexible skeleton, a framework accommodated to the new nature, the angelic nature, which one needs in order to live beauty. That other logic is the logic of aesthetic judgment, which unlike the syllogism inclines us to hope for, obliges us to demand, the miracle, the exception, salvation. A similar thing occurs in every poetic judgment, and shines forth in all its splendid power in the enlightenment of

From *Vasconcelos of Mexico: Philosopher and Prophet* by John H. Haddox. © 1967 by University of Texas Press. Reprinted by permission.

those who are profoundly inspired, and even in that of those who are less inspired, as one may note in the first verse of some chapters of the Koran: "In the name of mild and merciful God"—a sovereign cry that thunders as if a golden drum were deafening heaven with its music; wondrous rings expand; celestial trumpets tremble; and their echoes expand space limitlessly. Overhead, the abyss is enraptured with brightness, like an infinity which is but poorly imitated by the domes of the greatest mosques. The air is filled with fragrances, as if the gardens of paradise had opened their gates. "Mild and merciful God"—the resounding vibrancy of these magic words re-echoes, bringing into harmony with themselves all the echoes of creation. . . . True art is always thus, an open sesame that elevates us, with soul rejuvenated, to an improved and transcendental creation.

It has not thus far been possible to formulate the basis for an exact philosophy in which the subject and the object, science and religion, may be brought into harmony rather than into mutual opposition, simply because the aesthetic problem has stood in our way. We still have not been able to define the significance of this problem within the general process of knowing; nor even less, to show how it is a means to grace for the object itself. Therefore, we have frequently been in like error in judging aesthetics either as the goal of the living process or as a simple variant of biological energy. Hence, currently we have applied to it constantly the first logical method, the biological; but never its own, superior because it is genuinely spiritual.

Furthermore, we have time and again, in the case of art, confused form and content; holy creative inspiration needs forms in order to make itself apparent to our nature; but inspiration passes and the form remains; inspiration frequently remains unfulfilled; at other times, inspiration does not succeed in giving life, in transforming its mold, and then the mold reverts to its parallel, the intellectual form subject to the logic of reason, which is the logic of the object. Thus we see, for example, that in the classical Spanish theater the characters frequently discuss their love until they turn it into a dialectic; in the French theater it is even worse, for pathos becomes the golden mean, and one must turn to Shakespeare again to find the lyric tide which elevates the soul and the world beyond the mean, reason, and form.

The problem here is one of form as well as of essence, since emotion does not take on a fully material form, is not realized, except in concrete manifestations which emotion itself determines. Every river delves and slowly defines its own bed; each flood leaves its mark along the banks and its own particular channel on the bottom; just so does emotion constantly forge and alter its motifs; but never will the particular motif or the limited form be enough to retain all the contents of the emotion. Light cannot penetrate the cracks through which water may leak away; but in a cave the flow of water may be recognized by its mysterious music; light, in contrast, dances where not even clouds may ascend. None of the aspects of the object, none of its elements, no sensible impression, none of the senses, none of the forms of reason, no thought, no partial reality, will succeed in containing or capturing the entire course of the rivers and whirlpools of emotion which give birth to aesthetic creation. Only wonder accompanies the endless beauty of earth and heaven.

It is not a simple task to follow art's own law; creative artists are rare, and even they, if they allow themselves to be enthralled by their aesthetic emotion, run the risk of falling prey to passions, dances and orgies, until they are blinded and become as incapable of progress as a Persian Sufi or a howling dervish, despite the fact that their point of departure is sublime emotion. This means that in the human condition one has no right to delay for a long time, and that, hence, to achieve precise philosophical knowledge one must employ a method based upon attentive observation as well as upon a constant motivation toward higher conditions.

At any rate, the world of the philosopher is to be distinguished from the methodology of experimental science and from all specialized approaches, in that it is not limited to a single criterion but must combine all of them: a philosopher requires a super-criterion. He must constantly compare the discoveries of the mind with those of the senses, and with that which the emotions teach him.

Philosophy cannot disregard universal ancient knowledge without falling into the childishness of contemporary empirical systems; neither may it ignore contemporary discoveries relating to the material world and to our dealings with material things; but the supreme law must not be sought in a physical world. As soon as one affirms that practical convenience establishes the law, the instinct to transcend it is destroyed, and the greatest of the powers at philosophy's disposal is precisely the instinct to transcend the material world.

No philosophy, then, is valid unless it is based upon the harmony of all facets of universal knowledge, and it is up to the philosopher alone to establish the values and hierarchies which give meaning to that harmony; the method to achieve such a task must be, accordingly, multifold, and not isolated, but interrelated—both an interlacement of the cosmos and a sign of the spirit that transcends it.

In order to begin to conceive a system, it is fundamental that we recall that each one of the realms into which existence can be broken down possesses its own rhythm of development and perfection, and yet that none of them can by itself explain the universal process. To join the spokes to the hubs one must first observe how the change from one order to another takes place. Reality viewed from within by a judgment participating in its rhythms, but transcending them, reveals to us regular processes and leaps. Whenever existence passes from power to will, from will to enjoyment, and vice versa, judgment is filled with astonishment as if it were in the presence of something that lies without its realm; but emotion understands, and becomes intoxicated with miraculous power; then, under the full power of its own nature, it ascends a scale, the scale of emotions, and sees how, within a single essence, the object is clothed, as it were, in light, in the oppositions of different types of energy; the biological impulse is fulfilled and realized in pleasure, and the feeling of the soul is overwhelmed with divine joy. Here we have a glimpse of unity in the heterogeneous, a unity which takes in the three primary orders: object, intelligence, will.

Since emotion embraces more than intelligence, it is of prime necessity to assign it a place of honor among the means of knowledge. Thus we shall continue investigating and penetrating until we find a supreme unity, which can gather in all the currents without obliterating their identity, in order to bring into being by their means a new mode of existence. One word defines our method: concurrent. . . .

Let us now try this definition: emotional knowledge manifests itself when things and processes reveal a sudden identity or disparity with our innermost nature. When we perceive certain processes taking place in the outer world, such as the flow of melody, we feel arising in our consciousness as well a parallel flow, intangible but real, flexible, and almost free. At the same time we become aware that the flow within becomes more closely joined to the flow without, that one can influence the other. Moreover, rational knowledge works upon a substance that is a matter of indifference to me and whose development depends on its own nature, without my being able to change it fundamentally. On the other hand, the flow that I perceive with an internal sense of identity to it seems subject to my free will, and offers me at least the possibility of exerting my free will upon the thing and of affecting it in a parallel fashion.

A certain opposition between the two modes of knowledge, rational and emotional, that is, the one that discovers the rules of a process and the one that inquires into its nature and purpose, is no obstacle to their working cooperatively in the task of research. Pythagoras, without distinguishing the two modes, achieves their synthesis when, after defining the relationships of the triangle and the squares derived from it, and after finding the numerical combinations of the triad, the square, and so forth, he moves on to music to follow in it the development of the numerical rhythms; but it is necessary to note clearly that in the same instant that the move is made from numbers to music, one enters the field of aesthetics and one's judgment is no longer rational but emotional when one enters a realm of knowing through sympathies and differences based on emotion. By difference or by similarity of essence or of goal the two dramatic poles of every aesthetic contemplation are engendered: the subject and the object, no longer confronted for measurement by the rules of logical judgment, but suspended in the mutual mystery that separates them in a sort of morphological reality, while joining them through their involvement with the Absolute. . . .

It is evident, accordingly, that besides rational knowledge, which is a result of the exercise of the intelligence on the data of the internal and external sensitivity, or the sensitivity produced by both, we possess another means for penetrating reality, that is, another mode of knowing. The intuition of color as a scale of beauty, of sound as melody and mystery, the emotion of the presence and correspondence to us of things that are intimately related to us, although superficially farther from us than the water we drink or the air that replenishes our blood, all these experiences constitute a source of a specific type of knowledge that cannot be transferred to another category, but is closely linked to us in a sort of instinctive coordination and existential harmony.

Accordingly knowledge is not a synonym for thought but something still more inclusive than thought; that is, it involves bringing into the terms of consciousness elements that are most extraneous to it, making them part of our lives according to their affinities to the various powers of our personality so that all become joined in an awareness of super-existence and transcendence in which dissimilar elements are combined for the total achievement of harmony. Of course we are not proposing a type of harmony that will respect each unit of reality; on the contrary [we are proposing] a great, perhaps catastrophic, series of deep emotions and changes that will keep changing things, beings, and goals.

3.6   Feminist Politics and Epistemology: Justifying Feminist Theory

ALISON M. JAGGAR

Alison Jaggar (b. 1942) is a professor of Philosophy and Women's Studies at the University of Colorado at Boulder. She was formerly Wilson Professor of Ethics at the University of Cincinnati and has also taught at the University of Illinois at Chicago, the University of California at Los Angeles, and Rutgers University. Her books include *Feminist Frameworks*, co-edited with Paula Rothenberg; *Feminist Poli-*

tics and Human Nature, from which the following selection is taken; and *Gender/ Body/Knowledge: Feminist Reconstructions of Being and Knowing*, co-edited with Susan Bordo. She is currently working on several other books dealing with feminist ethics and epistemology, including *Toward a Feminist Conception of Practical Reason*, a book on feminist moral epistemology. Jaggar was a founding member of the Society for Women in Philosophy and is past chair of the American Philosophical Association Committee on the Status of Women. She works with a number of feminist organizations and sees feminist scholarship as inseparable from feminist activism.

In the following selection, Jaggar surveys the principal types of feminism that currently exist: liberal feminism, Marxist feminism, radical feminism, and socialist feminism. She contends that each type of feminism is tied to a distinctive conception of human nature, which in turn is connected to definite claims about the nature of knowledge and reality. Since these claims about knowledge and reality determine the meaning of such concepts as adequacy and objectivity, each type of feminism contains its own epistemological assumptions about how theories are to be justified. Not surprisingly, these epistemological assumptions theoretically justify themselves, while at the same time providing reasons for rejecting the other types of feminism. Obviously, this process of self-justification cannot ultimately claim to be either "neutral" or "objective." Indeed, as Jaggar points out, belief in the possibility of purely objective knowledge or a purely neutral observer is an epistemological assumption of liberal feminism.

Despite the impossibility of "objectively" choosing one type of feminism over the others, Jaggar does claim that there are grounds for committing oneself politically to one of them. Indeed, after describing the theoretical assumptions of each type of feminism, Jaggar argues that socialist feminism provides the best available framework for women's liberation. Her main reason for supporting socialist feminism is that it combines Marxist claims about the class determination of knowledge with the recognition of the special standpoint of women in the conceptualization of knowledge and reality. According to Jaggar, "The standpoint of women provides the basis for a more comprehensive representation of reality than the standpoint of men."

Questions for Thought

1. What do you think Jaggar means by feminism? How would you define this term?
2. Why does Jaggar reject the possibility of pure objectivity? Do you agree with her on this point? Why or why not?
3. In what ways do liberal feminism and Marxist feminism differ? What, if anything, do they have in common?
4. How does the worldview of radical feminism differ from the worldview of liberal feminism? Which of these worldviews seems most adequate to you?
5. Both radical feminism and socialist feminism claim that women have special modes of knowing. What are some of these special modes? Do you believe that women have special modes of knowing? Why or why not?
6. What are Jaggar's principal reasons for choosing socialist feminism over the other three types? Do you think this is the best choice?

THERE ARE MANY WAYS OF BEING A FEMINIST. Contemporary feminists are united in their opposition to women's oppression, but they differ not only in their views of how to combat that oppression, but even in their conception of what constitutes women's oppression in contemporary society. Liberal feminists . . . believe that women are oppressed insofar as they suffer unjust discrimination; traditional Marxists believe that women are oppressed in their exclusion from public production; radical feminists see women's oppression as consisting primarily in the universal male control of women's sexual and procreative capacities; while socialist feminists characterize women's oppression in terms of a revised version of the Marxist theory of alienation. Each of these analyses of women's oppression reflects a distinctive feminist perspective on contemporary society and each of them is associated with a characteristic conception of human nature. While these distinctive feminist perspectives have been in some ways cross-fertile, they are ultimately incompatible with each other. In other words, one cannot view contemporary society simultaneously from more than one of these perspectives. The question then arises which perspective one should choose. What are the reasons for preferring one feminist theory to another? . . .

On television commercials, the rational consumer is sometimes shown comparing one brand with another. In these comparisons, the consumer has a list of the qualities desired in the product and uses that list to determine which brand possesses most of these desiderata, be they fuel economy, clean lemon scent or gentle overnight action. In comparing different feminist theories to each other, the obvious procedure might seem to be to prepare a similar list of theoretical desiderata and then to check off which feminist theory possesses most of the desired qualities. In fact, however, this is not as simple as it sounds. While it is not difficult to reach agreement in general terms over the criteria of an adequate feminist theory, there is enormous controversy between feminists over what counts as satisfaction or fulfillment of these criteria of adequacy. One reason for this controversy is systematic disagreement over how the criteria should be interpreted and applied. . . .

Feminist disagreements over these metatheoretical issues are related conceptually to the rest of their political theory and in particular to their distinctive conceptions of human nature. This is because every conception of human nature involves a characteristic conception of human knowledge—its sources, its extent and the proper criteria for distinguishing truth from falsity. In other words, commitment to a theory of human nature carries with it commitment to a certain epistemology. Thus every political theory, like every other theory, involves at least an implicit commitment to a certain method for understanding social reality and to certain criteria for theoretical adequacy. In what follows, I shall explain the metatheoretical disagreements between various groups of feminists, linking these with the rest of their political theory and with their conceptions of human nature. I shall argue that the most politically appropriate and theoretically illuminating interpretations of theoretical desiderata are those associated with socialist feminism. Finally, I shall show, unsurprisingly, that socialist feminism best fulfills the criteria of theoretical adequacy thus interpreted, and so constitutes, despite its incompleteness, the best available theory of women's liberation.

Liberal Feminism and the Elimination of Bias

Liberal feminism rests on a conception of human nature that is radically individualistic. What this means, in part, is that human beings

Material from *Feminist Politics and Human Nature* is reprinted by permission of Rowman & Allanheld, a division of Rowman & Littlefield Publishers.

are conceived as isolated individuals who have no necessary connection with each other or even with non-human nature. Of course, liberals recognize that human individuals in fact engage in all kinds of interactions with each other and with non-human nature, but they do not see these interactions as essential to human beings. On the liberal view of humans as essentially separate rational agents, it would be logically possible for human individuals to exist in total isolation from each other and perhaps even from non-human nature.

Just as the individualistic conception of human nature sets the basic problems for the liberal political tradition, so it also generates the problems for the tradition in epistemology that is associated historically and conceptually with liberalism. This tradition begins in the seventeenth century with Descartes, and it emerges in the twentieth century as the analytic tradition. Because it conceives humans as essentially separate individuals, this epistemological tradition views the attainment of knowledge as a project for each individual on her or his own. The task of epistemology, then, is to formulate rules to enable individuals to undertake this project with success. Within this broad epistemological tradition, several different tendencies have emerged. The rationalist tendency, typified by Descartes, views knowledge as achieved by inference from indubitable first premises; by contrast, the British empiricist tendency views knowledge as achieved by inference from basic individual sense experiences. In either case, however, the attainment of knowledge is conceived as essentially a solitary occupation that has no necessary social preconditions.

The empiricist strand in Cartesian epistemology culminated in the theory of knowledge known as positivism. According to positivism, the paradigm of knowledge is physical science and positivism has a distinctive view of what constitutes the scientific enterprise and the proper method of scientific discovery. One basic assumption of this view is that all knowledge is constructed by inference from immediate sensory experiences. Thus knowledge, that is science, is atomistic in structure and the task of epistemology and the philosophy of science is to formulate the rules for making valid inferences from the basic sense experiences on which knowledge is thought to be founded. The assumption that knowledge is atomistic in structure means that a good scientific explanation must be reductionistic; that is, it must show how the characteristics of a complex entity are built up from its simplest components. . . .

On the positivist view, the adequacy of a scientific theory is thought to be guaranteed by its objectivity or lack of bias. The positivist conception of objectivity has several aspects. First, objectively produced claims are capable, in principle at least, of being verified by anyone. It is assumed that similar circumstances would stimulate similar perceptions in anyone with normal faculties of sensation, and from this assumption positivists conclude that, as long as they follow the same rules of valid inference, everyone should emerge with the same scientific conclusions. The possibility of intersubjective verification is thus part of what is meant by "objectivity." A second aspect of the positivist conception of objectivity is that it excludes any evaluative element. Positivism requires that scientists should take empirical observations as their only data and should scrupulously control their own values, interests and emotions, since these are viewed as biasing or distorting the results of scientific enquiry. For positivism, objectivity is defined by the inquiry's independence from the "subjective" values, interests and emotions of those who engage in scientific enquiry or who deal with its results. Positivists view this second requirement of value neutrality as necessary for fulfilling the first requirement of intersubjective verifiability. Since people, including scientists, have widely differing values, interests and emotions, intersubjective agreement is thought to be impossible unless these values, interests and emotions are prevented from directing the scientific enterprise.

On the positivist view, therefore, good scientists are detached observers and manipulators of nature who follow strict methodological rules, which enable them to separate themselves from the special values, interests and emotions generated by their class, race, sex or unique situation. Thus, the good scientist of positivism is the abstract individual of liberal political theory.

The narrow positivist paradigm excludes many aspects of human intellectual and cultural activity from the realm of knowledge; indeed, positivism's criteria for knowledge are so strict that many critics argue that they cannot be met even by the physical sciences. However that may be, positivists agree that value judgments cannot be part of genuine knowledge because value judgments cannot be justified empirically by the scientific method as they conceive that method. A consequence of this claim is that moral and political theories are not part of knowledge because value judgments are integral to such theories. The logical positivists of the mid-twentieth century accepted this consequence and declared the death of normative, that is, explicitly evaluative, moral and political philosophy, though not of the supposedly empirical political science.

In the latter part of the twentieth century, the more extreme versions of positivism have been rejected, explicitly normative moral and political philosophy has undergone a revival and the liberal tradition has been revitalized. Nevertheless, the conception of moral and political philosophy that dominates this revitalized tradition still retains some positivist or neo-positivist assumptions. One of the most important of these is the assumption that an adequate moral or political theory must be objective in the sense of being unbiased. In the case of normative theory, objectivity or lack of bias obviously cannot consist in independence from value judgments, since normative theories by definition express values. Instead, objectivity is defined to mean independence from the value judgments of any particular individual. Objective or unbiased value judgments are those that would be made by an individual who was impartial in the sense of giving no special weight to her own or to any other special interests. In other words, the good moral or political philosopher of the contemporary liberal tradition resembles the good scientist of positivism in being able to detach herself or himself from such "contingent" properties as race, class or sex. . . .

If the conception of objectivity that is held by the revitalized liberal/positivist tradition is used to evaluate the various contemporary feminist theories, one theory emerges as clearly superior. That one, of course, is liberal feminism. Unlike other versions of feminism, liberal feminism makes a sharp distinction between what it takes to be the normative and the empirical aspects of the theory. It does not rest on mystical notions of women's special relation to nature, nor does it rely on concepts such as alienation whose logical status, from the neo-positivist point of view, are quite unclear. In stating the non-empirical or normative aspects of its theory, moreover, liberal feminism relies on values that are claimed to be universal human values and which in consequence, liberal feminism assumes, cannot reflect only the special interests of a particular group. Most notably, liberal feminists insist that they seek no special privileges for women; they claim to demand only equal rights and equal opportunities for all. Their basic demand is that everyone should receive equal consideration with no discrimination on the basis of sex.

Given what they take to be the universal applicability of their values, liberal feminists assume that the validity of their theory will be evident to all who set aside their own special interests. In their view, after all, their version of feminism does not favor the interests of any one group or class over another. If men rationally think about why they should set aside their own special interests, they should be just as well able as women to see the soundness of liberal feminist arguments and there is no reason in principle why men should not be just as good feminists as women. In short, liberal feminists assume that their view reflects the impartial perspective of the rational, detached observer and consequently constitutes the most unbiased and objective feminist theory.

Other versions of feminism do not claim to be more objective than liberal feminism in the liberal/positivist sense of objectivity. Instead, they challenge precisely the conception of objectivity that liberals take as a primary condition of theoretical adequacy. In particular, they challenge the liberal assumption of a sharp fact/value distinction and they attack the claim that there is any such standpoint as that of the neutral observer.

Traditional Marxism and the Science of the Proletariat

The traditional Marxist conception of theoretical adequacy is in sharp contrast with the liberal conception. It is part of a theory of knowledge generated by a view of human nature that is quite different from liberal feminism's view.

Traditional Marxism conceives of human individuals as existing necessarily in dialectical interrelation with each other and with the nonhuman world. On this view, the essential activity of human beings is praxis and the development of knowledge is seen as just one aspect of praxis. In other words, knowledge is developed as part of human activity to satisfy human needs. Rather than viewing knowledge as the purely intellectual construct of a detached spectator, therefore, Marxism sees knowledge as emerging through practical human involvement in changing the world, an involvement which also changes human beings themselves. Moreover, since human productive activity always takes a definite historical form, all knowledge must be seen as growing out of a specific mode of production.

The Marxist conception of knowledge challenges two basic assumptions of liberal epistemology. First, since praxis is necessarily a social activity, it challenges the view that knowledge can be the achievement of a single isolated individual. Instead, Marxism views knowledge as socially constructed and the expansion of knowledge as a social product. Secondly, since knowledge is one aspect of human productive activity and since this activity is necessarily purposive, the basic categories of knowledge will always be shaped by human purposes and the values on which they are based. For this reason, Marxists conclude that even so-called empirical knowledge is never entirely value-free. The conceptual framework by which we make sense of ourselves and our world is shaped and limited by the interests and values of the society that we inhabit. Marxists express this by saying that all forms of knowledge are historically determined by the prevailing mode of production.[1]

At least since the inception of class society, however, societies have not been characterized by a single set of interests and values. Instead, societies have been composed of classes whose interests have been in opposition to each other and whose values have conflicted with each other. In such a situation, one cannot say that the prevailing world view or system of knowledge reflects the interests and values of society as a whole. Instead, one must specify which class's interests and values are reflected. Marxism's answer to this question is that the system of knowledge that is generally accepted within a society reflects the interests of the dominant class. . . . In class societies, the prevailing world view supports the interests of the ruling class by obscuring or by justifying the reality of domination. In this sense, Marxism views all existing claims to knowledge as "ideological," that is, as distorted representations of reality. Only a classless society will produce an undistorted and genuinely scientific representation of reality.

Although class societies are governed by a ruling system of ideas, they also contain some ideas that are subversive to that system: slaves perceive reality differently from their masters. As long as the society is relatively stable, however, subversive ideas will not be generally accepted or even understood; they will receive widespread consideration only during a period of social upheaval. During times of relative stability, the dominant ideology is imposed in a number of ways. The most obvious of these ways involve the direct suppression of potentially subversive observations or theories. One effective means of doing this is by denying a voice to those classes from which such ideas are likely to emerge. Those classes are denied education and even literacy, and their ideas are labeled as superstition. By contrast, honors are heaped on those who invent theories that can be used to justify the status quo, and their ideas are popularized in the mass media. Those who do develop subversive theories are ridiculed and denied jobs or research facilities. If their ideas seem to be gaining popularity anyway, the ruling class resorts to outright censorship and persecution; for instance, subversive groups may be prohibited from access to the media or denied the right to assemble.

In addition to direct forms of thought control, the plausibility of the dominant ideology is enhanced by the very structure of class society. Daily life itself tends to generate historically specific forms of false consciousness. In capitalist society, for instance, individuals are forced to compete with each other to survive, and the apparent universality of competition seems to confirm the view that humans are "naturally" aggressive and selfish. Similarly, the provision of inferior educational resources and facilities for the subordinate classes appears to provide confirmation of the view that the members of these classes are more lazy and/or stupid than members of the dominant class, and so seems to justify their subordinate position. The structure of capitalist society also seems to confirm the validity of the prevailing socioeconomic categories; for instance, it encourages the perception of capital as an independently existing object with its own properties, especially the property of generating capital, rather than as the expression of a certain system of social relations. . . .

According to this interpretation of Marxist epistemology, all systems of knowledge bear the marks of their social origin within a particular mode of production. This is true even of knowledge about knowledge. In class society, not only is there an ultimately ideological element, according to Marxism, in the concepts and categories through which we constitute our reality; there is also an ideological bias in the standards for determining what is to be accepted as knowledge or science and what is to be rejected as myth or superstition. . . .

The Marxist conception of existing claims to knowledge as ideological provides the conceptual basis for the enquiry known as the sociology of knowledge. Sociologists of knowledge study the way in which systems of thought are related to the social contexts from which they emerge. Investigations in the sociology of knowledge reveal that reality is perceived very differently by different groups and that these different perceptions depend not only on the social order that the groups inhabit but also on their position within that social order. Different social positions provide different vantage points from which some aspects of reality come into prominence and from which other aspects are obscured. . . .

Once we look at the real conditions in which knowledge is produced, Marxists believe that we will see that the ways in which we conceptualize the world are always shaped by our interactions with that world. Moreover, we will see that it is inevitable that all systems of thought should be constructed from some standpoint within the social world. There is no Archimedean point outside the world where we may stand to gain a perspective on reality that is neutral between the interests and values of existing social groups. Consequently, no knowledge can be objective in the liberal or positivist sense. . . .

On the traditional Marxist view, of course, Marxist theory itself constitutes the most comprehensive picture of the world from the standpoint of the proletariat. Precisely because it reflects the interests and values of the working class, which are thought to be those of the totality of humankind, Marxist theory provides the most-unbiased and objective available representation of social reality, as well as the most-useful method of investigating the non-human world. For this reason, Marxists sometimes describe their theory, perhaps with a slightly positivist ring, as the science of the proletariat. Proletarian science ultimately will defeat bourgeois science but the struggle will not be simply an intellectual one. The superiority of proletarian science will be demonstrated ultimately by the fact that it will enable the working class to abolish the class relations that have given rise to the forms of bourgeois consciousness. . . .

Given the epistemological framework of traditional Marxism, there is room for only two basic kinds of feminism. Inevitably, the dominant kind must be liberal or bourgeois feminism, which expresses the aspirations of upper- and middle-class women and which is grounded on the assumptions of capitalist ideology. By contrast, Marxist, or revolutionary, feminism expresses the aspirations of working-class women and is grounded on the science of the proletariat. On the traditional Marxist view, what appear to be independent versions of feminism, such as lesbian feminism, radical feminism, anarchist feminism, or socialist feminism, are simply distorted forms of one of the two major types. All versions of feminism are seen either as expressing ideals that are basically capitalist or as expressing "progressive" alternatives to capitalism, ideals which are flawed, however, by an incomplete understanding of Marxist science. The apparently ungendered categories of traditional Marxism, which do not allow women an independent class position, make it impossible for traditional Marxists to conceive that women might have their own epistemological standpoint. . . .

If contemporary society affords only two basic epistemological standpoints, then Marxist epistemology naturally recommends that feminists adopt the standpoint of the proletariat. Given Marxist epistemological presuppositions,

the political theory of liberal feminism is bound to be totally inadequate. By suggesting that women's liberation can be achieved primarily through legislative reform, liberal feminism obscures what Marxists take to be the fact that women's oppression is "built into the capitalist system."[2] Consequently, liberal feminism is unable to point the way to overthrowing the capitalist system which Marxists believe is the material base of women's contemporary subordination. Traditional Marxist feminism, by contrast, takes itself to be an epistemologically superior perspective because it reveals what Marxists claim to be the essential identity of interest between working-class women and working-class men. Marxist epistemology concludes that only the traditional Marxist conception of women's oppression provides the theory that will guide the simultaneous abolition of capitalism and women's oppression. As for the other varieties of feminism, traditional Marxist epistemology measures their adequacy by estimating how effectively they contribute to undermining the capitalist system and to strengthening the power of the working class as a whole.

Like liberal feminism, traditional Marxist feminism justifies itself on the basis of its own interpretation of the generally accepted criteria of theoretical adequacy. Just as traditional Marxism rejects the liberal interpretations of theoretical adequacy, however, so other versions of feminism reject the Marxist interpretations.

Radical Feminism and the Upward Spiral

Radical feminism is developing its own distinctive conception of what counts as reliable knowledge and how such knowledge may be achieved. Like a number of the foundational concepts of radical feminism, this conception of knowledge is nowhere expounded in a systematic or linear way. Instead, various authors mention various aspects of it in passing, often in the context of a critique of "patriarchal" conceptions of knowledge. From these scattered references, however, a number of common epistemological assumptions emerge. Not all radical feminists share all of these assumptions: in particular, some radical feminists accept mystical or spiritual experiences as a reliable source of knowledge, whereas others reject them. In spite of this and related disagreements, I think it is possible to identify the outlines of a fairly consistent radical feminist epistemology. This epistemology is in some ways strikingly similar to that of traditional Marxism, especially in its critique of the dominant conception of knowledge, a conception which radical feminists characterize as "patriarchal." In many ways, the radical feminist critique of patriarchal modes of knowing recalls traditional Marxist critiques of the liberal/positivist paradigm of knowledge. Like traditional Marxism, radical feminism seems to recognize a distinction between science and ideology and to assume that, in any society, the dominant group will impose its own distorted and mystifying version of reality. Radical feminist epistemology also generates an ontology that bears a remarkable resemblance to some aspects of traditional Marxist ontology. Unlike traditional Marxism, however, radical feminist epistemology is a self-conscious elaboration and justification of a specifically feminist view of reality.

Radical feminist epistemology starts from the belief that women know much of which men are ignorant and it takes one of its main tasks as being to explain why this should be so. Radical feminist epistemology explores the strategies women have developed for obtaining reliable knowledge and for correcting the distortions of patriarchal ideology. One of the best known of these strategies is the "consciousness-raising" process, a process that is often considered paradigmatic of the feminist method of inquiry. It was primarily through consciousness-raising groups that women involved in the contemporary women's liberation movement began to make visible, first to themselves, the hitherto invisible depths of their own oppression. . . .

Nancy Hartsock writes that the consciousness-raising method of gaining knowledge is remarkably close, in many respects, to the Marxist method of analysis. Certainly it is obvious that the knowledge gained through consciousness raising is a collective product and that the process of gaining it is guided by the special interests and values of the women in the group. It is clear, too, that the aim of such knowledge is ultimately practical. In addition, through the practice of consciousness raising, as Hartsock writes,

> Women have learned that it was important to build their analyses from the ground up, beginning with their own experiences. They examined their lives not only as thinkers but, as Marx would have suggested, with all their senses.[3]

In spite of these similarities, there are also important differences between the epistemologies of radical feminism and of traditional Marxism. One of these differences is the contemporary lack of radical feminist interest in political theory, as theory has been understood within the Marxist tradition. This lack of interest in theory construction is most marked among contemporary American radical feminists. . . .

Perhaps the most striking difference between radical feminist epistemology and the epistemology of the western tradition, both Marxist and non-Marxist, is that a conspicuous strain of radical feminism accepts the reliability of certain human faculties which are considered highly unreliable within the western (though not necessarily within the eastern) epistemological tradition. Many radical feminists believe that these faculties are especially well developed in women, although they do not make it clear whether this higher development is due to some special aptitude genetically inherited by women, or is simply due to the fact that the male culture inhibits men from developing those faculties whereas the female culture encourages their development in women. However that may be, one of the faculties that radical feminism regards as a special source of knowledge for women is the faculty of intuition, through which women are thought to have direct, non-inferential access to the feelings and motives of others. Women's intuition is both a cause and an effect of their special sensitivity to and empathy for others, capacities in which radical feminists take great pride. Another faculty that radical feminists accept as a source of special knowledge for women is the spiritual power of experiencing a mystical sense of connection or identification with other people or with the universe as a whole. . . . Finally, some radical feminists believe that women have the capacity for developing what are now viewed as parapsychological powers. . . .

Women's special modes of knowing encourage a conception of the world that is totally opposed to what radical feminists characterize as the patriarchal world view. According to radical feminism, patriarchal thought is characterized by divisions, distinctions, oppositions, and dualisms. Patriarchy opposes mind to matter, self to other, reason to emotion, and enquirer to object of enquiry. In each of these oppositions, one side of the dualism is valued more than the other side. For this reason, radical feminists claim that hierarchy is built into the fundamental ontology of patriarchy. . . .

By contrast with the dualistic and hierarchical ontology of patriarchy, radical feminism claims to be developing a world view that is non-dualistic and non-hierarchical. Instead, radical feminists conceive the world as an organic whole, in which "everything is connected to everything else."[4] . . . Not only is everything connected with everything else, but everything is always in a process of change. Radical feminists see the world "as structures of relations in process, a reality constantly in evolution."[5] . . .

The ontology and epistemology of radical feminism each imply the other, just as the atomistic liberal ontology and epistemology imply each other and just as the Marxist ontology of class both implies and is implied by the Marxist epistemological categories of class standpoint. Because radical feminist ontology conceives "everything as connected to everything else," Gerri Perreault points out that radical feminist epistemology is committed to the view that the observer is inseparable from the observed, the knower from the known.[6] If this is so, then it is both proper and inevitable for theory to be guided by practical interests and to be informed by feelings. . . .

Given this conception of how adequate theories are developed, radical feminists conclude that the liberal/positivist conception of objectivity is a myth. Knowledge does not grow in a linear way, through the accumulation of facts and the application of the hypothetico-deductive method, but rather resembles "an upward spiral, so that each time we re-evaluate a position or place we've been before, we do so from a new perspective."[7] Mary Daly uses the same image of spiraling to describe the growth of knowledge. She recommends that feminists spin a new web of ideas and then compares the spider's web to "a spiral net."[8] A few pages later, Daly writes: "Genuine Spinning is spiraling, which takes us over, under, around the baffle gates of godfathers into the Background."[9] . . .

By epistemological standards of liberal feminism, the political theory of radical feminism is totally inadequate. It makes no pretense of detached impartiality, and the more spiritually oriented versions of radical feminism rest on non-empirical claims about women's special closeness to each other and to non-human nature. Radical feminism also fails the epistemological tests of traditional Marxism, especially the tests imposed by the more positivistic interpretations, according to which radical feminism is mystical and non-scientific. . . . Traditional Marxists claim that, by dividing social reality according to the categories of male and female, patriarchal and feminist, radical feminism obscures the fundamental social division between the capitalist and the working class. It distorts the science of the proletariat and it implicitly strengthens the capitalist system by turning working-class men and women against each other.

By its own epistemological standards, however, radical feminism is indisputably the most adequate feminist theory. It is created directly from the experience of women, and it reflects women's pain and anger. It does not arbitrarily limit its sources of information, but utilizes women's special ways of knowing. Its nonlinear mode of exposition reflects the human learning process, and the highly charged language of its authors evokes an emotional response in its readers and helps to jolt their consciousness out of the conceptual framework of patriarchy and into a women-centered paradigm. It reveals men's domination of women and demystifies myths through which that domination is concealed. . . .

Like the other feminist theories that we have considered, radical feminism justifies itself though its own epistemological standards. Let us turn now to one more feminist theory of knowledge and examine one final interpretation of the generally accepted criteria for theoretical adequacy.

Socialist Feminism and the Standpoint of Women

The socialist feminist theory of human nature is structurally identical with that of traditional Marxism and so, consequently, is the structure of its epistemology. Like both traditional Marxists and radical feminists, socialist feminists view knowledge as a social and practical construct and they believe that conceptual frameworks are shaped and limited by their social origins. They believe that, in any historical period, the prevailing world view will reflect the interests and values of the dominant class. Consequently, they recognize that the establishment of a less mystified and more reliable world view will require not only scientific struggle and intellectual argument but also the overthrow of the prevailing system of social relations.

Where social feminist differs from traditional Marxist epistemology is in its assertion that the special social or class position of women gives them a special epistemological standpoint which makes possible a view of the world that is more reliable and less distorted than that available either to capitalist or to working-class men. Socialist feminists believe, therefore, that a primary condition for the adequacy of a feminist theory, indeed for the adequacy of any theory, is that it should represent the world from the standpoint of women. . . .

The political economy of socialist feminism establishes that, in contemporary society, women suffer a special form of exploitation and oppression. Socialist feminist epistemologists argue that this distinctive social or class position provides women with a distinctive epistemological standpoint. From this standpoint, it is possible to gain a less biased and more comprehensive view of reality than that provided either by established bourgeois science or by the male-dominated leftist alternatives to it. An adequate understanding of reality must be undertaken from the standpoint of women. As socialist feminists conceive it, however, the standpoint of women is not expressed directly in women's naive and unreflective world view. . . . [S]ocialist feminists recognize that women's perceptions of reality are distorted both by male-dominant ideology and by the male-dominated structure of everyday life. The standpoint of women, therefore, is not something that can be discovered through a survey of women's existing beliefs and attitudes—although such a survey should identify certain commonalities that might be incorporated eventually into a systematic representation of the world from women's perspective. Instead, the standpoint of women is discovered through a collective process of political and scientific struggle. The distinctive social experience of women generates insights that are incompatible with men's interpretations of reality and these insights provide clues to how reality might be interpreted from the standpoint of women. The validity of these insights, however, must be tested in political struggle and developed into a systematic representation of reality that is not distorted in ways that promote the interests of men above those of women.

Considerable work still needs to be done in elaborating the concept of women's standpoint. A number of arguments used to establish it are still speculative and require further development and investigation. Even so, the concept of women's standpoint promises to provide an important criterion for evaluating the adequacy of feminist theory. It is supported by a variety of arguments: by psychological research, which demonstrates that women's perceptions of reality are in fact different from those of men; by psychoanalytic theory, which offers an explanation of those differences in terms of the different infant experiences of girls and boys; by investigations in the sociology of knowledge, which link the distinctive social experience of women with distinctively feminine ways of perceiving the world; and by feminist critiques of existing knowledge, which reveal how prevailing systems of conceptualization are biased because they invalidate women's interests and promote the interests and values of the men who created them. Of course, the epistemological superiority of women's standpoint will be demonstrated conclusively only through a distinctively feminist reconstruction of reality in which women's interests are not subordinated to those of men. This reconstruction must be practical as well as theoretical. . . .

Of course, women have not yet been able to construct systematic alternatives to the prevailing masculine science and ideology. For one thing, they are still in process of discovering ways in which their thought is constrained on both conscious and unconscious levels by assumptions that reinforce male dominance. Powerful interests discredit women's ideas and minimal social resources are allocated to developing a science that is profoundly subversive. . . . Despite these obstacles, some theorists believe that it is possible to discern at least the outlines of a distinctively feminine perspective on reality and to see how these are generated by the sexual division of labor.

Within contemporary capitalism, the society with which they are concerned primarily, socialist feminist theorists remind us that the sexual division of labor assigns to women work that is very different from that of men. Dorothy Smith argues that women's work is primarily in what she calls "the bodily mode"; it focuses on the transformation of the immediate and concrete world. Men's work, by contrast, is in what Smith calls "the abstracted conceptual mode" which is the ruling mode in industrial society. The rulers are able to operate in the conceptual mode, abstracting from the concrete realities of daily existence, only because they participate in a system of social organization which assigns bodily work to others—others who also "produce the invisibility of that work."[10] . . .

Of course, women do not spend their whole lives as adults. Like men, their distinctively human labor in fact begins in infancy when they create their first conceptions of themselves, of other people and of the non-human world. According to the psychoanalytic tradition, this first labor is especially important because early infantile attitudes and conceptualizations often set the direction for adult life, becoming the unconscious and invisible foundation on which adult attitudes and conceptualizations are grounded. Psychoanalysts since Freud have claimed that girls typically tend to develop perceptions of reality that differ from those of boys because their infant experiences are different. . . . [A] number of socialist feminist theorists have drawn on psychoanalytic theory to explain the social formation and relative fixity of the masculine and feminine character structures that are typical of contemporary society. Some socialist feminist theorists also draw on psychoanalytic theory in attempts to identify the psychological links between gendered systems of conceptualization and the earliest experiences of girls and boys. . . .

Socialist feminist theorists argue that a consideration of the distinctive differences between the experience and work of women and the experience and work of men, both as infants and as adults, sheds light on certain distinctive differences in the way that each sex tends to conceptualize reality. Specifically, they claim that such a consideration can be used to explain why some systems of conceptualization distort reality in ways that are typically masculine and how the standpoint of women offers the possibility of correcting these distortions. . . .

Socialist feminist epistemology claims that the social experience of women is so different from that of men that it shapes and limits their vision in substantially different ways—in other words, that women's position in society provides the basis for an autonomous epistemological standpoint. Socialist feminist epistemology is not committed, however, to any specific account of the psychological relation between the sexual division of labor and the gender structuring of knowledge; it is quite compatible with socialist feminism for the gender-structured adult experience of women and men to be more influential than their infant experience in shaping their world view. Whenever and however this shaping occurs, growing empirical evidence shows that women tend to conceive the world differently from men and have different attitudes towards it. The discovery of the precise nature and causes of these differences is a task for feminist psychologists and sociologists of knowledge. The task for feminist scientists and political theorists is to build on women's experience and insights in order to develop a systematic account of the world, together with its potentialities for change, as it appears from the standpoint of women.

As we saw earlier, women are far from creating systematic alternatives to the prevailing male-dominant ways of conceptualizing reality. . . . Socialist feminist theorists claim, however, that women's experience has generated at least the outline of a distinctive world view, even though this outline is . . . sketchy and insubstantial. Nancy Hartsock provides this outline:

The female construction of self in relation to others, leads . . . toward opposition to dualisms of any sort, valuation of concrete, everyday life, sense of a variety of connectednesses and continuities both with other persons and with the natural world. If material life structures consciousness, women's relationally defined existence, bodily experience of boundary challenges, and activity of transforming both physical objects and human beings must be expected to result in a world view to which dichotomies are foreign.[11]

The standpoint of women generates an ontology of relations and of continual process. . . .

Even though we do not yet know how the world looks from the standpoint of women, I think that the socialist feminist concept of women's standpoint constitutes a valuable epistemological device for identifying certain necessary conditions of theoretical adequacy. It provides a politically appropriate and theoretically illuminating interpretation of such generally acknowledged conditions as impartiality, objectivity, comprehensiveness, verifiability and usefulness.

First, the concept of women's standpoint presupposes that all knowledge reflects the interests and values of specific social groups. Since this is so, objectivity cannot be interpreted to mean neutrality between conflicting interests. If these interpretations are ruled out, and given that we want to preserve the conditions of objectivity and impartiality, the question for epistemology becomes the following: if claims to knowledge are to be objective and impartial, whose interests should they reflect? Socialist feminists answer that they should reflect the interests of women. Women's subordinate status means that, unlike men, women do not have an interest in mystifying reality and so are likely to develop a clearer and more trustworthy understanding of the world. A representation of reality from the standpoint of women is more objective and unbiased than the prevailing representations that reflect the standpoint of men.

The concept of women's standpoint also provides an interpretation of what it is for a theory to be comprehensive. It asserts that women's social position offers them access to aspects or areas of reality that are not easily accessible to men. For instance, to use one of Hartsock's examples, it is only from the standpoint of women that household labor becomes visible as work rather than as a labor of love. The same might be said of socializing children, of empathizing with adults and even, often, of engaging in sexual relations. Thus the standpoint of women provides the basis for a more comprehensive representation of reality than the standpoint of men. Certain areas or aspects of the world are not excluded. The standpoint of women reveals more of the universe, human and non-human, than does the standpoint of men. . . .

Liberal feminist theory constitutes the first attempt to represent reality from the standpoint of women and the importance of this contribution cannot be overestimated. As we saw . . . , however, liberal feminism is still committed to the conceptual framework of traditional liberal theory, a frame-work that maintains rigid distinctions between mind and body, reason and emotion, fact and value, and public and private. Although apparently gender-neutral, these dichotomies justify a social system that perpetuates the subordination of women to men. For instance, they exclude from political consideration precisely that "private sphere" into which women historically have been relegated. Liberal feminism rests on an abstract conception of human nature that minimizes the importance of such "accidental" properties as class, sex, color and age. It focuses on a commitment to so-called human values that obscures the real conflict of interest between the oppressors and the oppressed, and especially between women and men. Viewed from the standpoint of women, liberal feminism is not impartial, comprehensive nor conformable with the experience of many groups of women. It is therefore inadequate as a feminist theory.

Although traditional Marxism is in many ways a contrast with liberalism, it shares some of the same assumptions. Like liberalism, traditional Marxism assumes that certain activities, such as childbearing and -rearing, housework and sexual activity, are more "natural" and less "human" than the making of physical objects. Like liberalism, therefore, although in a different way, traditional Marxism excludes these activities from serious political consideration by excluding them from the realm of political economy. Like liberalism's categories, the categories of traditional Marxism are apparently gender-neutral and, like those of liberalism, they divert attention away from men's domination of women. From the standpoint of women, therefore, traditional interpretations of Marxism are also inadequate as feminist theory. Rather than being impartial, they promote masculine interests; rather than being comprehensive, they systematically exclude important aspects of human life; and rather than being tested in experience, they disregard the experience of women.

Radical feminism is the first theory to recognize explicitly the need for a total reconceptualization of reality from the standpoint of women. It demonstrates the concealed masculine bias in the conceptual frameworks and dualisms that traditional political theory has used to justify the subordination of women. Its insight that the personal is political provides the basis for a political theory that is truly comprehensive rather than arbitrarily excluding "women's sphere." Radical feminism expresses the changes of attitude and consciousness that are needed to represent reality from the standpoint of women. In constructing this representation, however, many versions of American radical feminism are held back by assumptions unconsciously absorbed from the dominant culture: their theory shows tendencies toward biologism, toward idealism and toward the false universalization of women's experience. The effect of these tendencies is to minimize the effects of racism, classism and imperialism on women's lives, to encourage giving priority to "cultural" efforts to bring about social change and to eternalize the conflict of interest between women and men. As it currently exists in the United States, therefore, radical feminist theory tends to represent the standpoint only of certain relatively privileged women, rather than of all women. Nevertheless, if radical feminists were to recognize and explicitly renounce the assumptions that I have identified, as some are beginning to do, it is probable that radical feminist insights could be elaborated into a systematic reconceptualization of the world that truly represented the standpoint of women.

Such a development, in effect, is the theoretical project of socialist feminism. Since I have distinguished between radical and socialist feminism primarily in terms of their different methods, a change in the methodological assumptions of radical feminism may make this distinction no longer tenable. In the meantime, I think that socialist feminism offers the best available representation of reality from the standpoint of women. Its ideals and categories are designed to overcome the narrowness and masculine bias of prevailing theory by drawing directly on women's experience of their lives and labor. As we have seen, the socialist feminist analysis is incomplete and leaves many questions unanswered. Even so, it offers us the vision of a new society based on a much more comprehensive and less biased conception of what constitutes fully human activity. . . . Socialist feminism shows that to reconstruct reality from the standpoint of women requires a far more total transformation of our society and of ourselves than is dreamt of by a masculinist philosophy.

NOTES

1. On some interpretations of Marxism, the physical or "hard" sciences are exempted from this characterization. They are seen as being "objectively" true, and their fundamental categories are not thought to be tied to the social context from which they emerged. While the writings of Marx and Engels provide some evidence to support this positivistic interpretation, I believe that such an interpretation runs counter to the overriding epistemological orientation of Marxism. . . .

2. Barbara Winslow, "Women's Alienation and Revolutionary Politics" (a review of Anne Foreman, *Femininity as Alienation*), *International Socialism* 4 (Spring 1979): 9.

3. Nancy Hartsock, "Feminist Theory and the Development of Revolutionary Strategy," in Zillah R. Eisenstein, ed., *Capitalist Patriarchy and the Case for Socialist Feminism* (New York: Monthly Review Press, 1979), p. 59.

4. Mary Daly, *Gyn-Ecology: The Metaethics of Radical Feminism* (Boston: Beacon Press, 1978), p. 11.

5. Nancy Hartsock, "Fundamental Feminism: Process and Perspective," *Quest: A Feminist Quarterly*, 2, no. 2 (Fall 1975): 73.

6. Gerri Perreault, "Futuristic World Views: Modern Physics and Feminism. Implications for Teaching/Learning in Higher Education," pp. 15–16. This paper was presented at the Second Annual Conference of the World Future Society—Educational Section, October 18, 1979.

7. Robin Morgan, *Going Too Far: The Personal Chronicle of a Feminist* (New York: Random House, 1977), p. 14.

8. Daly, *Gyn-Ecology*, p. 401.

9. *Ibid.*, p. 405.

10. Dorothy Smith, "A Sociology for Women," in *The Prism of Sex: Essays in the Sociology of Knowledge* (Madison: University of Wisconsin Press, 1979), p. 166.

11. Nancy Hartsock, "The Feminist Standpoint: Developing the Ground for a Specifically Feminist Historical Materialism," in M. Hintikka and S. Harding, eds., *Discovering Reality: Feminist Perspectives on Epistemology, Metaphysics, Methodology and the Philosophy of Science* (Dordrecht: Reidel, 1983), p. 23 of typescript.

Ethics   4

$\mathbf{W}$hile your journey down the path of thinking about your self-identity could easily have led you to the path of thinking about creation and reality, it could also have led you to the path that we are about to consider, the path of ethical or moral thinking. It is easy to conceive that thinking about who you are could easily lead to questions about what you ought to do. Indeed, in the history of philosophy, this transition is often made. Deliberations about the nature of being human frequently lead to deliberations about the nature of ethics or morality.

Whether or not you were led to this latter path during your journey down the path of thinking about your self-identity, you have no doubt been on the path of ethical or moral thinking many times. At a very early age you were probably taught a set of rules dealing with how you were expected to act in certain circumstances. For example, your parents may have told you not to hit your little sister or brother. Or they may have told you that you had to share your toys with the friends that came over to your house to play. In addition to moral rules dealing with individual types of activity or particular people, you may also have been taught some more general ethical rules or principles. In Western society, some of the best-known general moral rules include the Ten Commandments and the golden rule, "Do unto others as you would have them do unto you."

As a child, you may have merely accepted these particular rules or general principles because of the authority of the person who taught them. (Of course, that didn't mean you always followed them.) At some point in your life, however, you probably asked yourself why you should follow these rules and not others. For example, you may have asked yourself why you shouldn't hit your little brother, especially if he was really bugging you. You might have even reasoned that a better moral rule would be "Never hit your little brother, unless he really deserves it."

Even if you never engaged in the type of moral reasoning described in the preceding paragraph, you probably had occasion to observe that not everyone was taught the same set of moral rules that you were. While your first reaction to this observation may have been merely to claim that your rules were obviously the right ones and the other person's rules were obviously wrong, deeper reflection may have shaken this initial confidence. You might have wondered exactly what it was that made your moral rules or principles the right ones and those that differed from yours the wrong ones.

Questions such as this have been as important in the history of philosophy as have questions about the nature of self-identity, the nature of creation and reality, and the nature of knowledge and truth. For example, the ancient Greek philosopher Socrates, who was mentioned in the introduction to Chapter 1 of this book, was extremely interested in the nature of morality. Indeed, in Plato's dialogues in which he often appears, Socrates is portrayed as the Athenian gadfly who goes about stinging his fellow citizens out of their moral complacency. In addition, we are also told that Socrates' quest for the good life, the only type of life that he considered worth living, ultimately led to his arrest, trial, and execution. Of course, being the philosophical hero that he was, Socrates remained loyal to his moral principles to the very end.

But this concern with moral questions and principles, which has been a major focus of Western thinking, did not originate with Socrates. Indeed, it was already evident in the earlier writings of Judaism, a religion that is often characterized by its concern with ethical principles and rules. One has only to glance at the so-called priestly writings, the last part of Exodus, all of Leviticus, Numbers, and Deuteronomy, to discover a host of moral commandments and regulations. Likewise, a cursory reading of the "Sermon on the Mount" shows that this Judeo-Socratic concern with the ethical dimension of human existence was just as important to Jesus as it was to Socrates and the authors of the priestly writings. A similarly cursory reading of the history of Western philosophy shows that the concern with ethics preoccupied, to one extent or another, most of the other major philosophical writers. From Aristotle's golden mean to Kant's categorical imperative, from Ayer's emotivism to Singer's call for animal liberation, traditional Western philosophers have attempted to formulate ethical theories and/or to resolve moral problems.

In the selections in this chapter, we see clearly that this concern with the ethical dimension of human existence is found in nontraditional writings as well. Indeed, all of these selections represent attempts to formulate ethical principles and/or to revise moral theory. Most of them also, to one extent or another, offer criticisms of the traditional moral theories with which we are most familiar. Whereas much of traditional Western ethical thinking has been anthropocentric, that is, has focused principally on humans as subjects of moral concern, the first two selections in this chapter suggest that our moral concern ought to extend to all living things, even to the earth itself. The next two selections criticize the Western tendency to view the world solely from the standpoint of natural science, a standpoint that reduces the world to an objective reality that stands outside of subjective experience. While the authors of these two selections do not agree on the nature of morality, Korn's notion of creative freedom and Radhakrishnan's claim that morality must be linked with mysticism are clearly intended as alternatives to certain Western ways of viewing the nature of morality.

The last three selections in this chapter, the selections by Gilligan, Daly, and Bunch, consist of critiques of traditional morality from the standpoint of women. Each of these writers also offers her own vision of the type of morality that should displace the male-dominated or patriarchal morality that currently exists. Gilligan argues that the traditional Western emphasis on individual rights has been used to deny equality to women and to devalue certain desirable moral traits, such as concern, caring, and community. However, she believes that now that women have achieved equal rights with men, the ethics of rights need not be viewed as oppressive to women. On the contrary, she claims that an ethics of rights can complement an ethics of care. In contrast to Gilligan, both Daly and Bunch argue that traditional Western morality is beyond redemption. Daly claims that traditional Western morality is inextricably linked to rape, genocide, and war, while Bunch adds that it inevitably leads to a logic of oppression. For this reason, both writers call for a transformation of human consciousness and experience, a transformation that will allow us to displace traditional morality with a morality free from domination or oppression.

Ahimsa: Respect for Life   4.1

FROM THE JAIN SCRIPTURES

The religion of Jainism arose in India in the sixth century B.C.E., at approximately the same time as Buddhism. Its founder was reportedly a man named Nataputta Vardhamana who was given the title "Mahavira," literally "great hero," by his followers. Many of the claims about the Mahavira's life are similar to those concerning the Buddha. Being the son of a minor ruler like the Buddha, the Mahavira also reportedly led a life of great luxury. Yet, also like the Buddha, he was not comforted by material wealth or social status. He thus renounced courtly life and sought a religious path to "salvation." Unlike the Buddha, however, the Mahavira found his answer in an extreme form of asceticism. This asceticism was coupled with a strong resolve not to injure life in any of its forms. Thus one of the popular images of the Jain monk shows him sweeping the path in front of him, so that he will not step on any of the crawling creatures that may lie in his way.

The depth of the Jain respect for life is expressed in the following selection, which is taken from the *Akaranga-sutra*. One of the striking features of this brief statement of Jain ethical principles is the fact that it lacks any element of anthropocentrism. Whereas most ancient ethical theories found in the West focus primarily on humans and human interests, Jain respect for life extends to all living creatures, even to the earth itself.

Questions for Thought

1. What exactly does the term *ahimsa* mean? Can you think of any Western ethical concept analogous to *ahimsa*?
2. What do you think the writer means by saying that "there are many souls embodied in water"? How is the concept of soul used in this selection?
3. In what ways, according to this writer, are plants and humans alike? Do you think you have anything in common with a plant? If so, what?
4. Do you agree with this writer that nonhuman animals deserve as much respect as humans? Why or why not?
5. Can you think of any good reasons why we should respect the earth? If so, what are the best ways to show this respect for the earth?
6. How is the concept of reciprocity used in this selection? How does this Jain concept compare with and differ from the golden rule?

EARTH IS AFFLICTED AND WRETCHED, IT IS HARD to teach, it has no discrimination. Unenlightened men, who suffer from the effects of past deeds, cause great pain in a world full of pain already, for in earth souls are individually embodied. If, thinking to gain praise, honor, or respect . . . or to achieve a good rebirth . . . or to win salvation, or to escape pain, a man sins against earth or causes or permits others to do so, . . . he will not gain joy or wisdom. . . . Injury to the earth is like striking, cutting, maiming, or killing a blind man. . . . Knowing this man should not sin against earth or cause or permit others to do so. He who understands the nature of sin against earth is called a true sage who understands karma. . . .

And there are many souls embodied in water. Truly water . . . is alive. . . . He who injures the lives in water does not understand the nature of sin or renounce it. . . . Knowing this, a man should not sin against water, or cause or permit others to do so. He who understands the nature of sin against water is called a true sage who understands karma. . . .

By wicked or careless acts one may destroy fire-beings, and moreover, harm other beings by means of fire. . . . For there are creatures living in earth, grass, leaves, wood, cowdung, or dustheaps, and jumping creatures which . . . fall into a fire if they come near it. If touched by fire, they shrivel up . . . lose their senses, and die. . . . He who understands the nature of sin in respect of fire is called a true sage who understands karma.

And just as it is the nature of a man to be born and grow old, so is it the nature of a plant to be born and grow old. . . . One is endowed with reason, and so is the other; one is sick, if injured, and so is the other; one grows larger and so does the other; one changes with time, and so does the other. . . . He who understands the nature of sin against plants is called a true sage who understands karma. . . .

All beings with two, three, four, or five senses, . . . in fact all creation, know individually pleasure and displeasure, pain, terror, and sorrow. All are full of fears which come from all directions. And yet there exist people who would cause greater pain to them. . . . Some kill animals for sacrifice, some for their skin, blood, . . . feathers, teeth, or tusks; . . . some kill them intentionally and some unintentionally; some kill because they have been previously injured by them, . . . and some because they expect to be

From *Sources of Indian Tradition*, ed. by William T. de Bary. Reprinted by permission of Columbia University Press.

injured. He who harms animals has not understood or renounced deeds of sin. . . . He who understands the nature of sin against animals is called a true sage who understands karma. . . .

A man who is averse from harming even the wind knows the sorrow of all things living. . . . He who knows what is bad for himself knows what is bad for others, and he who knows what is bad for others knows what is bad for himself.

This reciprocity should always be borne in mind. Those whose minds are at peace and who are free from passions do not desire to live [at the expense of others]. . . . He who understands the nature of sin against wind is called a true sage who understands karma.

In short he who understands the nature of sin in respect of all the six types of living beings is called a true sage who understands karma.

Mitakuye Oyasin: We Are All Related   4.2

ED MCGAA, EAGLE MAN

Ed McGaa, Eagle Man (b. 1936), was born on the Pine Ridge Reservation and received his early education in missionary schools. After earning an undergraduate degree in biology, he became a fighter pilot in the Marine Corps and volunteered for combat duty in Vietnam. As preparation for combat, he was called by Fools Crow, the Oglala holy man, for a warrior's preparation ceremony. After returning from Vietnam, Ed McGaa earned a law degree from the University of South Dakota, danced in several Oglala Sun Dances, and wrote a biography of the Oglala chief, Red Cloud.

In *Mother Earth Spirituality: Native American Paths to Healing Ourselves and Our World*, from which the following selection is taken, McGaa gives the following account of how he acquired his natural name: "Ben Black Elk, the interpreter of *Black Elk Speaks*, named me as a boy, *Wanblee Hoksila* (Eagle Boy). Later, when I became a fighter pilot and a warrior who returned to dance the Sun Dance, Ben, Bill Eagle Feather, and the Sun Dance chief, Fools Crow, named me *Wanblee Wichasha* (Eagle Man)." Eagle Man has recently published another work entitled *Rainbow Tribe: Ordinary People Journeying on the Red Road* (HarperCollins, 1992).

Throughout this selection, Eagle Man contrasts the value system of the European immigrants who came to America with the value system of the Native Americans. He notes that the European value system was based on conquest and acquisition, whereas the Native American value system was based on respect and sharing. As in the Benally selection reprinted in Chapter 3 of this text, Eagle Man discusses the importance of the four cardinal directions, and the good things that come from each of them. Tied in with the goods derived from the four directions are the four ethical commandments given by the Great Spirit: respect for the earth, for the Great Spirit, for our fellow humans, and for individual freedom. These four commandments are summarized in the concept of *Mitakuye Oyasin*, a concept that implies that we are interrelated to all living things as an extended family. This concept is, of course, quite similar to the Jain concept of *ahimsa* that was described in the preceding selection.

Questions for Thought

1. What are Eagle Man's main criticisms of European culture and values? What, if anything, does he praise about European culture?
2. How do the four commandments given by the Great Spirit compare with and differ from the ten commandments given by Yahweh or God?
3. Why, according to Eagle Man, is it crucial that humans accept some of the values taught by Native Americans? Do you agree with his analysis?
4. What is Eagle Man's attitude toward possessions? How do his views on this matter compare with your own?
5. What exactly does the concept of *Mitakuye Oyasin* mean? Do you think that this is an important ethical concept? Why or why not?
6. What do you think is the most important moral value? What makes this value so important?

THE PLIGHT OF THE NON-INDIAN WORLD IS THAT it has lost respect for Mother Earth, from whom and where we all come.

We all start out in this world as tiny seeds— no different from our animal brothers and sisters, the deer, the bear, the buffalo, or the trees, the flowers, the winged people. Every particle of our bodies comes from the good things Mother Earth has put forth. Mother Earth is our real mother, because every bit of us truly comes from her, and daily she takes care of us.

The tiny seed takes on the minerals and the waters of Mother Earth. It is fueled by *Wiyo*, the sun, and given spirit by *Wakan Tanka*.

This morning at breakfast we took from Mother Earth to live, as we have done every day of our lives. But did we thank her for giving us the means to live? The old Indian did. When he drove his horse in close to a buffalo running at full speed across the prairie, he drew his bowstring back and said as he did so, "Forgive me, brother, but my people must live." After he butchered the buffalo, he took the skull and faced it toward the setting sun as a thanksgiving and an acknowledgment that all things come from Mother Earth. He brought the meat back to camp and gave it first to the old, the widowed, and the weak. For thousands of years great herds thrived across the continent because the Indian never took more than he needed. Today, the buffalo is gone.

You say *ecology*. We think the words *Mother Earth* have a deeper meaning. If we wish to survive, we must respect her. It is very late, but there is still time to revive and discover the old American Indian value of respect for Mother Earth. She is very beautiful, and already she is showing us signs that she may punish us for not respecting her. Also, we must remember she has been placed in this universe by the one who is the All Powerful, the Great Spirit Above, or *Wakan Tanka*—God. But a few years ago, there lived on the North American continent people, the American Indians, who knew a respect and

Selected excerpts from pp. 203–209 from *Mother Earth Spirituality* by Ed McGaa.
© 1990 by Ed McGaa. Reprinted by permission of HarperCollins Publishers, Inc.

value system that enabled them to live on their native grounds without having to migrate, in contrast to the white brothers and sisters who migrated by the thousands from their homelands because they had developed a value system different from that of the American Indian. There is no place now to which we can migrate, which means we can no longer ignore the red man's value system.

Carbon-dating techniques say that the American Indian has lived on the North American continent for thousands upon thousands of years. If we did migrate, it was because of a natural phenomenon—a glacier. We did not migrate because of a social system, value system, and spiritual system that neglected its responsibility to the land and all living things. We Indian people say we were always here.

We, the American Indian, had a way of living that enabled us to live within the great, complete beauty that only the natural environment can provide. The Indian tribes had a common value system and a commonality of religion, without religious animosity, that preserved that great beauty that the two-leggeds definitely need. Our four commandments from the Great Spirit are: (1) respect for Mother Earth, (2) respect for the Great Spirit, (3) respect for our fellow man and woman, and (4) respect for individual freedom (provided that individual freedom does not threaten the tribe or the people or Mother Earth).

We who respect the great vision of Black Elk see the four sacred colors as red, yellow, black, and white. They stand for the four directions—red for the east, yellow for the south, black for the west, and white for the north.

From the east comes the rising sun and new knowledge from a new day.

From the south will come the warming south winds that will cause our Mother to bring forth the good foods and grasses so that we may live.

To the west where the sun goes down, the day will end, and we will sleep; and we will hold our spirit ceremonies at night, from where we will communicate with the spirit world beyond. The sacred color of the west is black; it stands for the deep intellect that we will receive from the spirit ceremonies. From the west come the life-giving rains.

From the north will come the white winter snow that will cleanse Mother Earth and put her to sleep, so that she may rest and store up energy to provide the beauty and bounty of springtime. We will prepare for aging by learning to create, through our arts and crafts, during the long winter season. Truth, honesty, strength, endurance, and courage also are represented by the white of the north. Truth and honesty in our relationships bring forth harmony.

All good things come from these sacred directions. These sacred directions, or four sacred colors, also stand for the four races of humanity: red, yellow, black, and white. We cannot be a prejudiced people, because all men and women are brothers and sisters and because we all have the same mother—Mother Earth. One who is prejudiced, who hates another because of that person's color, hates what the Great Spirit has put here. Such a one hates that which is holy and will be punished, even during this lifetime, as humanity will be punished for violating Mother Earth. Worse, one's conscience will follow into the spirit world, where it will be discovered that all beings are equal. This is what we Indian people believe.

We, the Indian people, also believe that the Great Spirit placed many people throughout this planet: red, yellow, black, and white. What about the brown people? The brown people evolved from the sacred colors coming together. Look at our Mother Earth. She, too, is brown because the four directions have come together. After the Great Spirit, *Wakan Tanka*, placed them in their respective areas, the *Wakan Tanka* appeared to each people in a different manner and taught them ways so that they might live in harmony and true beauty. Some men, some tribes, some nations have still retained the teachings of the

Great Spirit. Others have not. Unfortunately, many good and peaceful religions have been assailed by narrow-minded zealots. Our religious beliefs and our traditional Indian people have suffered the stereotype that we are pagans, savages, or heathens; but we do not believe that only one religion controls the way to the spirit world that lies beyond. We believe that *Wakan Tanka* loves all of its children equally, although the Great Spirit must be disturbed at times with those children who have destroyed proven value systems that practiced sharing and generosity and kept Mother Earth viable down through time. We kept Mother Earth viable because we did not sell her or our spirituality!

Brothers and sisters, we must go back to some of the old ways if we are going to truly save our Mother Earth and bring back the natural beauty that every person seriously needs, especially in this day of vanishing species, vanishing rain forests, overpopulation, poisoned waters, acid rain, a thinning ozone layer, drought, rising temperatures, and weapons of complete annihilation.

Weapons of complete annihilation? Yes, that is how far the obsession with war has taken us. These weapons are not only hydraheaded; they are hydroheaded as well, meaning that they are the ultimate in hydrogen bomb destruction. We will have to divert our obsession with defense and wasteful, all-life-ending weapons of war to reviving our environment. . . .

The quest for peace can be more efficiently pursued through communication and knowledge than by stealth and unending superior weaponry. If the nations of the world scale back their budgets for weaponry, we will have wealth to spend to solve our serious environmental problems. Our home planet is under attack. It is not an imagined problem. This calamity is upon us now. We are in a real war with the polluting, violating blue man of Black Elk's vision.

Chief Sitting Bull advised us to take the best of the white man's ways and to take the best of the old Indian ways. He also said, "When you find something that is bad, or turns out bad, drop it and leave it alone."[1]

The fomenting of fear and hatred is something that has turned out very badly. This can continue no longer; it is a governmental luxury maintained in order to support pork-barrel appropriations to the Department of Defense, with its admirals and generals who have substituted their patriotism for a defense contractor paycheck after retirement. War has become a business for profit. In the last two wars, we frontline warriors—mostly poor whites and minorities—were never allowed to win our wars, which were endlessly prolonged by the politicians and profiteers, who had their warrior-aged sons hidden safely away or who used their powers, bordering on treason, to keep their offspring out of danger. The wrong was that the patriotic American or the poor had to be the replacement. The way to end wars in this day and age is to do like the Indian: put the chiefs and their sons on the front lines.

Sitting Bull answered a relative, "Go ahead and follow the white man's road and do whatever the [Indian] agent tells you. But I cannot so easily give up my old ways and Indian habits; they are too deeply ingrained in me."[2]

My friends, I will never cease to be an Indian. I will never cease respecting the old Indian values, especially our four cardinal commandments and our values of generosity and sharing. It is true that many who came to our shores brought a great amount of good to this world. Modern medicine, transportation, communication, and food production are but a few of the great achievements that we should all appreciate. But it is also true that too many of those who migrated to North America became so greedy and excessively materialistic that great harm has been caused. We have seen good ways and bad ways. The good way of the non-Indian way I am going to keep. The very fact that we can hold peace-seeking communication and that world leaders meet and communicate for peace shows the wisdom of the brothers and sisters of this time. By all means, good technology should not be curtailed, but care must be taken lest our water, air, and earth become irreparably harmed. The good ways I will always respect and support. But, my brothers and sisters, I say we must give up this obsession with excess consumption and materialism, especially when it causes the harming of the skies surrounding our Mother and the pollution of the waters upon her. *She is beginning to warn us!*

Keep those material goods that you need to exist, but be a more sharing and generous person. You will find that you can do with less. Replace this empty lifestyle of hollow impressing of the shallow ones with active participation for your Mother Earth. At least then, when you depart into the spirit world, you can look back with pride and fulfillment. Other spirit beings will gather around you, other spirits of your own higher consciousness will gather around you and share your satisfaction with you. The eternal satisfaction of knowing you did not overuse your Mother Earth and that you were here to protect her will be a powerful satisfaction when you reach the spirit world.

Indian people do not like to say that the Great Mystery is exactly this or exactly that, but we do know there is a spirit world that lies beyond. We are allowed to know that through our ceremonies. We know nothing of hell-fire and eternal damnation from some kind of unloving power that placed us here as little children. None of that has ever been shown to us in our powerful ceremonies, conducted by kind, considerate, proven, and very nonmaterialistic leaders. We do know that everything the Great Mystery makes is in the form of a circle. Our Mother Earth is a very large, powerful circle.

Therefore, we conclude that our life does not end. A part of it is within that great circle. If there is a hell, then our concept of hell would be an eternal knowing that one violated or took and robbed from Mother Earth and caused this suffering that is being bestowed upon the generations unborn. This then, if it were to be imprinted upon one's eternal conscience, this would surely be a terrible, spiritual, mental hell. Worse, to have harmed and hurt one's innocent fellow beings, and be unable to alter (or conceal) the harmful

actions would also be a great hell. Truth in the spirit world will not be concealed, nor will it be for sale. Lastly, we must realize that the generations unborn will also come into the spirit world. Let us be the ones that they wish to thank and congratulate, rather than eternally scorn.

While we are shedding our overabundant possessions, and linking up with those of like minds, and advancing spiritual and environmental appreciations, we should develop a respect for the aged and for family-centered traditions, even those who are single warriors, fighting for the revitalization of our Mother on a lone, solitary, but vital front. We should have more respect for an extended family, which extends beyond a son or daughter, goes beyond to grandparents and aunts and uncles, goes beyond to brothers, sisters, aunts, and uncles that we have adopted or made as relatives—and further beyond, to the animal or plant world as our brothers and sisters, to Mother Earth and Father Sky and then above to *Wakan Tanka*, the *Unci/Tankashilah*, the Grandparent of us all. When we pray directly to the Great Spirit, we say *Unci* (Grandmother) or *Tankashilah* (Grandfather) because we are so family-minded that we think of the Great Power above as a grandparent, and we are the grandchildren. Of course, this is so because every particle of our being is from Mother Earth, and our energy and life force are fueled by Father Sky. This is a vital part of the great, deep feeling and spiritual psychology that we have as Indian people. It is why we preserved and respected our ecological environment for such a long period. *Mitakuye oyasin!* We are all related!

In conclusion, our survival is dependent on the realization that Mother Earth is a truly holy being, that all things in this world are holy and must not be violated, and that we must share and be generous with one another. You may call this thought by whatever fancy words you wish—psychology, theology, sociology, or philosophy—but you must think of Mother Earth as a living being. Think of your fellow men and women as holy people who were put here by the Great

Spirit. Think of being related to all things! With this philosophy in mind as we go on with our environmental ecology efforts, our search for spirituality, and our quest for peace, we will be far more successful when we truly understand the Indians' respect for Mother Earth.

NOTES

1. John F. McBride, *Modern Indian Psychology* (Vermillion, SD: University of South Dakota, Indian Studies Department, 1971), p. 1.

2. David Humphreys Miller, *Ghost Dance* (Lincoln, NE: University of Nebraska Press, 1959), p. 65.

4.3   Creative Freedom

ALEJANDRO KORN

Alejandro Korn (1860–1936) was born in San Vicente, Argentina. After attending medical school where he specialized in psychiatry, Korn practiced medicine for several years, eventually becoming the director of a hospital for the insane. After discovering the works of Schopenhauer, Korn became more and more interested in philosophy and less and less interested in the practice of psychiatry. This change of direction in his life eventually led him to become a member of the School of Philosophy and Letters of Buenos Aires in 1906. Korn, who described himself as having "a Latin mind and a German heart," then dedicated himself to teaching and to developing his own distinctive philosophical views. These views were mapped out in his three principal philosophical works: *La libertad creadora* ("Creative Freedom"), *Axiología* ("Axiology"), and *Apuntes filosóficos* ("Notes on Philosophy"). Korn is also known for his important cultural history of Argentina, *Influencias filosóficas en la evolución nacional* ("Philosophic Influences in the Evolution of the Nation").

In the following selection from his collected works, Korn uses a sophisticated conception of the nature of consciousness to support his contention that creative freedom is the ultimate sanction and goal of human existence. Rejecting both subjectivism and realism, Korn argues that the subjective and the objective are poles within consciousness, and that human existence is characterized by continual movement from one pole to the other. Whereas philosophical analysis may attempt to isolate the purely subjective or the purely objective, Korn insists that all such attempts distort the true nature of consciousness and reality. Such attempts also pervert the true nature of human action and morality—on the one hand by suggesting that values are purely subjective and therefore relative, or on the other hand by claiming that values are purely objective and therefore transcendental.

In opposition to such distortions, Korn claims that the sanction of moral values is found within consciousness, but that it is nonetheless common to all human beings. This shared moral situation is the continuous struggle to maintain freedom in the face of both external and internal obstacles. In other words, he argues that morality requires that we achieve dominion over the external world (what he calls "economic freedom") and that we achieve dominion over our internal drives and desires (what he calls "ethical freedom"). Unlike certain philosophers who would assert that one might achieve ethical freedom even if one were economically oppressed, Korn asserts that there can be no true ethical freedom without economic freedom. Unlike other philosophers who claim that the reason for being moral lies in some eternal reward, Korn claims that morality carries its own justification. The person who struggles to actualize his or her freedom and the freedom of others, the person who is indeed guided by the principle of creative freedom, is the person who is truly fulfilled.

Questions for Thought

1. How does Korn describe the nature of consciousness? Does his description seem accurate to you?
2. Why does Korn reject the concept of reality? Do you think that the concept of reality makes sense? If so, how would you describe it?
3. Do you agree with Korn's claim that there can be no ethical freedom without economic freedom? Why or why not?
4. How would you define human freedom? To what extent are you truly free?
5. What does Korn mean when he says that "an ethics without sanction is an absurd concept"? What constitutes moral sanction for Korn?
6. Do you believe that we can clearly distinguish between moral and immoral acts? If so, on what basis is this distinction drawn?

Consciousness and Reality

NO SOPHISTRY CAN ABOLISH THE FUNDAMENTAL distinction between the I and the not-I, between the subjective and the objective orders. Such an absurdity never occurred to the Greeks, despite their having exhausted almost every possible philosophical position. It was Descartes, who, identifying thought with the I, inoculated modern philosophy with that pernicious germ, which soon proliferated monstrously in the German idealistic systems. They confound consciousness with my consciousness, take the part for the whole—thus making possible the conclusion that "life is a dream," that the world is only the "veil of Maya" or the "cinematographic film" which passes through our consciousness.

It is the merit of the realistic schools that they opposed this fallacious conception. In demonstrating the independence of object and subject they celebrate their worthiest triumph, because they base themselves upon an indisputable fact of consciousness. Unfortunately, they hasten to negative it by trying to submit the subject to a noumenal world. Certainly, the objective world is outside the I, but it is not outside of the consciousness. When we call something external, we refer ourselves to the I and not to an uncognizable reality. Why must we substitute an imagined reality for known reality?

In truth, consciousness expands into two orders—the one objective, the other subjective. We cannot say more about what we know, but we know this in an immediate and final fashion.

From *Contemporary Latin-American Philosophy*, trans. by Willard R. Trask, pp. 54–67. Reprinted by permission of University of New Mexico Press.

Consciousness and Duality

Apparently the cognoscitive capacity should precede cognition, but in fact the latter is equally inconceivable without the cognizable. Cognition consists precisely in the act of cognizing and cannot precede itself. Subject and object in isolation are abstractions, the one does not exist without the other. When conscious activity is polarized, it opposes the one to the other, but without ceasing to keep them united by mutual relations, which are necessarily both subjective and objective in nature. Here there is neither an *a priori* nor an *a posteriori*; there is a confluence and a concordance, a simultaneous common action which the most subtle abstraction could not accurately report.

Hence ratiocination can deduce the necessary concepts both of the subjective order and of the objective order, with equally valid arguments. Here, as always, confusion is introduced by the egocentric error, which regards cognition as a function of the I instead of seeing that cognition is equivalent to the content of the consciousness in its totality. Hence the sterile disquisitions of realism and of subjective idealism. Evident as it is that being is identical with thinking, it is equally so that thinking is not exclusively subjective.

The precise line of demarcation between the two orders, the subjective and the objective, is an interesting psychological subject; its satisfactory solution is highly problematic. We know perfectly well what, *grosso modo*, falls on one side or the other: sensations on the one hand, affections, volitions, and judgments on the other. But to distinguish matter and form in the consciousness, and to attribute the latter to the subject, is hazardous. The form is as necessary a part of the object as its matter. In the language of Kant, and contradicting him, we would say: we are given the matter, and also the form.

The subject distinguishes what is its own from what is foreign to it and does not attribute to itself the function of giving form to cognition, as for example, it attributes attention to itself. This is not a naive impression which could be corrected, because we never acquire the immediate consciousness of such a capacity. It appears to me that the matter of cognition is no more than a shadow of the material matter of realist dualism: pure sensations do not exist.

The old scholastic distinction between the material and formal elements of cognition reduces itself to abstracting the primary from the secondary elements; but both together constitute the objective order opposed to the I. The psychic process takes place in its own forms, not through intervention of the subject, but necessarily; and perhaps despite the subject. What characterizes the objective order and distinguishes it from the subjective order is spatiality.

Reality and Actuality

So far, we have worked with an equivocal concept, and it must now be abandoned. The term reality comes from the Latin *res* (thing) and involves the idea of stability. But the fact is that there is nothing stable. In consciousness we observe only a process, an action, a becoming, a flowing and meeting which are continuous. If we do not keep this fact in mind, we run the risk of again postulating things and entities where there are only acts. Subject and object are nothing but synthetic operations in which the complex of psychic states or the fascicle of sensations is unified. As for the *substratum* which we suppose for them—matter or spirit—it is only a concept and not a thing.

In place of reality, then, we have an actuality, and this is the right word, which Aristotle taught us. Events are actualized, not realized. Consciousness itself is not an entity, but action, and not even abstract action, but concrete action. A pure consciousness would be a consciousness without content, that is, an action without activity—a perfect example of absurdity. We must cure ourselves of all realism, not only of naive realism.

Reality, in philosophy, is a fossil concept, that is, a superstition. Let us reserve the word, with an agreed value, especially to distinguish the indubitable event from the imagined or desired event. To be logical, a philosophical treatise should be written entirely in verbs, without using a single substantive.

The rigidity of nouns, their excessive solidity and compactness, does not lend itself to transmitting the idea of a dynamic process which is movement, vibration, unfolding of energies and rhythms. Around the two poles of consciousness, themselves mobile and unstable, contrary or parallel currents gyrate in ebullition, are reconciled or resist one another and at every moment create a new event which never existed before and will not be repeated. The need to systematize the mass of events makes it necessary to isolate them, to pigeonhole them, and with them the psychic process is deprived precisely of this synthetic life, in which each element is a function of all the others. The reader's intuition must continuously maintain the unity and correlation which the account destroys, because analysis necessarily converts the active unity of cogitation into the discrete series of the cogitated and replaces living reality with bygone phantoms.

Necessity and Freedom

If the only difference between objective and subjective activity were spatiality, it would, though extremely difficult, be possible to subordinate the one to the other, as the monistic systems have so perseveringly attempted to do. In reality there is a much more basic difference between these two opposed currents of conscious activity.

The objective world obeys necessary norms, obeys laws. The subjective world is without laws, is free. In the former, a series of necessary events, which can be foreseen, unrolls mechanically. In the latter there acts a will which seeks what it desires and whose resolves cannot be foreseen. The former obeys causes lost in the past, the latter ends projected into the future. Confronting the physical mechanism stands the autonomous I. Pray excuse the redundance: *autos* means neither more nor less than the I itself; the autonomy of the I is autonomy par excellence.

The physical order is actualized; it inexorably links an effect to its cause, without purpose, without finality, amoral and insensible. The subject, meanwhile, feels itself agitated by pains and pleasures, affirms or denies, formulates purposes, frames ideals, establishes values, and subordinates its conduct to the ends which it pursues.

But its freedom is to desire, not to accomplish. The free expansion of the will is restrained by the coercion of necessity and the latter permits no infraction of the law. The subject is autonomous, but not sovereign; its power is not equal to its will, and hence it tends ceaselessly to increase it. The aspiration to actualize all its freedom never forsakes the eternal rebel. Nature must submit to the master, and the instrument of this liberation is science and technology.

It is not for freedom to flaunt itself in a vacuum. Kant's dove imagined that, without the resistance of the air, it would fly even higher. It would fall to the ground, as our freedom would do, were it not supported by the resistance which opposes it. This is the condition of subjective endeavor, and freedom does not pretend to abolish it; its sole pretension is to elude coercion in order to attain its own ends. Dominion over the objective order emancipates from material servitude and constitutes economic freedom, in the broadest sense of the term. Its conquest was begun by whomever first broke open the recalcitrant coconut with a stone and invented the hammer.

But the subject feels itself restrained not only by the objective world but also by its own conditions. Its action is disturbed by impulses, affections, and errors. From these too it desires to emancipate itself. To dominion over nature it must, then, add dominion over itself. Only the autarchy, which encloses the will in a discipline established by itself, gives us ethical freedom.

Thus, beside economic finality, there is established a moral finality, to which, without any diminution of self-determination, conduct must submit. It is symbolized in a concept whose content and whose names vary but which for the present we shall call the ethical concept. It comes to be the most perfect expression of the personality, the final objective of free action, engaged in submitting the natural order to a moral order. Though within an unacceptable metaphysics, no one has better described ethical freedom than Spinoza in the fourth and fifth chapters of his fundamental work, which treat, respectively, of servitude and freedom.

Yet what a difference there is between the moral law and the physical law! We suffer the latter, we dictate the former; the latter is the expression of a necessary order, the former a postulate of our free will. We cannot imagine the law of gravity failing in a single instance; when we rise into space and apparently contravene it, we are obeying it. Not so with the moral law which we infringe, because we retain the monstrous capacity of disobeying it.

Indeed, freedom and ethics are correlative concepts. The mechanistic conception, by extending physical determination to the subject, robs it of the privileges of personality. It usurps the place of autonomy; and no parade of dialectics is able, on that basis, to construct an ethics.

Economic freedom, dominion over the objective world, and ethical freedom, dominion over oneself, together constitute human freedom, which, far from being transcendent, is actualized in proportion to our knowledge and capacity. They interpenetrate and presuppose each other, one cannot exist without the other, because both are bases of the unfolding of the personality. It is not the struggle for existence which is the preeminent principle, it is the struggle for freedom; at every turn the former is sacrificed to the latter. Freedom becomes. From

the depths of the consciousness the I emerges like a torso: brow free, arms free, resolved to free the rest.

Economic Freedom and Ethical Freedom

Economic freedom is as fundamental as ethical freedom, but that is no reason for confusing the corresponding concepts. The useful is not always the good, nor the good the useful. One term refers to the object and the other to the subject.

Taking the useful for the good is the aim of every utilitarian ethics and the error proper to those systems which tend to deny autonomous personality. To insist solely upon the ethical concept is not to recognize the fact that the full expansion of the personality is possible only in a subjected world.

The lack of economic freedom leads to rejecting ethical freedom for the mess of pottage, and the absence of ethical freedom surrenders us to the dominion of instincts and dogmas. The lack of both subjects us to powers foreign to ourselves, annihilates our personality, prevents us from living our proper life.

The close correlation between economic freedom and ethical freedom is reflected in language. All the words which express servitude have at the same time a pejorative moral acceptation: slave, villain, lackey, etc. To sweep away all economic subjection is, then, the antecedent condition of freedom. But not the only one.

The desire to discover the basis of our conduct and distinguish the lawful from the unlawful has obsessed the human mind from its first dawnings. In this case too, as in all others, the religious solution was the first. The norms of conduct were put under the protection of divine authority. A vicious aftereffect of this primitive position is the constantly renewed attempt to solve this grave problem by the intervention of transcendent factors. No doubt an ethics supposes, as indispensable elements, a free and responsible subject and a sanction. If the first is lacking, we have only the unfolding of a process determined beforehand, of which we should be useless witnesses; if the second were lacking, it would be a matter of indifference whether we decided for good or for evil. But what have we to do with a metaphysical freedom or with a posthumous sanction, after the individual existence vanishes? The grotesque postulate of an immortality of the individual was a necessary consequence of the transcendental interpretation.

The anti-metaphysical schools, in turn, in pointing out the emptiness of these fictions, attempted the construction of a purely human ethics, but they fell into hedonism or utilitarianism, and the logical development of their deterministic principles led them to a morality without freedom, without responsibility, and without sanction; that is, though they do not admit it, to the negation of ethics. On such bases it is possible to write a manual of good conduct or of rules for obtaining the greatest success in business, but not to clear up the age-old problem which vexes the human soul.

To show that our actual ethical concepts are the result of a biological or social evolution is of the greatest interest, but it has nothing to do with the case. It is not the historical fact of this evolution, but the reason for it that we are investigating, the principle which guides and informs it. All these positivist systems are beside the question.

Biological systematization, in reminding us that we derive from the animal, ought to tell us why we have surpassed the animal and tend to get rid of our animal residuum. Or does it perchance believe that we should return to our original?

The work of the gregarious instinct, the consequences of social existence, are worthy of examination; but to base an ethics upon them is to forget that the social organization of the moral and the immoral is equally strong. This little truth is concealed from sociological moralists, and it would be good for them, from time to time, to reread Rousseau's paradox.

Historical materialism is, beyond doubt, the most coherent and important doctrine of the positivist period, since the influence of Hegel is still perceptible in it. But it is one-sided, it faces only half of the problem, and does not consider that its dogmatic application would strip us of spiritual freedom.

Neither the determinism of the objective world nor the dominion of utilitarian egotism can be denied. But neither can consciousness of our freedom and responsibility be abolished. To seek to abolish this duality is a vain endeavor, is to ignore the psychic conflict in which the human personality struggles in defense of its dignity and in order to gain an increasingly wider freedom. For us to make use of objective determinism is only a pragmatic means of realizing our material freedom. But for us to limit ourselves to that intention is to make ourselves slaves of the machine we have invented. Let us remember the profound saying in the Gospels: "For what shall it profit a man, if he gain the whole world, and lose his own soul?"

Ethics and Sanction

An ethics without a sanction is an absurd concept. It is to suppose acts devoid of finality. Even a utilitarian morality has to suppose that an act brings useful or harmful consequences. Now, are good or evil to be matters of indifference?

No one casts doubt upon the pragmatic effects of error or prudence, of ignorance or knowledge. Our acts, consequently, prove to be efficacious or harmful, and in that fact they carry a very explicit sanction.

As for the ethical act as such, it cannot have a utilitarian sanction, because it would cease to be a pure ethical act. In this it resembles esthetic pleasure, which has no objective utility either. Should we therefore give up being good, or are we to contemn beauty? In these cases the sanction is confined to the domain of the subjective, but it is not therefore less important, since it affects the development of life, and indeed in its most intimate sphere. If the ethical finality is to realize freedom, the sanction of the immoral act is precisely deprivation of freedom, the degradation of human freedom. In turn, the good act contains its reward within itself, that is, in the consciousness of freedom actualized.

Let us remember Spinoza: "I call servitude man's impotence to moderate and govern his affections; for a man carried away by his affections is not under his own dominion but under fortune's; which has such power over him that often, though he sees what is better for him, he does what is worse."

If the useful receives its economic sanction and the ethical its subjective sanction, we must not forget, however, that life is not made up of these abstractions but of the series of concrete acts, which, in varying proportions, are at once useful and ethical. We must not fail to realize to what a degree the ethical nature of the personality influences the solution of practical problems. Through that directing influence, the ethical attitude also has its share in the moral sanction which accompanies every human life.

The intuitive instinct of the people has never ceased to believe that the punishment is in the crime, that he who calls the tune pays the piper, that he who slays with the sword dies by the sword.

When, with a wide experience of life, we contemplate it from a certain elevation, we get the sense of an immanent, an almost inexorable justice, and the balance struck by existence appears as the difference between our virtues and our faults.

This does not imply falling into a cheap optimism or believing that the rewards of virtue or the punishments of vices are continuously distributed, according to the casuistry of a bourgeois code. It is not a matter of an arithmetical relation, or of anything mensurable, but of an intimate fact of consciousness which permits us to verify that, in the conflict of life, it is no mean undertaking to fortify the soul and conquer freedom of spirit. Even before the fortuitous event, it arms us with virile integrity, as the inevitable does the Stoic.

If we related the pain of existence with its faults, we should perhaps discover a compensation, which we shall certainly not consider just in our particular case, but often in the case of others. How many reproaches we utter, which, before a sincere examination of conscience, become reproaches to our own weakness!

There is a close and constant relation between the ethical development of life and the evils that afflict it. In the profound theory of Karma, the world is at every moment the expression of its ethical value. So the Hindus can maintain, because for them the individual I and the universal I are identical. We of the West would be inclined to translate this thought into less mystical language and would say: Life is at every moment the expression of its ethical value. According to the vulgar superstition of transmigration, each lives the Karma of a previous existence; in reality, each lives his own Karma, or, to drop the exotic terminology and use plain everyday language: each is the child of his own works.

Will and Freedom

Long before Darwin announced the "struggle for existence" as the cause of biological development, Schopenhauer believed that he had found the noumenal principle of the universe in the "will to live."

He was undoubtedly right in regarding the will as the most perfect expression of the I. But not in identifying it with cosmic energy, because the subject and the object, which are opposed, cannot be reduced to a single principle except on condition of doing away with one of the two.

In effect, the will—which is a teleological agent—cannot be confused with energy subsumed under the category of causality. Schopenhauer, then, no less than other romanticists whom he so denigrated, is involved in the difficulty of combining the necessity of the phenomenal process with a supposed transcendent freedom.

The will, almost synonymous with the I, belongs entirely to the domain of the subjective, affirms or denies. But it cannot be admitted that in its highest manifestation it is solely will to live, mere affirmation of existence. If fear of relapsing into the old anthropocentric error did not cause the predominance of a tendency to equate man with the animal, the simplest sort of reflection would call to mind how, at every moment, life is sacrificed to a higher value.

This is a historical fact and a fact of daily observation. The very possibility of suicide, which is observed only in the human species, proves that that species can reach the point of negating—and not merely in theory—this supposed fundamental principle. Man, as an individual or as a collectivity, continually hazards existence for motives which may be serious or trifling but which in reality are unnecessary. Indeed, excessive clinging to life, cowardice, is by universal consent evaluated as contemptible.

For the developed mental organization, life has ceased to be an end and is reduced to a means of realizing purposes without which it is not valued. The Stoics knew this in their time; our liberal positivist contemporaries do not know it.

It is not fatuous boasting if man has always considered himself different from the animal or if, at least, he aspires to be different. It is his consciousness of his freedom which reveals itself in this old presumption and which enables him to die for his ideals or his superstitions.

Nietzsche saw clearly in this matter and wished to replace freedom to live by the "will to power," the condition for the development of a superior human type. This concept, however, lends itself to an infamous interpretation, which was never in Nietzsche's mind, despite his affected immoralism. The will to power is nothing but the will to actualize freedom in all its fullness, because, in man, the will to live has risen to be the will to live free. . . .

Freedom as Creative Principle

Conscious action is the alpha and omega, the beginning and the end, the creative energy of the existent. It unrolls the cosmic panorama in the infinite variety of its pictures, and it opposes to it the infinite scale of the most inward emotions. Beyond it nothing is conceivable. It is, then, the absolute, the eternal.

We men, however, know only the inextensive instant between the past and the future; a perpetual and fugitive present. We know only the incessant passing of particular and relative events. Neither the eternal nor the absolute are within our intuition.

If we knew the absolute with certainty, if the essential nexus of events were more than a concept, intellectual tranquillity should pervade us, the last doubt would be hushed, and Being would cease to be a problem. We are witnesses of the action active in consciousness, but we do not know it in itself; we intuit only the process of its manifestations; indeed, even less: the series which unrolls in the individual consciousness. Are we to take this fragment for the universe?

No egolatry has reached that extreme. The evidence of our relativity troubles us too acutely, and aspiration toward the absolute springs up imperiously, like a logical exigency, as a longing of sentiment, as a desired end; never as an actualized fact. No intuition, no empirical datum, no ratiocination illuminates the concept of the absolute for us, though it is the inescapable complement of the relative.

Penned by methodical doubt in the solipsism of the egocentric position, Descartes appeals to our consciousness of our relativity and transfers it to the absolute. He says this in the language of his time and of his principles, and it is possible that, stripped of such contingencies, the argument may be convincing to many.

For our part, we do not run into the embarrassment of solipsism, inevitable for subjective idealism, because we have not identified the I with the totality of the existent. Nevertheless, the difficulty remains, because even though the existence of the absolute be affirmed and believed, we have only its abstract concept, completely empty if we place it outside of the consciousness. It has been given a hundred different names—conclusive proof that we do not know the true one.

In the consciousness, the absolute presents itself as aspiration, as a tendency toward an end which we evaluate as the supreme and ultimate end, as the overcoming of the duality subject–object. In this sense we can base ourselves on the very nature of the conscious process to determine the absolute. We know that this process is a conflict, a ceaseless struggle between freedom and necessity. To actualize absolute freedom by conquering economic do-minion over nature and ethical self-dominion, to subdue necessity to freedom, to attain the full development of one's own personality: this is the goal which is not imposed by outside forces, not invented by the fancy, because it is the very root of becoming.

We struggle for our freedom from the moment we extricate ourselves from the darkness of animality; we continue to assert our right to it. When the conquest is concluded, necessity and freedom will have been conciliated. The consciousness will rest in its own peace, the last doubt will be stilled. But not as yet: philosophy does not have the last word, because life is action, a perpetual task, and not a theorem. *Cosa fatta capo ha.* Theory limps along behind events. But the principle which moves them, we have pointed out: let us call it creative freedom.

4.4   Mysticism and Ethics in Hindu Thought

SARVEPALLI RADHAKRISHNAN

Sarvepalli Radhakrishnan (1888–1975), who was born in south India, held chairs in philosophy at the University of Mysore, at the University of Calcutta, and at Benares Hindu University. In addition, Radhakrishnan taught for many years at Oxford. On returning to India after independence was obtained in 1947, he became very active in Indian political affairs. His political offices included ambassador to the Soviet Union, vice president, and then president of India. Radhakrishnan was also a prolific writer. In his various writings he championed the philosophy of Hinduism and became a strong advocate of the philosophical dialogue between Eastern and Western philosophical traditions. His better-known writings include *Indian Philosophy, The Hindu View of Life*, and *Eastern Religions and Western Thought*. Radhakrishnan was also the co-editor of the widely used *A Sourcebook in Indian Philosophy*, which was published by Princeton University Press in 1957.

In the following selection, which was taken from *Eastern Religions and Western Thought*, Radhakrishnan begins, as Korn did, by arguing that an ethical theory must be grounded on a certain view of the nature of knowledge and reality. However, in opposition to Korn, Radhakrishnan goes on to argue that all attempts to ground ethics in a this-worldly, humanistic metaphysics are destined to fail because they do not take account of the true nature of human existence. In adopting the Hindu conception of self-identity (expressed in the selection from the Upanishads in Chapter 1 of this text), Radhakrishnan claims that human beings contain a divine spark that links them to a reality higher than the reality of the everyday, empirical world. Our connection to this higher, other-worldly reality allows us to attain our highest moral ideals. As Radhakrishnan states, "If goodwill, pure love, and disinterestedness are our ideals [and he thinks they should be], then our ethics must be rooted in other-worldliness." While claiming that this need not lead to either the neglect or the negation of this-worldly life, Radhakrishnan does argue that the empirical world has value only insofar as it is the reflection of the higher spiritual universe. For this reason, the higher moral life requires that we liberate ourselves from "sense addiction" and see the historical process as a "succession of spiritual opportunities."

Questions for Thought

1. How would you describe Radhakrishnan's metaphysics? Do you agree with his claim that "ethical theory must be grounded in metaphysics"?
2. What is the foundation of your own moral views? In what ways, if any, is your foundation similar to that of Radhakrishnan?
3. What are the essential differences between Korn's views and those of Radhakrishnan? Which of them comes closest to your own position?
4. What are Radhakrishnan's principal reasons for claiming that a this-worldly ethics will ultimately prove unsatisfactory? Do you agree with his analysis?
5. Would you describe history as "a succession of spiritual opportunities"? If not, what significance, if any, does the historical process have for you?

ANY ETHICAL THEORY MUST BE GROUNDED IN metaphysics, in a philosophical conception of the relation between human conduct and ultimate reality. As we think ultimate reality to be, so we behave. Vision and action go together. If we believe absurdities, we shall commit atrocities. A self-sufficient humanism has its own metaphysical presuppositions. It requires us to confine our attention to the immediate world of space and time and argues that moral duty consists in conforming to nature and modeling our behavior in accordance with the principles of her working. It attempts to perfect the causes of human life by purely natural means. The subject of ethics is treated as a branch of sociology or a department of psychology. Scientific materialism and mystical nationalism are two types of humanist ethics, interpreted in a narrow sense. They look upon man as a purely natural phenomenon whose outlook is rigorously confined by space and time. They encourage a cynical subservience to nature and historical process and an acquiescence in the merely practicable. Renunciation, self-sacrifice, disinterested service of humanity are not stimulated by the workings of natural law.

An abundance of material things will not help to make life more interesting. The rich of the world are among those who find life stale, flat, and unprofitable. Even the social conscience that

Reprinted from *Eastern Religions and Western Thought* by Sarvepalli Radhakrishnan (2nd ed. 1940) by permission of Oxford University Press.

urges us to extend the benefits of a material civilization cannot be accounted for by the principles of scientific naturalism. The material basis, while essential, is still too narrow for real living. The collective myths of Nazism, Fascism, and Communism propose to make life seem rich and significant by asking us to banish all considerations of reason and humanity and to worship the State. Man is not merely an emotional being. The Nation-State falls short of the human and the universal in man which is postulated with increasing force by the advance of science and which the well-being of human society demands.

The question has its center in the nature of man. Is he only a body which can be fed, clothed, and housed, or is he also a spirit that can aspire? The feeling of frustration experienced even by those who are provided with all the comforts and conveniences which a material civilization can supply indicates that man does not live by bread or emotional excitement alone. Besides, progress is not its own end. If it is the ultimate reality, it cannot ever be completed. We can draw nearer and nearer the goal, but cannot reach it. Its process has neither a beginning nor an end. It starts nowhere and leads nowhere. It has no issue, no goal. Senseless cycles of repetition cannot give meaning to life. It may be argued that, although the universe may have no purpose, items in the universe such as nations and individuals may have their purposes. The rise and fall of nations, the growth and crash of individuals may be quite interesting, and the universe may be viewed as an infinite succession of finite purposes. But this cannot be regarded as a satisfactory goal of ethics. Does not the humanist hope to build a terrestrial paradise inhabited by a perfect race of artists and thinkers? What is the good of telling us that though our sun, moon, and stars will share in the destruction of earthly life, other suns, moons, and stars will arise? We long for a good which is never left behind and never superseded. Man's incapacity to be satisfied with what is merely relative and remain permanently within

the boundaries of the finite and empirical reality cannot be denied. Man stands before the shrine of his own mystery. He enters it the moment he becomes aware of his own eternity. Apart from eternity there is nothing that can, strictly speaking, be called human. A meaningful ethical ideal must be transcendent to the immediate flow of events.

Again, in view of the enigmatic character of the actual, is moral life possible? There are some thinkers who exhort us to do what is right even though we may not know whether it can be realized or not. Moral enthusiasm is possible only if our motive includes the expectation of being able to contribute to the achievement of moral ideals. If we are not certain that active service of the ideals will further their actualization, we cannot be sure of their worthwhileness.

We cannot help asking ourselves whether our ideals are mere private dreams of our own or bonds created by society, or even aspirations characteristic of the human species. Only a philosophy which affirms that they are rooted in the universal nature of things can give depth and fervor to moral life, courage and confidence in moral difficulties. We need to be fortified by the conviction that the service of the ideals is what the cosmic scheme demands of us, that our loyalty or disloyalty to them is a matter of the deepest moment not only to ourselves or to society, or even to the human species, but to the nature of things. If ethical thought is profound, it will give a cosmic motive to morality. Moral consciousness must include a conviction of the reality of ideals. If the latter is religion, then ethical humanism is acted religion. When man realizes his essential unity with the whole of being, he expresses this unity in his life. Mysticism and ethics, otherworldliness and worldly work go together. In the primitive religions we have this combination. Otherworldliness appears as *mana*, which the savage derives from an innate sense of some mysterious power within the phenomena and behind the events of the visible world, and morality appears as taboo, and the sense of sacredness in things and persons, which with its inhibitions controls the whole range of his conduct. In the higher religions of mankind, belief in the transcendent and work in the natural have grown together in close intimacy and interaction. Religion is the soul's attitude, response, and adjustment in the presence of the supreme realities of the transcendent order; ethics deal with the right adjustment of life on earth, especially in human society. Both are motivated by a desire to live in the light of ideals. If we are satisfied with what exists, there is no meaning in "ought"; if we are a species of passing phenomena, there is no meaning in religion. Religion springs from the conviction that there is another world beyond the visible and the temporal with which man has dealings, and ethics require us to act in this world with the compelling vision of another. With our minds anchored in the beyond we are to strive to make the actual more nearly like what it ought to be. Religion alone can give assurance and wider reference to ethics and a new meaning to human life. We make moral judgments about individual lives and societies simply because we are spiritual beings, not merely social animals.

If there is one doctrine more than another which is characteristic of Hindu thought, it is the belief that there is an interior depth to the human soul, which, in its essence, is uncreated and deathless and absolutely real. The spirit in man is different from the individual ego; it is that which animates and exercises the individual, the vast background of his being in which all individuals lie. It is the core of all being, the inner thread by being strung on which the world exists. In the soul of man are conflicting tendencies: the attraction of the infinite, which abides for ever, changeless, unqualified, untouched by the world; and the fascination of the finite, that which like the wind-beaten surface of the waters is never for a moment the same. Every human being is a potential spirit and represents, as has been well said, a hope of God and is not a mere fortuitous concourse of episodes like the changing forms of clouds or the patterns of a kaleidoscope. If the feeling for God were not in man, we could not implant it any more than we could squeeze blood from a stone. The heart of religion is that man truly belongs to another order, and the meaning of man's life is to be found not in this world but in more than historical reality. His highest aim is release from the historical succession denoted by birth and death. So long as he is lost in the historical process without a realization of the super-historical goal, he is only "once born" and is liable to sorrow. God and not the world of history is the true environment of our soul. If we overlook this important fact, and make our ethics or world affirmation independent of religion or world negation, our life and thought become condescending, though this condescension may take the form of social service or philanthropy. But it is essentially a form of self-assertion and not real concern for the well-being of others. If goodwill, pure love, and disinterestedness are our ideals, then our ethics must be rooted in other-worldliness. This is the great classical tradition of spiritual wisdom. The mystery cults of Greece had for their central doctrine that man's soul is of divine origin and is akin to the spirit of God. The influence of these mystery cults on Socrates and Plato is unmistakable. When Jesus tells Nicodemus that until a man is begotten from above he cannot see or enter the Kingdom of God, when Paul declares that "he that soweth to the flesh shall of the flesh reap corruption; but he that soweth to the spirit shall of the spirit reap everlasting life," they are implying that our natural life is mortal and it is invaded by sin and death, and that the life of spirit is immortal. St. John in the First Epistle says: "the world passeth away, and the lust thereof: but he that doeth the will of God abideth for ever." We are amphibious beings, according to Plotinus. We live on earth and in a world of spirit.

Although the view about the coexistence of the human and the divine in close intimacy and interpenetration may be true, does not Hindu thought declare that life is empty and unreal, and that it has no purpose or meaning? Schweitzer tells us that for the Upanishads "the world of the senses is a magic play staged by the universal soul for itself. The individual soul is brought into this magic play under a spell. By reflection about itself it must become capable of seeing through the deception. Thereupon it gives up taking part in the play. It waits quietly and enjoys its identity with the universal soul until, at death, the magic play for it ceases to be." "Man cannot engage in ethical activity in a world with no meaning." "For any believer in the *maya* doctrine ethics can have only a quite relative importance." This account is by no means a fair representation of the position of the Upanishads. The long theistic tradition interprets the doctrine of the Upanishads in a way directly opposed to this account. . . . Religious experience, by its affirmation that the basic fact in the universe is spiritual, implies that the world of sound and sense is not final. All existence finds its source and support in a supreme reality whose nature is spirit. The visible world is the symbol of a more real world. It is the reflection of a spiritual universe which gives to it its life and significance.

What is the relation of absolute being to historical becoming, of eternity to time? Is succession, history, progress, real and sufficient in its own right, or does man's deep instinct for the unchanging point to an eternal perfection which alone gives the world meaning and worth? Is the inescapable flux all, or is there anything which abides? Religious consciousness bears testimony to the reality of something behind the visible, a haunting beyond, which both attracts and disturbs, in the light of which the world of change is said to be unreal. The Hebrews contrasted the abidingness of God with the swift flow of human generations. "Before the mountains were brought forth or ever Thou hadst formed the earth and the world even from everlasting to everlasting, Thou art God." The psalmist cries to his God: "They [i.e., heaven and earth] shall

be changed: but Thou art the same, and Thy years shall have no end." The Christian exclaims: "The things which are seen are temporal; but the things which are not seen are eternal." The mutability of things which is part of the connotation of the word "*maya*" is a well-known theme in the world's literature. The saying that "time and chance happeneth to them all" of Ecclesiastes is the refrain we hear often.

Gaudapāda argues that "whatever is non-existent at the beginning and in the end is non-existent in the middle also." In other words, the things of the world are not eternal. The world is *maya*, i.e., passes away, but God is eternal. Change, causality, activity are finite categories and the Eternal is lifted above them. God is not a mere means to explain the universe or improve human society.

Śaṁkara, who is rightly credited with the systematic formulation of the doctrine of *maya*, tells us that the highest reality is unchangeable, and therefore that changing existence such as human history has not ultimate reality (*pāramārthika sattā*). He warns us, however, against the temptation to regard what is not completely real as utterly illusory. The world has empirical being (*vyāvahārika sattā*) which is quite different from illusory existence (*prātibhāsika sattā*). Human experience is neither ultimately real nor completely illusory. Simply because the world of experience is not the perfect form of reality, it does not follow that it is a delusion, without any significance. The world is not a phantom, though it is not real. Brahman is said to be the real of the real, *satyasyasatyam*. In all objective consciousness, we are in a sense aware of the real.

Similarly, all knowledge presupposes the knower who is constant, while the known is unsteady. When Plato tells us that we bring universal ideas with us from the world in which we lived before our birth, he is referring to the nonphenomenal, time-transcending power in us which belongs to a different world from the observed phenomena. The "nous" which organizes the facts of experience and interprets them is not itself a fact of experience. It must have had its origin in and belong to another world. It beholds by virtue of its own nature eternal realities. This presence in us is an assurance that we are in touch with reality. Spirit is real being and the rest its limited activity. The spirit is pure existence, self-aware, timeless, spaceless, unconditioned, not dependent for its being on its sense of objects, not dependent for its delight on the gross or subtle touches of outward things. It is not divided in the multitude of beings. Śaṁkara's *advaita* or non-duality has for its central thesis the non-difference between the individual self and Brahman. As for difference or multiplicity (*nānātva*), it is not real. Its self-discrepant character shows that it is only an appearance of the real. All schools of *advaita* are agreed on these two propositions. Differences arise when the nature of the actuality of the manifold world as distinct from the reality is described. Śaṁkara accepts the empirical reality of the world, which is negated only when perfect insight or intuition of the oneness of all is attained. Until then it has empirical validity or pragmatic justification. There are *advaitins* who argue that the world of difference has not even empirical validity. Śaṁkara, however, tells us that so long as we are in the world of *maya* and occupy a dualistic standpoint, the world is there, standing over against us, determining our perceptions and conduct.

Besides, the world we see and touch is not independent and self-sufficing. It carries no explanation of itself. It is a world reflecting the condition of our minds, a partial construction made from insufficient data under the stress of self-conscious individuality with its cravings and desires. What is perceived and shaped into meaning depends on the powers of apprehension we employ and the interests we possess. Our passion-limited apprehension gives us the world of common sense. Take the apparent facts of the universe. Matter is not primal. It is a thing made, not self-existent. It is not unreal, but is

being as it forms itself to sense. It is not a baseless fiction, but at the lowest it is a misrepresentation of truth; at the highest it is an imperfect representation or translation of the truth into a lower plane. Even as our knowledge implies the presence of a constant consciousness, the object of our knowledge implies the reality of pure being. Our conceptions of the universe answer to our degrees of consciousness. As our consciousness increases in its scope, we see more clearly. We now see partly as an animal and partly as a human being. Sometimes the world is viewed as one of self-satisfaction, at other times as an object of curiosity and contemplation. To see it in truth, one has to free oneself from sense addiction and concentrate the whole energy of one's consciousness on the nature of reality. It is the only way by which we can attain a clear consciousness of reality as it is and get a true picture of the world instead of partial sketches. Knowledge which we now obtain through senses and reason cannot be regarded as complete or perfect. It is flawed with antinomies and contradictions. Through the force of *avidya* (not knowing) we impose on the reality of the one the multiplicity of the world. Being which is one only appears to the soul as manifoldness, and the soul beholds itself as entangled in the world of *samsara*, in the chain of birth and death. This *avidya* is natural (*naisargika*) to the human mind, and the world is organically connected with it. It is not therefore mere waking dream.

Maya is not solipsism. It does not say that suns and universes are the invention of the solitary mind. Śaṁkara proclaims his opposition to Vijñānavāda or mentalism. He argues that waking experiences are distinct from dreamstates, though neither can be regarded as real metaphysically. Our world of waking experience is not the ultimate reality, but neither is it a shadow-show. We are surrounded by something other than ourselves, which cannot be reduced to states of our own consciousness. Though the world is always changing, it has a unity and a meaning. These are revealed by the reality present all through it. This reality lies not in the facts but in the principle which makes them into a whole. We are able to know that the world is imperfect, finite, and changing, because we have a consciousness of the eternal and the perfect. It is by the light of this consciousness that we criticize ourselves or condemn the world. Even as the human individual is a complex of the eternal and the temporal, the world which confronts him contains both. It is for Śaṁkara a mixture of truth and illusion. It partakes of the characteristics of being and non-being (*sadasadātmaka*). Although, therefore, it has a lower form of reality than pure spirit, it is not non-existent. While Śaṁkara refuses to acquiesce in the seeming reality of the actual, he does not dismiss it as an unreal phantasmagoria. It is not determinable either as real or unreal. Its truth is in being, reality, truth (*sat*); its multiplicity and division, its dispersal in space and time is untrue (*an-ṛtam*). In the world itself we have change. Śaṁkara does not tell us that the process of the world is perpetual recurrence, in which events

of past cycles are repeated in all their details. If everything is recurrent, perpetually rotating, and governed by a law of cyclic motion, there is nothing new, no meaning in history. But there is an historical fulfillment and destiny for the cosmic process. Mankind is engaged in a pursuit that tends towards a definite goal. Truth will be victorious on earth, and it is the nature of the cosmic process that the finite individual is called upon to work through the exercise of his freedom for that goal through ages of struggle and effort. The soul has risen from the sleep of matter, through plant and animal life, to the human level, and is battling with ignorance and imperfection to take possession of its infinite kingdom. It is absolute not in its actual empirical condition but in its potentiality, in its capacity to appropriate the Absolute. The historical process is not a mere external chain of events, but offers a succession of spiritual opportunities. Man has to attain a mastery over it and reveal the higher world operating in it. The world is not therefore an empty dream or an eternal delirium.

4.5   Women's Rights and Women's Judgment

CAROL GILLIGAN

Carol Gilligan (b. 1936) is a professor of Education in the Graduate School of Education at Harvard University. She has published several articles on developmental psychology, as well as her influential work, *In a Different Voice*. Gilligan has also co-edited several anthologies published by Harvard University Press, including *Making Connections: The Relational Worlds of Adolescent Girls at Emma Willard School* (1990), and she is co-author of a recent work entitled *Meeting at the Crossroads: Women's Psychology and Girls' Development* (Harvard University Press, 1992).

In the following selection from *In a Different Voice*, Gilligan begins by discussing the Seneca Falls Declaration of Sentiments (issued in 1848) and other calls for the equal rights of women. She notes that such calls immediately gave rise to concerns about the possible conflict between women's virtue, which at the time was viewed in terms of selflessness and self-sacrifice, and women's rights, which depended on the possibility of self-development and autonomy. This concern, according to Gilligan, was the basis for the traditional claim that an ethics of rights was incompatible with an ethics of care.

Turning to an analysis of more recent debates about women's rights, Gilligan claims that concern about this same conflict between self-sacrifice and self-development can be found there as well. However, using two literary sources as support— George Eliot's *The Mill on the Floss* (1860) and Margaret Drabble's *In the Waterfall* (1969)—Gilligan argues that women's moral judgments have been changed by the attainment of rights. While women are still concerned about balancing the morality of individual rights and the morality of care, women's moral judgments have become more complex. Part of this modern complexity is due to the fact that in attaining rights, women have come to see that self-assertion and independence are not incompatible with care. Indeed, by divorcing the ethics of care from its earlier association with selflessness and self-sacrifice, women have come to realize that the ethics of care extends to oneself as well as to others. This realization, according to Gilligan, is what has allowed modern women to find a moral voice of their own, a voice that joins "the heart and the eye in an ethic that ties the activity of thought to the activity of care."

Questions for Thought

1. What does Gilligan mean by an ethic of rights? What does she mean by an ethic of responsibility or care?
2. What moral rights do you think you have? Can you think of a case in which an ethic of responsibility or care could justify suspending or overriding a moral right?
3. What was the common moral dilemma in the two novels that Gilligan described? Which heroine do you think made the right decision? Why do you think she made the better choice?
4. Do you think that self-sacrifice is a moral virtue? Why or why not?
5. How, according to Gilligan, have women's moral judgments been changed by the attainment of women's rights? Do you find her analysis compelling?
6. Do you think that there are any essential differences between the moral judgments of women and the moral judgments of men? Why or why not?

WHEN IN THE SUMMER OF 1848 Elizabeth Cady Stanton and Lucretia Mott convened a conference at Seneca Falls, New York, to consider "the social, civil and religious condition and rights of women," they presented for adoption a Declaration of Sentiments, modeled on the Declaration of Independence. The issue was simple, and the analogy made their point clear: women are entitled to the rights deemed natural and inalienable by men. The Seneca Falls

Reprinted by permission of the publishers from *In a Different Voice: Psychological Theory and Women's Development* by Carol Gilligan, Cambridge, Mass.: Harvard University Press. © 1982 by Carol Gilligan.

Conference was spurred by the exclusion of Stanton and Mott, along with other female delegates, from participation in the World Anti-Slavery Convention held in London in 1840. Outraged by their relegation to the balconies to observe the proceedings in which they had come to take part, these women claimed for themselves in 1848 only what they had attempted eight years previously to claim for others, the rights of citizenship in a professedly democratic state. Anchoring this claim in the premise of equality and drawing on the notions of social contract and natural rights, the Seneca Falls Declaration argues no special consideration for women but simply holds "these truths to be self-evident: that all men and women are created equal; that they are endowed by their Creator with certain inalienable rights; that among these are life, liberty, and the pursuit of happiness."

But the claim to rights on the part of women had from the beginning brought them into a seeming opposition with virtue, an opposition challenged by Mary Wollstonecraft in 1792. In "A Vindication of the Rights of Women," she argues that liberty, rather than leading to license, is "the mother of virtue," since enslavement causes not only abjectness and despair but also guile and deceit. Wollstonecraft's "arrogance" in daring "to exert my own reason" and challenge "the mistaken notions that enslave my sex" was subsequently matched by Stanton's boldness in telling a reporter to "put it down in capital letters: SELF-DEVELOPMENT IS A HIGHER DUTY THAN SELF-SACRIFICE. The thing which most retards and militates against women's self-development is self-sacrifice." Countering the accusation of selfishness, the cardinal sin in the ladder of feminine virtue that reached toward an ideal of perfect devotion and self-abnegation, in relation not only to God but to men, these early proponents of women's rights equated self-sacrifice with slavery and asserted that the development of women, like that of men, would serve to promote the general good.

As in claiming rights women claimed responsibility for themselves, so in exercising their reason they began to address issues of responsibility in social relationships. This exercise of reason and the attempt of women to exert control over conditions affecting their lives led, in the latter half of the nineteenth century, to various movements for social reform, ranging from the social purity movements for temperance and public health to the more radical movements for free love and birth control. All of these movements joined in support of suffrage, as women, claiming their intelligence and, to varying degrees, their sexuality as part of their human nature, sought through the vote to include their voices in the shaping of history and to change prevailing practices that were damaging to present and future generations. While the disappointment of suffrage is recorded in the failure of many women to vote and the tendency of others in voting only to second their husbands' opinions, the twentieth century has in fact witnessed the legitimation of many of the rights the early feminists sought.

Given these changes in women's rights, the question arises as to their effect, a question pointed at present both by the renewed struggle for women's rights and by the centennial celebrations of many of the women's colleges to which the feminists' call for women's education gave rise. In tying women's self-development to the exercise of their own reason, the early feminists saw education as critical for women if they were to live under their own control. But as the debate over the current Equal Rights Amendment repeats many of those that occurred in the past, so the issue of women's self-development continues to raise the specter of selfishness, the fear that freedom for women will lead to an abandonment of responsibility in relationships. Thus the dialogue between rights and responsibilities, in its public debate and its psychic representation, focuses the conflicts raised by the inclusion of women in thinking about responsibility and relationships. While this dialogue elucidates some of the more puzzling aspects of women's opposition to women's rights, it also illuminates how the concept of rights engages women's thinking about moral conflict and choice.

The century marked by the movement for women's rights is spanned roughly by the publication of two novels, both written by women and posing the same moral dilemma, a heroine in love with her cousin Lucy's man. In their parallel triangles these novels provide an historical frame in which to consider the effects of women's rights on women's moral judgments and thus offer a way of addressing the centennial question as to what has changed and what has stayed the same.

In George Eliot's novel *The Mill on the Floss* (1860), Maggie Tulliver "clings to the right." Caught between her love for her cousin Lucy and her "stronger feeling" for Stephen, Lucy's fiancee, Maggie is unswerving in her judgment that, "I must not, cannot, seek my own happiness by sacrificing others." When Stephen says that their love, natural and unsought, makes it "right that we should marry each other," Maggie replies that while "love is natural, surely pity and faithfulness and memory are natural too." Even after "it was too late already not to have caused misery," Maggie refuses to "take a good for myself that has been wrung out of [others'] misery," choosing instead to renounce Stephen and return alone to St. Oggs.

While the minister, Mr. Kenn, considers "the principle upon which she acted as a safer guide than any balancing of consequences," the narrator's judgment is less clear. George Eliot, having placed her heroine in a dilemma that admits no viable solution, ends the novel by drowning Maggie, but not without first cautioning the reader that "the shifting relation between passion and duty is clear to no man who is capable of apprehending it." Since "the mysterious complexity of our life" cannot be "laced up in formulas," moral judgment cannot be bound by "general rules" but must instead be informed "by a life vivid and intense enough to have created a wide, fellow-feeling with all that is human."

Yet given that in this novel the "eyes of intense life" that were Maggie's look out in the end from a "weary, beaten face," it is not surprising that Margaret Drabble, steeped in the tradition of nineteenth century fiction but engaged in the issues of twentieth century feminism, should choose to return to Eliot's story and explore the possibility of an alternative resolution. In *The Waterfall* (1969) she recreates Maggie's dilemma in *The Mill on the Floss* but, as the title implies, with the difference that the societal impediment has been removed. Thus Drabble's heroine, Jane Grey, clings not to the right but to Lucy's husband, renouncing the renunciations and instead "drowning in the first chapter." Immersed in a sea of self-discovery, "not caring who should drown so long as I should reach the land," Jane is caught by the problem of judgment as she seeks to apprehend the miracle of her survival and to find a way to tell that story. Her love for James, Lucy's husband, is narrated by two different voices, a first and a third person who battle constantly over the issues of judgment and truth, engaging and disengaging the moral questions of responsibility and choice.

Though the balance between passion and duty has shifted between 1860 and 1969, the moral problem remains in both novels the same. Across the intervening century, the verdict of selfishness impales both heroines. The same accusation that compels Maggie's renunciation orchestrates Jane's elaborate plea of helplessness and excuse: "I was merely trying to defend myself against an accusation of selfishness, judge me leniently, I said, I am not as others are, I am sad, I am mad, so I have to have what I want." But the problem with activity and desire that the accusation of selfishness implies not only leads Jane into familiar strategies of evasion and disguise but also impels her to confront the underlying premise on which this accusation is based. Taking apart the moral judgment of the past that had made it seem, "in a sense, better to re-nounce myself than them," Jane seeks to recon-stitute it in a way that could "admit me and encompass me." Thus she strives to create "a new ladder, a new virtue," one that could in-clude activity, sexuality, and survival without abandoning the old virtues of responsibility and care: "If I need to understand what I am doing, if I cannot act without my own approbation— and I must act, I have changed, I am no longer capable of inaction—then I will invent a moral-ity that condones me. Though by doing so, I risk condemning all that I have been."

These novels thus demonstrate the continu-ing power for women of the judgment of self-ishness and the morality of self-abnegation that it implies. This is the judgment that regularly appears at the fulcrum of novels of female ado-lescence, the turning point of the *Bildungsro-man* that separates the invulnerability of childhood innocence from the responsibility of adult participation and choice. The notion that virtue for women lies in self-sacrifice has com-plicated the course of women's development by pitting the moral issue of goodness against the adult questions of responsibility and choice. In addition, the ethic of self-sacrifice is directly in conflict with the concept of rights that has, in this past century, supported women's claim to a fair share of social justice.

But a further problem arises from the tension between a morality of rights that dissolves "nat-ural bonds" in support of individual claims and a morality of responsibility that knits such claims into a fabric of relationship, blurring the distinc-tion between self and other through the repre-sentation of their interdependence. This problem was the concern of Wollstonecraft and Stanton, of Eliot and Drabble. This concern emerged as well in interviews with college women in the 1970s. All of these women talked about the same conflict, all revealed the enor-mous power of the judgment of selfishness in women's thought. But the appearance of this judgment in the moral conflicts described by

contemporary women brings into focus the role that the concept of rights plays in women's moral development. These conflicts demonstrate the continuation through time of an ethic of re-sponsibility as the center of women's moral con-cern, anchoring the self in a world of relationships and giving rise to activities of care, but also indicate how this ethic is transformed by the recognition of the justice of the rights ap-proach. . . .

In one sense, then, not much has changed. George Eliot, observing that "we have no mas-ter-key that will fit all cases" of moral decision, returns to the casuists in whose "perverted spirit of minute discrimination" she sees "the shadow of a truth to which eyes and hearts are too often fatally sealed—the truth that moral judgments must remain false and hollow unless they are checked and enlightened by a perpetual refer-ence to the special circumstances that mark the individual lot." Thus moral judgment must be informed by "growing insight and sympathy," tempered by the knowledge gained through ex-perience that "general rules" will not lead peo-ple "to justice by a ready-made patent method, without the trouble of exerting patience, dis-crimination, impartiality, without any care to as-sure whether they have the insight that comes from a hardly-earned estimate of temptation or from a life vivid and intense enough to have cre-ated a wide, fellow feeling with all that is human."

And yet, for Eliot, at least in this novel, the moral problem remains one of renunciation, a question of "whether the moment has come in which a man has fallen below the possibility of a renunciation that will carry any efficacy, and must accept the sway of a passion against which he had struggled as a trespass." The opposition of passion and duty thus binds morality to an ideal of selflessness, the "perfect goodness" to-ward which Maggie Tulliver aspired.

Both this opposition and this ideal are called into question by the concept of rights, by the assumption underlying the idea of justice that self and other are equal. Among college students in the 1970s, the concept of rights entered into their thinking to challenge a morality of self-sacrifice and self-abnegation. Questioning the stoicism of self-denial and replacing the illusion of innocence with an awareness of choice, they struggled to grasp the essential notion of rights, that the interests of the self can be considered legitimate. In this sense, the concept of rights changes women's conceptions of self, allowing them to see themselves as stronger and to consider directly their own needs. When assertion no longer seems dangerous, the concept of relationships changes from a bond of continuing dependence to a dynamic of interdependence. Then the notion of care expands from the paralyzing injunction not to hurt others to an injunction to act responsively toward self and others and thus to sustain connection. A consciousness of the dynamics of human relationships then becomes central to moral understanding, joining the heart and the eye in an ethic that ties the activity of thought to the activity of care.

Thus changes in women's rights change women's moral judgments, seasoning mercy with justice by enabling women to consider it moral to care not only for others but for themselves. The issue of inclusion first raised by the feminists in the public domain reverberates through the psychology of women as they begin to notice their own exclusion of themselves. When the concern with care extends from an injunction not to hurt others to an ideal of responsibility in social relationships, women begin to see their understanding of relationships as a source of moral strength. But the concept of rights also changes women's moral judgment by adding a second perspective to the consideration of moral problems, with the result that judgment becomes more tolerant and less absolute.

As selfishness and self-sacrifice become matters of interpretation and responsibilities live in tension with rights, moral truth is complicated by psychological truth, and the matter of judgment becomes more complex. Drabble's heroine, who sought to write "a poem as round and hard as a stone," only to find that words and thoughts obtrude, concludes that "a poem so round and smooth would say nothing" and sets out to describe the variegated edges of an event seen from angles, finding in the end no unified truth. Instead, through a final shift in perspective, she relegates her suspicions to "that removed, third person" and, no longer fending off the accusation of selfishness, identifies herself with the first person voice.

Transvaluation of Values: The End of Phallic Morality   4.6

MARY DALY

Mary Daly (b. 1928) has been a leading spokesperson for radical feminism since her provocative text *Beyond God the Father* was published by Beacon Press in 1973. Daly has expanded on and supplemented the ideas found in this text in two equally provocative works, *Gyn/Ecology: The Metaethics of Radical Feminism* (1978) and *Pure Lust: Elemental Feminist Philosophy* (1984). More recent publications include *Websters' First New Intergalactic Wickedary of the English Language* (1987), which was co-authored by Jane Caputi, and *Women and Poverty* (1989). Her latest work,

Outercourse: The Bedazzling Voyage, was published by HarperCollins in 1993. Daly, who received doctorates in theology and philosophy from the University of Fribourg in Switzerland, is an associate professor of Theology at Boston College.

In the following selection, taken from *Beyond God the Father*, Daly describes the re-creation of values that she believes will result from radical feminism. Unlike Gilligan, who sees some value in traditional rights-oriented ethics, Daly offers a thorough-going critique of traditional Western morality, a morality that she describes as "phal-locentric" and "patriarchal." She argues that this traditional morality was based on a dualism of stereotypical sexual roles, the eternal masculine and the eternal feminine, and that its main values, such as chastity, meekness, humility, and selflessness, resulted from a reaction to stereotypically male excesses. Moreover, this traditional Western emphasis on "feminine" or passive virtues has served to reinforce the oppres-sion of women and to mask the real motives behind aggressive male behavior. As she shows through her analysis of historical and literary examples, it has also been intimately connected with "The Most Unholy Trinity," that is, with rape, genocide, and war.

Daly believes that the only philosophy capable of moral transvaluation, of over-coming the oppression of this Most Unholy Trinity, is radical feminism. Since tradi-tional morality has been "feminine" in nature, Daly claims that feminists, who have suffered most from the effects of such a passive morality, are best suited to see through the logic of oppression that is embedded in it. In freeing themselves from this logic of oppression (or in "castrating the phallic ethic," as Daly says elsewhere), women will be able to realize a new type of existence that is no longer characterized by psychic, sexual, or social alienation. This new type of existence, which will tran-scend the stereotypical sex roles of traditional morality, will allow women to elimi-nate oppression in all its forms. Most important, it will allow women to truly comprehend and to actualize the "Most Holy and Whole Trinity of Power, Justice and Love," and thus to overcome rape, genocide, and war.

Questions for Thought

1. What does Daly mean by "phallic morality"? Do you think that traditional Western moral-ity has been phallic? Why or why not?
2. In what ways, according to Daly, has traditional morality been hypocritical? Can you think of any examples from your own experience that might substantiate her claim that traditional morality has been hypocritical?
3. How are the terms *Apollonian* and *Dionysian* used in this selection? Are you familiar with any other uses of these terms?
4. What is Daly's point in quoting several passages from the Bible? What do you make of these passages?
5. Do you agree with Daly's claim that we need a transvaluation of values? Why or why not? Do you think Gilligan would agree with this claim?
6. How does Daly envision the new type of human being that emerges from the overcoming of phallocentric morality? In what ways, if any, does this new type of human existence dif-fer from your own existence?

If the first woman God ever made was strong enough to turn the world upside down, all alone—these together ought to be able to turn it back and get it rightside up again: and they is asking to do it. The men better let 'em.

—SOJOURNER TRUTH (1851)

See
That no matter what you have done
I am still here.
And it has made me dangerous, and wise.
And brother,
You cannot whore, perfume and suppress
     me anymore.
I have my own business in this skin
And on this planet.

—GAIL MURRAY (1970)

A transvaluation of values can only be accomplished when there is a tension of new needs, and a new set of needy people who feel all old values as painful—although they are not conscious of what is wrong.

—FRIEDRICH NIETZSCHE

IN ORDER TO UNDERSTAND THE POTENTIAL IMpact of radical feminism upon phallocentric morality it is important to see the problem of structures of alienation on a wide scale. Some contemporary social critics of course have seen a need for deep psychic change. Herbert Marcuse, for example, encourages the building of a society in which a new type of human being emerges. He recognizes that unless this transformation takes place, the transition from capitalism to socialism would only mean replacing one form of domination by another. The human being of the future envisaged by Marcuse would have a new sensibility and sensitivity, and would be physiologically incapable of tolerating an ugly, noisy, and polluted universe.[1] Norman O. Brown, recognizing that the problem of human

oppression is deeply linked with the prevalence of the phallic personality, quotes King James who in 1603 said: "I am the husband and the whole island is my lawful wife."[2] The statement calls to mind the traditional insistence of ecclesiastics that the church is "the bride of Christ." For Theodore Roszak, such imagery poses a dilemma:

> Does social privilege generate the erotic symbolism? Does the erotic symbolism generate social privilege? . . . Politically, it poses the question of how our liberation is to be achieved. How shall we rid ourselves of the king or his dominating surrogates?[3]

The point is not missed by any of these authors that the desired psychic change is related to overcoming sexual alienation. What is lacking is adequate recognition of the key role of women's becoming in the process of human liberation. When this crucial role is understood and experienced, it can be seen that there are ways of grappling with the problems of psychic/social change that are concrete and real. As distinct from the speculations of Marcuse, Brown, and other social philosophers, the analysis developing out of feminism has a compelling power deriving from its concreteness and specificity. It speaks precisely out of and to the experience of the sexually oppressed and has an awakening force that is emotional, intellectual, and moral. It changes the fabric of lives, affecting also the consciousness of the men related to the women whose consciousness it is changing.

The dynamics of the psychic/social revolution of feminism involve a twofold rejection of patriarchal society's assumptions about "women's role." First, there is a basic rejection of what Alice Rossi calls the pluralist model of sex roles, which involves a rigid "equal but different" ideology and socialization of the sexes.[4] The assumption of such "pluralism" is that there is and should be "complementarity," based not upon individual differences but upon sex stereotyping. Feminists universally see through the fallaciousness and oppressiveness of the "complementarity" theme at least to some degree. However, there are "levels and levels" of perception of this, and permitting oneself to have deep insight is threatening to the self. Thus, it is possible to stop at a rather surface level of denying this stereotypic pluralism, by reducing the problem to one of "equal pay for equal work," or (in the past) acquisition of the right to vote, or passage of the Equal Rights Amendment. In the present wave of feminism, a second and deeper rejection of patriarchal assumptions is widespread. This is rejection of what Rossi calls the "assimilation model." Radical feminists know that "50/50 equality" within patriarchal space is an absurd notion, neither possible nor desirable. The values perpetuated within such space are seen as questionable. When the myth of the eternal feminine is seen through, then the brutalization implied in the eternal masculine also becomes evident. Just as "unveiling" the eternal feminine logically entails revealing the true face of the eternal masculine, the whole process, if carried through to its logical conclusion, involves refusal of uncritical assimilation into structures that depend upon this polarization. The notion of a fifty percent female army, for example, is alien to the basic insights of radical feminism.

Intrinsic to the re-creative potential of the women's movement, then, is a new naming of values as these have been incarnated in society's laws, customs, and arrangements. This means that there will be a renaming of morality which has been false because [it has been] phallocentric, denying half the species the possibility not only of naming but even of *hearing* our own experience with our own ears.

Hypocrisy of the Traditional Morality

Much of traditional morality in our society appears to be the product of reactions on the part of men—perhaps guilty reactions—to the behavioral excesses of the stereotypic male. There has been a *theoretical* one-sided emphasis upon charity, meekness, obedience, humility, self-abnegation, sacrifice, service. Part of the problem with this moral ideology is that it became accepted not by men but by women, who hardly have been helped by an ethic which reinforces the abject female situation. Of course, oppressed males are forced to act out these qualities in the presence of their "superiors." However, in the presence of females of the oppressed racial or economic class, the mask is dropped. Basically, then, the traditional morality of our culture has been "feminine" in the sense of hypocritically idealizing some of the qualities imposed upon the oppressed.

A basic irony in the phenomenon of this "feminine" ethic of selflessness and sacrificial love is the fact that the qualities that are *really* lived out and valued by those in dominant roles, and esteemed by those in subservient roles, are not overtly held up as values but rather are acted out under pretense of doing something else. Ambitious prelates who have achieved ecclesiastical power have been praised not for their ambition but for "humility." Avaricious and ruthless politicians often speak unctuously of sacrifice, service and dedication. Not uncommonly such pronouncements are "sincere," for self-deceit is encouraged by a common assumption that the simple fact of having an office proves that the incumbent truly merits it. The Judeo-Christian ethic has tended to support rather than challenge this self-legitimating facticity, by its obsession with obedience and respect for authority. Since the general effect of Christian morality has been to distort the real motivations and values operative in society, it hinders confrontation with the problems of unjust acquisition and use of power and the destructive effects of social conditioning. Since it fails to develop an understanding and respect for the aggressive and creative virtues, it offers no alternative to the hypocrisy-condoning situation fostered by its one-sided and unrealistic ethic.

A mark of the duplicity of this situation is the fact that women, who according to the fables of our culture (the favorable ones, as opposed to those that stress the "evil" side of the stereotype) should be living embodiments of the virtues it extols, are rarely admitted to positions of leadership. It is perhaps partial insight into the inconsistency of this situation that has prompted Christian theologians to justify it not only by the myth of feminine evil but also by finding a kind of tragic flaw in women's natural equipment. Commonly this flaw has been seen as an inherent feebleness of the reasoning power, linked, of course, to emotional instability. Typically, Thomas Aquinas argued that women should be subject to men because "in man the discretion of reason predominates."[5] This denial of rationality in women by Christian theologians has been a basic tactic for confining them to the condition of moral imbecility. Inconsistently, women have been blamed for most of the evil in the world, while at the same time full capacity for moral responsibility has been denied to females.

Feminism Versus the "Feminine" Ethic

While Christian morality has tended to deny responsibility and self-actualization to women by definition, it has also stifled honesty in men. I have pointed out that the pseudo-feminine ethic—which I also call the passive ethic—conceals the motivations and values that are actually operative in society. While it is true that there has been an emphasis upon some of the aspects of the masculine stereotype, for example, control of emotions by "reason" and the practice of courage in defense of the prevailing political structure or of a powerful ideology (the courage of soldiers and martyrs), these have been tailored to serve mechanisms that oppress, rather than to liberate the self. The passive ethic, then, whether stressing the so-called feminine qualities or the so-called masculine qualities does not challenge exploitativeness but supports it. This kind of morality lowers consciousness so that "sin" is basically equated with an offense against those in power, and the structures of oppression are not recognized as evil.

Feminism has a unique potential for providing the insight needed to undercut the prevailing moral ideology. Striving for freedom involves an awakening process in which layer upon layer of society's deceptiveness is ripped away. The process has its own dynamics: after one piece of deception is seen through the pattern can be recognized elsewhere, again and again. What is equally important, women build up a refusal of self-deception. The support group, which is the cognitive minority going through the same process, gains in its power to correlate information and refute opposing arguments. Nietzsche, the prophet whose prophecy was short-circuited by his own misogynism, wanted to transvaluate Judeo-Christian morality, but in fact it is women who will confront patriarchal morality as *patriarchal*. It is radical feminism that can unveil the "feminine" ethic, revealing it to be a phallic ethic.

Existential Courage and Transvaluation

The Aristotelian theory of moral virtue, which was assumed into Christian theology, centered around the virtue of prudence, the "queen" of the moral virtues. Prudence presumably is "right reason about things to be done," enabling one to judge the right and virtuous course.[6] Since moral virtue was understood as the mean between two extremes, prudence was understood as a virtue in the intellect which enabled one to steer between two opposed vices.

As Sam Keen and others have pointed out, a theory of moral virtue so dominated by the motif of prudence is basically Apollonian. It presupposes a view of human life in which the emotions are considered inferior to "reason," which is at the summit of the hierarchy of human faculties. Aquinas, following Aristotle, believed that prudence involved a kind of practical knowledge by which one was enabled to judge in a particular set of circumstances what would be the best course of action. Since prudential knowledge was understood to be connatural and nonideological, it would seem that there should have been hope for an ethic thus envisaged to be free of subservience to authoritarian structures. However, it did not work out this way. In the opinion of Aquinas and of all "main line" Catholic moralists the prudent person would accept guidance from the moral teachings of the church and attempt to apply these in the given situation. Ecclesiastical ideology, then, did work itself into one's prudential decision about how to act.

A major difficulty with all of this arises from the fact that the moral teachings designed to guide the Christian in making prudential decisions have to a large extent been the products of technical reason, that is, the capacity for "reasoning" about means for achieving ends, cut off from the aesthetic, intuitive, and practical functions of the mind. As Tillich realized, when the reasoning process about means is cut off from the deep sources of awareness in the human mind (ontological reason), then the ends to which the means are uncritically directed are provided by other nonrational forces external to the self.[7] These may be traditions or authoritarian structures or ideologies that have become so embedded in the psyche that they have rendered themselves invisible. In any case the result is blindness concerning the ends or goals which are actually behind the whole reasoning process and which are motivating the selection of certain premises that will determine what other data, that is, what other possible premises, will be excluded from consideration in the reasoning process.

It is precisely this unconsciousness of ends and motivations which makes so much of Christian doctrine about morality suspect. While Tillich and others have seen the problem of heteronomy conflicting with autonomy in a general way, it is feminist women who now are gaining insights about *specific* ways in which prudential ethics has lent itself to the service of patriarchal power and about *specific* issues that have been clouded by this. Patriarchal systems demand precisely this: cautious execution of means on the part of those who are in bondage to such systems, without application of the mind's powers to the work of criticizing their purposes. This blotting out of critical power involves a desensitizing to elements in human experience which, if heeded, would challenge the "reasonableness" of the dominant ethic.

Classical and medieval moralists did of course put a great deal of emphasis upon the role of the end or goal in determining the morality of a human act. However, in Christian scholastic ethics especially, the greatest attention was paid to the *ultimate* end of human acts, that is, "eternal happiness." Intermediate ends did not receive the kind of scrutiny that a revolutionary morality requires. The built-in assumption was that these goals should be determined by authority and receive unquestioning assent from subordinates. Such assumptions still dominate a great deal of "modern" ethical theory. . . . The potential that radical feminism has for breaking their demonic power has its source in the awakening of existential courage in women, which can give rise to a Dionysian feminist ethic.

Although repudiation of the passive and Apollonian ethic of authoritarian religion is not entirely new, there is a qualitative newness arising from the fact that women are beginning to *live* this repudiation personally, corporately, and politically. Those who have been socialized most profoundly to live out the passive ethic are renouncing it and starting to affirm a style of human existence that has existential courage as its dominant motif.

It may be asked what this qualitative newness means. In what does it consist? Aren't there "situation ethicists" around already challenging the Old Morality? . . .

Clues to fundamental differences between the Dionysian feminist ethic that is beginning to be lived and spoken about by some women and the "New Morality" of situation ethics can be found in the work of Joseph Fletcher, author of *Situation Ethics*. Fletcher insists upon labeling what he is doing as "Christian situation ethics."[8] One may well ask why the label "Christian" is necessary. What does it add to "situation ethics"? Fletcher himself responds to this question by saying that what makes it different from other moralities is a theological factor, "the faith affirmation that God himself suffered for man's sake to reconcile the world in Christ."[9] This means that, however valuable many of the author's insights may be, there is here a basic affirmation of sacrificial love morality. Fletcher feels constrained to give priority to "the desire to satisfy the neighbor's need, not one's own."[10] As the primordial victims of this kind of unrealistic and destructive moral ideal, women—once consciousness has been liberated—can see that this kind of "New Morality" is very much like the old. It does not move us beyond the good and evil of patriarchy because it does not get us out of the bind of scapegoat psychology. Those who have actually been scapegoats and have said No to being victims any longer are in a position to say NO to this modernized Christolatrous morality, in which "love" is always privatized and lacking a specific social context, and in which the structures of oppression are left uncriticized.

Out of this "No" to the morality of victimization, which women share with all the oppressed, comes a "Yes" to an ethic which transcends the most basic role stereotypes, those of masculine/feminine. Janice Raymond points out that this ethic upholds as its ideal "a dynamic metaphysical process of becoming, in which what has been traditionally circumscribed as masculine and feminine is divested of its sex-typing and categorization and is brought together into a new reality of being, a new wholeness of personhood." Far from being "unisex," in the sense of universal sameness, it involves a revolt against standardization.[11] As

another feminist writer has pointed out, terms such as "masculinize" or "feminize" would then come to mean a process of warping children to develop only half of their potentialities. In these terms a man of our culture now seen as "masculine" would be seen to have been masculinized, that is, to have lost half of himself.[12]

Before the androgynous world can begin to appear, however (a world in which even the term "androgynous" itself would be rendered meaningless because the word reflects the archaic heritage of psycho-sexual dualism), women will have to assume the burden of castrating the phallic ethic (which "appears" as a feminine ethic or a passive ethic) by calling forth out of our experience a new naming in the realm of morality. To do this it will be necessary to understand the dynamics of the false naming in the realm of ethics that has been encased in patriarchy's definitions of good and evil. . . .

The Most Unholy Trinity: Rape, Genocide, and War

The first dimension of what I have baptized as The Most Unholy Trinity is rape. It is clear that there has always been a connection between the mentality of rape and the phenomenon of war, although there is much unseeing of this connection when the war is perceived as "just." An example within recent times was the horrible treatment of the women of Bangladesh. Many horrendous stories came out at the time of the civil war between East and West Pakistan, but scant reference was made to "the heartbreaking reports that as many as 200,000 Bengali women, victims of rape by West Pakistani soldiers, had been abandoned by their husbands, because no Moslem will live with a wife who has been touched by another man."[13] Joyce Goldman, a writer who discovered such a reference buried in a postwar "return to normality" article, decided that if male reporters would not investigate, she would attempt to do so. The experience of reading her account is unforgettable. A Pakistani officer is quoted as saying: "We used the girls until they died." Many of the women imprisoned in barracks (to be used by soldiers as "cigarette machines," as one government official described it), tried to commit suicide. Goldman cites reports of a town named Camilla, near Dacca, where women were raped and then thrown from the rooftops like rubbish. "One eight-year-old girl who was found too childsmall for the soldiers' purposes was slit to accommodate them, and raped until she died."[14] Goldman points to the obvious cruel irony in the fact that these victims were then abandoned by their husbands as unclean, which is an obvious corollary of looking upon women as objects and possessions, for then they must have only one possessor. Most significantly she shows that the concept of a raped woman as damaged is only a morbid exaggeration of "our" own attitudes, for the women of Bangladesh have suffered "collectively, exaggeratedly what individual women in this and other 'advanced' countries know from their own experience."[15] . . .

"Informed" Christians and Jews may protest that rape and brutality are alien to our own heritage. The reader, then, should refer to biblical passages which tell a different story, namely that there is precedent for looking upon women as spoils of war. In the Book of Numbers, Moses, after the campaign against Midian, is described as enraged against the commanders of the army for having spared the lives of all the women:

> So kill all the male children. Kill also all the women who have slept with a man. Spare the lives only of the young girls who have not slept with a man, and take them for yourselves. (Numbers 31:17–18).

The story continues:

> Moses and Eleazar the priest did as Yahweh had ordered Moses. The spoils, the remainder of the booty captured by the soldiers, came to six hundred and seventy-five thousand head of small stock, seventy-two thousand head of cattle, sixty-one thousand donkeys, and in persons, women who had never slept with a man, thirty-two thousand in all. (Numbers 31:31–35)

In Deuteronomy, the advice given to the Hebrews is that when they go to war and Yahweh delivers the enemy into their power, they may choose a wife from among them.

> Should she cease to please you, you will let her go where she wishes, not selling her for money: you are not to make any profit out of her, since you have had the use of her. (Deuteronomy 21:14)

Even outside the context of war (if such a context is imaginable in a patriarchal world), the value placed upon women in the Old Testament is illustrated in the story of the crime of the men of Gibeah. A man who was giving hospitality to a Levite and his concubine was having dinner with them. Scoundrels came to the house demanding to have the guest, in order to abuse him. The response of the host was to offer them his daughter as substitute for the guest. The devoted father is reported to have said:

> Here is my daughter; she is a virgin; I will give her to you. Possess her, do what you please with her, but do not commit such an infamy against this man. (Judges 19:24)

Since the visitors refused this offer, the guest gallantly offered them his concubine as a replacement for himself. They raped her all night and she died. Tastefully the guest, when he had returned home with her, cut her into twelve pieces and sent all these around Israel with a message about the crime. The text offers no negative judgment upon the host or his guest. The crime was seen as an offense against men, not against their female property.

The second dimension of The Most Unholy Trinity is genocide. It should require no great imaginative leap to perceive a deep relationship between the mentality of rape and genocide. The socialization of male sexual violence in our culture forms the basis for corporate and military interests to train a vicious military force. It would be a mistake to think that rape is reducible to the physical act of a few men who are rapists. This ignores the existence of the countless armchair rapists who vicariously enjoy the act through reading pornography or news stories about it. It also overlooks the fact that all men have their power enhanced by rape, since this instills in women a need for protection. Rape is a way of life. Since this is the case, police do not feel obliged to "believe" women who report rape. Typical of police attitudes was the statement of Police Captain Vincent O'Connell of Providence, Rhode Island, concerning women who attempt to report rape: "We are very skeptical when we first interview them. We feel there's a tendency for women not to tell the truth."[16]

The politics of domination are everywhere. E. Ionesco wrote:

> The world of the concentration camps . . . was not an exceptionally monstrous society. What we saw there was the image, and in a sense the quintessence, of the infernal society in which we are plunged every day.[17]

This "everyday world" is fundamentally a world of sexual dominance and violation.

The logical extension of the mentality of rape is the objectification of all who can be cast into the role of victims of violence. Rape is the primordial act of violation but it is more than an individual act. It is expressive of a basic alienation within the psyche and of structures of alienation within society. Rape is an act of group against group: male against female. As I have pointed out, it is also an act of male against male, in which the latter is attacked by the pollution of his property. Rape is expressive of group-think, and group-think is at the core of racial prejudice whose logical conclusion and final solution is genocide.

Writing of Vietnam, Paul Mayer pointed out that the United States [conducted] the same kind of genocide against the Indochinese as the Nazis once ordered against European Jewry.

"The method has changed from the gas chambers of Auschwitz to those crematoria that rain burning death and terror from the skies, particularly on civilians."[18] Mr. Mayer's dismay that American Catholics and Jews [did] not see the parallel [appeared] to spring from his not seeing the fundamental patriarchal character of these traditions. The record of the church in Nazi Germany is well known. Guenter Lewy writes:

> When thousands of German anti-Nazis were tortured to death in Hitler's concentration camps, when the Polish intelligentsia was slaughtered, when hundreds of thousands of Russians died as a result of being treated as Slavic *Untermenschen*, and when 6,000,000 human beings were murdered for being "non-Aryan," Catholic Church officials in Germany bolstered the regime perpetrating these crimes.[19]

With characteristic insight, Lewy points out that the hold of the church upon the faithful is precarious and that this prevents it from risking confrontation with a state that tramples upon human dignity and freedom. Lewy asserts that the situation is worsened when the clergy are infected with an alien creed. I would point out that the creed of totalitarian governments is not all that "alien." As Lewy himself notes, theologians such as Michael Schmaus and Joseph Lortz saw basic similarities between the Nazi and the Catholic *Weltanschauung*.[20] At any rate, whether one wishes to call the affinity an infection or a recognition of some dimension of secret sameness, the alliance of hierarchical Catholicism with the demonic forces is a familiar pattern. . . .

Silence in the face of genocide or open support of this is hardly foreign to Protestant Christianity. In Nazi Germany, there was the Nazi-approved National Church, or *Reich* church, co-opted by Hitler. This fact is not obliterated by the compensatory fact that there existed also the "Confessing Church," which refused to cooperate with the Nazis, nor is it wiped out by the lives of Protestant heroes such as Dietrich Bonhoeffer, who was hanged by the Nazis. For that matter, there were also Catholic heroes and martyrs such as Franz Jägerstätter, the peasant who was beheaded, and Alfred Delp, a priest killed by the Nazis. The fact is that the United States, at the peak of its genocidal mania, was a predominantly Protestant nation. Nor should it be forgotten that Christianity, Catholic and Protestant, has deep roots in the Judaic tradition, in which the people of Yahweh were able to see themselves as different from "the Other"—the worshipers of "false gods." If, then, many American Jews have allowed themselves not to see the parallels between American genocide and Auschwitz, this phenomenon is not totally contradictory, for the mentality of rape is also embedded in the Hebrew tradition itself.

The third dimension of The Most Unholy Trinity is war. Theodore Roszak writes of "the full and hideous flowering of the politics of masculine dominance" which from the late nineteenth to the mid-twentieth centuries became more candid than ever before.[21] Such diverse figures as Teddy Roosevelt, General Homer Lea, Patrick Pearse, and the Spanish political philosopher Juan Donoso-Cortés agreed in associating war with "the manly and adventurous virtues" and the civilized horror of war with loss of manhood. This masculine metaphysical madness was lived out in Nazism and Fascism. It is being lived out today to an even greater extent, but the language of violence has become disguised, mathematized, and computerized. There are occasional linguistic lapses that are gross enough to make tragic absurdity visible, as when a military officer made the famous statement that it was necessary to destroy a (Vietnamese) village in order to save it. Such lapses briefly jolt the consciences of a few, but the majority, drugged by the perpetual presence of the politics of rape on the TV screen, sees it all but sees nothing. The horrors of a phallocentric world have simultaneously become more visible and more invisible. . . .

The Most Unholy Trinity of Rape, Genocide, and War is a logical expression of phallocentric power. These are structures of alienation that are self-perpetuating, eternally breeding further estrangement. The circle of destruction generated by the Most Unholy Trinity and reflected in the Unwhole Trinitarian symbol of Christianity will be broken when women, who are by patriarchal definition objects of rape, externalize and internalize a new self-definition whose compelling power is rooted in the power of being. The casting out of the demonic Trinities *is* female becoming. . . .

The Most Holy and Whole Trinity: Power, Justice, and Love

Tillich has rightly shown that "all problems of love, power, and justice drive us to an ontological analysis."[22] What his analysis leaves out is the essential fact that division by socialization into sex roles divides the human psyche itself, so that love cut off from power and justice is pseudo-love, power isolated from love and justice is inauthentic power of dominance, and justice is a meaningless facade of legalism split off from love and real power of being. Without a perception of the demonic divisiveness of sex role socialization, an "ontological" analysis of these problems remains hopelessly sterile and removed from the concrete conditions of existence. It is not really ontological.

Given this multiple dividedness, "love" is restricted to a private sphere. The theory of the "two kingdoms," according to which "love" holds a prominent place in the private order whereas power reigns in the political order, has been a common idea in Lutheran theology. Expressed in other "language systems" than that of the "two kingdoms," this is a common idea in our whole culture. The idea that these realities can be separated and still be real is, of course, a mirage. Women's movement theorists have shown that "the personal is political," that the power structures get into the fabric of one's psyche and personal relationships: this is "sexual politics." Power split off from love makes an obscenity out of what we call love, forcing us unwillingly to destroy ourselves and each other. R. D. Laing has given us a terrible insight into the destructiveness of this privatized love which is ultimately public, reflecting the alienated consciousness shared by all. He writes of the menace to those trying to break out of alienated consciousness coming precisely from those who "love" them:

> And because they are humane, and concerned, and even love us, and are very frightened, they will try to cure us. They may succeed, but there is still hope that they will fail.[23]

When extended outside the sphere of familial and personal relationships the "love" that serves patriarchal power sometimes is the impotent do-gooder quality that is conveyed by such expressions as "charity bazaar" or "charity case." Sometimes it is the mask of absolute violence, as in the case of the American "love" for the people of South Vietnam who [were] being "protected."

Genuine love, which is not blindly manipulable by political power of domination, seeks to overcome such power by healing the divided self. Sexist society maintains its grasp over the psyche by keeping it divided against itself. Through stereotyping it harnesses the power of human becoming. It is commonly perceived that on the deepest ontological level love is a striving toward unity, but the implications of this unity have not been understood by the philosophers of patriarchy. It means the becoming of new human beings, brought forth out of the unharnessed energy of psychically androgynous women, whose primary concern is not giving birth to others but to ourselves.

A qualitatively different understanding of justice also emerges when the peculiar rigidities of the stereotypic male no longer dominate the scene. Tillich has written of transforming or creative justice, which goes beyond calculating in

fixed proportions. Unfortunately, he tries to uphold the idea that "the religious symbol for this is the kingdom of God."[24] I suggest that as long as we are under the shadow of a *kingdom*, real or symbolic, there will be no creative justice. The transforming and creative element in justice has been intuited and dimly expressed by the term "equity." Aristotle defined this as a correction of law where it is defective owing to its "universality."[25] What this leaves out is the dynamic and changing quality of justice which does not presuppose that there are fixed and universal essences, but which is open to new data of experience.

The falsely universal and static quality of patriarchal thought which allows no breakthrough beyond "equity" reaches the ultimate state of sclerotic rigidity when the subject under consideration is the female half of the species. An example of this sclerosis which has prevented anything like creative justice in relation to women from emerging in Christian thought is the approach of renowned theologian Helmut Thielicke who, in his *The Ethics of Sex*, writes:

> It is, so to speak, the "vocation" of the woman to be lover, companion, and mother. And even the unmarried woman fulfills her calling in accord with the essential image of herself only when these fundamental characteristics, which are designed for wifehood and motherhood, undergo a sublimating transformation, but still remain discernible.[26]

Further on, Thielicke gets even worse, opining that "woman" is oriented monogamously because she is profoundly stamped by the sexual encounter, insisting that she is marked by the first man who "possesses" her:

> One must go even further and say that even the first meeting with this first man possesses the faculty of engraving and marking the women's being, that it has, as it were, the character of a *monos* and thus tends toward monogamy.[27]

For Thielicke, clearly, the male is God in relation to women. His language betrays him at every step. He claims that numerous psychopathological symptoms are "determined" by this "structure" of feminine sexuality. A woman's "frigidity" as well as the "vampire insatiability of the strumpet" are traced to her first sexual encounter. Creative justice, which could break through this dualistic sort of ethics, is not likely to come from those whose status benefits so totally from stereotypic rigidity.

The sterility and rigidity of noncreative justice that classifies and remains closed to change is reflected not only in ethics but also in legal systems as well as in the attitudes of those who interpret the law. Patriarchal rigidity expressed in law, moreover, carries over from women to other disadvantaged groups (and it is important to remember that over fifty percent of all of these segments of humanity—for example, blacks, the Third World—are women). Gunnar Myrdal, in his famous Appendix Five of *An American Dilemma*, wrote:

> In the earlier common law, women and children were placed under the jurisdiction of the paternal power. When a legal status had to be found for the imported Negro servants in the seventeenth century, the nearest and most natural analogy was the status of women and children.[28]

Myrdal cites George Fitzhugh, who in his *Sociology for the South* (1854) categorizes together wives, apprentices, lunatics, and idiots, asserting that a man's wife and children are his slaves.

As marginal beings whose authentic personal interest is not served by the rigidities of patriarchal power, women have the potential to see through these. Some men have seen this, of course, but the tendency has been to capture the insight into stereotypes which reinforce the separation of love and justice and therefore support the demonic usages of political power. This can be seen in the cliche: "Man is the head, woman is the heart." At least one renowned legal authority, however, tried (very timidly) to suggest the possibility of overcoming the dichotomy by bringing more women into the legal profession. Justice Jerome Frank suggested that there might be a connection between the inflexibility of the Roman legal system and the fact that the power of the father (*patria potestas*) was a dominant characteristic of Roman society. He points out that in Greek society, in which the power of the father had diminished, the legal system was more flexible:

> I suggest that it is barely possible that, as a result, the role of the mother emerged as an influence on Greek legal attitudes, so that equity, greater lenience, more attention to "circumstances that alter cases" in the application of rules, became an accepted legal ideal.[29]

Although Frank had tendencies to be both apologetic and stereotypic in his exposition of his opinion that women could bring flexibility into the legal system, his view is hardly totally bereft of insight. In support of it, he cited Henry Adams's passages about the role of Mary in the twelfth and thirteenth centuries. Adams saw Mary as functioning symbolically as the only court of equity capable of overruling strict law (symbolized in the Trinity):

> The mother alone was human, imperfect, and could love. . . . The Mother alone could represent whatever was not Unity; whatever was irregular, exceptional, *outlawed* [emphasis mine]; and this was the whole human race.[30]

The church has harnessed (but not succeeded in destroying) this power of diversity, irregularity, and exceptionality by standardizing it into its bland and monolithic image of Mary. It has captured this power of diversity and imprisoned it in a symbol. The real diversity and *insight* into diversity is in existing rebellious women, whose awareness of power of being is emerging in refusal to be cast into a mold. The primordial experiencers of powerlessness and victims of phallic injustice, fixed in the role of practitioners of servile and impotent "love," having been aroused from our numbness, have something to say about the Most Holy and Whole Trinity of Power, Justice, and Love. Grounded in ontological unity this Trinity can overcome Rape, Genocide, and their offspring, the Unholy Spirit of War, which together they spirate in mutual hate.

Women are beginning to be able to say this because of our conspiracy—our breathing together. It is being said with individuality and diversity, in the manner of *outlaws*—which is exactly what radical feminists are. It is being said in the diverse words of our lives, which are just now being spoken.

NOTES

1. Herbert Marcuse, "Marxism and the New Humanity: An Unfinished Revolution," *Marxism and Radical Religion*, ed. by John C. Raines and Thomas Dean (Philadelphia: Temple University Press, 1970), pp. 7–9.

2. Norman O. Brown, *Love's Body* (New York: Random House, 1966), pp. 132–133.

3. Theodore Roszak, *The Making of the Counter Culture* (New York: Doubleday, 1969), p. 86.

4. Alice Rossi, "Sex Equality: The Beginning of Ideology," *Masculine/Feminine*, ed. by Betty Roszak and Theodore Roszak, Harper Colophon Books (New York: Harper and Row, 1969), pp. 173–186.

5. Thomas Aquinas, *Summa theologiae* I, q. 92, a. 1, ad 2. For Aquinas, this inferiority was so inherent in female nature that women even would have been in a state of subjection before the Fall, which he understood as an historical event of the past.

6. *Ibid.*, II–II, q. 47, a. 2. See Aristotle, *Nichomachean Ethics* vi, 5.

7. See Tillich, *Systematic Theology* I, pp. 72–73.

8. Joseph Fletcher, *Situation Ethics* (Philadelphia: Westminster Press, 1966), p. 59.

9. *Ibid.*, p. 156.

10. *Ibid.*, p. 104.

11. Janice Raymond, "Beyond Male Morality," a paper delivered at the International Congress of Learned Societies in the Field of Religion, Los Angeles, September 1–5, 1972. Published by the American Academy of Religion (University of Montana) in *Proceedings of the Working Group on Women and Religion*, 1972, ed. by Judith Plaskow Goldenberg, pp. 83–93.

12. Linda Thurston, "On Male and Female Principle," *The Second Wave* I (Summer 1971), p. 39.

13. See Joyce Goldman, "The Women of Bangladesh," *Ms.* I (August 1972), p. 84.

14. *Ibid.*, p. 88. While Daly cites atrocities that were committed against women in a war that happened over twenty years ago, similar atrocities are still occurring. Recent reports from Bosnia graphically illustrate this point.—ED.

15. *Ibid.*

16. Quoted in *The Providence Sunday Journal*, January 16, 1972, p. E–1.

17. E. Ionesco, in *Nouvelle Revue Française*, July 1956, as quoted in Herbert Marcuse, *One Dimensional Man* (Boston: Beacon Press, 1964), p. 80.

18. Paul Mayer, "Jeremiah and Jesus," *American Report*, October 23, 1972, p. 2.

19. Guenter Lewy, *The Catholic Church and Nazi Germany* (New York: McGraw-Hill, 1964), p. 341.

20. *Ibid.*, p. 107.

21. Theodore Roszak, "The Hard and the Soft," in *Masculine/Feminine*, pp. 91–92.

22. Paul Tillich, *Love, Power, and Justice: Ontological Analyses and Ethical Applications*, Galaxy Books (New York: Oxford University Press, 1960), p. 18.

23. R. D. Laing, *The Politics of Experience* (New York: Ballantine Books, 1968), p. 168.

24. Tillich, *Love, Power, and Justice*, p. 65.

25. Aristotle, *Nichomachean Ethics*, Book V, ch. 10.

26. Helmut Thielicke, *The Ethics of Sex*, trans. by John W. Doberstein (New York: Harper and Row, 1964), p. 81.

27. *Ibid.*, p. 84.

28. Gunnar Myrdal, Appendix 5, "A Parallel to the Negro Problem," *An American Dilemma* (New York: Harper and Row, 1944, 1962), p. 1073.

29. Jerome Frank, *Courts on Trial: Myth and Reality in American Justice* (New York: Atheneum, 1971), pp. 384–385.

30. Henry Adams, *Mont Saint-Michel and Chartres* (New York: Collier Books, 1963), p. 260.

A Global Perspective on Feminist Ethics and Diversity

CHARLOTTE BUNCH

Charlotte Bunch (b. 1944) has been on the frontlines of the women's movement for over twenty years. An organizer, author, and teacher, Bunch was the first woman resident fellow at the Institute for Policy Studies, and co-founder of D.C. Women's Liberation. During the 1970s, she founded and edited the journal *Quest: A Feminist Quarterly*. She has also edited seven anthologies of feminist writings. Her most recent book is *Passionate Politics: Feminist Theory in Action*.

Bunch, who worked on global feminism and the U.N. Decade for Women with a variety of organizations during the 1980s, is currently a professor of Planning and Public Policy at Rutgers University, where she also serves as director of the Douglass College Center for Women's Global Leadership. The center, which works to enhance the leadership of women on global issues, recently coordinated the Global Campaign for Women's Human Rights at the 1993 United Nations World Conference on Human Rights in Vienna.

In the following essay, Bunch argues for the necessity of a global perspective for feminist ethics. She claims that feminists must be aware not only of the bias that results from viewing the world from a male or patriarchal perspective, but also of bias resulting from family, race, class, cultural, and professional differences. In addition to being aware of such bias, Bunch suggests that feminists need to examine the way in which difference is understood in Western society. She argues that whereas we have been socialized to view difference as a justification for exclusion, inequality, and domination, we must come to see difference and diversity in a positive manner. As she says, "There could be no more fundamental, ethical revolution in how we see ourselves than altering this dynamic, this model by which all differences are viewed as a matter of fear and domination." This statement is, of course, very close to Daly's call for a new type of human being.

Throughout her article, Bunch links her theoretical analysis of the requirements for developing a global perspective with accounts of her own personal growth. She claims that a global perspective requires that we move beyond perspectives limited by political or economic divisions to a view of the world that is holistic and that sees the interconnectedness of events that have traditionally been separated. She also claims that a global perspective requires that we see diversity as a "richness of possibility," whereby we can truly learn from those who are different from us, rather than merely tolerating them.

Questions for Thought

1. What does Bunch mean by seeing things from a global perspective? Why does she think that it is necessary to attain such a perspective?

2. Do you see things from a global perspective? If not, what is your perspective on the world?
3. How did the civil rights movement serve to broaden Bunch's perspective? Can you think of something in your life that has helped to broaden your own philosophical or ethical perspective?
4. How, according to Bunch, is difference traditionally viewed? How does she view difference? Which of the two views is closer to your own way of understanding difference?
5. In what ways are Bunch's criticisms of traditional morality like Daly's criticisms? In what ways are they different?
6. If you were to ask Bunch which moral values she considered most important, what do you think she would say? Which moral values do you consider to be most important?

I WANT TO BEGIN WITH A STORY I ONCE HEARD about Gandhi being interviewed by the British press during the Indian Independence struggle. When asked "What do you think of Western civilization?" he is said to have paused and replied: "What a wonderful idea!"

This story illustrates the importance of the question of perspective, of how our view of reality is shaped by our experiences and by where we stand in relation to the issues being discussed. One fundamental objective of feminism has been exposing the limitations of male-biased perspectives where women's views have been left out. But women sometimes critique male distortions without seeing race, class, age, heterosexual, ablebodied and cultural biases as well. Here I focus primarily on ethnocentric bias not because it is more important than other distortions, but because addressing it seems urgent for the development of feminism at this time.

The question of perspective is central to one of the basic tenets of feminism: "the personal is political." As the Indian feminist Gita Sen has noted, "Seen through a woman's eyes the personal is always political. It is perhaps as profound a sign as any of the fragmentation of identity that is a hallmark of our times that we have had to say so. And to justify our saying so."[1] The concept of the personal as political reflects a vital insight of feminism, but the personal is not all we need for our politics. We must also learn from the experiences of others since each of our perspectives is necessarily limited and culture-bound. While feminism begins with our own lives, we need to see how our personal experiences have been shaped and perspectives distorted by society, by the limitations and biases of our families, our race, our class, our culture, and our professions.

Another problem with understanding the implications of the personal as political is reflected in confusion between ethical principles/values and whether one's behavior is politically correct in a narrow individualistic sense—whether that's about how you cut your hair or where you go shopping. It is important to think about the political aspects of personal behavior, but the emphasis on such correctness has often led women to become obsessed with individual guilt, rather than to develop a political perspective on what can be done about these things. Trying to be politically correct often has a moralistic tone that implies if you do all the "right" things, then you can wash your hands of responsibility for being part of an oppressive culture. But there is no way to deny that responsibility, no matter how correct one's personal behavior. There is, however, the possibility of being ethical or taking responsibility for doing whatever one can about society. Ethics is, then, a critical part of politics not to be confused with moralism; ethics should inform political decisions which then embody and make concrete ethical commitments.

Today it is critical that we learn to think about such feminist questions globally. This is not a luxury or something one does as a hobby, but must be incorporated into our everyday lives. There is a tendency in the U.S. to view international as totally other than local, but that is a separation we cannot afford. Developing a global perspective is not learning a body of facts, it is a matter of one's approach. No one person can give you a global perspective, including me. But I can share reflections on my own journey as a WASP USAmerican seeking to understand the world from the perspectives of "other" experiences.

My global journey began in the 1960s in the civil rights movement in North Carolina, which first taught me that I could more profoundly understand myself by learning about the world as viewed by black people in the South. The reconstruction of my view of the world begun then led to the process of reconceptualizing myself. Since then I have tried to put myself in situations where I could see, experience, and learn from difference. I have sought to understand other ways of seeing reality through my choice of reading, conversations, public events, actions to take, and so on. Even whom you listen to and are around informally shapes how you perceive the world. For example, I watched the 1988 Democratic and Republican conventions with Latin Americans. It was embarrassing to look through their eyes at rhetoric like "Keeping America Number One" or "they can't do that to an American," implying that we have rights that other citizens in the world don't deserve. There are many opportunities in the U.S. to hear various views of this country from the outside since there are many foreign students, scholars, visitors, refugees, and immigrants here.

Speaking of U.S. elections, a feminist ethics from a global perspective reminds us that when we vote, we don't vote just for ourselves. We vote in solidarity and on behalf of all those in the world who can't vote in U.S. elections but whose lives will be affected by them. Thus a global perspective is more than just going to another country. It means looking at whatever one does here—in an election or direct action or a classroom—and seeking to understand the global implications of that situation. A global perspective requires seeing beyond the domestic versus international split and moving beyond nation-state boundaries as the defining parameters of our lives.

Global also means *integral*, taken from its Spanish definition as holistic, not just seeing the parts of a question as separate but seeing how things are connected. It means looking for the relationship between various factors usually thought of in isolation—political, economic, cultural, and spiritual—or how what happens in one part of the world is connected to another. For example, we see the inter-connectedness of women's economic and sexual subordination or of how violence against women is related to the violence of militarism. Thus we see that all forms of violence reinforce each other, from racism and homophobia to sexual assault and warfare—all are based in the dynamic of domination of one group by another backed up by physical and economic force.

A global perspective on feminist ethics requires a global vision of feminism—a feminism that is inclusive and seeks to reflect a wide diversity of women's experiences and views. It is possible to work toward this today because the 1980s brought an enormous growth in women's movements around the world, making feminism more reflective of women's diversity. One group that has articulated the significance of these movements is DAWN—Development Alternatives with Women in a New Era. This group of Third World women activists and researchers prepared a book for the 1985 End of the Decade Women's World Conference in Nairobi, declaring:

There is and must be a diversity of feminisms, responsive to the different needs and concerns of different women, and defined by them for themselves. This diversity builds on a common opposition to gender oppression and hierarchy which, however, is only the first step in articulating and acting upon a political agenda.

For many women of the world, problems of nationality, class and race are inextricably linked to their specific oppression as women. Their definition of feminism to include the struggle against all forms of oppression is legitimate and necessary. In many instances gender equality must be accompanied by changes on those other fronts as well. But, at the same time, the struggle against gender subordination cannot be compromised in the struggle against other forms of oppression, or be relegated to a future when they may be wiped out. . . . This is why we need to affirm that feminism strives for the broadest, deepest development of society and human beings, free of all systems of domination.[2]

This process of diversification and particularization of feminism has surfaced in groups not often heard about before. One example is the Network of Women Living under Muslim Laws, with women from North Africa, the Middle East, South Asia and Europe working to see what forms of feminism are meaningful to women's evolving struggles in their varying cultures. The network has exchanges among women from different Muslim communities coming together for meetings or going to work with groups in other countries for a short period. Through the efforts of such women, a body of work about what it means to be feminist in a Muslim context is emerging.

Another example is a lesbian feminist network in Latin America, which has evolved in the past decade, with groups in Brazil, Chile, Peru, Mexico, Costa Rica, and the Dominican Republic among others. Their first regional conference in Mexico in 1987 brought together over 250 Latina lesbians, many of whom are building an ongoing network of women challenging the particular forms that heterosexism takes in their region. The Muslim women and the lesbians in Latin America are some of the many women's voices speaking out today that the media ignore when they keep trying to declare feminism in decline. Yet, such global activism has been the cutting edge of feminism in the last decade.

Much emphasis in this decade has been on diversity, but there has also been recognition of commonality. The DAWN statement, for example, talks about common opposition to gender subordination and to domination in all its forms. The global feminist vision of justice seeks to end gender subordination along with other forms of domination to which it is connected. On the individual level, a common goal has been the empowerment of every woman to gain more control over her life.

This global approach to feminist ethics requires seeing feminism as a standpoint or a political perspective on the world. It is a way of understanding ourselves and the world around us, of interpreting our reality and guiding our actions. It begins with any woman's experiences that have been denied, and moves from there to a broader view of diverse women's experiences. It also reinterprets men's experiences and definitions of reality from the point of view of women. For, though a feminist standpoint starts with women's lives at the center, it is not synonymous with being female or just about a single set of issues; rather, it is about reinterpreting any issue from this approach, which anyone can choose to develop.

The Issue of Difference

In looking at feminist writings on ethics, I felt there was not enough attention paid to the question of diversity and difference among women. The issue of differences among people is probably the key question for feminism today. The way our societies deal with differences of race, class, culture, nation, sex, sexual preference, and so on, and those between people and the rest of nature, is part of the cycle of patriarchal domination and destruction that is bringing the planet to the point of self-destruction. This question of differences in all its manifestations is quite simply a question of survival. It is an issue not only of differences within feminist groups, which is often how it gets discussed, but also of how we challenge the basic ways we've been socialized to view the question of difference. It's not only that we need to learn more about different people, but also that we have to learn how to view diversity differently. We need new ways of thinking about the issue of difference.

For example, much of the debate about feminism has focused on the nature versus nurture question of whether differences of sex are innate or socially constructed. My assumption is that they are not biological, or at least that we cannot know much about what's innate for some time because our gender concepts are deeply ingrained. But what interests me more is why we are so focused on that question.

I see the crucial question as: Why does difference have to mean inequality? The basic issue is not whether gender differences are biological—even if we should discover they are, why does that have to lead to inequality? Our fears in looking at the issue of biological differences are rooted in patriarchal culture, where we know only difference as inequality. We know little about societies where diversity is respected as truly complementary and equal. There's often been rhetoric about women and men as being complementary, but we know that's usually a cover-up for female oppression. The question therefore is whether it is possible to separate issues of diversity from domination. Is it possible to think and live in a way that relates to difference from another set of assumptions? If we could separate difference from domination, we could move toward a genuine discussion of the biology, nature–nurture question in which we wouldn't have to fear the results, because they would no longer be so loaded.

Talk about diversity can fall into sloppy pluralism in which everything is diverse and nothing matters. But if we do not equate difference with inequality and domination, it is possible to have genuine debate about differences without carrying power-over baggage. We could argue with respect over what is most effective and liberating, rather than fall into our culture's obsession with who is number one/correct and therefore has the right to dominate others.

For example, we wouldn't be talking after a presidential debate about who won, but of how much the debate showed us about the candidate's character or of the direction he might take the nation. What does winning the debate have to do with being a good president? It doesn't tell us who expressed the values and concerns we have. The emphasis should be on whose vision and plans we see as the most humane, motivating, or viable, rather than on who won the contest. This example reveals how the dynamic of domination distorts public life.

There could be no more fundamental, ethical revolution in how we see ourselves than altering this dynamic, this model by which all differences are viewed as a matter of fear and domination. Violence throughout the world is fueled by this dynamic, which leads people to concentrate on who is going to be on top, who is going to dominate and who will lose, rather than on how we might all survive better together.

Positive Approaches to Diversity

I would like to suggest positive ways of thinking about diversity because there is a tendency to see it as a problem to be solved. This reminds me of the way people once talked about "the woman question," or "the negro problem," mistakenly implying that the problem was women or blacks, rather than understanding that the problem was racism and sexism. So too with the issue of diversity, there is nothing inherently problematic or wrong about the existence of differences between people. On the contrary, differences can be a source of richness, insight, and variety. But many fear and avoid differences because of this negative assumption that one side has to be right or better or dominate the other.

This difficulty with difference occurs not only around identity issues such as sex or race but also in relation to political differences. For example, in feminist debates over whether sex, race, or class was the most important factor of oppression, there was often little space to discuss the really vital issue of how the three interact in affecting women's lives. Or in arguments over feminist ethics, it's not a question of whether justice or caring is more important, but of whether we can create a more equal relationship between these principles.

Feminist ethics that builds on interrelatedness and balances differing values requires that we live with complexity and see diversity positively. The problem is not diversity but how we approach differences and the power, privilege, and prejudice that our culture has structured around it. Audre Lorde has illuminated this question:

> As a 49-year-old Black lesbian feminist socialist mother of two, including one boy, and a member of an interracial couple, I usually find myself part of some group defined as other, deviant, inferior or just plain wrong. . . . Certainly there are very real differences between us, differences of race, of age, of sex and sexual preference. But it is not those differences between us that are separating us. It is rather our refusal to recognize those differences and to examine the distortions which result from our misnaming them and their effects upon human behavior and expectation.[3]

In stating that it is not the differences, but the way in which we relate to them that is the problem, Lorde points us toward examining how people deny diversity or pretend it doesn't have a social or political impact on all of us. Only through acknowledging diversity and dealing with the problems that society has created around it can we begin to have unity through respecting and valuing diversity. In order for diversity to function fully as a creative source of richness and possibility, it must be de-coupled

from economic, political, and social power and privileges. Differences will divide us as long as they are the basis upon which any group is denied power and resources. This de-coupling is the critical political task; the personal work is to change how each of us thinks about and functions with regard to these issues. The two tasks go hand in hand.

When diversity is understood as richness of possibility, it is possible to move beyond tolerance toward a genuine engagement around difference. Don't get me wrong—I'm for tolerance over intolerance any day. But feminist appreciation of diversity must move beyond tolerance to valuing diversity not by condescendingly allowing others to live but by learning from them. This helps us see the changes necessary in the world more clearly and broadens our perspective on ourselves. This approach to diversity is not always easy or comfortable to carry out, but it is both politically necessary and personally rewarding to try it.

In the effort to learn from and value diversity, we must put it at the center of our inquiries. Too often in women's studies and movements, diversity is something that gets added on at the end. For example, a class studies "women" and then looks at "other" groups of women—lesbians, older women, Latinas, and so on—which implies that the first study of white, middle-class, heterosexual U.S. women of a certain age is the norm and all the rest (the majority of the female population) is added on to that essence of womanhood.

We must not assume that there is any one female core experience and, instead, view the diversity of women as the center from which we then explore commonness. To look at a question in this way, one might start with a nondominant group's experience rather than from the dominant position. As bell hooks has pointed out in *Feminist Theory: From Margin to Center*, in viewing that which is defined as marginal one comes to understand the norm more profoundly and to understand the impact of the norm and its distortion of reality.[4] For example, in discussing motherhood, begin with lesbian mothers or teenage mothers. Starting with those who don't fit the norm and seeing the institution from that perspective will alter how one views the issue.

Global Feminist Ethics

Following this approach to diversity, it is useful to look at feminist ethics as discussed in other countries. Gita Sen, in "Ethics in Third World Development: A Feminist Perspective," declares that the ethics of development in our time has to do with the simple survival of human beings and of humanness. Thus she speaks of ethics not as a secondary or academic matter, but as the heart of human survival. She suggests that by looking at women's survival efforts in the Third World, we see not only women's ethics coming out of that struggle but also the basis for developing values for the culture.[5]

Sen's is not an abstract inquiry; she states that she is trying to convince government and development planners to listen to poor, Third World women as the source of ideas that could provide solutions to the problems of development in their countries. She challenges them to see that the way in which poor women have managed to survive in spite of incredible odds is by coming up with creative strategies that can also be useful to government planning. She does not claim that every survival strategy is therefore a feminist ethic or that every poor woman is more moral. Rather she says that these women's experiences have produced new ways of looking at and solving their countries' problems.

I sought to apply this approach by looking at insights and strategies that have emerged from the survival struggles of various disenfranchised groups. For example, the black civil rights movement created a context for looking at the world from the perspective of the oppressed that opened the way for many changes in U.S. culture. It offered a view of how racial domination distorted society and its concept of humanness that not only affected blacks but changed the way many of us saw the world in other areas as well. The way we saw U.S. involvement in Vietnam changed. The way we saw ourselves as women changed.

Within the U.S. feminist movement a similar development took place when lesbians reinterpreted women's reality from the perspective of the marginalized. Lesbians provided insights about what it means to be woman-identified and how male identification restrained women's search for identity and options. Being outside the dominant institution of heterosexuality, lesbians could see not just our experience of it but also how its compulsory structure affected women generally. Thus we could suggest that if every woman did not mind being called a lesbian and refused to run away from the issue, it would lose its power to control us and there would be a powerful upsurge in women's self-image and freedom. Whether one is lesbian or straight, if that fear restrains women's activities, homophobia affects us. Some women have acted on these insights from the margins while others haven't, but the ideas are now there for all to draw on.

Women of color and Third World women have been doing something similar for feminism in the eighties. They have been producing insights in many areas that women in the dominant culture often don't see, but that all of us can learn from. I'm not focusing on such women as the most oppressed or as victims— even though we must never forget that many have been brutally victimized. I'm talking about Third World women as actors who are struggling to change their lives and who have found keys to survival for themselves and in so doing are producing ideas useful to all concerned with change. This is not about some mythological, super-oppressed superwomen who are going to rise up and save the world, but about how insights and social alternatives are born from the struggles of everyday life.

Let me illustrate. During the recent dictatorship in Argentina, the women of the Plaza de

Mayo—mostly mothers and grandmothers of people who disappeared during the crackdown on dissidents—began a silent vigil every week in the Plaza holding placards with photos and names of their missing loved ones. In the midst of a ruthless dictatorship, when most were denying that anything was wrong, this simple act was a courageous ethical stand taken out of the pain in these women's lives. They refused to be silent and stood up to power, bearing witness to a reality that was being denied.

That action had an impact throughout the world as an example of a nonviolent way to stand up to militarism. The women did not single-handedly bring down the dictatorship, but they played an important role in bringing people to see the ethical necessity of facing up to what was happening. They opened up space in a closed society and provided the impetus for expanding the concept of human rights in such situations. Before that, disappearances weren't recognized as a form of human-rights abuse, just as violence against women is not understood as a human-rights abuse today, since there is no clear understanding of government responsibility for individual violations of human rights. The work of the women of the Plaza de Mayo will also help in the effort to broaden the understanding of human rights of women generally.

Another example is the movement of women in Peru and other Andean countries around "comedores populares"—community dining rooms where poor women band together to feed their families communally. They not only meet the survival needs of their families better, but also through taking action together, an empowering process occurs. Working together in the communal kitchens, the women talk about their lives and become politically active around issues ranging from food prices to domestic violence. One group passed out whistles to women in the neighborhood so that if anyone was being beaten, she could blow a whistle, or if one heard another being beaten, she blew her whistle until many women in the community were blowing their whistles to shame the man and stop the violence.

I could talk about many more examples of women taking action to break the silent acceptance of domination and bring change in their situations. In Kenya women of the Greenbelt movement have planted trees where the desertification process threatens to destroy more land and leave many families with no work or food. In India the Chipko movement was led by tribal women who literally hugged trees that were to be chopped down for "development" to prevent their destruction, which would have led to the destruction of their communities. In these actions, women are demanding an ethical accounting for the human costs of development, forcing governments and planners to consider people's needs.

Women are also bringing change in basic concepts that define how we see issues. In Chile feminists initiated a slogan that has caught on throughout Latin America: "democracia en el pais y en la casa" (democracy in the country and in the home). This concept shows the link between democracy as a public issue, which is important to people in the region, and democracy as a concept of the right to self-determination in the home. In this country we call that linkage "the personal is political" and talk about connections between the public and the private sphere. By connecting feminism to the concept of democracy, the Chileans have created a more powerful way to talk about women's rights in the language of ideals that are important to the region.

Feminists are also examining human-rights discourse and struggling with the question of whether feminist ethics is based too much on individualism. Human rights is a useful concept for defending women's rights, but women are also seeking a different relationship between individual and community rights. Here, too, we may benefit from insights from other cultures. A woman from West Africa explained that gaining the right to abortion in her country must be based on getting the community to understand that a woman's control over her body is in the interest of the community. Our challenge as feminists is not to give up such individual human rights, but to find ways to move away from the idea that these are isolated and separate from the needs of the community. How do we bring more integration of community and individual needs/rights? This is one of the areas where feminists hope to move beyond old dichotomies and dualisms that separate issues of concern. Is there not some way to reconceptualize these things that doesn't put them in opposition?

Many feminist discussions about ethics seek to bring what our society poses as opposites, such as a nurturing ethic versus a justice ethic, into a new relationship. Ways to get beyond our cultural binds may well come from seeing the issues as they are viewed by women in other countries. The next step in the discourse about feminist ethics should be to look at how questions are being addressed in other places and see what we can both learn from others as well as offer from our work. A global feminist ethic of respect for diversity is required if we are to learn from each other. This means building an exchange based on respect that grows out of acknowledging the richness of our differences while also struggling against the ways in which these divide us through an imbalance of power and privilege. Such an exchange does not deny any of our realities but it pushes us to learn to understand them more broadly by seeing other aspects of the world as well. An ethic of responsibility for our actions and solidarity and reciprocity in our interactions with each other can lay the groundwork for this exchange to become a truly global, feminist movement.

NOTES

1. Gita Sen, "Ethics in Third World Development: A Feminist Perspective." The Rama Mehta Lecture, Radcliffe College, Harvard University, April 28, 1988, manuscript p. 4.

2. Gita Sen and Caren Grown (for DAWN), *Development, Crises and Alternative Visions: Third World Feminist Perspectives* (New York: Monthly Review Press, 1987), pp. 18–19.

3. Audre Lorde, "Age, Race, Class and Sex: Women Redefining Difference," *Sister Outsider* (Trumansburg, N.Y.: The Crossing Press, 1984), pp. 114–115.

4. bell hooks, *Feminist Theory: From Margin to Center* (Boston: South End Press, 1984).

5. Sen, "Ethics," 14. Another useful look at feminist ethics from other cultures is *Speaking of Faith: Global Perspectives on Women, Religion, and Social Change*, Diana L. Eck and Devaki Jain, eds. (New Delhi: Kali for Women Press, 1986).

Politics

5

Having completed our journey down the thorny path of thinking about morality, we are now ready to embark on what might be an even more perilous path, the path of thinking about politics. Indeed, as you are no doubt well aware, the path of politics is marked by many dangers. First, there is the danger of disagreement, that is, the danger that the path of thinking about politics may end up like one of those political talk shows on CNN where the guests and commentators (usually divided into those from the left and those from the right) can't seem to agree on anything. Second, there is the danger of disloyalty, the danger that the path of political thinking may lead to conflict with some of the patriotic beliefs that you have been taught to accept unquestioningly. Third, there is the danger of dullness. While you may be one of those rare individuals who finds political discussion and argument fascinating, it is more likely that you are among those countless others who prefer to amuse themselves in almost any other way.

Why, then, should you be forced to journey down the path of political thinking? Perhaps I could convince you by appealing to Thomas Jefferson's claim that a democracy cannot thrive without well-informed and politically astute citizens. Since you live in a democracy, it is your duty to become well informed and politically astute. Or I might use the more ancient argument of Aristotle that man (this now includes women as well, even if Aristotle saw fit to exclude them) is a political animal. Since it is part of your nature, you have no choice but to journey down the path of political thinking.

Of course, despite the fact that Americans are often viewed as being apolitical, you have likely already begun this journey. In reading the preceding paragraph, you no doubt knew who Thomas Jefferson was, and it is likely that you have read at least a portion of his "Declaration of Independence." Also, you probably knew what a democracy was; and although you may have disagreed with Jefferson's claim that you have a duty to become well informed and politically astute, you had some idea of what it means to have a social duty.

In pursuing the path of political thinking in this chapter, we could choose to further discuss or define some of these concepts. We might explore the nature and legitimacy of government and spell out more carefully the exact nature of democracy as contrasted with other forms of government. Or we might look at differing theories of the nature of duty and try to figure out the exact nature of the duties that each theory implies. While these are only two of the possible directions that we might take, they are directions that have provided a primary focus for much of traditional Western political thinking.

However, while such abstract reflections on the nature of government and social duty can be found in nontraditional writings as well, these abstract reflections are not as prevalent in nontraditional political thinking as they are in Western political thinking. One important reason for this is that many nontraditional writers find themselves in a climate of political repression, and thus much of their writing is devoted to analyzing the cause of this repression and to suggesting strategies by which it can be overcome.

Analyzing the nature of political oppression and formulating practical strategies by which it can be overcome is the common theme and task that runs through all of the selections found in this chapter. Indeed, while each of the writers indulges in a certain amount of theoretical speculation, all of them are more concerned with practical political problems and solutions. This is perhaps most evident in Guevara's "We Are Practical Revolutionaries," an essay in which he shows how abstract Marxist theory was adapted in one concrete historical situation, namely, the revolutionary movement in Cuba that led to the overthrow of the Batista regime. But even in the most theoretical essay found in the chapter, West's "Philosophy, Politics, and Power: An Afro-American Perspective," the goal of the author's rather abstract analysis of the history of modern philosophy is to prepare the way for the overcoming of oppression. As West clearly says, "The principal task of the Afro-American philosopher is to keep alive the idea of a revolutionary future, a better future different from the deplorable present, a state of affairs in which the multifaceted oppression of Afro-Americans (and others) is, if not eliminated, alleviated." If we were to substitute the appropriate self-defining term into West's statement for each of the other authors in this chapter, it would be an excellent description of their tasks as well.

That this is the case with the first two authors should be immediately apparent. While Gandhi and Fanon disagree on the means for ending political oppression (Gandhi argues for the use of *satyagraha*, or nonviolence, while Fanon claims that violence is often necessary), both of them agree that political oppression must be resisted. Indeed, both of their arguments are made in the context of their own practical struggles to oust colonial governments.

Moreover, it should be equally obvious that West's statement fits the other three selections as well. In one of them, Carmichael explains the history and philosophy of black power, but he does so while providing a stinging indictment of racism and economic exploitation. In the next selection, hooks analyzes the cultural and theoretical assumptions of feminism in the United States, and provides some harsh criticisms of the women's movement. But her ultimate goal in doing so is to reform the movement so that it can ultimately lead to "feminist revolution." Finally, Rose explains the psychological and philosophical underpinnings of whiteshamanism, but her main reason for doing so is to defend the cultural and literary integrity of Native American and other peoples who have suffered from what she calls "cultural imperialism."

From these brief descriptions, it should be evident that all of the writers included in this chapter not only emphasize practical concerns over theoretical ones, but also are engaged in resistance against some form of repression or exploitation. Although this focus may be only one of the many directions that the path of political thinking might take, it seems to me that it is an important and interesting one, one that at least avoids the danger of dullness. Whether it also avoids the dangers of disagreement and disloyalty, only you can decide. However, you should keep in mind that both thinking and personal growth involve a certain amount of risk and danger, and that a life without thinking and personal growth is precisely the type of life that all of the writers in this chapter are struggling to overcome.

Principles of Nonviolence   5.1

MOHANDAS K. GANDHI

Mohandas K. Gandhi (1869–1948), also known as Mahatma ("Great-Souled"), led the Indian movement for independence from British rule. Gandhi was raised in a deeply religious home, and his parents taught him to value pacifism and the sanctity of all living things (*ahimsa*) above all else. After studying law in England, he went to South Africa to seek work. Shocked by the separatist policies that he found there, Gandhi led a series of protests against the South African government. In 1919, he returned to India to work on human rights issues in his native country. He became head of the Indian National Congress and led a famous march to the sea in 1930 to protest a British-imposed tax. Although Gandhi was arrested many times in both South Africa and India, he consistently advocated a policy of nonviolence or *satyagraha*. In 1947, he successfully negotiated with the British for Indian independence. However, just a few months after his people had won their independence, Gandhi was killed by an assassin's bullet.

In the following excerpts from his writings, which were arranged in *sutra* form by D. S. Sarma, Gandhi explains the concept of *satyagraha*, the term that he coined to refer to Indian resistance to segregation and racism in South Africa. Gandhi states that *satyagraha* is not merely passive resistance, for it is the result of an active decision to resist oppression. Moreover, whereas passive resistance has sometimes included acts of violence, Gandhi claims that *satyagraha* excludes violence in any form. Rather, *satyagraha* is the use of "soul force" or "truth force," not bodily force, to bring about social change. Indeed, Gandhi argues that in order to actualize *satyagraha* in his or her life, a person must eliminate all vestiges of anger or ill will through self-analysis and self-purification. Once this is done, the person will no longer resist violence with violence. As Gandhi says, "A *satyagrahi* will always try to overcome evil by good, anger by love, untruth by truth, *himsa* by *ahimsa*." Rejecting concern for the body and bodily pleasures, the *satyagrahi* becomes a force for social change that cannot ultimately be defeated.

Questions for Thought

1. What does Gandhi mean by *satyagraha*? Can you think of anyone other than Gandhi who has promoted and/or practiced *satyagraha*?
2. Do you think that *satyagraha* is an effective way of bringing about social change? Why or why not?
3. Why, according to Gandhi, have historians failed to note the role that *satyagraha* has played in world history? Do you think his analysis of history is accurate? Why or why not?
4. What are Gandhi's views on the relationship of the soul to the body? What is the connection between these views and the practice of *satyagraha*?
5. Can you think of anything in contemporary society that ought to be changed? If so, what strategies would you use to change it?

53

I SEE SO MUCH MISAPPREHENSION ABOUT *SATYA-graha* amongst us, as well as amongst Englishmen that, though I have said and written much about it, I think it proper to say something even at the risk of repetition.

Satyagraha was a word coined in South Africa to name a certain movement. First, even the Gujarati word for the great movement that our countrymen in South Africa were carrying on was "passive resistance." Once I happened to address a meeting of Europeans in connection with the movement, and on that occasion the European president of the meeting said there was nothing active in the power of the Indians—who were voteless and unarmed—to offer passive resistance, which could only be a weapon of the weak. He was my friend. He expressed these views without meaning any insult to us, but I felt humiliated. I was conscious that the nature of the fight that the Indians were offering in South Africa was not the result of their weakness. They had purposely decided on that sort of agitation. I took the earliest opportunity to correct my friend's views and demonstrate to him that it was beyond the power of weak men to put up a fight of the nature the Indians in South Africa were doing. They were exhibiting greater courage than that required of a soldier.

Whilst I was in England, in connection with the same movement, I saw that the suffragist women were burning buildings and whipping officers and calling their agitation "passive resistance," and the people also called it so. In the agitation of the Indians in South Africa there was no room for these violent acts. I thus saw that to let our movement be known by the name of "passive resistance" was fraught with dangers. I could not find an English word that could correctly express our movement. In the meeting of Europeans above referred to I called our movement one of "soul force." But I did not dare to make the word current as expressive of our movement. Some capable Englishmen could see the imperfectness of the words "passive resistance," but they could not suggest a better phrase. I now see that "Civil Resistance" is the phrase which can correctly express our movement. Some time ago I somehow hit upon this phrase, and so I have now been using it in English. "Civil Resistance" expresses much more than is conveyed by the phrase "Civil Disobedience," though it expresses much less than *satyagraha*.

I also saw that in South Africa, truth and justice were our only weapons, that the force we were putting forth was not brute force but soul force, be it ever so little. This force is not found to be within the power of brutes, and as truth ever contains soul force, the South African agitation began to be known in our vernacular by the name of *satyagraha*.

That *satyagraha* is thus based on purity is no exaggeration. We can now understand that *satyagraha* is not merely Civil Disobedience. At times, it may be *satyagraha* not to offer Civil Disobedience. When it appears to us to be our duty to offer Civil Disobedience—when not to offer it seems to us derogatory to our manliness and to our soul—then only Civil Disobedience can be *satyagraha*.

This *satyagraha* can be offered not only against Government but against family and society. In short, *satyagraha* may be used as between husband and wife, [between] father and son, and between friends. We may use this weapon in any sphere of life and to get redress of any grievance. The weapon purifies the one who uses it as well as the one against whom it is used. A good use of the weapon can never be undesirable and it is ever infallible. If *satyagraha* is converted into *duragraha* and thus becomes fruitful of evil results, *satyagraha* cannot be blamed.

This sort of *satyagraha* consciously or unconsciously appears to be used mostly in families. That is to say, if a son finds that his father is unjust to him, he does not put up with the injustice, and he pays the penalty with pleasure. In the end he succeeds in winning over his callous father and in having justice from him. But a deadening inertia prevents us from carrying *satyagraha* beyond the family sphere. And I have therefore thought the use of *satyagraha* in the political and social sphere to be a new experiment. Tolstoy in one of his letters drew attention to the fact that this was a new experiment.

There are some who believe that *satyagraha* may be used only in the religious sphere. My wide experience points to a contrary conclusion. We may use it in other spheres and spiritualize them, and by so doing we hasten the victory and are saved many a false thing. I am firmly of the opinion that *satyagraha* contains the observance of the manifest laws of economics, and therefore I believe *satyagraha* to be a practical affair. *Satyagraha* being, as I have shown above, a new weapon, it may take time to be understood and accepted by the people—and things pregnant with results great and good do take time—but when it pervades the land, then political and social reforms, which today take very long to be achieved, will be obtained in comparatively less time, the gulf that separates rulers and the ruled will be bridged over, and trust and love will take the place of distrust and estrangement.

There is only one thing needful for a wide propagation of *satyagraha*. If the leaders understand it correctly and put it before the people, I am sure the people are ready to welcome it. To understand its true beauty one should have unflinching faith in Truth and nonviolence. Truth does not require to be explained. I do not mean to enter here into a minute explanation of nonviolence. It means, in brief, that we should not be actuated by spite against him from whom we seek to obtain justice, that we should never think of obtaining anything from him by any violence to his person, but by pure civility. If we can trust ourselves to be equal to only this much nonviolence, the required reforms can be easily achieved.

When the whole nation adopts *satyagraha* as an eternal weapon, all our movements will take a new form. We shall be spared much of the hubbub and stump oratory, much of the petition making and passing of resolutions, and much of our mean selfishness. I see nothing in which lies social, economic, and political advancement of the nation so much as in *satyagraha*.

Satyagraha differs from Passive Resistance as the North Pole from the South. The latter has been conceived as a weapon of the weak and does not exclude the use of physical force or violence for the purpose of gaining one's end. Whereas, the former has been conceived as a weapon of the strongest and excludes the use of violence in any shape or form. . . .

Satyagraha is utter self-effacement, greatest humiliation, greatest patience, and brightest faith. It is its own reward. . . .

54

Its [*satyagraha's*] root meaning is holding on to Truth, hence Truth force. I have called it Love force or Soul force. I discovered in the earliest stages that pursuit of Truth did not admit of violence being inflicted on one's opponent, but that he must be weaned from error by patience and sympathy. For, what appears to be Truth to the one may appear to be error to the other. And patience means self-suffering. So the doctrine came to mean vindication of Truth, not by infliction of suffering on the opponent, but on oneself.

When I refuse to do a thing that is repugnant to my conscience, I use soul force. For instance, the government of the day has passed a law which is applicable to me. I do not like it. If, by using violence, I force the government to repeal the law, I am employing what may be termed body force. If I do not obey the law, and accept the penalty for its breach, I use soul force. It involves sacrifice of self.

Soul force begins when man recognizes that body force, be it ever so great, is nothing compared to the force of the soul within, which pervades not only him but all creation.

55

The fact that there are so many men still alive in the world shows that it is based not on the force of arms but on the force of truth or love. Therefore, the greatest and most unimpeachable evidence of the success of this force is to be found in the fact that, in spite of the wars of the world, it still lives on.

Thousands, indeed tens of thousands, depend for their existence on a very active working of this force. Little quarrels of millions of families in their daily lives disappear before the exercise of this force. Hundreds of nations live in peace. History does not and cannot take note of this fact.

56

History is really a record of every interruption of the even working of the force of love or of the soul. Two brothers quarrel, one of them repents and reawakens the love that was lying dormant in him, the two again begin to live in peace; nobody takes note of this. But if the two brothers, through the intervention of solicitors or for some other reason, take up arms or go to law—which is another form of the exhibition of brute force—their doings would be immediately noticed in the press, they would be the talk of their neighbors and would probably go down in history.

And what is true of families and communities is true of nations. There is no reason to believe that there is one law for families and another for nations. History, then, is a record of interruptions in the course of nature. Soul force, being natural, is not noted in history.

57

I have more than once dilated in my writings on the limits of *satyagraha*. *Satyagraha* presupposes self-discipline, self-control, self-purification, and a recognized social status in the person offering it. A *satyagrahi* must never forget the distinction between evil and the evil-doer. He must not harbor ill will or bitterness against the latter. He may not even employ needlessly offensive language against the evil person, however unrelieved his evil might be. For it should be an article of faith with every *satyagrahi* that there is no one so fallen in this world but can be converted by love. A *satyagrahi* will always try to overcome evil by good, anger by love, untruth by truth, *himsa* by *ahimsa*. *There is no other way of purging the world of evil.* Therefore, a person who claims to be a *satyagrahi* always tries by close and prayerful self-introspection and self-analysis to find out whether he is himself completely free from the taint of anger, ill will and such other human infirmities, whether he is not himself capable of those very evils against which he is out to lead a crusade. In self-purification and penance lies half the victory of a *satyagrahi*. A *satyagrahi* has faith that the silent and undemonstrative action of truth and love produces far more permanent and abiding results than speeches or such other showy performances. . . .

60

It is a fundamental principle of *satyagraha* that the tyrant whom the *satyagrahi* seeks to resist has power over his body and material possessions, but he can have no power over the soul. The soul can remain unconquered and unconquerable even when the body is imprisoned. The whole science of *satyagraha* was born from a knowledge of this fundamental truth.

61

Defeat has no place in the dictionary of nonviolence.

The path of a *satyagrahi* is beset with insurmountable difficulties. But in true *satyagraha* there is neither disappointment nor defeat. As truth is all-powerful, *satyagraha* can never be defeated.

There is no time limit for a *satyagrahi*, nor is there a limit to his capacity for suffering. Hence, there is no such thing as defeat in *satyagraha*. The so-called defeat may be the dawn of victory. It may be the agony of birth. . . .

64

The triumph of *satyagraha* consists in meeting death in the insistence on Truth.

65

From the standpoint of pure Truth, the body too is a possession. It has been truly said that desire for enjoyment creates bodies for the soul. When this desire vanishes, there remains no further need for the body, and man is free from the vicious cycle of births and deaths. The soul is omnipresent; why should she care to be confined within the cagelike body or do evil and even kill for the sake of that cage? We thus arrive at the ideal of total renunciation and learn to use the body for the purposes of service so long as it exists, so much so that service, and not bread, becomes with us the staff of life. We eat and drink, sleep and wake, for service alone. Such an attitude of mind brings us real happiness and the beatific vision in the fullness of time. . . .

70

The man who is saturated with the spirit of nonviolence has never any quarrel with a single individual. His opposition is directed to a system, to the evil in man, not against the man himself.

Concerning Violence

FRANTZ FANON

Frantz Fanon (1925–1961) was born on the island of Martinique in the French Antilles. After studying medicine in France, where he specialized in psychiatry, Fanon became a leading spokesperson for the colonized peoples of the world. From his studies of the psychology of racism and oppression, he concluded that humans could be transformed only after society was transformed, and that social transformation could not occur without violence. His first book, *Black Skin, White Masks*, chronicles the (mis)treatment of the peoples of the Antilles. When the French government assigned him to a hospital in Algeria during the Algerian attempt to win independence from France, Fanon found that his sympathies lay with the Algerian rebels. In 1956, he began working with the Algerian liberation movement, serving as an editorial writer for its underground newspaper *El Moudjahid*. In 1960, Fanon was appointed ambassador to Ghana by the Algerian Provisional Government. His work in Algeria led to two additional works dealing with the philosophy and politics of colonization, *L'An V de la Revolution Algerienne* (published in English as *A Dying Colonialism*) and *The Wretched of the Earth*. Fanon died of leukemia at age thirty-six in Washington D.C.

In the following selection from *The Wretched of the Earth*, Fanon describes colonization as a system of oppression that establishes a Manichean or dualistic world through continuous applications of force and violence. Unlike the capitalist world where the need to use police and military force against the oppressed is lessened by the educational system and by the establishment of a morality that emphasizes loyalty, the settlers' domination of the native population in the colonial world depends on the unmitigated use of brute force. This use of force is "justified" by viewing the native population as savage, that is, as an absolute other who represents the very negation of values.

Because of this absolute opposition between the settlers and the native population, Fanon argues that decolonization can never result from a rational decision to resolve differences. Rather, in clear contrast to Gandhi's emphasis on nonviolence, Fanon claims that decolonization can result only from a murderous struggle whereby the downtrodden native population seizes the power and privileges of the settlers. Born of violence and maintained by it, the colonial world can be overcome only by violence. As Fanon provocatively puts it, "The naked truth of decolonization evokes for us the searing bullets and bloodstained knives which emanate from it."

Questions for Thought

1. How does Fanon describe the colonized world? Does his description match what you know about colonization?
2. In what ways is life in the United States different from life in the colonized world that Fanon describes? In what ways is life in the United States the same?

3. Why does Fanon believe that violence is necessary for decolonization? Do you agree with his analysis?
4. What are the basic differences between Fanon's views and those of Gandhi? Can you think of any similarities between the two?
5. When, if ever, do you think that violence is justified?

NATIONAL LIBERATION, NATIONAL RENAISSANCE, the restoration of nationhood to the people, commonwealth: whatever may be the headings used or the new formulas introduced, decolonization is always a violent phenomenon. At whatever level we study it—relationships between individuals, new names for sports clubs, the human admixture at cocktail parties, in the police, on the directing boards of national or private banks—decolonization is quite simply the replacing of a certain "species" of men by another "species" of men. Without any period of transition, there is a total, complete, and absolute substitution. It is true that we could equally well stress the rise of a new nation, the setting up of a new state, its diplomatic relations, and its economic and political trends. But we have precisely chosen to speak of that kind of *tabula rasa* which characterizes at the outset all decolonization. Its unusual importance is that it constitutes, from the very first day, the minimum demands of the colonized. To tell the truth, the proof of success lies in a whole social structure being changed from the bottom up. The extraordinary importance of this change is that it is willed, called for, demanded. The need for this change exists in its crude state, impetuous and compelling, in the consciousness and in the lives of the men and women who are colonized. But the possibility of this change is equally experienced in the form of a terrifying future in the consciousness of another "species" of men and women: the colonizers.

Decolonization, which sets out to change the order of the world, is, obviously, a program of complete disorder. But it cannot come as a result of magical practices, nor of a natural shock, nor of a friendly understanding. Decolonization, as we know, is a historical process: that is to say that it cannot be understood, it cannot become intelligible nor clear to itself except in the exact measure that we can discern the movements which give it historical form and content. Decolonization is the meeting of two forces, opposed to each other by their very nature, which in fact owe their originality to that sort of substantification which results from and is nourished by the situation in the colonies. Their first encounter was marked by violence and their existence together—that is to say the exploitation of the native by the settler—was carried on by dint of a great array of bayonets and cannons. The settler and the native are old acquaintances. In fact, the settler is right when he speaks of knowing "them" well. For it is the settler who has brought the native into existence and who perpetuates his existence. The settler owes the fact of his very existence, that is to say, his property, to the colonial system.

Decolonization never takes place unnoticed, for it influences individuals and modifies them fundamentally. It transforms spectators crushed with their inessentiality into privileged actors, with the grandiose glare of history's floodlights upon them. It brings a natural rhythm into existence, introduced by new men, and with it a new language and a new humanity. Decolonization is the veritable creation of new men. But this creation owes nothing of its legitimacy to any supernatural power; the "thing" which has been colonized becomes man during the same process by which it frees itself.

In decolonization, there is therefore the need of a complete calling in question of the colonial situation. If we wish to describe it precisely, we might find it in the well-known words: "The last shall be first and the first last." Decolonization is the putting into practice of this sentence. That is why, if we try to describe it, all decolonization is successful.

The naked truth of decolonization evokes for us the searing bullets and bloodstained knives which emanate from it. For if the last shall be first, this will only come to pass after a murderous and decisive struggle between the two protagonists. That affirmed intention to place the last at the head of things, and to make them climb at a pace (too quickly, some say) the well-known steps which characterize an organized society, can only triumph if we use all means to turn the scale, including, of course, that of violence.

You do not turn any society, however primitive it may be, upside down with such a program if you have not decided from the very beginning, that is to say from the actual formulation of that program, to overcome all the obstacles that you will come across in so doing. The native who decides to put the program into practice, and to become its moving force, is ready for violence at all times. From birth it is clear to him that this narrow world, strewn with prohibitions, can only be called in question by absolute violence.

The colonial world is a world divided into compartments. It is probably unnecessary to recall the existence of native quarters and European quarters, of schools for natives and schools for Europeans; in the same way we need not recall apartheid in South Africa. Yet, if we examine closely this system of compartments, we will at least be able to reveal the lines of force it implies. This approach to the colonial world, its ordering and its geographical layout, will allow us to mark out the lines on which a decolonized society will be reorganized.

The colonial world is a world cut in two. The dividing line, the frontiers are shown by barracks and police stations. In the colonies it is the policeman and the soldier who are the official, instituted go-betweens, the spokesman of the settler and his rule of oppression. In capitalist societies the educational system, whether lay or clerical, the structure of moral reflexes handed down from father to son, the exemplary honesty of workers who are given a medal after fifty years of good and loyal service, and the affection which springs from harmonious relations and good behavior—all these aesthetic expressions of respect for the established order serve to create around the exploited person an atmosphere of submission and of inhibition which lightens the task of policing considerably. In the capitalist countries a multitude of moral teachers, counselors and "bewilderers" separate the exploited from those in power. In the colonial countries, on the contrary, the policeman and the soldier, by their immediate presence and their frequent and direct action maintain contact with the native and advise him by means of rifle butts and napalm not to budge. It is obvious here that the agents of government speak the language of pure force. The intermediary does not lighten the oppression, nor seek to hide the domination; he shows them up and puts them into practice with the clear conscience of an upholder of the peace; yet he is the bringer of violence into the home and into the mind of the native.

The zone where the natives live is not complementary to the zone inhabited by the settlers. The two zones are opposed, but not in the service of a higher unity. Obedient to the rules of pure Aristotelian logic, they both follow the principle of reciprocal exclusivity. No conciliation is possible, for of the two terms, one is superfluous. The settlers' town is a strongly built town, all made of stone and steel. It is a brightly lit town; the streets are covered with asphalt, and the garbage cans swallow all the leavings, unseen, unknown and hardly thought about.

The settler's feet are never visible, except perhaps in the sea; but there you're never close enough to see them. His feet are protected by strong shoes although the streets of his town are clean and even, with no holes or stones. The settler's town is a well-fed town, an easygoing town; its belly is always full of good things. The settlers' town is a town of white people, of foreigners.

The town belonging to the colonized people, or at least the native town, the Negro village, the medina, the reservation, is a place of ill fame, peopled by men of evil repute. They are born there, it matters little where or how; they die there, it matters not where, nor how. It is a world without spaciousness; men live there on top of each other, and their huts are built on top of each other. The native town is a hungry town, starved of bread, of meat, of shoes, of coal, of light. The native town is a crouching village, a town on its knees, a town wallowing in the mire. It is a town of niggers and dirty Arabs. The look that the native turns on the settler's town is a look of lust, a look of envy; it expresses his dreams of possession—all manner of possession: to sit at the settler's table, to sleep in the settler's bed, with his wife if possible. The colonized man is an envious man. And this the settler knows very well; when their glances meet he ascertains bitterly, always on the defensive, "They want to take our place." It is true, for there is no native who does not dream at least once a day of setting himself up in the settler's place.

This world divided into compartments, this world cut in two is inhabited by two different species. The originality of the colonial context is that economic reality, inequality, and the immense difference of ways of life never come to mask the human realities. When you examine at close quarters the colonial context, it is evident that what parcels out the world is, to begin with, the fact of belonging to or not belonging to a given race, a given species. In the colonies the economic substructure is also a superstructure. The cause is the consequence; you are rich because you are white, you are white because you are rich. This is why Marxist analysis should always be slightly stretched every time we have to do with the colonial problem.

Everything up to and including the very nature of pre-capitalist society, so well explained by Marx, must here be thought out again. The serf is in essence different from the knight, but a reference to divine right is necessary to legitimize this statutory difference. In the colonies, the foreigner coming from another country imposed his rule by means of guns and machines. In defiance of his successful transplantation, in spite of his appropriation, the settler still remains a foreigner. It is neither the act of owning factories, nor estates, nor a bank balance which distinguishes the governing classes. The governing race is first and foremost those who come from elsewhere, those who are unlike the original inhabitants, "the others."

The violence which has ruled over the ordering of the colonial world, which has ceaselessly drummed the rhythm for the destruction of native social forms and broken up without reserve the systems of reference of the economy, the customs of dress and external life, that same violence will be claimed and taken over by the native at the moment when, deciding to embody history in his own person, he surges into the forbidden quarters. To wreck the colonial world is henceforward a mental picture of action which is very clear, very easy to understand and which may be assumed by each one of the individuals which constitute the colonized people. To break up the colonial world does not mean that after the frontiers have been abolished lines of communication will be set up between the two zones. The destruction of the colonial world is no more and no less than the abolition of one zone, its burial in the depths of the earth or its expulsion from the country.

The natives' challenge to the colonial world is not a rational confrontation of points of view. It is not a treatise on the universal, but the untidy affirmation of an original idea propounded as an absolute. The colonial world is a Manichean world. It is not enough for the settler to delimit physically, that is to say with the help of the army and the police force, the place of the native. As if to show the totalitarian character of colonial exploitation the settler paints the native as a sort of quintessence of evil.[1] Native society is not simply described as a society lacking in values. It is not enough for the colonist to affirm that those values have disappeared from, or still better never existed in, the colonial world. The native is declared insensible to ethics; he represents not only the absence of values, but also the negation of values. He is, let us dare to admit, the enemy of values, and in this sense he is the absolute evil. He is the corrosive element, destroying all that comes near him; he is the deforming element, disfiguring all that has to do with beauty or morality; he is the depository of maleficent powers, the unconscious and irretrievable instrument of blind forces. . . .

A world divided into compartments, a motionless, Manicheistic world, a world of statues: the statue of the general who carried out the conquest, the statue of the engineer who built the bridge; a world which is sure of itself, which crushes with its stones the backs flayed by whips: this is the colonial world. The native is a being hemmed in; apartheid is simply one form of the division into compartments of the colonial world. The first thing which the native learns is to stay in his place, and not to go beyond certain limits. This is why the dreams of the native are always of muscular prowess; his dreams are of action and of aggression. I dream I am jumping, swimming, running, climbing; I dream that I burst out laughing, that I span a river in one stride, or that I am followed by a flood of motorcars which never catch up with me. During the period of colonization, the native never stops achieving his freedom from nine in the evening until six in the morning.

The colonized man will first manifest this aggressiveness which has been deposited in his bones against his own people. This is the period when the niggers beat each other up, and the police and magistrates do not know which way to turn when faced with the astonishing waves of crime in North Africa. . . . When the native is confronted with the colonial order of things, he finds he is in a state of permanent tension. The settler's world is a hostile world, which spurns the native, but at the same time it is a world of which he is envious. We have seen that the native never ceases to dream of putting himself in the place of the settler—not of becoming the settler but of substituting himself for the settler. This hostile world, ponderous and aggressive because it fends off the colonized masses with all the harshness it is capable of, represents not merely a hell from which the swiftest flight possible is desirable, but also a paradise close at hand which is guarded by terrible watchdogs.

The native is always on the alert, for since he can only make out with difficulty the many symbols of the colonial world, he is never sure whether or not he has crossed the frontier. Confronted with a world ruled by the settler, the native is always presumed guilty. But the native's guilt is never a guilt which he accepts; it is rather a kind of curse, a sort of sword of Damocles, for, in his innermost spirit, the native admits no accusation. He is overpowered but not tamed; he is treated as an inferior but he is not convinced of his inferiority. He is patiently waiting until the settler is off his guard to fly at him. The native's muscles are always tensed. You can't say that he is terrorized, or even apprehensive. He is in fact ready at a moment's notice to exchange the role of the quarry for that of the hunter. The native is an oppressed person whose permanent dream is to become the persecutor. The symbols of social order—the police, the bugle calls in the barracks, military parades and the waving flags—are at one and the same time inhibitory and stimulating: for they do not convey the message "Don't dare to budge"; rather, they cry out "Get ready to attack." And, in fact, if the native had any tendency to fall asleep and to forget, the settler's hauteur and the settler's anxiety to test the strength of the colonial system would remind him at every turn that the great showdown cannot be put off indefinitely.

NOTES

1. We have demonstrated the mechanism of this Manichean world in *Black Skin, White Masks* (New York: Grove Press, 1967).

Power and Racism   5.3

STOKELY CARMICHAEL

Stokely Carmichael (b. 1941) was born in Port-of-Spain, Trinidad. His parents immigrated to the United States in 1952. In 1960, Carmichael joined CORE (the Congress of Racial Equality) and became involved with the Freedom Rides that were organized to protest segregation on public buses in the South. Carmichael then entered Howard University, from which he graduated in 1964. In 1966, he became chairperson of the Student Nonviolent Coordinating Committee (SNCC), and he later served as prime minister of the Black Panther Party. In 1969, after becoming further disillusioned with the racist attitudes that still prevailed in many areas of the United States, Carmichael and his wife, Miriam Makeba, emigrated to Guinea, where he still resides. Carmichael has adopted the African name Kwame Turé.

In the following article, which was written in 1966 when he was chairperson of SNCC, Carmichael explains the concept of black power as a response to the pervasive racism that existed in the United States at that time. Carmichael criticizes the civil rights movement, which had adopted a philosophy of nonviolence similar to that espoused by Gandhi, for operating from a position of weakness. He also criticizes the struggle for integration as a subterfuge for the maintenance of white supremacy.

In place of nonviolence and integration, Carmichael calls for the acquisition of political and economic power. After describing the movement to attain voting rights in the South and acknowledging its ultimate failure, Carmichael argues that racism can be overcome only by shaking the very foundations of the American economy. Progressive people, blacks as well as whites, must learn to recognize the United States as an "octopus of exploitation," whereby "a powerful few have been maintained and enriched at the expense of the poor and voiceless colored masses." By recognizing that racism and hypocrisy extend to the very core of political and economic life in the United States, it may be possible to slay this octopus of exploitation and replace it with a new society in which "the spirit of community and humanistic love prevail."

Questions for Thought

1. What does Carmichael mean by black power? Do you think that black power is an important political concept? Why or why not?
2. How do you think Carmichael would respond to Gandhi's notion of *satyagraha*?
3. What reasons does Carmichael give for claiming that the United States is an "octopus of exploitation"? Can you think of any historical examples that might support this claim?
4. To what extent do you think contemporary society is racist? Do you believe that it is more or less racist than when Carmichael wrote this article?
5. What is the point of Carmichael's remarks about Tarzan? Do you think that the example of Tarzan is well chosen?
6. Why does Carmichael reject the call for integration? How would you define integration? Do you agree with Carmichael's criticisms of the value of integration? Why or why not?

ONE OF THE TRAGEDIES OF THE STRUGGLE against racism is that up to now there has been no national organization which could speak to the growing militancy of young black people in the urban ghetto. There has been only a civil rights movement, whose tone of voice was adapted to an audience of liberal whites. It served as a sort of buffer zone between them and angry young blacks. None of its so-called leaders could go into a rioting community and be listened to. In a sense, I blame ourselves—together with the mass media—for what has happened in Watts, Harlem, Chicago, Cleveland, and Omaha.[1] Each time the people in those cities saw Martin Luther King get slapped, they became angry; when they saw four little black girls bombed to death, they were steaming.[2] We had nothing to offer that they could see, except to go out and be beaten again. We helped build their frustration.

For too many years, black Americans marched and had their heads broken and got shot. They were saying to the country, "Look, you guys are supposed to be nice guys and we are only going to do what we are supposed to do—why do you beat us up, why don't you give us what we ask, why don't you straighten your-selves out?" After years of this, we are at almost the same point—because we demonstrated from a position of weakness. We cannot be expected any longer to march and have our heads broken in order to say to whites: come on, you're nice guys. For you are not nice guys. We have found you out.

An organization which claims to speak for the needs of a community—as does the Student Nonviolent Coordinating Committee—must speak in the tone of that community, not as somebody else's buffer zone. This is the significance of black power as a slogan. For once, black people are going to use the words they want to use—not just the words whites want to hear. And they will do this no matter how often the press tries to stop the use of the slogan by equating it with racism or separatism.

An organization which claims to be working for the needs of a community—as SNCC does—must work to provide that community with a position of strength from which to make its voice heard. This is the significance of black power beyond the slogan.

Black power can be clearly defined for those who do not attach the fears of white America to their questions about it. We should begin with the basic fact that black Americans have two problems: they are poor and they are black. All other problems arise from this two-sided reality: lack of education, the so-called apathy of black men. Any program to end racism must address itself to that double reality.

Almost from its beginning, SNCC sought to address itself to both conditions with a program aimed at winning political power for impoverished Southern blacks. We had to begin with politics because black Americans are a propertyless people in a country where property is valued above all. We had to work for power, because this country does not function by morality, love, and nonviolence, but by power. Thus we determined to win political power, with the idea of moving on from there into activity that would have economic effects. With power, the masses could *make or participate in making* the decisions which govern their destinies, and thus create basic change in their day-to-day lives.

But if political power seemed to be the key to self-determination, it was also obvious that the key had been thrown down a deep well many years earlier. Disenfranchisement, maintained by racist terror, made it impossible to talk about organizing for political power in 1960. The right to vote had to be won, and SNCC workers devoted their energies to this from 1961 to 1965. They set up voter registration drives in the Deep South. They created pressure for the vote by holding mock elections in Mississippi in 1963 and by helping to establish the Mississippi Freedom Democratic Party (MFDP) in 1964. That struggle was eased, though not won, with the passage of the 1965 Voting Rights Act. SNCC workers could then address themselves to the question: "Who can we vote for, to have our needs met—how do we make our vote meaningful?"

SNCC had already gone to Atlantic City for recognition of the Mississippi Freedom Democratic Party by the Democratic convention and been rejected; it had gone with the MFDP to Washington for recognition by Congress and been rejected. In Arkansas, SNCC helped thirty Negroes to run for School Board elections; all but one were defeated, and there was evidence of fraud and intimidation sufficient to cause their defeat. In Atlanta, Julian Bond ran for the state legislature and was elected—twice—and unseated—twice. In several states, black farmers ran in elections for agricultural committees which make crucial decisions concerning land use, loans, etc. Although they won places on a number of committees, they never gained the majorities needed to control them. . . .

Ultimately, the economic foundations of this country must be shaken if black people are to control their lives. The colonies of the United States—and this includes the black ghettos within its borders, north and south—must be liberated. For a century, this nation has been like an octopus of exploitation, its tentacles stretching from Mississippi and Harlem to South America, the Middle East, southern Africa, and Vietnam; the form of exploitation varies from area to area but the essential result has been the same—a powerful few have been maintained and enriched at the expense of the poor and voiceless colored masses. This pattern must be broken. As its grip loosens here and there around the world, the hopes of black Americans become more realistic. For racism to die, a totally different America must be born.

This is what the white society does not wish to face; this is why that society prefers to talk about integration. But integration speaks not at all to the problem of poverty, only to the problem of blackness. Integration . . . means the man who "makes it," leaving his black brothers behind in the ghetto as fast as his new sports car will take him. It has no relevance to the Harlem wino or to the cottonpicker making three dollars a day. As a lady I know in Alabama once said, "The food that Ralph Bunche eats doesn't fill my stomach."

Integration, moreover, speaks to the problem of blackness in a despicable way. As a goal, it has been based on complete acceptance of the fact that *in order to have* a decent house or education, blacks must move into a white neighborhood or send their children to a white school. This reinforces, among both black and white, the idea that "white" is automatically better and "black" is by definition inferior. This is why integration is a subterfuge for the maintenance of white supremacy. It allows the nation to focus on a handful of Southern children who get into white schools, at great price, and to ignore the 94 percent who are left behind in unimproved all-black schools. Such situations will not change until black people have power—to control their own school boards, in this case. Then Negroes become equal in a way that means something, and integration ceases to be a one-way street. Then integration doesn't mean draining skills and energies from the ghetto into white neighborhoods; then it can mean white people moving from Beverly Hills into Watts, white people joining the Lowndes County Freedom Organization. Then integration becomes relevant.[3]

In April 1966, before the furor over black power, Christopher Jencks wrote in a *New Republic* article on white Mississippi's manipulation of the antipoverty program:

> The war on poverty has been predicated on the notion that there is such a thing as *a community* which can be defined geographically and mobilized for a collective effort to help the poor. This theory has no relationship to reality in the Deep South. In every Mississippi county there are *two* communities. Despite all the pious platitudes of the moderates on both sides, these two communities habitually see their interests in terms of conflict rather than cooperation. Only when the Negro community can muster enough political, economic and professional strength to compete on somewhat equal terms, will Negroes believe in the possibility of true cooperation and whites accept its necessity. En route to integration, the Negro community needs to develop greater independence—a chance to run its own affairs and not

cave in whenever "the man" barks. . . . Or so it seems to me, and to most of the knowledgeable people with whom I talked in Mississippi. To OEO, this judgment may sound like black nationalism.

Mr. Jencks, a white reporter, perceived the reason why America's antipoverty program has been a sick farce in both North and South. In the South, it is clearly racism which prevents the poor from running their own programs; in the North, it more often seems to be politicking and bureaucracy. But the results are not so different. . . . Behind it all is a federal government which cares far more about winning the war on the Vietnamese than the war on poverty; which has put the poverty program in the hands of self-serving politicians and bureaucrats rather than the poor themselves; which is unwilling to curb the misuse of white power but quick to condemn black power.

To most whites, black power seems to mean that the Mau Mau are coming to the suburbs at night. The Mau Mau are coming, and whites must stop them. Articles appear about plots to "get Whitey," creating an atmosphere in which "law and order must be maintained." Once again, responsibility is shifted from the oppressor to the oppressed. Other whites chide, "Don't forget—you're only 10 per cent of the population; if you get too smart, we'll wipe you out." If they are liberals, they complain, "What about me?—don't you want my help any more?" These are people supposedly concerned about black Americans, but today they think first of themselves, of their feelings of rejection. Or they admonish, "You can't get anywhere without coalitions," without considering the problems of coalition with whom?; on what terms? (coalescing from weakness can mean absorption, betrayal); when? Or they accuse us of "polarizing the races" by our calls for black unity, when the true responsibility for polarization lies with whites who will not accept their responsibility as the majority power for making the democratic process work.

White America will not face the problem of color, the reality of it. The well-intended say: "We're all human, everybody is really decent, we must forget color." But color cannot be "forgotten" until its weight is recognized and dealt with. White America will not acknowledge that the ways in which this country sees itself are contradicted by being black—and always have been. Whereas most of the people who settled this country came here for freedom or for economic opportunity, blacks were brought here to be slaves. When the Lowndes County Freedom Organization chose the black panther as its symbol, it was christened by the press "the Black Panther Party"—but the Alabama Democratic Party, whose symbol is a rooster, has never been called the White Cock Party. No one ever talked about "white power" because power in this country *is* white. All this adds up to more than merely identifying a group phenomenon by some catchy name or adjective. The furor over that black panther reveals the problems that white America has with color and sex; the furor over "black power" reveals how deep racism runs and the great fear which is attached to it.

Whites will not see that I, for example, as a person oppressed because of my blackness, have common cause with other blacks who are oppressed because of blackness. This is not to say that there are no white people who see things as I do, but that it is black people I must speak to first. It must be the oppressed to whom SNCC addresses itself primarily, not to friends from the oppressing group.

From birth, black people are told a set of lies about themselves. We are told that we are lazy—yet I drive through the Delta area of Mississippi and watch black people picking cotton in the hot sun for fourteen hours. We are told, "If you work hard, you'll succeed"—but if that were true, black people would own this country. We are oppressed because we are black—not because we are ignorant, not because we are lazy, not because we're stupid (and got good rhythm), but because we're black.

I remember that when I was a boy, I used to go to see Tarzan movies on Saturday. White Tarzan used to beat up the black natives. I would sit there yelling, "Kill the beasts, kill the savages, kill 'em!" I was saying: Kill *me*. It was as if a Jewish boy watched Nazis taking Jews off to concentration camps and cheered them on. Today, I want the chief to beat hell out of Tarzan and send him back to Europe. But it takes time to become free of the lies and their shaming effect on black minds. It takes time to reject the most important lie: that black people inherently can't do the same things white people can do, unless white people help them.

The need for psychological equality is the reason why SNCC today believes that blacks must organize in the black community. Only black people can convey the revolutionary idea that black people are able to do things themselves. Only they can help create in the community an aroused and continuing black consciousness that will provide the basis for political strength. In the past, white allies have furthered white supremacy without the whites involved realizing it—or wanting it, I think. Black people must do things for themselves; they must get poverty money they will control and spend themselves, they must conduct tutorial programs themselves so that black children can identify with black people. This is one reason Africa has such importance: The reality of black men ruling their own nations gives blacks elsewhere a sense of possibility, of power, which they do not now have.

This does not mean we don't welcome help, or friends. But we want the right to decide whether anyone is, in fact, our friend. In the past, black Americans have been almost the only people whom everybody and his momma could jump up and call their friends. We have been tokens, symbols, objects—as I was in high school to many young whites, who liked having "a Negro friend." We want to decide who is our friend, and we will not accept someone who comes to us and says: "If you do X, Y, and Z, then I'll help you." We will not be told whom we should choose as allies. We will not be isolated from any group or nation except by our own choice. We cannot have the oppressors telling the oppressed how to rid themselves of the oppressor.

I have said that most liberal whites react to "black power" with the question, What about me?, rather than saying: Tell me what you want me to do and I'll see if I can do it. There are answers to the right question. One of the most disturbing things about almost all white supporters of the movement has been that they are afraid to go into their own communities—which is where the racism exists—and work to get rid of it. They want to run from Berkeley to tell us what to do in Mississippi; let them look instead at Berkeley. They admonish blacks to be nonviolent; let them preach nonviolence in the white community. They come to teach me Negro history; let them go to the suburbs and open up freedom schools for whites. Let them work to stop America's racist foreign policy; let them press this government to cease supporting the economy of South Africa.

There is a vital job to be done among poor whites. We hope to see, eventually, a coalition between poor blacks and poor whites. That is the only coalition which seems acceptable to us, and we see such a coalition as the major internal instrument of change in American society. . . . It is purely academic today to talk about bringing poor blacks and whites together, but the job of creating a poor-white power bloc must be attempted. The main responsibility for it falls upon whites. Black and white can work together in the white community where possible; it is not possible, however, to go into a poor Southern town and talk about integration. Poor whites everywhere are becoming more hostile—not less—partly because they see the nation's attention focused on black poverty and nobody coming to them.[4] . . .

Black people do not want to "take over" this country. They don't want to "get whitey"; they just want to get him off their backs, as the saying goes. It was for example the exploitation by Jewish landlords and merchants which first created black resentment toward Jews—not Judaism. The white man is irrelevant to blacks, except as an oppressive force. Blacks want to be in his place, yes, but not in order to terrorize and lynch and starve him. They want to be in his place because that is where a decent life can be had.

But our vision is not merely of a society in which all black men have enough to buy the good things of life. When we urge that black money go into black pockets, we mean the communal pocket. We want to see money go back into the community and used to benefit it. We want to see the cooperative concept applied in business and banking. We want to see black ghetto residents demand that an exploiting landlord or storekeeper sell them, at minimal cost, a building or a shop that they will own and improve cooperatively; they can back their demand with a rent strike, or a boycott, and a community so unified behind them that no one else will move into the building or buy at the store. The society we seek to build among black people, then, is not a capitalist one. It is a society in which the spirit of community and humanistic love prevail. The word love is suspect; black expectations of what it might produce have been betrayed too often. But those were expectations of a response from the white community, which failed us. The love we seek to encourage is within the black community, the only American community where men call each other "brother" when they meet. We can build a community of love only where we have the ability and power to do so: among blacks.

As for white America, perhaps it can stop crying out against "black supremacy," "black nationalism," "racism in reverse," and begin facing reality. The reality is that this nation, from top to bottom, is racist; that racism is not primarily a problem of "human relations" but of an exploitation maintained—either actively or through silence—by society as a whole. Camus and Sartre have asked, can a man condemn himself? Can whites, particularly liberal whites, condemn themselves? Can they stop blaming us, and blame their own system? Are they capable of the shame which might become a revolutionary emotion?

We have found that they usually cannot condemn themselves, and so we have done it. But the rebuilding of this society, if at all possible, is basically the responsibility of whites—not blacks. We won't fight to save the present society, in Vietnam or anywhere else. We are just going to work, in the way *we* see fit, and on goals *we* define, not for civil rights but for all our human rights.

NOTES

1. When Carmichael wrote this article, all of these cities had just experienced periods of urban rioting, resulting in much death and destruction.—ED.

2. Carmichael is referring to the bombing of the Sixteenth Street Baptist Church in Birmingham, Alabama, on September 15, 1963. Four young girls, Addie Mae Collins, Denise McNair, Carole Robertson, and Cynthia Wesley, were killed by the explosion.—ED.

3. One might still wonder today, over twenty years after this was written, whether the type of meaningful integration that Carmichael envisions has been realized on a broad scale.—ED.

4. Recent attacks on affirmative action programs, as well as increased incidences of hate crimes throughout the United States, suggest that this problem still exists. Of course in many places today, much of the resentment is directed toward recent immigrants, such as Mexicans and Southeast Asians, rather than African Americans.—ED.

Racism and Feminism   5.4

BELL HOOKS

bell hooks (b. 1952) is the pseudonym of Gloria Watkins, a writer, speaker, and teacher who grew up in Kentucky. Hooks, who received her B.A. from Stanford University and her Ph.D. from the University of California, Santa Cruz, is currently a professor of English and Women's Studies at Oberlin College. She has also taught in the African American Studies Department at Yale University.

Hooks has published extensively in progressive periodicals, including *Aurora, Catalyst, Discourse, Sage,* and *Zeta.* Her books include *Black Looks: Race and Representation; Yearning: Race, Gender, and Cultural Politics; Feminist Theory: From Margin to Center; Ain't I a Woman: Black Women and Feminism; Talking Back: Thinking Feminist, Thinking Black;* and *Breaking Bread: Insurgent Black Intellectual Life* (with Cornel West).

In the following excerpt from *Ain't I a Woman,* hooks examines the way in which racism pervades the lives of American women. She argues that women are socialized to perceive racism in terms of race hatred and prejudice, and not in terms of political ideology or imperialism. Because of this, women are not only prevented from recognizing the way in which racism has served as an essential cornerstone of the American economic system, they are also prevented from acknowledging the extent to which their own psyches have been warped by racist and classist assumptions.

Hooks goes on to argue that these racist and classist assumptions are nowhere more evident than in the women's rights movement. In her examination of classical and contemporary feminist writings, hooks notes that there has been a definite tendency to exclude women of color by assuming that the white woman's experience is representative of women's experience as a whole. Moreover, both classical and contemporary feminists have refused to distinguish between levels of oppression, and have thus inappropriately used the oppression of black men as a metaphor for their own oppression. Finally, by viewing liberation in terms of the right to work and by failing to denounce capitalist exploitation, feminists have generally ignored the plight of the working poor.

Despite these shortcomings, hooks believes that a feminist revolution is both a possibility and a necessity. This revolution, however, can be achieved only if women are willing to acknowledge the extent to which they have been socialized to be racist, classist, and sexist. They must also recognize that the attempt to define liberation in terms of economic status has been largely determined by the white male power structure, a structure that "denies unity, denies common connections and is inherently divisive." If women are to achieve true liberation, this divisiveness must be overcome, and racism, as one form of this divisiveness, must be eliminated.

Questions for Thought

1. How, according to hooks, have women been socialized to be racist? Do you agree with her analysis?
2. In what ways is hooks's critique of American society similar to that of Carmichael? In what ways is it different?
3. What reasons does hooks give to support her claim that the women's rights movement has been racist and classist? Are her reasons convincing?
4. Like Gandhi, hooks criticizes history books for being biased. Do you think that your history books have given you an accurate picture of American and world history? Why or why not?
5. Does hooks consider work to be oppressive or liberating? What is her attitude toward capitalism?
6. Why do you think hooks favors a feminist revolution? Can you think of any reasons of your own for favoring a feminist revolution?

AMERICAN WOMEN OF ALL RACES ARE SOCIALIZED to think of racism solely in the context of race hatred. Specifically in the case of black and white people, the term racism is usually seen as synonymous with discrimination or prejudice against black people by white people. For most women, the first knowledge of racism as institutionalized oppression is engendered either by direct personal experience or through information gleaned from conversations, books, televi-

Reprinted by permission of South End Press.

sion, or movies. Consequently, the American woman's understanding of racism as a political tool of colonialism and imperialism is severely limited. To experience the pain of race hatred or to witness that pain is not to understand its origin, evolution, or impact on world history. The inability of American women to understand racism in the context of American politics is not due to any inherent deficiency in woman's psyche. It merely reflects the extent of our victimization.

No history books used in public schools informed us about racial imperialism. Instead we were given romantic notions of the "new world," the "American dream," America as the great melting pot where all races come together as one. We were taught that Columbus *discovered* America; that "Indians" were scalphunters, killers of innocent women and children; that black people were enslaved because of the biblical curse of Ham, that God "himself" had decreed they would be hewers of wood, tillers of the field, and bringers of water. No one talked of Africa as the cradle of civilization, of African and Asian people who came to America before Columbus. No one mentioned mass murders of Native Americans as genocide, or the rape of Native American and African women as terrorism. No one discussed slavery as a foundation for the growth of capitalism. No one described the forced breeding of white wives to increase the white population as sexist oppression.

I am a black woman. I attended all-black public schools. I grew up in the south where all around me was the fact of racial discrimination, hatred, and forced segregation. Yet my education as to the politics of race in American society was not that different from that of white female students I met in integrated high schools, in college, or in various women's groups. The majority of us understood racism as a social evil perpetuated by prejudiced white people that could be overcome through bonding between blacks and liberal whites, through militant protest, changing of laws or racial inte-

gration. Higher educational institutions did nothing to increase our limited understanding of racism as a political ideology. Instead professors systematically denied us truth, teaching us to accept racial polarity in the form of white supremacy and sexual polarity in the form of male dominance.

American women have been socialized, even brainwashed, to accept a version of American history that was created to uphold and maintain racial imperialism in the form of white supremacy and sexual imperialism in the form of patriarchy. One measure of the success of such indoctrination is that we perpetuate both consciously and unconsciously the very evils that oppress us. I am certain that the black female sixth grade teacher who taught us history, who taught us to identify with the American government, who loved those students who could best recite the pledge of allegiance to the American flag was not aware of the contradiction; that we should love this government that segregated us, that failed to send schools with all black students supplies that went to schools with only white pupils. Unknowingly she implanted in our psyches a seed of the racial imperialism that would keep us forever in bondage. For how does one overthrow, change, or even challenge a system that you have been taught to admire, to love, to believe in? Her innocence does not change the reality that she was teaching black children to embrace the very system that oppressed us, that she encouraged us to support it, to stand in awe of it, to die for it.

That American women, irrespective of their education, economic status, or racial identification, have undergone years of sexist and racist socialization that has taught us to blindly trust our knowledge of history and its effect on present reality, even though that knowledge has been formed and shaped by an oppressive system, is nowhere more evident than in the recent feminist movement. The group of college-educated white middle and upper class women who came together to organize a women's movement brought a new energy to the concept of women's rights in America. They were not merely advocating social equality with men. They demanded a transformation of society, a revolution, a change in the American social structure. Yet as they attempted to take feminism beyond the realm of radical rhetoric and into the realm of American life, they revealed that they had not changed, had not undone the sexist and racist brainwashing that had taught them to regard women unlike themselves as Others. Consequently, the Sisterhood they talked about has not become a reality, and the women's movement they envisioned would have a transformative effect on American culture has not emerged. Instead, the hierarchical pattern of race and sex relationships already established in American society merely took a different form under "feminism": the form of women being classed as an oppressed group under affirmative action programs further perpetuating the myth that the social status of all women in America is the same; the form of women's studies programs being established with all-white faculty teaching literature almost exclusively by white women about white women and frequently from racist perspectives; the form of white women writing books that purport to be about the experience of American women when in fact they concentrate solely on the experience of white women; and finally the form of endless argument and debate as to whether or not racism was a feminist issue.

If the white women who organized the contemporary movement toward feminism were at all remotely aware of racial politics in American history, they would have known that overcoming barriers that separate women from one another would entail confronting the reality of racism, and not just racism as a general evil in society but the race hatred they might harbor in their own psyches. Despite the predominance of patriarchal rule in American society, America was colonized on a racially imperialistic base and not on a sexually imperialistic base. No degree of patriarchal bonding between white male colonizers and Native American men overshadowed white racial imperialism. Racism took precedence over sexual alliances in . . . the white world's interaction with Native Americans and African Americans, just as racism overshadowed any bonding between black women and white women on the basis of sex. Tunisian writer Albert Memmi emphasizes in *The Colonizer and the Colonized* the impact of racism as a tool of imperialism:

> Racism appears . . . not as an incidental detail, but as a consubstantial part of colonialism. It is the highest expression of the colonial system and one of the most significant features of the colonialist. Not only does it establish a fundamental discrimination between colonizer and colonized, a sine qua non of colonial life, but it also lays the foundation for the immutability of this life.

While those feminists who argue that sexual imperialism is more endemic to all societies than racial imperialism are probably correct, American society is one in which racial imperialism supersedes sexual imperialism.

In America, the social status of black and white women has never been the same. In 19th and early 20th century America, few if any similarities could be found between the life experiences of the two female groups. Although they were both subject to sexist victimization, as victims of racism black women were subjected to oppressions no white woman was forced to endure. In fact, white racial imperialism granted all white women, however victimized by sexist oppression they might be, the right to assume the role of oppressor in relationship to black women and black men. From the onset of the contemporary move toward feminist revolution, white female organizers attempted to minimize their position in the racial caste hierarchy of American society. In their efforts to disassociate themselves from white men (to deny connections based on shared racial caste), white women involved in the move toward feminism have charged that racism is endemic to white male patriarchy and have argued that they cannot be held responsible for racist oppression. Commenting on the issue of white female accountability in her essay "'Disloyal to Civilization': Feminism, Racism, and Gynephobia," radical feminist Adrienne Rich contends:

> If Black and White feminists are going to speak of female accountability, I believe the word racism must be seized, grasped in our bare hands, ripped out of the sterile or defensive consciousness in which it so often grows, and transplanted so that it can yield new insights for our lives and our movement. An analysis that places the guilt for active domination, physical and institutional violence, and the justifications embedded in myth and language, on white women not only compounds false consciousness; it allows us all to deny or neglect the charged connection among black and white women from the historical conditions of slavery on, and it impedes any real discussion of women's instrumentality in a system which oppresses all women and in which hatred of women is also embedded in myth, folklore, and language.

No reader of Rich's essay could doubt that she is concerned that women who are committed to feminism work to overcome barriers that separate black and white women. However, she fails to understand that from a black female perspective, if white women are denying the existence of black women, writing "feminist" scholarship as if black women are not part of the collective group American women, or discriminating against black women, then it matters less that North America was colonized by white patriarchal *men* who institutionalized a racially imperialistic social order than that white women who purport to be feminists support and actively perpetuate anti-black racism.

To black women the issue is not whether white women are more or less racist than white men, but that they are racist. If women committed to feminist revolution, be they black or white, are to achieve any understanding of the "charged connections" between white women and black women, we must first be willing to examine woman's relationship to society, to race, and to American culture as it is and not as we would ideally have it be. That means confronting the reality of white female racism. Sexist discrimination has prevented white women from assuming the dominant role in the perpetuation of white racial imperialism, but it has not prevented white women from absorbing, supporting, and advocating racist ideology or acting individually as racist oppressors in various spheres of American life.

Every women's movement in America from its earliest origin to the present day has been built on a racist foundation—a fact which in no way invalidates feminism as a political ideology. The racial apartheid social structure that characterized 19th and early 20th century American life was mirrored in the women's rights movement. The first white women's rights advocates were never seeking social equality for all women; they were seeking social equality for white women. Because many 19th century white women's rights advocates were also active in the abolitionist movement, it is often assumed they were anti-racist. Historiographers and especially recent feminist writings have created a version of American history in which white women's rights advocates are presented as champions of oppressed black people. This fierce romanticism has informed most studies of the abolitionist movement. In contemporary times there is a general tendency to equate abolitionism with a repudiation of racism. In actuality, most white abolitionists, male and female, though vehement in their anti-slavery protest, were totally opposed to granting social equality to black people. . . .

The fact that the majority of white women reformers did not feel political solidarity with black people was made evident in the conflict over the vote. When it appeared that white men might grant black men the right to vote while leaving white women disenfranchised, white suffragists did not respond as a group by demanding that all women and men deserved the right to vote. They simply expressed anger and outrage that white men were more committed to maintaining sexual hierarchies than racial hierarchies in the political arena. Ardent white women's rights advocates like Elizabeth Cady Stanton who had never before argued for women's rights on a racially imperialistic platform expressed outrage that inferior "niggers" should be granted the vote while "superior" white women remained disenfranchised. Stanton argued:

> If Saxon men have legislated thus for their own mothers, wives and daughters, what can we hope for at the hands of Chinese, Indians, and Africans? . . . I protest against the enfranchisement of another man of any race or clime until the daughters of Jefferson, Hancock, and Adams are crowned with their rights.

White suffragists felt that white men were insulting white womanhood by refusing to grant them privileges that were to be granted black men. They admonished white men not for their sexism but for their willingness to allow sexism to overshadow racial alliances. Stanton, along with other white women's rights supporters, did not want to see blacks enslaved, but neither did she wish to see the status of black people improved while the status of white women remained the same. . . .

Relationships between white and black women were charged by tensions and conflicts in the early part of the 20th century. The women's rights movement had not drawn black and white women close together. Instead, it exposed the fact that white women were not willing to relinquish their support of white supremacy to support the interests of all women. Racism in the women's rights movement . . . was a constant reminder to black women of the distances that separated the two experiences, distances that white women did not want bridged. When the contemporary movement toward feminism began, white women organizers did not address the issue of conflict between black and white women. Their rhetoric of sisterhood and solidarity suggested that women in America were able to bond across both class and race boundaries—but no such coming together had actually occurred. The structure of the contemporary women's movement was no different from that of the earlier women's rights movement. Like their predecessors, the white women who initiated the women's movement launched their efforts in the wake of the 60s black liberation movement. As if history were repeating itself, they also began to make synonymous their social status and the social status of black people. And it was in the context of endless comparisons of the plight of "women" and "blacks" that they revealed their racism. In most cases, this racism was an unconscious, unacknowledged aspect of their thought, suppressed by their narcissism—a narcissism which so blinded them that they would not admit two obvious facts: one, that in a capitalist, racist, imperialist state there is no one social status women share as a collective group; and second, that the social status of white women in America has never been like that of black women or men.

When the women's movement began in the late 60s, it was evident that the white women who dominated the movement felt it was "their" movement, that is the medium through which a white woman would voice her grievances to society. Not only did white women act as if feminist ideology existed solely to serve their own interests because they were able to draw public attention to feminist concerns. They were unwilling to acknowledge that nonwhite women were part of the collective group women in American society. They urged black women to join "their" movement or in some cases the women's movement, but in dialogues and writings, their attitudes toward black women were both racist and sexist. Their racism did not assume the form of overt expressions of hatred; it was far more subtle. It took the form of simply ignoring the existence of black women or writing about them using common sexist and racist stereotypes. From Betty Friedan's *The Feminine Mystique* to Barbara Berg's *The Remembered Gate* and on to more recent publications like *Capitalist Patriarchy and the Case for Socialist Feminism*, edited by Zillah Eisenstein, most white female writers who considered themselves feminist revealed in their writing that they had been socialized to accept and perpetuate racist ideology.

In most of their writing, the white American woman's experience is made synonymous with *the* American woman's experience. While it is in no way racist for any author to write a book exclusively about white women, it is fundamentally racist for books to be published that focus solely on the American white woman's experience in which that experience is assumed to be *the* American woman's experience. . . .

In America, white racist ideology has always allowed white women to assume that the word "woman" is synonymous with white woman, for women of other races are always perceived as Others, as de-humanized beings who do not fall under the heading woman. White feminists who claimed to be politically astute showed themselves to be unconscious of the way their use of language suggested they did not recognize the existence of black women. They impressed upon the American public their sense that the word "woman" meant white woman by drawing endless analogies between "women" and "blacks." . . .

White feminists did not challenge the racist–sexist tendency to use the word "woman" to refer solely to white women; they supported it. For them it served two purposes. First, it allowed them to proclaim white men world oppressors while making it appear linguistically that no alliance existed between white women and white men based on shared racial imperialism. Second, it made it possible for white women to act as if alliances did exist between themselves and non-white women in our society, and by so doing they could deflect attention away from their classism and racism. Had feminists chosen to make explicit comparisons between the status of white women and that of black people, or more specifically the status of black women and white women, it would have been more than obvious that the two groups do not share an identical oppression. It would have been obvious that similarities between the status of women under patriarchy and that of any slave or colonized person do not necessarily exist in a society that is both racially and sexually imperialistic. In such a society, the woman who is seen as inferior because of her sex can also be seen as superior because of her race, even in relationship to men of another race. Because feminists tended to evoke an image of women as a collective group, their comparisons between "women" and "blacks" were accepted without question. This constant comparison of the plight of "women" and "blacks" deflected attention away from the fact that black women were extremely victimized by both racism and sexism—a fact which, had it been emphasized, might have diverted public attention away from the complaints of middle and upper class white feminists.

Just as 19th century white women's rights advocates attempted to make synonymous their lot with that of the black slave to draw attention away from the slave toward themselves, contemporary white feminists have used the same metaphor to attract attention to their concerns. Given that America is a hierarchical society in which white men are at the top and white women are second, it was to be expected that should white women complain about not having rights in the wake of a movement by black people to gain rights, their interests would overshadow those of groups lower on the hierarchy, in this case the interests of black people. No other group in America has used black people as metaphors as extensively as white women involved in the women's movement. . . .

When white women talked about "Women as Niggers," "The Third World of Women,"

"Woman as Slave," they evoked the sufferings and oppressions of non-white people to say "look at how bad our lot as white women is, why we are like niggers, like the Third World." Of course, if the situation of upper and middle class white women were in any way like that of the oppressed people in the world, such metaphors would not have been necessary. And if they had been poor and oppressed, or women concerned about the lot of oppressed women, they would not have been compelled to appropriate the black experience. It would have been sufficient to describe the oppression of woman's experience. A white woman who has suffered physical abuse and assault from a husband or lover, who also suffers poverty, need not compare her lot to that of a suffering black person to emphasize that she is in pain. . . .

If white women in the women's movement needed to make use of a black experience to emphasize woman's oppression, it would seem only logical that they focus on the black female experience—but they did not. They chose to deny the existence of black women and to exclude them from the women's movement. When I use the word "exclude" I do not mean that they overtly discriminated against black women on the basis of race. There are other ways to exclude and alienate people. Many black women felt excluded from the movement whenever they heard white women draw analogies between "women" and "blacks." For by making such analogies white women were in effect saying to black women: "We don't acknowledge your presence as women in American society." Had white women desired to bond with black women on the basis of common oppression they could have done so by demonstrating any awareness or knowledge of the impact of sexism on the status of black women. Unfortunately, despite all the rhetoric about sisterhood and bonding, white women were not sincerely committed to bonding with black women and other groups of women to fight sexism. They were primarily interested in drawing attention to their lot as white upper and middle class women.

It was not in the opportunistic interests of white middle and upper class participants in the women's movement to draw attention to the plight of poor women, or the specific plight of black women. A white woman professor who wants the public to see her as victimized and oppressed because she is denied tenure is not about to evoke images of poor women working as domestics receiving less than the minimum wage struggling to raise a family single-handedly. Instead it is far more likely she will receive attention and sympathy if she says, "I'm a nigger in the eyes of my white male colleagues." She evokes the image of innocent, virtuous white womanhood being placed on the same level as blacks and most importantly on the same level as black men. It is not simply a coincidental detail that white women in the women's movement chose to make their race–sex analogies by comparing their lot as white women to that of black men. . . .

Whenever black women tried to express to white women their ideas about white female racism or their sense that the women who were at the forefront of the movement were not oppressed women they were told that "oppression cannot be measured." White female emphasis on "common oppression" in their appeals to black women to join the movement further alienated many black women. Because so many of the white women in the movement were employers of non-white and white domestics, their rhetoric of common oppression was experienced by black women as an assault, an expression of the bourgeois woman's insensitivity and lack of concern for the lower class woman's position in society. . . .

Despite the reality that white upper and middle class women in America suffer from sexist discrimination and sexist abuse, they are not as a group as oppressed as *poor* white, or black, or yellow women. Their unwillingness to distinguish between various degrees of discrimination or oppression caused black women to see them as enemies. As many upper and middle class white feminists who suffer least from sexist oppression were attempting to focus all attention on themselves, it follows that they would not accept an analysis of woman's lot in America which argued that not all women are equally oppressed because some women are able to use their class, race, and educational privilege to effectively resist sexist oppression.

Initially, class privilege was not discussed by white women in the women's movement. They wanted to project an image of themselves as victims and that could not be done by drawing attention to their class. In fact, the contemporary women's movement was extremely class bound. As a group, white participants did not denounce capitalism. They chose to define liberation using the terms of white capitalist patriarchy, equating liberation with gaining economic status and money power. Like all good capitalists, they proclaimed work as the key to liberation. This emphasis on work was yet another indication of the extent to which the white female liberationists' perception of reality was totally narcissistic, classist, and racist. Implicit in the assertion that work was the key to women's liberation was a refusal to acknowledge the reality that, for masses of American working class women, working for pay neither liberated them from sexist oppression nor allowed them to gain any measure of economic independence. . . .

As concerned black and white individuals tried to stress the importance to the women's movement of confronting and changing racist attitudes because such sentiments threatened to undermine the movement, they met with resistance from those white women who saw feminism solely as a vehicle to enhance their own individual, opportunistic ends. Conservative, reactionary white women, who increasingly represented a large majority of the participants, were outspoken in their pronouncements that the issue of racism should not be considered worthy of attention. They did not want the issue of

racism raised because they did not want to deflect attention away from their projection of the white woman as "good," i.e., non-racist victim, and the white man as "bad," i.e., racist oppressor. For them to have acknowledged woman's active complicity in the perpetuation of imperialism, colonialism, racism, or sexism would have made the issue of women's liberation far more complex. To those who saw feminism solely as a way to demand entrance into the white male power structure, it simplified matters to make all men oppressors and all women victims. . . .

Animosity between black and white women's liberationists was not due solely to disagreement over racism within the women's movement; it was the end result of years of jealousy, envy, competition, and anger between the two groups. Conflict between black and white women did not begin with the 20th century women's movement. It began during slavery. The social status of white women in America has to a large extent been determined by white people's relationship to black people. It was the enslavement of African people in colonized America that marked the beginning of a change in the social status of white women. Prior to slavery, patriarchal law decreed white women were lowly inferior beings, the subordinate group in society. The subjugation of black people allowed them to vacate their despised position and assume the role of a superior. . . .

Throughout American history white men have deliberately promoted hostility and divisiveness between white and black women. The white patriarchal power structure pits the two groups against each other, preventing the growth of solidarity between women and ensuring that woman's status as a subordinate group under patriarchy remains intact. To this end, white men have supported changes in the white woman's social standing only if there exists another female group to assume that role. Consequently, the white patriarch undergoes no radical change in his sexist assumption that woman is inherently inferior. He neither relinquishes his dominant position nor alters the patriarchal structure of society. He is, however, able to convince many white women that fundamental changes in "woman's status" have occurred because he has successfully socialized her, via racism, to assume that no connection exists between her and black women.

Because women's liberation has been equated with gaining privileges within the white male power structure, white men—and not women, white or black—have dictated the terms by which women are allowed entrance into the system. One of the terms male patriarchs have set is that one group of women is granted privileges that they obtain by actively supporting the oppression and exploitation of other groups of women. White and black women have been socialized to accept and honor these terms, hence the fierce competition between the two groups; a competition that has always been centered in the arena of sexual politics, with white and black women competing against one another for male favor. This competition is part of an overall battle between various groups of women to be the chosen female group.

The contemporary move toward feminist revolution was continually undermined by competition between various factions. In regards to race, the women's movement has become simply another arena in which white and black women compete to be the chosen female group. This power struggle has not been resolved by the formation of opposing interest groups. Such groups are symptomatic of the problem and are no solution. Black and white women have for so long allowed their idea of liberation to be formed by the existing status quo that they have not yet devised a strategy by which we can come together. They have had only a slave's idea of freedom. And to the slave, the master's way of life represents the ideal free lifestyle.

Women's liberationists, white and black, will always be at odds with one another as long as our idea of liberation is based on having the power white men have. For that power denies unity, denies common connections, and is inherently divisive. It is woman's acceptance of divisiveness as a natural order that has caused black and white women to cling religiously to the belief that bonding across racial boundaries is impossible, to passively accept the notion that the distances that separate women are immutable. Even though the most uninformed and naive women's liberationist knows that Sisterhood as political bonding between women is necessary for feminist revolution, women have not struggled long or hard enough to overcome the societal brainwashing that has impressed on our psyches the belief that no union between black and white women can ever be forged. The methods women have employed to reach one another across racial boundaries have been shallow, superficial, and destined to fail.

Resolution of the conflict between black and white women cannot begin until all women acknowledge that a feminist movement which is both racist and classist is a mere sham, a cover-up for women's continued bondage to materialist patriarchal principles, and passive acceptance of the status quo. The sisterhood that is necessary for the making of feminist revolution can be achieved only when all women disengage themselves from the hostility, jealousy and competition with one another that has kept us vulnerable, weak, and unable to envision new realities. That sisterhood cannot be forged by the mere saying of words. It is the outcome of continued growth and change. It is a goal to be reached, a process of becoming. The process begins with action, with the individual woman's refusal to accept any set of myths, stereotypes, and false assumptions that deny the shared commonness of her human experience; that deny her capacity to bridge gaps created by racism, sexism, or classism; that deny her ability to change. The process begins with the individual woman's acceptance that American women, without exception, are socialized to be racist, classist, and sexist, in varying degrees, and that labeling ourselves feminists does not change the fact that we must consciously work to rid ourselves of the legacy of negative socialization.

If women want a feminist revolution—ours is a world that is crying out for feminist revolution—then we must assume responsibility for drawing women together in political solidarity. That means we must assume responsibility for eliminating all the forces that divide women. Racism is one such force. Women, all women, are accountable for racism continuing to divide us. Our willingness to assume responsibility for the elimination of racism need not be engendered by feelings of guilt, moral responsibility, victimization, or rage. It can spring from a heartfelt desire for sisterhood and the personal, intellectual realization that racism among women undermines the potential radicalism of feminism. It can spring from our knowledge that racism is an obstacle in our path that must be removed. More obstacles are created if we simply engage in endless debate as to who put it there.

We Are Practical Revolutionaries   5.5

ERNESTO CHE GUEVARA

Ernesto Che Guevara (1928–1967) was born in Rosario, Argentina. Although his family was middle class and entrepreneurial, both of Guevara's parents were politically leftist in their thinking. Guevara thus spent many of his holidays traveling in Latin America and observing the abject poverty of most of the Latin American people. After receiving his M.D. degree from the University of Buenos Aires in 1953, Guevara went to Guatemala, which was governed by the socially progressive regime of Jacobo Arbenz. However, when the Arbenz regime was overthrown in 1954 by a CIA-supported coup, Guevara moved to Mexico, where he met Fidel and Raúl Castro. Guevara joined the Castros in their attempt to overthrow the Batista dictatorship in Cuba, serving first as a medical officer, and eventually as commander of one of the most important guerrilla columns. When the revolutionary forces claimed victory in 1959, Guevara became a Cuban citizen and served the new government in several important positions, including the position of minister of industry. As a representative of the Cuban government, Guevara wrote and delivered many speeches in which he formulated and defended Cuba's new form of Marxism. In the mid-1960s, Guevara suddenly disappeared from public life so that he could better implement his revolutionary ideas. After traveling to the Congo where he helped organize the Patrice Lumumba Battalion, Guevara went to Bolivia to lead a guerrilla group there. In October of 1967, Guevara's group was attacked by a detachment of the Bolivian army. Guevara was wounded, captured, and then shot. Guevara's best-known writing was *La guerra de guerrillas* (1960), which was translated into English as *Guerrilla Warfare* in 1961.

In the following selection, which is taken from *Venceremos! The Speeches and Writings of Ernesto Che Guevara*, Guevara describes the events leading up to the successful overthrow of the Batista regime. Although he acknowledges the importance of Marxist theory in this revolutionary movement, he emphasizes the fact that the revolution was practical rather than theoretical. Guevara also suggests that the revolution was marked by a transformation of consciousness, as well as by a change of political systems. While the revolutionaries began with the theoretical assumption that the people would rise up in mass against the dictatorship and with a profound misunderstanding and mistrust of the *campesinos*, they came to realize both the necessity of prolonged guerrilla struggle and the importance of *campesino* participation.

Guevara attributes the success of the revolution to two factors. First, whereas the guerrillas were fighting for survival, land, and liberation, the government troops were fighting for a paycheck and pension. This difference in motivation meant that the guerrillas were willing to risk their lives, whereas the government troops generally were not. Second, because of the nature of the struggle and the goals of the revolution, the guerrillas were able to forge a unity between intellectuals, *campesinos*, and workers. Because of its oppressive nature, however, the Batista regime was never able to create such unity. Thus, the revolutionaries were able to overcome the much larger and better equipped government army, and the people ultimately prevailed.

Questions for Thought

1. Can you tell from Guevara's account what caused the Cuban Revolution? What do you think caused this revolution?
2. Do you think there were any similarities between the Cuban Revolution and the American Revolution? If so, what were they?
3. How does the Cuban Revolution compare with and differ from the feminist revolution that hooks calls for in the preceding selection?
4. What is Guevara's attitude toward Marxism? Do you think that Marxism represents a viable political philosophy? Why or why not?
5. Under what conditions, if any, do you think revolution would be justified?

CUBA'S IS A UNIQUE REVOLUTION, WHICH SOME people maintain contradicts one of the most orthodox premises of the revolutionary movement, expressed by Lenin: "Without a revolutionary theory there is no revolutionary movement." It would be suitable to say that revolutionary theory, as the expression of a social truth, surpasses any declaration of it; that is to say, even if the theory is not known, the revolution can succeed if historical reality is interpreted correctly, and if the forces involved are utilized correctly. Every revolution always incorporates elements of very different tendencies, which nevertheless coincide in action and in the revolution's most immediate objectives.

It is clear that if the leaders have an adequate theoretical knowledge prior to the action, they can avoid trial and error whenever the adopted theory corresponds to the reality.

The principal actors of this revolution had no coherent theoretical criteria; but it cannot be said

Reprinted with the permission of Macmillan Publishing Company from *Venceremos! The Speeches and Writings of Ernesto Che Guevara* by John Gerassi, editor. ©1968 by John Gerassi.

that they were ignorant of the various concepts of history, society, economics, and revolution which are being discussed in the world today.

Profound knowledge of reality, a close relationship with the people, the firmness of the liberator's objective, and the practical revolutionary experience gave to those leaders the chance to form a more complete theoretical concept.

The foregoing should be considered as introduction to the explication of this curious phenomenon which has intrigued the entire world: the Cuban Revolution. It is a deed worthy of study in contemporary world history: the how and the why of a group of men who, shattered by an army enormously superior in technique and equipment, first managed to survive, soon became strong, later become stronger than the enemy in the battle zones, still later moved into new zones of combat, and finally defeated that enemy on the battlefield, even though their troops were still very inferior in number.

Naturally, we who often do not show the requisite concern for theory will not run the risk of expounding the truth of the Cuban Revolution as though we were its masters. We will simply try to give the bases from which one can interpret this truth. In fact, the Cuban Revolution must be separated into two absolutely distinct stages: that of the armed action up to January 1, 1959, and the political, economic, and social transformations since then.

Even these two stages deserve further subdivisions; however, we will not take them from the viewpoint of historical exposition, but from the viewpoint of the evolution of revolutionary thought of its leaders through their contact with the people. Incidentally, here one must introduce a general attitude toward one of the most controversial terms of the modern world: Marxism. When asked whether or not we are Marxists, our position is the same as that of a physicist or a biologist when asked if he is a "Newtonian," or if he is a "Pasteurian."

There are truths so evident, so much a part of people's knowledge, that it is now useless to discuss them. One ought to be "Marxist" with the same naturalness with which one is "Newtonian" in physics, or "Pasteurian" in biology, considering that if facts determine new concepts, these new concepts will never divest themselves of that portion of truth possessed by the older concepts they have outdated. Such is the case, for example, of Einsteinian relativity or of Planck's "quantum" theory with respect to the discoveries of Newton. They take nothing at all away from the greatness of the learned Englishman. Thanks to Newton, physics was able to advance until it had achieved new concepts of space. The learned Englishman provided the necessary stepping-stones for them.

The advances in social and political science, as in other fields, belong to a long historical process whose links are connecting, adding up, molding, and constantly perfecting themselves. In the origin of peoples, there exists a Chinese, Arab, or Hindu mathematics. Today mathematics has no frontiers. In the course of history there was a Greek Pythagoras, an Italian Galileo, an English Newton, a German Gauss, a Russian Lobatchevsky, an Einstein, etc. Thus in the field of social and political sciences, from Democritus to Marx, a long series of thinkers added their original investigations and accumulated a body of experience and of doctrines.

The merit of Marx is in suddenly producing a qualitative change in the history of social thought. He interprets history, understands its dynamics, predicts the future, but in addition to predicting it (which would satisfy his scientific obligation), he expresses a revolutionary concept: The world must not only be interpreted, it must be transformed. Man ceases to be the slave and tool of his environment and converts himself into the architect of his own destiny. At that moment Marx puts himself in a position where he becomes the necessary target of all who have a special interest in maintaining the old—similar to Democritus before him, whose work was burned by Plato and his disciples, the ideologues of Athenian slave aristocracy. Beginning with the revolutionary Marx, a political group with concrete ideas establishes itself. Basing itself in the giants, Marx and Engels, and developing through successive steps with personalities like Lenin, Stalin, Mao Tse-tung, and the new Soviet and Chinese rulers, it establishes a body of doctrine and, let us say, examples to follow.

The Cuban Revolution takes up Marx at the point where he himself left science to shoulder his revolutionary rifle. And it takes him up at that point, not in a revisionist spirit, of struggling against that which follows Marx, of reviving "pure" Marx, but simply because up to that point Marx, the scientist, placed himself outside of the history he studied and predicted. From then on Marx the revolutionary could fight within history. We, practical revolutionaries, initiating our own struggle, simply fulfill laws foreseen by Marx, the scientist. We are simply adjusting ourselves to the predictions of the scientific Marx as we travel this road of rebellion, struggling against the old structure of power, supporting ourselves in the people for the destruction of this structure, and having the happiness of this people as the basis of our struggle. That is to say—and it is well to emphasize this once again—the laws of Marxism are present in the events of the Cuban Revolution, independently of what its leaders profess or fully know of those laws from the theoretical point of view. Those events began before the landing of the "Granma," and continued long after, and included the landing itself, the setting up of the second guerrilla column, the third and the fourth, the invasion of the Sierra de Cristal, the establishment of the second front, the general strike of April and its failure, the setback of the great offensive, and the invasion of Las Villas.

Each of those brief historical moments in the guerrilla warfare framed distinct social concepts and distinct appreciations of the Cuban reality; they outlined the thought of the military leaders of the Revolution—those who in time would also take their position as political leaders.

Before the landing of the "Granma," a mentality predominated that to some degree might be called "subjectivist": blind confidence in a rapid popular explosion; enthusiasm and faith in the power to liquidate the Batista regime by a swift, armed uprising combined with spontaneous revolutionary strikes and the subsequent fall of the dictator. The movement was the direct heir of the Orthodox party, and its main slogan was "Shame Against Money," that is to say, administrative honesty as the principal concern of the new Cuban Government. . . .

After the landing came the defeat, the almost total destruction of the forces, and their regrouping and integration as guerrillas. Characteristic of those few survivors, imbued with the spirit of struggle, was the understanding that to count upon spontaneous outbursts throughout the island was a deception, an illusion. They understood also that the fight would have to be a long one, and that it would need vast *campesino* participation. At this point, the *campesinos* entered the guerrilla war for the first time. Two forces—hardly important in terms of the number of combatants, but of great psychological value—were unveiled. First, the antagonism that the city people, who comprised the central guerrilla group, felt toward the *campesinos* was erased. The *campesinos* had distrusted the group and, above all, feared the barbarous reprisals of the government. Two facts revealed themselves at this stage, both very important for the interrelated factors: to the *campesinos*, the bestialities of the army and all the persecution would not be sufficient to put an end to the guerrilla war, even though the army was certainly capable of liquidating the *campesinos'* homes, crops, and families. To take refuge with those in hiding was a good solution. In turn, the guerrilla fighters learned the necessity, each time more pointed, of winning over the *campesino* masses, which required, obviously, that they be offered something they desired very much. And there was nothing that a *campesino* sought more than land.

After that came a nomadic stage in which the rebel army kept gaining zones of influence. It could not remain in these areas for any length of time, but then, neither could the enemy. As a result of a series of combats a rather fluid front was mapped. Then, on May 28, 1957, at Ubero, an attack was launched against a well-armed, well-situated garrison, which had ready access to reinforcements, due to its position by the sea and its airport. The rebel victory was very costly: some 30 per cent of the rebel forces were killed or wounded. But it showed that the forces could sweep down from the mountains and wage successful battles in the fields, that they could come after the enemy rather than wait for it to pursue them.

Shortly thereafter, the first segregation took place, and a second rebel column was organized. It went into combat immediately. The two columns attacked Estrada Palma the twenty-sixth of July, and five days later, Bueycito, which is thirty kilometers away. From then on the battles were more important. We were beginning to stand firm against enemy counter-attacks. We resisted all its attempts to penetrate the Sierra. And we maintained our vast front areas. . . .

Our successes became known, as they filtered through government censorship, and the people of Cuba began to look forward, for the first time, to a rebel victory. It is then that from Havana the idea of a nationwide struggle was discussed, specifically developing the idea of a general revolutionary strike.

The function of the rebel army would then be mainly one of an "irritating thorn," or catalyst, for the over-all struggle. In those days, our guerrillas became increasingly more daring and successful, and it is then that the heroic legend of Camilo Cienfuegos was born, as his column went into combat, successfully, in the lowlands of Oriente for the first time—under strict central orders.

Nevertheless, the general strike was badly organized and planned, for it did not take into account the workers' own struggle, their unity, or their concept of revolutionary activity. The general call for the strike was launched over a clandestine radio, but the specific date, to be kept secret until the last minute, was to be announced by word-of-mouth, and this manner of communication was not capable of reaching all of the people. The strike not only failed, but many valiant and dedicated revolutionary leaders were gunned down in the process. . . .

In any case, the failure of the strike made it clear that only through armed struggle could the government be toppled. It became imperative, therefore, that such a struggle be accelerated and intensified and that it lead to the final confrontation and defeat of the government forces on the field of battle.

By then, of course, we had established close bonds with the *campesinos*. In the liberated areas we had established a rebel administration, with civil and penal codes. We set up a judicial system, distributed foodstuffs, and levied taxes. Neighboring zones also felt our influence, and in the next two months we waged three major offensives, which caused a thousand deaths among the enemy, completely demoralizing it, which increased our strength from new volunteers by six hundred actual fighters.

It was then clear that we could not be defeated; every path in Oriente became a sieve for enemy casualties. All counteroffensives by the enemy failed. And then, Camilo Cienfuegos, leading column number two, and I, in charge of column number eight, named for another hero of our revolution, Antonio Maceo, were ordered to cross the province of Camaguey in order to establish ourselves in Las Villas and thus cut the enemy's communication lines. . . .

It may seem strange, incomprehensible, and even incredible that two columns of such small size [80 men in one, 140 in the other]—without communications, without mobility, without the most elemental arms of modern warfare—could fight against well-trained, and above all, well-armed troops. Basic was the characteristic of each group: The more uncomfortable the guerrilla fighter is, and the more he is initiated into the rigors of nature, the more he feels himself at home;

his morale is higher; his sense of security, greater. At the same time he has learned to risk his life in every circumstance that might arise, to trust it to luck like a tossed coin. In general, as a result of this kind of combat, it matters little to the individual guerrilla whether or not he survives.

The enemy soldier in the Cuban example which at present concerns us, is the junior partner of the dictator; he is the man who gets the last crumbs left by a long line of profiteers that begins in Wall Street and ends with him. He is disposed to defend his privileges, but he is disposed to defend them only to the degree that they are important to him. His salary and his pension are worth some suffering and some dangers, but they are never worth his life: If the price of maintaining them will cost it, he is better off giving them up; that is to say, withdrawing from the face of guerrilla danger. From these two concepts and these two moralities springs the difference which would cause the crisis of December 31, 1958, Batista's downfall.

Meanwhile, the superiority of the rebel army became clearly evident, as did, with our arrival in Las Villas, the popularity of the 26th of July Movement with everyone: the revolutionary directorate, the second front of Las Villas, the Popular Socialist party, and even some small guerrilla bands of the Authentic Organization. This was due in great part to the magnetic personality of our leader, Fidel Castro, but also to the just cause of our revolutionary line.

Here ended the insurrection. But the men who arrived in Havana after two years of arduous struggle in the mountains and plains of Oriente, in the lowlands of Camaguey, and in the mountains, plains, and cities of Las Villas, were not the same men, ideologically, who landed on the beaches of Las Coloradoas, or who took part in the first phase of the struggle. Their distrust of the *campesino* had been converted into affection and respect for his virtues; their total ignorance of life in the country had been converted into a knowledge of the needs of our *guajiros;* their flirtations with statistics and with

theory had been solidified by the cement which is practice.

With the banner of agrarian reform, the execution of which began in the Sierra Maestra, these men confronted imperialism. They knew that the agrarian reform was the basis upon which the new Cuba must build itself. They also knew that the agrarian reform would give land to all the dispossessed, and that it would dispossess its unjust possessors; and they knew that the greatest of the unjust possessors were also influential men in the State Department or in the government of the United Stated of America. But they had learned to conquer the difficulties with bravery, with audacity, and above all, with the support of the people; and they had now seen the future of liberation which awaited us on the other side of our sufferings.

To reach these conclusions, we traveled far and we changed a lot. As our armed struggle changed qualitatively in the course of the actual battle, so too did the social composition of the guerrillas and the ideological understanding of our leaders. This happened inevitably, because each battle, each confrontation, broadens, widens and therefore changes its participants. And this is the revolutionary process, to mature from each event. The *campesino* learns to believe in his own vigor. He gives the revolutionary army his capacity to suffer, his knowledge of the terrain, his love of the land, his hunger for the agrarian reform. The intellectual, of whatever type, throws in his mite, beginning to mold the theoretical framework on this knowledge. The worker contributes his sense of organization, of unity. Above all these, there is the rebel army, which proves to be much more than just an "irritating thorn," but on the contrary contributes the most important lesson, leading the masses to experience it, that all men can get rid of their fear of torment.

Never before was the concept of interaction so clear to us. We could feel with our bones how this concept deepened and matured in us, teaching us the value of armed insurrection, the strength that any man has when, with a weapon in his hand and the will to win in his heart, he confronts other men who are out to destroy him. And we learned from the *campesinos* that there is no limit to the efforts, to the sacrifices that we can all make when we are fighting for the destiny of the people.

Thus, when bathed in *campesino* sweat, with a horizon of mountains and clouds, beneath the radiant sun of the island, the rebel chief and his men entered Havana, a new "history climbed from the winter's garden with the feet of the people."

Philosophy, Politics, and Power: An Afro-American Perspective

5.6

CORNEL WEST

Cornel West (b. 1953), professor of religion and director of the Afro-American Studies Program at Princeton University, was born in Tulsa, Oklahoma. However, because his father's job as a civilian in air force administration required frequent moves, West's childhood was spent in several different locales. The family eventually settled in Sacramento, California, where West was greatly influenced by the theology of the Baptist church and by the political philosophy of the Black Panther party.

At age seventeen, West entered Harvard University. Although he was forced to work at odd jobs to help finance his education, West nevertheless completed his undergraduate degree in three years. He graduated *magna cum laude* with a major in Near Eastern languages and literature. Then, after a two-year stint in the Ph.D. program at Princeton, West completed his doctorate at Harvard as a Du Bois Fellow.

West has taught at the Union Theological Seminary, the Yale Divinity School, and the University of Paris. He has combined his teaching duties with a sustained commitment to social activism. He has also published extensively in both academic and nonacademic journals. His books include *Prophesy Deliverance! An Afro-American Revolutionary Christianity* (1982); *Prophetic Fragments* (1988); *The American Evasion of Philosophy: A Genealogy of Pragmatism* (1989); *The Ethical Dimension of Marxist Thought* (1991); and *Race Matters* (1993).

In the following essay, West examines the history of modern philosophy as the prelude to defining a distinctively Afro-American perspective on the nature of philosophizing. He notes that because of certain developments in recent Western culture, namely, the demythologizing of science, the demystifying of authority, and the disclosure of a deep sense of impotence and despair, the very nature and existence of philosophy have been called into question.

West argues that this crisis in recent philosophy is both necessary and healthy. Following such critics of philosophy as Kierkegaard, Marx, Nietzsche, and Foucault, West argues that philosophy must be resituated in the practical world, that it must "see itself as a form of praxis-in-the-world-of-politics-and-power." Specifically from an Afro-American perspective, philosophy must be linked to the possibility of the idea of a revolutionary and better future, a future in which racist and economic oppression are overcome.

Questions for Thought

1. Why, according to West, have many recent philosophical thinkers called for an end to philosophy?
2. What does West say about the origins of modern science and capitalism? What seems to be his attitude toward modern science and capitalism?
3. What are West's basic criticisms of contemporary culture? Do you agree with his analysis?
4. What, according to West, has been the basic relationship between modern philosophy and politics or power? How does West's view of this relationship compare with and differ from the views of the various philosophers that he discusses?
5. How does West perceive the task of the contemporary Afro-American philosopher? What do you think the principal task of philosophy should be?
6. How does West's view of the role of philosophy compare with and differ from that of hooks?

IS IT A MERE COINCIDENCE THAT THE MAJOR philosophical thinkers in the modern West—Marx, Kierkegaard, and Nietzsche in the nineteenth century and Wittgenstein, Heidegger, and Derrida in the twentieth century—call for an end to philosophy? What do these post-philosophical voices have to do with Afro-Americans engaged in the philosophical enterprise?

I suggest that the calls for an end to philosophy are symptomatic of fundamental cultural transformations in the modern West. These transformations primarily consist of three salient developments in modern Western culture. First, the demythologizing of the institution of science—still in its rudimentary stage—renders the status of philosophy problematic. This demythologizing is not a discrediting of the achievements of science, but an undermining of its legitimacy regarding its alleged monopoly on truth and reality. Second, the demystifying of the role of authority makes the function of philosophy suspect. This demystifying is not simply a revolt against intellectual, social, and political authority, it calls into question the very notion of and need for authority. Third, the disclosure of a deep sense of impotence tends to support the view that philosophy is superfluous. This disclosure is not only a recognition of dominant ironic forms of thinking and narcissistic forms of living, but a pervasive despair about the present and lack of hope for the future.

These three developments require that philosophy—both as a professional discipline and as a mode of thinking—either redefine itself or bring itself to an end. In this historical moment, Afro-Americans engaged in the philosophical enterprise can contribute to the redefining of philosophy principally by revealing why and showing how philosophy is inextricably linked to politics and power—to structures of domination and mechanisms of control. This important task does not call for an end to philosophy. Rather it situates philosophical activity in the midst of personal and collective struggles in the present.

Revaluations of the Philosophical Past

In order to understand the prevailing crisis of philosophy in the modern West, it is necessary to examine the beginnings of modern Western philosophy. Modern philosophy emerged alongside modern science. The basic aim of modern philosophy was to promote and encourage the legitimacy of modern science. Descartes, the famous mathematician and scientist, was the father of modern philosophy. He tried to show that modern science not merely provides more effective ways of coping with the world, but also yields objective, accurate, value-free copies of the world. Descartes attempted to do this by putting forward rational foundations for knowledge independent of theological grounds and moral concerns. For the first time, epistemological matters became the center around which philosophical reflection evolved. Henceforth, the principal thrust of modern philosophy would be toward the justification of and rationale for belief. Modern philosophy became a disinterested quest for certainty regulated by a conception of truth that stands outside the world of politics and power—a prop that undergirds the claims of modern science.

The emergence of the capitalist mode of production, with its atomistic individualism and profit-oriented dispositions toward nature and people, partly accounts for the way in which Descartes chose to defend modern science. This defense takes the form of a justification of knowledge that starts with the self-consciousness of the individual, the immediate awareness of the subject, the *cogitatio* of the ego. Descartes' methodological doubt, a search for certainty that begins in radical doubt, rests upon the only mental activity that cannot be doubted: the activity of doubt itself. In his view, such doubting presupposes an agent who doubts, that is, a thinking in-

dividual, subject, or ego. Only by validly inferring from this indubitable activity of doubting—the only certainty available—can claims about God, the world, and the bodily self be justified. Like the new literary genre of early capitalist culture—the novel—Descartes' viewpoint supports the notion that we have access to, arrive at, and acquire knowledge of the world through the autonomous individual. Therefore, the primacy of the individual, subject, or ego who accurately copies the world or validly makes inferences about the world serves as the foundation of knowledge, the philosophical basis of modern science.

The obsession of the early modern philosophers with science (especially Newton) partly explains the empiricist twist given to Descartes' subjectivist turn in philosophy. For Locke, Berkeley, and Hume, the primacy of the thinking subject, or ego remained, but experience (understood as sensations and perceptions) became the major candidate for the foundation of knowledge. Yet the ambitious project faltered. When Berkeley rejected the substantial self—the subject to which attributes are attached—and called on God to ground it as spirit, philosophical havoc set in. Hume, who had little philosophical use for God, explicitly articulated the skeptical result: the idea that knowledge has no empirical foundation. Instead, knowledge is but the (philosophically unjustifiable) imaginative constructs enacted by thinking individuals, subjects, or egos. Yet these thinking individuals, subjects, or egos are but themselves bundles of sensations and perceptions. Hence the subject and object of knowledge is rendered problematic—and modern philosophy found itself in a quandary.

Kant, the first modern professional philosopher in the West, rescued modern philosophy by providing transcendental grounds for truth outside of politics and power—by locating the justification of what we know in the conditions for the possibility of knowing. These conditions are neither deductively arrived at nor empirically grounded. Rather they are transcendental in that they consist of the universal and necessary conceptual scheme people employ in order to know and hence have experience. Although Kant rejected the rationalist inference-making activity of Descartes, he deepened Descartes' subjectivist turn by locating the universal and necessary conceptual scheme in the thinking activity of the subject. Although Kant criticized the empiricist perspectives of Locke, Berkeley, and especially Hume, he accepted Hume's skepticism by holding that the universal and necessary conceptual scheme constitutes an objective world, but not the real world. In addition, Kant's architectonic project tried to link science, morals and aesthetics—Truth, Goodness, and Beauty—while arguing for their different foundations.

With the appearance of Hegel, modern philosophy drifted into a deep crisis. This was so primarily because of the emergence of historical consciousness. This consciousness was threatening to modern philosophy because it acknowledged the historical character of philosophy itself. This acknowledgment presented a major challenge to modern philosophy because it implied that the very aim of modern philosophy— the quest for certainty and search for foundations of knowledge—was an ahistorical enterprise. Hegel's historicizing of Kant's universal and necessary conceptual scheme questioned the very content and character of modern philosophy.

It is no accident that the first modern calls for the end of philosophy were made by the two major thinkers who labored under the shadow of Hegel: Kierkegaard and Marx. Both accepted Hegel's historicizing of the subjectivist turn in philosophy, his emphasis on activity, development, and process, his dialectical approach to understanding and transforming the world, and his devastating critiques of Cartesian and Kantian notions of substance, subject, and the self. Kierkegaard rejected Hegel's intellectualist attempt to link thought to concrete, human existence and put forward a profound existential dialectic of the self. Marx discarded Hegel's ide-

alistic project of resolving the dominant form of alienation in the existing order and presented a penetrating materialistic dialectic of capitalist society. Both Kierkegaard and Marx understood philosophy as an antiquated, outmoded form of thinking, a mere fetter that impeded their particular praxis-oriented projects of redemption. Kierkegaard noted that, "philosophy is life's dry nurse, it can stay with us but not give milk." And Marx stated that, "philosophy stands in the same relation to the study of the actual world as masturbation to sexual love."

Afro-American philosophers should take heed of the radical antiphilosophical stances of Kierkegaard and Marx, not because they are right but rather because of the concerns that motivate their viewpoints. Both stress the value-laden character of philosophical reflection; the way in which such reflection not only serves particular class and personal interest, but also how it refuses to see itself as a form of praxis-in-the-world-of-politics-and-power. This refusal conceals the complex linkages of philosophical reflection to politics and power by defining itself as above and outside politics and power. By viewing itself as the queen of the disciplines that oversee the knowledge-claims of other disciplines, modern philosophy elides its this-worldly character, its role and function in the world of politics and power.

Despite Hegel's historicizing efforts, academic philosophers managed to overthrow Hegelianism, ignore Kierkegaard and Marx (both nonacademics!), and replace Hegelianism either with the analytical realism of Bertrand Russell and G. E. Moore in England; the diverse forms of returns to Kant (neo-Kantians) and Descartes (phenomenology) in Germany; and the various modes of vitalism (Bergson) and religious-motivated conventionalism (Pierre Duhem) in France. The only kind of professional philosophizing that took Hegel seriously was Dewey's version of American pragmatism, yet even Dewey wrote as if Kierkegaard and Marx never lived. In short, the professionalization of modern philosophy in the

West shielded the academy from the powerful antiphilosophical perspectives of post-Hegelian figures, especially that of Nietzsche.

Since Nietzsche is first and foremost a philosopher of power—who links philosophy to power, truth to strategic linguistic tropes, and thinking to coping techniques—he has never been welcomed in the philosophical academy. This is so primarily because—like Kierkegaard and Marx—his understanding of the power dimensions of knowledge and the political aspects of philosophy calls into question the very conception of philosophy that legitimates philosophical reflection in the academy. Ironically, the recent developments in philosophy and literary theory—antirealism in ontology, antifoundationalism in epistemology, and the detranscendentalizing of the subject—were prefigured by Nietzsche.[1] Yet the relation of these developments to politics and power is ignored.

Repetition in the Post-Philosophical Present

The contemporary philosophical scene can be viewed as a repetition of Hegel's historicizing efforts—but with a difference. This crucial difference primarily consists of retranslating Hegel's stress on History as an emphasis on Language. The Hegelian notions of origins and ends of history, of homogeneous continuities in and overarching totalizing frameworks for history, are replaced by beginnings and random play of differences within linguistic systems, heterogeneous discontinuities in and antitotalizing deconstructions of linguistic discourses. This repetition of Hegel—the replacement of history with language—is mediated by three central-European processes in this century: the nihilistic Death-of-God perspective conjoined with Saussurean linguistics, which radically questions the meaning and value of human life (best portrayed in contemporary literature); the rise of fascism and totalitarianism, which tempers efforts for social change; and the sexual revolution, which un-

leashes hedonistic and narcissistic sensibilities on an unprecedented scale. These three processes circumscribe the repetition of Hegel within the perimeters of philosophical nihilism, political impotence, and hedonistic fanfare. Professional philosophy finds itself either radically historicized and linguisticized, hence vanishing, or holding on to the Kantian tradition for dear life.[2]

On a philosophical plane, the repetition of Hegel takes the form of an antirealism in ontology, [an] antifoundationalism in epistemology, and a detranscendentalizing of the Kantian subject. The antirealism in ontology leaves us with changing descriptions and versions of the world, which come from various communities as responses to problematics, as fallible attempts to overcome specific situations, and as means to satisfy particular needs and interests. The antifoundationalism in epistemology precludes notions of privileged representations that correctly correspond to the world, hence ground our knowledge; it leaves us with sets of transient social practices that facilitate our survival as individuals and members of society. The detranscendentalizing of the Kantian subject—the historical and linguistic situating of ourselves as knowers and doers—focuses our attention no longer on the mental activity of thinking individuals, but rather on the values and norms of historical and linguistic groups. Kierkegaard and Marx, like their master Hegel, held such antirealist, antifoundationalist, detranscendentalist views, but they did so with a sense of engagement in the present and hope for the future. The repetition of Hegel holds similar postphilosophical views yet despairs of the present and has little hope, if any, for the future.

This post-philosophical despair and hopelessness—with its concomitant forms of ironic and apocalyptic thinking and narcissistic living—is inextricably linked to the fundamental cultural transformations I noted earlier: the demythologizing of the institution of science, the demystifying of the role of authority, and the disclosure of a deep sense of impotence. Since modern philosophy at its inception was the handmaiden of science, it is not surprising that the demythologizing of science occurs alongside the vanishing of modern philosophy. Just as the Enlightenment era witnessed the slow replacement of the authority of the church with that of science, so we are witnessing a displacement of science, but there is no replacement as of yet. The *philosophes* of the Enlightenment—the propagandists for science and ideologues for laissez-faire capitalism—had a vision of the future; whereas the professional avant-gardists—propagandists against "bourgeois" science and ideologues against monopoly capitalism—rarely present a project for the future. The neo-Marxist Frankfurt school, including Max Horkheimer, Theodor Adorno, and Herbert Marcuse, along with creative followers like Stanley Aronowitz and Michel Foucault, are pioneers of this novel perspective of philosophy.[3] Yet, with the exception of Aronowitz and Marcuse at times, the hopelessness for the future is overwhelming. Nevertheless, these figures are much further along than their contemporaries, as illustrated by Quine's outdated neo-positivist veneration of physics or Rorty's nostalgic longing for pre-professional humanistic "conversation" among men and women of letters.

The demystifying of the role of authority—promoted by the "hermeneutics of suspicion" of Marx, Nietzsche, and Freud and encouraged by the antifoundationalism in contemporary philosophy—can be traced to the more general problem of the deep crisis of legitimacy in postmodern capitalist civilization. Of course, the breakdown of scientific, technocratic culture also affects the socialist world, but the crisis of legitimacy is in many ways a phenomenon rooted in the processes of monopoly capitalist societies. By undermining traditional forms of authority—church, family, school—owing to the profit-motivated promotion of hedonistic sensibilities, capitalist societies can legitimate themselves principally by satisfying the very needs they help activate. These societies keep the populace loyal to their authority primarily by "delivering the goods," often luxury consumer goods that are rendered attractive by means of ingenious advertising. These goods do not merely pacify the populace; they also come to be viewed as the basic reason, in contrast to moral, religious or political reasons, that people have for acquiescence to capitalist authority. Hence, the crisis of legitimacy—the undermining of the work ethic, the collapse of the family, anarchy in public schools, and the proliferation of sexually-oriented advertisements, commercials, movies, and television shows—becomes part and parcel of the very legitimizing processes of monopoly capitalist societies.

The disclosure of a deep sense of impotence sits at the center of the post-philosophical present: the sense of reaching an historical dead end with no foreseeable way out and no discernible liberating projects or even credible visions in the near future. This disclosure is related to the de-transcendentalizing of the Kantian subject in the sense that the emergence of the transcendental subject—the creative and conquering romantic hero—signifies the sense of optimistic triumph of early modern capitalist civilization. The de-transcendentalizing of the subject portrays the sense of pessimistic tragedy of post-modern capitalist civilization, with the primary redemptive hope for this civilization, Marx's collective subject, the proletariat, remaining relatively dormant and muted.

The dominant forms of intellectual activity, especially philosophical reflection, enact this sense of impotence: analytical philosophy makes a fetish of technical virtuosity and uses it as a measure to regulate the intense careerism in the profession; antiacademic professional avant-gardists fiercely assault fellow colleagues and fervently attack notions of epistemological privilege yet remain relatively silent about racial, sexual, and class privilege in society at large; and poststructuralists perennially decenter prevailing discourse and dismantle philosophical and literary texts yet valorize a barren, ironic disposition by deconstructing, hence disarming and discarding, any serious talk about praxis. In this way, the repetition of Hegel is, from an Afro-American perspective, meretricious: attractive on a first glance but much less substantive after careful examination.

Recommendations for a Revolutionary Future

The principal task of the Afro-American philosopher is to keep alive the idea of a revolutionary future, a better future different from the deplorable present, a state of affairs in which the multifaceted oppression of Afro-Americans (and others) is, if not eliminated, alleviated. Therefore the Afro-American philosopher must preserve the crucial Hegelian (and deeply Christian) notions of negation and transformation of what is in light of a revolutionary not-yet.[4] The notions of negation and transformation—the pillars of the Hegelian process of *Aufhebung*—promote the activity of resistance to what is and elevate the praxis of struggle against existing realities. In this way, Afro-American philosophers must wage an intense intellectual battle in the form of recovering the revolutionary potential of Hegel against the ironic repetition of Hegel, which dilutes and downplays this potential. The revolutionary potential of Hegel—indigenously grounded in the prophetic religious and progressive secular practices of Afro-Americans—can be promoted by a serious confrontation with the Marxist tradition and, among others, the recent work of Michel Foucault.

Foucault's exorbitant reaction to his former vulgar Marxism and past Communist allegiances often leads him to embody the worst of the repetition of Hegel: precluding any talk about a better future and downplaying the activity of resistance and struggle in the present. Despite these limitations, certain aspects of Foucault's work can contribute to a revolutionary future, notably his attempt to construct "a new politics of truth." For Foucault, the Western will to truth has not been truthful about itself. Only with the appearance of Hegel and later Kierkegaard, Marx, and Nietzsche, has the this-worldly character of truth—its rootedness in politics and power—been disclosed and dissected. Foucault, who views his own work as "philosophical fragments put to work in a historical field of problems," begins his philosophical reflections with two basic questions: How are the conditions for the possibility of knowledges—the rules, conventions, and operations that circumscribe fields of discourse wherein notions, metaphors, categories, and ideas are rendered intelligible and comprehensible—ensconced in particular sets of power-relations? How are these conditions articulated in discursive practices and elaborated (in the sense in which Antonio Gramsci defines this crucial term) in nondiscursive formations? These questions are answered neither by abstract philosophical arguments nor by systematic theoretical treatises, but rather by detailed analytical descriptions—containing arguments and explanations—that constitute a genealogy of moral and political technologies, a genealogy that lays bare the workings of structures of domination and mechanisms of control over human bodies. Foucault's genealogical approach eschews the philosophical past and shuns the ironic repetition of Hegel in the present; he writes a subversive history of this past and present by discerning and detaching "the power of truth from the forms of hegemony, social, economic, and cultural, within which it operates."[5]

Foucault's perspective can be valuable for Afro-American philosophers whose allegiance is to a revolutionary future. With the indispensable aid of sophisticated neo-Marxist analysis, Foucault's viewpoint can be creatively transformed and rendered fruitful for a genealogy of modern racism, in both its ideational and material forms. This genealogy would take the form of detailed, analytical descriptions of the battery of notions, categories, metaphors, and concepts that regulate the inception of modern discourse, a discourse that constituted the idea of white supremacy in a particular way (e.g. inaugurated the category of "race") and excluded the idea of black equality in beauty, culture, and character from its discursive field.[6] Unlike Foucault, this Afro-American genealogical approach also would put forward an Afro-American counter-discourse, in all its complexity and diversity, to the modern European racist discourse and examine and evaluate how the Afro-American response promotes or precludes a revolutionary future.[7] In addition, a more refined effort would even delve into the political content of Afro-American everyday life and disclose the multivarious Afro-American cultural elements that debilitate or facilitate an Afro-American revolutionary future.

If Afro-American philosophers are to make a substantive contribution to the struggle for Afro-American freedom, it is imperative that we critically revaluate the grand achievements of the past philosophical figures in the West and avoid falling into their alluring traps, traps that disarm Afro-American philosophers and render us mere colorful presences in the glass menagerie of the academy in monopoly capitalist USA. Afro-American philosophers must understand the repetition of Hegel in the present time as inescapable yet of highly limited value owing to its nihilistic outlooks; outlooks that implicitly presuppose luxury and explicitly preclude any serious talk about a future better than the inferno-like present. Lastly Afro-American philosophers must articulate and elaborate recommendations for a revolutionary future. This articulation and elaboration requires a recovery of the revolutionary potential of Hegel, a deepening of the Marxist tradition, and a concrete grounding in the indigenous prophetic and progressive practices of Afro-Americans. This calling of Afro-American philosophers—this vocation of service—permits us to take our place alongside, not above, other committed Afro-Americans who continue to hold up the blood-stained banner, a banner that signifies the Afro-American struggle for freedom.

NOTES

1. Cornel West, "Nietzsche's Prefiguration of Postmodern American Philosophy," *Boundary 2: A Journal of Postmodern Literature*, Special Nietzsche issue, vols. 9, 10, nos. 1, 3 (Fall–Winter 1980–1981), pp. 241–270.

2. The most penetrating and provocative examination of these two options for contemporary philosophy is Richard Rorty's *Philosophy and the Mirror of Nature* (Princeton, 1979). For a sympathetic yet biting critique of this book, see my review in *Union Seminary Quarterly Review*, vol. 37, nos. 1, 2 (Fall–Winter 1981–1982).

3. The central works on this subject are Max Horkheimer and Theodor Adorno, *Dialectic of Enlightenment* (New York, 1972); Herbert Marcuse, *One-Dimensional Man: Studies in the Ideology of Advanced Industrial Society* (Boston, 1964); Stanley Aronowitz, *The Crisis in Historical Materialism: Class, Politics and Culture in Marxist Theory* (New York, 1981); Michel Foucault, *Discipline and Punish: The Birth of the Prison*, trans. Alan Sheridan (New York, 1977).

4. For a brief treatment of these two basic notions as a basis for prophetic Christian and progressive Marxist praxis, see Cornel West, *Prophesy Deliverance! An Afro-American Revolutionary Christianity* (Philadelphia, 1982), "Introduction: The Sources and Tasks of Afro-American Critical Thought."

5. Michel Foucault, *Power/Knowledge: Selected Interviews and Other Writings 1972–1977* (New York, 1980), p. 133.

6. For a rudimentary effort at such a genealogical approach, see Cornel West, *Prophesy Deliverance! An Afro-American Revolutionary Christianity* (Philadelphia, 1982), Chapter 2.

7. For a humble attempt at such a project, see Cornel West, "Philosophy and the Afro-American experience," *The Philosophical Forum*, vol. IX, nos. 2–3 (Winter–Spring 1977–1978), pp. 117–148, and, with additions and revisions, Cornel West, *Prophesy Deliverance! An Afro-American Revolutionary Christianity* (Philadelphia, 1982), Chapter 3.

The Great Pretenders:
Further Reflections on Whiteshamanism

WENDY ROSE

Wendy Rose (b. 1948) began writing poetry as a teenager in California during the 1960s. Several of her early poems, which were written under the penname Cheron Khanshendel, appeared in anthologies devoted to the works of young Native American poets. Since then she has published many books of poetry under her own name. These include *Hopi Roadrunner Dancing*; *Long Division: A Tribal History*; *Academic Squaw: Reports to the World from the Ivory Tower*; *What Happened When the Hopi Hit New York*; *Halfbreed Chronicles and Other Poems*; and *Lost Copper*, which was nominated for a Pulitzer Prize in 1980. In addition to writing poetry, Rose paints and teaches anthropology. She is currently coordinator of the Native American Studies Program at Fresno City College.

In the following essay, Rose describes and criticizes what she calls cultural imperialism or cultural colonialism. She claims that this form of colonialism, like other forms, is tied to the Eurocentric belief in superiority and "Manifest Destiny." Using personal experiences to support her claim, Rose argues that Eurocentrism, which includes belief in the universality of European models of knowledge and European philosophical conceptions, systematically devalues the culture and philosophy of non-European peoples. The ultimate expression of this devaluation is the claim that Euroamericans are "uniquely qualified to explain the rest of humanity, not only to Euroamerica, but to everyone else as well."

One particular instance of Eurocentrism and cultural imperialism is what Rose identifies as whiteshamanism. The term *whiteshaman* refers to a group of non-Indian writers who claim to have derived their voices and authority from Native American sources. Rose argues that whiteshamans, like their European forebears, are expropriating the culture of Native Americans for personal gain. And in remaking Native American culture in their own image, whiteshamans not only are distorting Native American traditions, but also are silencing "the genuine voice of Native America." Despite her criticisms of Eurocentrism and whiteshamanism, Rose ends her essay by holding out the possibility of a complementary relationship between European and Native American culture. However, for such a complementary relationship to become a reality, Rose believes that both Europeans and Native Americans must reclaim their distinctive cultural traditions. Getting beyond the European call for universality and the suppression of ethnicity, Rose believes that we must honestly admit our differences and learn to value diversity.

Questions for Thought

1. What does Rose mean by "whiteshamanism"? Why does she believe that whiteshamanism represents a form of cultural imperialism?

2. Do you agree with Rose's claim that cultural colonialism is as objectionable as economic, political, or military colonialism? Why or why not?
3. What, according to Rose, are the essential differences between the European and Native American conceptions of freedom? Which of these two conceptions comes closer to your own views about freedom?
4. Do you agree with Rose's claim that the academic canon is Eurocentric? Would you describe the subject matter in your high school classes as Eurocentric? What about the college classes you have taken?
5. What is Rose's position concerning ethnocentrism? How important is your ethnicity in determining who you are?
6. How does Rose conclude her essay? In what ways, if any, is her conclusion similar to the conclusions of hooks and Guevara?

They came for our land, for what grew or could be grown on it, for the resources in it, and for our clean air and pure water. They stole these things from us, and in the taking they also stole our free ways and the best of our leaders, killed in battle or assassinated. And now, after all that, they've come for the very last of our possessions; now they want our pride, our history, our spiritual traditions. They want to rewrite and remake things, to claim them for themselves. The lies and thefts just never end.

—Margo Thunderbird, 1988

I AM THAT MOST SCHIZOPHRENIC OF CREATURES, an American Indian who is both poet and anthropologist. I have, in fact, a little row of buttons up and down my ribs that I can press for the appropriate response: *click*, I'm an Indian; *click*, I'm an anthropologist; *click*, I'll forget the whole thing and write a poem. I have also been a critic of the "whiteshaman movement," to use the term coined by Geary Hobson, Cherokee critic. The term "whiteshaman," he says, rightly belongs to "the apparently growing number of small-press poets of generally white, Euro-Christian American background, who in their poems assume the persona of the shaman, usually in the guise of an American Indian medicine man. To be a poet is simply not enough; they

must claim a power from higher sources."[1] Actually, the presses involved are not always small, as is witnessed by the persona adopted by Gary Snyder in his Pulitzer Prize-winning book of verse, *Turtle Island*.[2] . . .

I would expand upon Hobson's definition by observing that not all whiteshamans are Americans, poets, nor even white. A perfect example is that of Carlos Castaneda, author of the best-selling series of "Don Juan" epics purporting to accurately reveal the "innermost secrets" of a purely invented "Yaqui sorcerer."[3] I would further add that whiteshamans pretending to higher sources may or may not refer to themselves as shamanic. Some of those within the movement have professed more secular intimacies with Native American cultures and traditions. This is well illustrated by Ruth Beebe Hill, who pretended in her book *Hanta Yo* to have utilized her association with a single American Indian man—"Chunksa Yuha," otherwise known as Alonzo Blacksmith—to uncover not only 19th-century social, sexual, and spiritual forms, but an "archaic dialect" of the Lakota language unknown to the Lakota themselves.[4]

Such claims, whether sacred or secular, are uniformly made with none of the community ac-

Reprinted from Wendy Rose, "The Great Pretenders: Further Reflections on Whiteshamanism," in *The State of Native America*, ed. by M. Annette James, by permission of South End Press.

knowledgment and training essential to the positions in question. Would it not be absurd to aver to be a Rabbi if one were neither Jewish nor even possessed an elementary knowledge of Judaism? Or that one were a jet aircraft pilot without having been inside an airplane? Yet, preposterous as whiteshaman assertions may be on the face of it, there seems to be an unending desire on the part of the American public to absorb such "knowledge" as the charlatans care to produce. Further, the proliferation of such "information" typically occurs to the exclusion of far more accurate and/or genuinely native material, a matter solidly reinforcing the profound ignorance of things Indian afflicting most of society. As the Lakota scholar Vine Deloria, Jr. has put it:

> The realities of Indian belief and existence have become so misunderstood and distorted at this point that when a real Indian stands up and speaks the truth at any given moment, he or she is not only unlikely to be believed, but will probably be contradicted and "corrected" by the citation of some non-Indian and totally inaccurate "expert." More, young Indians in universities are now being trained to see themselves and their cultures in terms prescribed by such experts rather than in the traditional terms of the tribal elders. . . . In this way, the experts are perfecting a system of self-validation in which all semblance of honesty and accuracy is lost. This is not only a travesty of scholarship, but it is absolutely devastating to Indian societies.[5]

Hobson and others have suggested that the assumption of shaman status or its secular counterparts by non-native writers is part of a process of "cultural imperialism" directly related to other claims on Native American land and lives. By appropriating indigenous cultures and distorting them for its own purposes, their reasoning goes, the dominant society can neatly eclipse every aspect of contemporary native reality, from land rights to issues of religious freedom. Pam Colorado, an Oneida Scholar working at the University of Calgary in Canada, frames the matter:

> The process is ultimately intended to supplant Indians, even in areas of their own customs and spirituality. In the end, non-Indians will have complete power to define what is and is not Indian, even for Indians. We are talking here about an absolute ideological/conceptual subordination of Indian people in addition to the total physical subordination [we] already experience. When this happens, the last vestiges of real Indian society and Indian rights will disappear. Non-Indians will then "own" our heritage and ideas as thoroughly as they now claim to own our land and resources.[6]

Whiteshamans and their defenders, assuming a rather amazing gullibility on the part of American Indians, usually contend they are "totally apolitical." Some have pointed out that the word "shaman" is itself of Tungus (Siberian) origin and insist that their use of it thus implies nothing specifically Native American, either in literal content or by impression. They often add the insulting caveat that American Indian writers know less of their ancestral traditions and culture than non-Native anthropologists. Finally, most argue that "artistic license" or "freedom of speech" inherently empowers them to do what they do, no matter whether Indians like it (and, ultimately, no matter the cost to native societies). Native American scholars, writers, and activists have heard these polemics over and over again. It is time to separate fact from fantasy in this regard.

Anatomy of Whiteshamanism

First, it must be noted that the term "shaman" is one of convenience, as are the terms "Indian," "American Indian," "Native American," and so on. The Siberian origin of the word is in this sense irrelevant at best and, more often, polemically obfuscatory. Moreover, whiteshamans do not construct their writings or antics after the Siberian model, even when they use the term "shaman" to describe themselves and the processes of their craft. Their works, whether poetic, novelistic, or theoretical, are uniformly designed and intended to convey conceptions of "Indian-ness" to their readers. This remains true regardless of the literal content of the material at issue, as is readily evident in "Blackfoot/Cherokee" author Jamake Highwater's (aka: Jay Marks, a non-Indian) extended repackaging of Greek mythology and pop psychology in the garb of supposed "primal Native American legends."[7]

Further, during performances, whiteshamans typically don a bastardized composite of pseudo-Indian "style" buckskins, beadwork, headbands, moccasins, and sometimes paper masks intended to portray native spiritual beings such as Coyote or Raven. They often appear carrying gourd rattles, eagle feathers, "peace pipes," medicine bags, and other items reflective of native ceremonial life. Their readings are frequently accompanied by the burning of sage, "pipe ceremonies," the conducting of chants and beating of drums of vaguely native type, and the like. One may be hard-pressed to identify a particular indigenous culture being portrayed, but the obviously intended effect is American Indian. The point is that the whiteshaman reader/performer aspires to "embody the Indian," in effect "becoming" *the* "real" Indian even when actual native people are present. Native reality is thereby subsumed and negated by imposition of a "greater" or "more universal" contrivance.

This leads to a second major point. Whiteshamanism functions as a subset of a much broader assumption within the matrix of contemporary Eurocentric domination holding that non-Indians always (inherently) know more about Indians than do Indians themselves. It is from this larger whole that whiteshamanism draws its emotional and theoretical sustenance and finds the sense of empowerment from which it presumes to extend itself as "spokesperson" for Indians, and ultimately to substitute itself for Indians altogether. Illustrations of this abound, especially within anthropology, linguistics, and the various social sciences. Allow me to recall, by way of example, a few of my own experiences as an employee of a large, university-connected anthropology museum during the mid-to-late 1970s.

- One famous anthropologist whose specialty is northern California insisted that northwestern California Indians were no longer familiar with their ancient form of money, long shells called "dentalia" or tooth-shells. The comment was stimulated by the fact that I was wearing some of these very same shells—which had been given to me by a Yurok woman as payment for a painting—around my neck.

- A basket specialist assured me that basket-hats are no longer worn by California Indian women. Yet, nearly every weekend such women attended the same social functions as I, wearing basket-hats that had been passed down through their families and, more importantly, were still being made.

- A woman who was both anthropologist and art collector told me that pottery was no longer produced at Laguna Pueblo. She continued to insist on this, even after I told her the names of the women who produce it there.

- A famous ethnohistorian informed me that I'd never see a California Indian woman with chin tattoos. I have seen them, albeit rarely.

- A very well known linguist asked me to escort a group of Yuki elders around the museum, and then confided to me that it was a shame no one spoke Yuki anymore. The elders spoke to one another in Yuki the entire time they were there.

- The "expert" on Laguna Pueblo pottery said to me, face to face, that Indians only *think* they know more about themselves than anthropologists. She wanted to impress upon me how "pathetic" my own people really were, and how much more enlightened and superior were her own.

Taken singly, these episodes are not important. But taken together, and added to the enormous pile of similar events and conversations Indians might collectively recount, it is apparent that a pattern exists: taken as a group, Euroamericans consider themselves to be uniquely qualified to explain the rest of humanity, not only to Euroamerica, but to everyone else as well. Coupled to this bizarre notion, whiteshamanism is simply the acting out of a much greater dynamic of cultural usurpation, employing a peculiarly "ritualistic" format.

The Pioneer Spirit

What are the implications of this? Consider that a working (if often sublimated) definition of "universality" is very much involved. It is reflected perfectly in the presumed structure of knowledge and in the real structure of "universities" through which this knowledge is imparted in contemporary society. The "core" of information constituting the essential canon of every discipline in academe—from philosophy to literature, from history to physical science, from art to mathematics—is explicitly derived from thought embodied in the European tradition. This is construed as encapsulating all that is fundamentally meaningful within the "universal attainment of human intellect." The achievements and contributions of all other cultures are considered, when they are considered at all, only in terms of appendage (filtered through the lens of Eurocentric interpretation), adornment (to prove the superiority of the Euro-derived tradition), esoteric specialization (to prove that other traditions, unlike those derived from Europe, are narrow and provincial rather than broad and universal).[8]

Always and everywhere, the inclusion of non-European intellectual content in the academy is absolutely predicated upon its conformity to sets of "standards" conceived and administered by those adhering to the basic precepts of Euro-derivation. The basic "qualification" demanded by academe of those who would teach non-European content is that they first receive "advanced training" and "socialization" in doctoral programs steeped in the supposed universality of Euro-derivation. Non-European subject matters are thus intrinsically subordinated to the demands of Eurocentrism at every level within U.S. institutions of higher learning. There are no exceptions: the intended function of such inclusion is to fit non-European traditions into positions assigned them by those of the Eurocentric persuasion. The purpose is to occupy and consume other cultures just as surely as their land and resources have been occupied and consumed.

Such circumstances are quite informative in terms of the more generalized socio-cultural situation. In the construction at hand, those who embrace the Euro-derivation of "universal knowledge" are considered by definition to be the normative expression of intellectual advancement among all humanity. They are "citizens of the world," holders of the "big picture," having inherent rights to impose themselves and their "insights" everywhere and at all times, with military force if need be. The rest of us are consigned by the same definition to our "parochialism" and "provinciality," perceived as "barriers to progress" in many instances, "helped" by our intellectual "betters" to overcome our "conceptual deficiencies" in others. The phenomenon is integral to Euroamerican culture, transcending all ideological boundaries demarcating conservatism and progressivism; a poster popular among science fiction readers of both political persuasions shows a 15th-century European ship sailing a star-map and asks: "What would have happened if Ferdinand and Isabella had said no?"

If, as the academics would have it, Indians "no longer really know" or at least lack access to their traditions and spirituality (not to mention land tenure), then it follows that they are no longer "truly" Indian. If culture, tradition, spirituality, oral literature, and land are not theirs to protect, then such things are free for the taking. An anthropologist or folklorist hears a story or a song and electronically reproduces it, eventually catalogs it, and perhaps publishes it. According to the culture of the scholar, it is then *owned* by "science" in exactly the same fashion as native land, once "settled" by colonizers, is said to be owned by them. Stories, songs, ceremonies, and other cultural ingredients can be—and often are—stolen as surely as if they were tangible objects removed by force. There is a stereotype about the "savage" who is afraid that a camera will steal his soul. It will indeed, and much more, as will the tape recorder, the typewriter, and the video cassette. The process is as capable, and as purposeful, in first displacing and then replacing native people within their own cultural contexts as were earlier processes of "discovery" and "settlement" in displacing us from and replacing us upon our land. What is at issue is the extension across intellectual terrain of the more physically oriented 19th-century premise of "Manifest Destiny."

Anthropologists often contend they do not have any appreciable effect upon their own societies, but the fact is that the public does swallow and regurgitate anthropological concepts, usually after about twenty years. At that point, one generally finds efforts undertaken to put to popular use the cultural territory that anthropology had discovered, claimed, and tentatively expropriated in behalf of the dominant society. The subsequent popular endeavors serve to settle and "put to good use" this new cultural territory. This is the role of the whiteshamans. Theirs is a fully sanctioned, even socially mandated activity within the overall imperial process of Eurocentrism. It should thus come as no surprise to serious students of American culture that editors, publishers, reviewers, and most readers greatly prefer the nonsense of whiteshamanism to the genuine literature of American Indians. The situation is simply a continuation of the "Pioneer Spirit" in American life.

Appropriation and Denial

The anthropologist of me is always a little embarrassed. When I am called upon to speak anthropologically, I find myself apologizing or stammering that I'm not *that* kind of anthropologist. I feel like the housewife–prostitute who must go home to clean the house for her unknowing husband. She must lie or she must admit her guilt. Native Americans expect me to reflect the behavior they have come to anticipate from non-Native anthropologists. If I live in *their* camp, the native reasoning goes, it follows that I must have joined ranks with them; it is therefore expected that I will attempt to insinuate myself into tribal politics where I have no business. Non-native anthropologists expect me either to be what Delmos Jones has called a "superinformant" or a spy for the American Indian Movement, watching their every action with the intention of "causing trouble."

The irony of all this is that I'm really NOT that kind of anthropologist. My dissertation involves a cultural–historical perspective on published literature by American Indians. Such a degree should be, perhaps, granted by the English or literature departments, but such is not the case. At the university where I worked toward my doctorate in anthropology, the English Department refused to acknowledge two qualified Native American applicants for a position during the 80's, with the statement—made to the Coordinator of Native American Studies—that "Native American literature is not part of American literature." In the same English Department, a non-Indian graduate student was also awarded a degree on the basis of a dissertation on "Native American Literature." The student focused on four authors, *none* of whom was an Indian. The four writers were all known whiteshamans.

Native American literature is considered (by Euroamericans) to be "owned" by anthropology, as American Indians themselves are seen as "owned" by anthropologists. Our literature is merely ethnographic, along with our material culture and kinship systems. This is not, of course, restricted to Native American societies; Fourth World peoples everywhere are considered copyrightable in the same way. Maori, Native Hawaiian, Papuan, Cuna, Thai, and other people around the globe have been literarily colonized just as they have been economically, politically and militarily colonized. Not so the literature of the Euro-derived (with certain exceptions, such as homosexuals, prisoners, etc.— all groups not "normal"). My position is that all literature must be viewed ethnographically. All literatures provide information about the culture of both writer and subject. All literatures are potential tools for the anthropologist—but not one "type" of literature more than any other. What literature is not ethnic? What person has no ethnicity? American Indians are not "more ethnic" than Polish-Americans or Anglo-Americans; they are simply called upon more frequently and intensively to deal with their ethnicity. . . .

Freedom (with Reservations)

While the Indian of me is bent double from the force of being hit by the literary-colonial canon, the anthropologist of me is always looking for cultural explanations for whiteshamanism and its emotional impact. Feelings run deep on both sides and people tend to take sides on the issue, even if they are not otherwise interested in literary matters. I have found that much of the controversy over whiteshamanism involves fundamental, cherished concepts held by Europeans and Euroamericans involving art, freedom, and what it means to be an artist. These ideas do not, as is often claimed by their advocates, deviate from—much less transcend—the more directly and overtly imperialist manifestations discussed above. To the contrary, they dovetail

quite nicely with the rest of the Pioneer Spirit.

All of us, Native and non-Native, are ethnocentric at our deepest levels. No amount of anthropological training or insight can abolish ethnocentrism, although we can become aware of it and learn to take it into consideration on a day-to-day basis. The problem is that the notion of intrinsic universalism lodged within Euro-derived tradition usually precludes those of that tradition from acknowledging either the fact or the meaning of their own ethnicity. I've encountered literally scores of white students over the years who have professed in various ways to have "no culture." Sometimes they bemoan this circumstance, sometimes they appear to take a certain pleasure in it. Either way, they purport to inhabit "reality," while culture is a habitat reserved exclusively for those whose heritage deviates from their own. Ethnicity, for the mainstream, is thus specifically the domain of Others. The attitude is absolutely pervasive: A short time ago, I even saw a section in a variety store advertising its products for "ethnic hair."

Rather than taking pride in their own deeply rooted ethnicity, most Euroamericans feel duty-bound to sublimate it. Instead of being proud of who they are, they run about making liberal statements about "loving everybody," believing everyone to be "the same under the skin," and so on. The fact is that even the most avowedly progressive Euroamericans seem to want a Disney-ish world in which everyone is a different shade of the same thing, everyone a member of the same cultural "reality" except for things which are "safely" different: food, dress, dancing, and crafts; sometimes language. Beyond these distinctions, they hold that we should *all* be "entitled" to "share equally" in what they hold to be the loftiest and "most natural" aspiration of humanity: Freedom, the more total the better. In noting this to be the case, Edmund Carpenter observed: "The message is clear: we should love them because they are like us. But the statement has its questioning brother: what if they *aren't* like us?"[9]

What Euroamerican, other than those of fascistic persuasion, can be comfortable with the notion that total freedom is a pathological concept? Yet my father's Hopi people see it that way. In the Hopi view, no one would want to be that completely alone and uncontrolled unless there was something seriously wrong with them. In the Hopi Way, and in most other native traditions, to want to be away from people is seen as a form of madness. The very worst punishment indigenous societies can inflict, much worse than death or imprisonment, is exile or to be stigmatized by your people. Conversely, to be allowed to participate in society represents the essence of fulfillment: To be assigned responsibility and acknowledged by the group as having made a useful contribution is the highest accolade. Acceptance by and inclusion among the people are the highest principles governing native life.

By contrast, the typical Euro-derived pattern, in an ideal state, would be for people to live absolutely "free" or "unbound." Euroamericans define freedom in a certain way, primarily politically, and no longer think to question whether it's bad or good. Freedom is why their ancestors left Europe. Freedom is why their ancestors fought for independence from Europe. Freedom is why they continuously penetrated "the frontier." Freedom is why they came in the California and Yukon gold rushes; if you have enough money, you can "live free." Freedom is why they save up (or compulsively spend) that money today. Freedom is why they went to college, send their kids to college. Freedom is why they retire at a certain age. And yet "freedom" as they envision it is an extremely culture-specific value.

Likewise, "art" and being "an artist" are culture-specific ideas that relate to freedom; the "freest" individuals in society are supposed to be artists. Artists can be eccentric, they can act however they wish, only to be forgiven because they are artists and therefore free. It is freedom and not creativity that arouses jealousy among Euroamerican non-artists. When a Euroamerican hears that I give poetry readings all over the country, she or he invariably turns wistful and remarks: "You're so lucky. You have all that freedom to travel. I sure wish I could." (Could what? Write poetry? No, freely travel.) Native people, on the other hand, often extend genuine condolences that my work forces me to spend so much time so far from home, away from the obligations and responsibilities which lend a central meaning to life. The dichotomy in values couldn't be clearer. These ideas about art and freedom are at the center of the conflict about whiteshamanism.

In Euro-derived society, art is separated from everyday life. For instance, an artist typically works at night instead of when other people work. Art is special, elite (much of it requiring specialized training in "appreciation"), non-utilitarian, self-expressive, solitary, ego-identified, self-validating, innovative (to make it perpetually "new"), unique, and—in its "highest" forms—"without rules." It is a hallmark of the greatest artists, those who "change history," that they break rules, discarding everything "old." Scholars and critics refer to a favored artist as "breaking the mold" or "flying in the face of tradition." The whiteshaman says to the American Indian critic, "You can't tell me what to write. I have a right to do whatever I want. This is art; there are no rules." Within the context of whiteshaman culture, truth and freedom are at stake. He or she honestly views the Indian critic as abusing artistic freedom (or "poetic license"), as trying to restrict the unrestrictable, as *trespassing*. The pioneer cannot allow the native to say "go home."

Native American views are different regarding freedom and art. We are not a uniform people, of course, from arctic to tropic, and coast to coast, and so my statements must be generalizations, more or less true for most American Indian societies. In life and art, there are rules, and this is good. These rules were given to us, they belong to us, and we must not only follow them, but guard them. Rules exist governing form, content, context, and personnel. Of these, context may be the most important, and yet for the Euro-derived artist it seems to be of negligible significance. A white male art teacher once said to me, "Art is everywhere." Even the many movements which call themselves "countercultural" or "revolutionary" have bought into the European system enough to revolt against it and to use its structure to fuel the revolt. The "alternatives" are merely extensions of the European tradition. They are not, and have never been, "a whole new thing."

American Indian views on art tend to be trans-tribal, especially now when so many diverse native cultures are united by a single colonial language and electronic media. Art must be community-oriented (it may be sacred, but not supernatural; *nothing* is supernatural), it must be useful, it must be beautiful and functional at the same time (the ideas are inseparable, for functioning is part of beauty, and vice versa), it is good if more than one person has a hand in its production, and its completion is always an excellent excuse for a party. There are occasions where the party (or feast or ceremony) is part of the art form. The artist is not above or otherwise separated from the rest of society; she or he feels no particular desire to be recognized alone or considered different from the other people. The artist contributes a particular skill to the welfare and survival, not to mention the happiness, of the community.

Native American art is fitted into a continuum where it may or may not change, but certainly will not be pressured to be innovative. Innovation is a consideration that is more often than not rejected by the group, but a successful, acceptable, useful innovation is always welcome. The point is that the artist does not innovate just for the sake of innovating; by itself, innovation is not part of the criteria for "good art." The artist is not expected to be eccentric or any way noticeably different from anyone else. Quite the contrary. These ideas—the Euroamerican

and American Indian—are obviously in fundamental conflict. It is equally obvious that people on both sides will not normally think about them as I have presented them; people just don't sit down and analyze their behavior in a cultural context. So the conflicts go on unrecognized, the whiteshaman and the Native American writer occupying the same turf, but running according to a different set of rules.

Displacement

Aside from the psychological and spiritual impact of whiteshamans on American Indian writers, there are practical effects as well. Indian writers are struggling like others in an age of budget cuts and lack of respect for literature. Most Indians write in English and use literary forms that are European and Asian in origin. These forms are generally combined with images, subject matter, and philosophy drawn from the native heritage. Few of us consciously think about what part of a particular poem came from what heritage, but the combinations are there to be studied. Not only have we adopted aspects of form and style that are non-native, but many of us have adopted the concept of what it *means* to be a writer. Even while this concept is in conflict with native sensibilities, we understand that, as professional writers, we are entitled to earn a living if we work hard enough and well enough, that we may profit from earning degrees in college, that if we give a reading and do a good job we will receive applause and people will say nice things about us in public.

Still, behind all this is the native idea that, if we succeed as writers, we are making a valuable contribution to our communities. We become role models for younger people, we speak at community gatherings (and may be asked to do so by those who respect our special skills with words), and the like. When we are in our communities, we are artists, or storytellers, or historians, in the native tradition. We are accepted, found worthy and useful. We fit in, and are thereby fulfilled. And yet, being of peoples who are now physically colonized, we must also sustain ourselves in other ways. So, when we go out to the lecture halls of fancy universities, we must become artists in a much more Euro-derived sense (though not all the way, because we never actually believe in it). To do this, we want and need our work to be read by both natives and non-natives, to be respected, to be reviewed, and to sell. Ours is always the balancing act between selling and selling out; the market for sellouts is invariably a good one.

As a poet, I am continually frustrated by the restrictions placed on my work by the same people who insist that poets should not be restricted. It is expected—indeed, *demanded*—that I do a little "Indian-dance," a shuffle and scrape to please the tourists (as well as the anthropologists). Organizers of readings continually ask me to wear beadwork and turquoise, to dress in buckskin (my people don't wear much buckskin; we've cultivated cotton for thousands of years), and to read poems conveying pastoral or "natural" images. I am often asked to "tell a story" and "place things in a spiritual framework." Simply *being* Indian—a real, live, breathing, up-to-date Indian person—is not enough. In fact, other than my genetics, this is the precise opposite of what is desired. The expectation is that I adopt, and thereby validate, the "persona" of some mythic "Indian being" who never was. The requirement is that I act to negate the reality of my—and my people's—existence in favor of a script developed within the fantasies of our oppressors.

I can and do refuse. Sometimes, I am invited to read anyway. More often, I am told that there are other poets "out there" who will prove to be more compliant with the needs of the organizers and, frequently, of their audiences. Invariably, by this is meant that there are non-Indian poets ready and willing to assume the role of what "real Indians" are "supposed" to be like. As an Indian, I am rendered "unreal." By the same token, the non-Indians displace me

as "Indian reality." On more than one occasion when I ended up sharing a podium with whiteshamans, I have been told pointblank that I am only a prop to make them look more "authentic." Even in the best of settings, when I read poetry about a political issue or anything else that is not a part of native culture (as perceived by non-natives), people frequently express disappointment, even outrage. Every other American Indian poet I know has undergone exactly the same sorts of experiences.

A logical consequence of these circumstances is that when "Indian content" is sought in a literary event, non-Indians are far more likely than Indians to be solicited to participate in the representation of "Indian-ness." Whiteshamans attract far more invitations to read their "Indian poetry" than do actual Indian poets. Correspondingly, because of their relative celebrity, they tend to accrue larger fees and honoraria for readings than do Indian poets, even when appearing in the same programs. A further consequence is that they are placed in positions from which to publish their "Indian" material, in larger press runs, often at higher prices and at higher royalty rates, than are most Indian writers. The "Indian biz" has proven quite lucrative for a number of whiteshamans. Not so the careers of all but a scant handful of Native American writers. The result has been a marked stilling of the genuine voice of Native America and its replacement by the utterances of an assortment of hucksters and carnival barkers. . . .

Fear and Loathing Among the Literati

Before closing, I would like to talk about certain misunderstandings regarding criticism by Native Americans of the whiteshamans and their followers. The fear exists among non-native writers that we are somehow trying to bar them from writing about Indians at all, that Indian people might be "staking a claim" as the sole interpreters of Indian cultures, most especially of that which is sacred, and asserting that only Indians can make valid observations on themselves. Such fears are not based in fact; I know of no Indian who has ever said this. Nor do I know of any who secretly think it. We accept as given that whites have as much prerogative to write and speak about us and our cultures as we have to write and speak about them and theirs. The question is how this is done and, to some extent, why it is done.

The problem with whiteshamans is one of integrity and intent, not topic, style, interest, or experimentation. Many non-Indian people have—from the stated perspective of the non-native viewing things native—written honestly and eloquently about any number of Indian topics, including those we hold sacred. We readily acknowledge the beauty of some poetry by nonnatives dealing with Indian people, values, legends, or the relationship between human beings and the American environment. A non-native poet is obviously as capable of writing about Coyote and Hawk as an Indian poet. The difference is in the promotion, so to speak. A non-native poet cannot produce an *Indian* perspective on Coyote or Hawk, cannot see Coyote or Hawk in an Indian way, and cannot produce a poem expressing Indian spirituality. What can be produced is another perspective, another view, another spiritual expression. The issue, as I said, is one of integrity and intent.

The principle works in both directions. As an Indian person who was deeply impressed with the oral literature of the Catholic Church during my childhood, I might compose verse based in this poetic form. I might go on to publish the poems. I might also perform them, with proper intonation, as in Mass. All of this is appropriate and permissible. But I would not and *could* not claim to be a priest. I could not tell the audience they were actually experiencing the transmutation that occurs during Mass. At the point I did endeavor to do such things, a discernible line of integrity—both personal and artistic—would have been crossed. Artistic freedom and emotional identification would not make me a priest,

nor would the "uplifting" of my audience—no matter how gratifying to them, and to me—make them participants in Mass. To evoke my impression of the feel of the Mass and its liturgy does not necessitate my lying about it.

There is a world of difference between a non-Indian man like Frank Waters writing about Indians and a non-Indian man like Jamake Highwater claiming through his writing that he has in fact *become* "an Indian." Similar differences exist between a non-Indian woman like Marla N. Powers who expresses her feelings about native spirituality honestly, stating that they are her perceptions, and white women like Lynn Andrews and "Mary Summer Rain" perpetrating the fraud of having been appointed "mediums" of Indian culture. And, of course, the differences between non-Indians like John Neihardt who rely for their information upon actual native sources, and those like Andrews and Castaneda who simply invent them, should speak for themselves. As an Indian, as a poet, and as an anthropologist, I can wholeheartedly and without inconsistency accept the prerogatives claimed by the former in each case while rejecting the latter without hesitancy or equivocation. And I know of no American Indian aligned with his or her own heritage and traditions who would react otherwise.

Conclusion

So what is to be done about all this? For starters, readers of this essay should take the point that whiteshamanism is neither "okay," "harmless," nor "irrelevant," no more than any other form of racist, colonialist behavior. Correspondingly, they must understand that there is nothing "unreasonable" or "unfair" about the Indian position on the matter. As concerns the literary arena, we demand only informational and artistic integrity and mutual respect. It is incumbent upon Euroamerica, first and foremost, to make the whiteshamans and their followers understand that their "right" to use material from other cultures stems from those cultures, not from themselves. It must be impressed on them in no uncertain terms that there is nothing innately superior separating them from the rest of humanity, entitling them to trample upon the rights of others, or enabling them to absorb and "perfect" unfamiliar material better than the originators of that material. The only *right* they have when dealing with native-derived subject matters is to present them honestly, accurately, and—if the material is sensitive or belongs to another group or specific person—with permission. If their response to what they've seen, heard, or otherwise experienced is subjective and interpretive, we insist only that they make this known from the outset, so as not to confuse their impressions with the real article.

Application of a bit of common sense by the public would prove helpful. Those who have a genuine desire to learn about American Indians should go out of their way to avoid being *misled* into thinking they are reading, seeing, or hearing a native work. Most whiteshamans have demonstrated a profound ignorance of the very traditions they are trying to imitate or subsume, and so they have mostly imitated each other. Many of them claim to deploy an authentically Native American model, but speak rhetoric about "inventing their own myths," a literal impossibility within *real* indigenous traditions. Any mythology stemming from experiences in a university or along city streets is unlikely to include any recognizable coyotes, and confusion in this area precludes genuine intercultural communication faster and more thoroughly than any other single factor. Until such communication is realized, we are all going to remain very much mired in the same mess in which we now collectively find ourselves, interculturally speaking.

Adoption of a proactive attitude in this regard on the part of avowed progressives would likely prove effective. If they are truly progressive, they will demand—loudly and clearly—that not only authors, but publishers and organizers of events make it plain when "the facts" are being interpreted by a representative of a non-native culture. The extension of misinformation along these lines should be treated as seriously as any other sort of propaganda, and transgressors discredited—branded as liars, or perhaps sued for fraud—when revealed. It follows that bookstores—especially alleged "alternative" outlets—need to hear, with emphasis, that their progressive clientele objects to both their stocking of whiteshaman trash *and* to the absence of real Native American material on their shelves. Those who queue up to participate in, defend, or apologize for whiteshamanism must at last be viewed and treated as what they are. An unequivocally negative response to this sort of cultural imperialism on the part of large numbers of non-Indians would undoubtedly go far toward ending at least the worst of the practices at issue.

Native people, on the other hand, must come to understand that whiteshamans did not just pop up out of the blue and decide to offend Indians. They are responding, at least to some extent, to a genuinely felt emotional need within the dominant society. The fact that they are concomitantly exploiting other people for profit according to the sanctions and procedures of their own culture does not alter this circumstance. In spite of itself, whiteshamanism has touched upon something very real. An entire population is crying out for help, for alternatives to the spiritual barrenness they experience, for a way out of the painful trap in which their own worldview and way of life have ensnared them. They know, perhaps intuitively, that the answers—or part of the answers—to the questions producing their agony may be found within the codes of knowledge belonging to the native peoples of this land. Despite what they have done to us during the past 500 years, it would be far less than Indian of us were we not to endeavor to help them. Such are our Ways, and have always been our Ways.

Perhaps we can treaty now. Perhaps we can regain a balance that once was here, but now seems lost. If poets and artists are the prophets and expressers of history—as thinkers of both the American Indian and Euro-derived traditions have suggested in different ways—then it may well be that our task is simply to take back our heritage from the whiteshamans, shake it clean and bring it home. In doing so, we not only save ourselves from much that is happening to us, but empower ourselves to aid those who have stolen and would continue to steal so much from us, to help them locate their *own* power, their *own* traditions as human beings among human beings, as relatives among relatives not only of the human kind. Perhaps then they can come into themselves as they might be, rather than as they have been, or as they are. Perhaps then we can at last clasp hands, not as people on this land, but of this land, and go forward together. As Seattle, leader of the Suquamish people, once put it, "Perhaps we will be brothers after all. . . . We shall see."

NOTES

1. Geary Hobson, "The Rise of the White Shaman as a New Version of Cultural Imperialism," in Geary Hobson, ed., *The Remembered Earth* (Albuquerque: Red Earth Press, 1978), pp. 100–108. An interesting, if unintended, history of the evolution of whiteshamanism in American letters may be found in Michael Castro, *Interpreting the Indian: Twentieth Century Poets and the Native American* (Albuquerque: University of New Mexico Press, 1983).

2. Gary Snyder, *Turtle Island* (New York: New Directions Publishers, 1974). It should be noted that Snyder may have set the entire whiteshaman phenomenon in motion with his "shaman songs" included in his *Myths and Texts*, (New York: Totem Press, 1960).

3. The Castaneda books in question are *The Teachings of Don Juan: A Yaqui Way of Knowledge* (1968); *A Separate Reality: Further Conversations with Don Juan* (1971); *Journey to Ixtlan: The Lessons of Don Juan* (1972); *Tales of Power* (1974); and *The Second Ring of Power* (1977). All of Castaneda's assertions were "academically validated" through his publication of a "scholarly paper" entitled "The didactic uses of hallucinogenic plants: An examination of a system of teaching," in *Abstracts of the 67th Annual Meeting of the American Anthropological Association* in 1968, and UCLA's 1973 award of a Ph.D. in anthropology to Castaneda on the basis of a dissertation entitled *Sorcery: A Description of the World* (actually a retitled manuscript of *Journey to Ixtlan*).

4. Ruth Beebe Hill, *Hanta Yo: An American Saga* (Garden City, N.Y.: Doubleday Publishers, 1977). For detailed American Indian criticism, see Vine Deloria Jr., "Hanta Yo: Super Hype," *Co-Evolution Quarterly*, Fall 1979, and "The Twisted World of Hanta Yo," *Minority Notes*, 1 (1), Spring 1979. Also see Beatrice Medicine, "Hanta Yo: A New Phenomenon," *The Indian Historian*, 12 (2), Spring 1979, and Allan R. Taylor, "The Literary Offenses of Ruth Beebe Hill," *American Indian Culture and Research Journal*, 4 (3), Summer 1980.

5. Vine Deloria, Jr., lecture presented during American Indian Awareness Week, University of Colorado at Boulder, as quoted by Ward Churchill in "A Little Matter of Genocide: Native American Spirituality and New Age Hucksterism," *Bloomsbury Review*, 8 (5), September/October 1988, pp. 23–24.

6. Pam Colorado, as quoted in Churchill, op. cit.

7. The books in question are Highwater's *Ritual of the Wind* (1977); *Anpao: An American Indian Odyssey* (1977); *The Sweetgrass Lives On: Fifty Contemporary Indian Artists* (1980); *The Sun, He Dies: The End of the Aztec World* (1980); and especially *The Primal Mind: Vision and Reality in Indian America* (1981). The Grecian content of Highwater's "interpretations" of American Indian mythos has been exhaustively demonstrated by Assiniboin-Sioux scholar Hank Adams in a manuscript entitled *Cannibal Green*. Adams's material has, of course, gone unpublished, other than an extract printed in the native rights journal *Akwesasne Notes* in early 1985. All the better to allow promoters such as David Jackson to pen pieces such as "Jamake Highwater's Native Intelligence," *Village Voice*, May 3, 1983, pp. 37–39.

8. For an in-depth examination of these assumptions, see Martin Carnoy, *Education as Cultural Imperialism* (New York: David McKay Publishers, 1974).

9. Edmund Carpenter, *Oh, What a Blow That Phantom Gave Me!* (New York: Holt, Rinehart, and Winston Publishers, 1972), p. 97.

6 Religion

In the introduction to the last chapter, I mentioned three dangers associated with the path of political thinking: the danger of disagreement, the danger of disloyalty, and the danger of dullness. As you now prepare to journey down the final philosophical path in this text, the path of thinking about religion, I should warn you that these same dangers are to be found on this path as well. Like political dialogue, religious dialogue often seems to be marked by endless argument and confrontation. Of course, recent ecumenical movements have tried to move beyond this state of affairs, but they have not been totally successful. Thus, there still remains much disagreement, not only between different religions (consider, for example, the recent confrontations between Hindus and Muslims in India), but between different divisions of the same religion as well.

Moreover, while an increasing number of my students have been reared in a purely secular environment and thus are able to discuss religion without facing the fear of disloyalty, others have grown up within a strong religious tradition that prohibits questioning of certain assumptions. If you fall into this latter category, then the danger of disloyalty may be even more worrisome on the path of thinking about religion than it was on the path of political thinking.

Finally, just as many people find political thinking and discussion to be terribly dull, others feel the same way about religion. I believe that one reason for this is that, at least in the Judeo-Christian tradition, much thinking about religion has taken the form of debates about abstract theological questions. Students are often introduced to religious thinking by being bombarded with arguments about the nature of God or with arguments trying to prove (or disprove) the existence of God.

If you get beyond such abstract theological debates, however, the path of thinking about religion becomes existentially exciting. Indeed, like the path of political thinking, the path of thinking about religion can be a path of personal and social transformation. In examining religious literature, you will find numerous examples of radical personal transformation, like the case of Prince Gautama who gave up a life of luxury to become the Buddha, or the case of the New Testament writer Paul who went from being an adamant persecutor of members of the early Christian sect to one of its foremost defenders and missionaries. And history offers a large number of social transformations as well, from Zarathustra's religious transformation of ancient Persian society and culture to the Islamic Revolution in Iran in the early 1980s.

The possibility of achieving personal and/or social transformation through religious thinking or experience is a common motif of the selections contained in this chapter. In the first selection, "The Great Announcement to Mankind," Bahá'u'lláh, who has himself experienced a radical personal transformation of a religious nature, urges that religion be used for the transformation of society. In a similar vein, Black Elk, in the second selection, describes part of the great vision that he received from the spirit world, and explains how this vision became a source of personal and social healing.

Selections three and four, both from a Christian perspective, criticize certain traditional Christian beliefs and practices, while offering a version of Christianity filled with the possibility of empowerment and liberation. In a defense of his civil rights activities in the "Letter from Birmingham Jail," Martin Luther King, Jr. contrasts the apathy and obstructionism of the white churches in the South with the "inner spiritual church," which offers genuine hope for freedom, and encouragement for those struggling to attain it. In a parallel manner, Gustavo Gutierrez criticizes the complicity of the Latin American church with the oppressive powers that maintain the status quo, and formulates the outlines of a theology of liberation that recognizes the plight of the poor and engages in the revolutionary movement to end poverty and injustice.

The next two writings, in contrast to the selections by King and Gutierrez, argue that true liberation, especially for women, cannot be achieved within the confines of the Judeo-Christian tradition. As the title to her essay indicates, Carol P. Christ argues that women need the imagery and symbolism of the Goddess, that is, myths and rituals affirming the sacredness of the female principle, if they are to overcome the negative portrayal and treatment of women associated with patriarchal religious beliefs and practices. This claim, which is echoed in the following essay by Starhawk, is forcefully supported by Starhawk's account of the persecution of witches (most of whom were women) by the Christian church. Starhawk goes on to contrast witchcraft, which she believes encourages independence and the development of women's spiritual and economic power, with the hierarchical and authoritarian structure of Christianity.

Finally, in a brief account of his personal journey from Christianity to paganism, Lin Yutang suggests that the theological beliefs of Christianity are less satisfying than the philosophy of paganism. Like both Christ and Starhawk, Lin believes that Christianity devalues earthly existence and encourages people to remain immature and psychologically dependent.

As you read and discuss these selections, keep in mind that their ultimate value lies in the role that they play in your own psychological and spiritual development. Indeed, this can be said for all of the selections in this text. As I suggested throughout all my introductions, if the path of philosophical reflection is not to be a path of lifeless abstractions, then it must be linked to self-analysis and personal growth.

6.1   The Great Announcement to Mankind

BAHÁ'U'LLÁH

Bahá'u'lláh (Arabic for "the glory of God") is the religious name of Husayn Ali (1817–1892). Husayn Ali, who was the son of one of the most distinguished families in Persia, became a member of the movement known as the Babis, a sect of Shi'ite Islam that looked for the coming of a savior figure who would establish a universal religion. After the leader of this group (known as Bāb-ub-Dīn or "the gate of faith") was publicly executed for political and religious reasons in 1850, Husayn Ali was imprisoned in Tehran and later in Baghdad. While in prison he had a powerful religious experience in which it was revealed to him that he was the savior figure of which the Bāb-ub-Dīn had foretold. In 1863, on the eve of his departure from Baghdad to forced exile in Constantinople, Husayn Ali publicly declared that he was this promised savior. At this point, he became Bahá'u'lláh, and his followers became known as Baha'is.

For the rest of his life Bahá'u'lláh was subjected to continuous exile and imprisonment in various cities throughout the Middle East. At his final destination, the Turkish prison city of Akko in Palestine, Bahá'u'lláh was eventually allowed the freedom to write, to receive visitors, and to send out missionaries. Among his writings were a series of letters, like the one printed below, which announced his mission and called for a universal religion of peace. He also wrote several books, including the *Kitab-i-Iqan* ("The Book of Certitudes"), the *Kitab-i-Aqdas* ("The Most Holy Book"), and *The Hidden Words*.

In his "Great Announcement to Mankind," Bahá'u'lláh proclaims that the day of the fulfillment of scripture, the day in which humanity can behold the Promised One (the Mahdi), has arrived. He calls upon all people to recognize the oneness of God, and claims that the fundamental goal of religion is to establish unity and harmony among all peoples. Thus, all sources of dissension, including those that arise from religious differences, must be eliminated from the face of the earth. To eliminate dissension and to promote unity, Bahá'u'lláh calls for the establishment of a new world order. This new world order, which would be governed by a great universal assembly and which would teach a universal language, would displace the political boundaries and divisions that currently exist. For, as Bahá'u'lláh forcefully says, "The earth is but one country, and mankind its citizens."

Questions for Thought

1. How does Bahá'u'lláh's proclamation compare with and differ from the pronouncements of other religious leaders with which you are familiar?
2. Do you agree with Bahá'u'lláh that the fundamental purpose of religion should be to promote unity and harmony? If not, how would you describe the fundamental purpose of religion?
3. Assuming that the fundamental purpose of religion is the promotion of unity and harmony, how successful has religion been in achieving this purpose?
4. What does Bahá'u'lláh mean by the new world order? Do you agree that such an order is needed? Why or why not?
5. Assuming that a new world order is needed, how do you think it could be achieved? What role, if any, would religion have in your new world order?
6. What would be the advantages of having a universal language? Can you think of any disadvantages?

THE TIME FORE-ORDAINED UNTO THE PEOPLES and kindreds of the earth is now come. The promises of God, as recorded in the holy Scriptures, have all been fulfilled. Out of Zion hath gone forth the Law of God, and Jerusalem, and the hills and land thereof, are filled with the glory of His Revelation. Happy is the man that pondereth in his heart that which hath been revealed in the Books of God, the Help in Peril, the Self-Subsisting. Meditate upon this, O ye beloved of God, and let your ears be attentive unto His Word, so that ye may, by His grace and mercy, drink your fill from the crystal waters of constancy, and become as steadfast and immovable as the mountain in His Cause.

Verily I say, this is the Day in which mankind can behold the Face, and hear the Voice, of the Promised One. The Call of God hath been raised, and the light of His countenance hath been lifted up upon men. It behoveth every man to blot out the trace of every idle word from the tablet of his heart, and to gaze, with an open and unbiased mind, on the signs of His Revelation, the proofs of His Mission, and the tokens of His glory.

Great indeed is this Day! The allusions made to it in all the sacred Scriptures as the Day of God attest its greatness. The soul of every Prophet of God, of every Divine Messenger, hath thirsted for this wondrous Day. All the divers kindreds of the earth have, likewise, yearned to attain it. No sooner, however, had the Day Star of His Revelation manifested itself in the heaven of God's Will, than all, except those whom the Almighty was pleased to guide, were found dumbfounded and heedless.

O thou that hast remembered Me! The most grievous veil hath shut out the peoples of the earth from His glory, and hindered them from hearkening to His call. God grant that the light of unity may envelop the whole earth, and that the seal, "the Kingdom is God's," may be stamped upon the brow of all its peoples.

Reprinted by permission from *The Proclamation of Bahá'u'lláh* (Haifa: Bahá'i World Center, 1967), pp. 111–22.

O ye children of men! The fundamental purpose animating the Faith of God and His Religion is to safeguard the interests and promote the unity of the human race, and to foster the spirit of love and fellowship amongst men. Suffer it not to become a source of dissension and discord, of hate and enmity. This is the straight Path, the fixed and immovable foundation. Whatsoever is raised on this foundation, the changes and chances of the world can never impair its strength, nor will the revolution of countless centuries undermine its structure. Our hope is that the world's religious leaders and the rulers thereof will unitedly arise for the reformation of this age and the rehabilitation of its fortunes. Let them, after meditating on its needs, take counsel together and, through anxious and full deliberation, administer to a diseased and sorely-afflicted world the remedy it requires. . . . It is incumbent upon them who are in authority to exercise moderation in all things. Whatsoever passeth beyond the limits of moderation will cease to exert a beneficial influence. Consider for instance such things as liberty, civilization and the like. However much men of understanding may favourably regard them, they will, if carried to excess, exercise a pernicious influence upon men. . . . Please God, the peoples of the world may be led, as the result of the high endeavours exerted by their rulers and the wise and learned amongst men, to recognize their best interests. How long will humanity persist in its waywardness? How long will injustice continue? How long is chaos and confusion to reign amongst men? How long will discord agitate the face of society? The winds of despair are, alas, blowing from every direction, and the strife that divideth and afflicteth the human race is daily increasing. The signs of impending convulsions and chaos can now be discerned, inasmuch as the prevailing order appeareth to be lamentably defective. I beseech God, exalted be His glory, that He may graciously awaken the peoples of the earth, may grant that the end of their conduct may be profitable unto them, and aid them to accomplish that which beseemeth their station.

O contending peoples and kindreds of the earth! Set your faces towards unity, and let the radiance of its light shine upon you. Gather ye together, and for the sake of God resolve to root out whatever is the source of contention amongst you. Then will the effulgence of the world's great Luminary envelop the whole earth, and its inhabitants become the citizens of one city, and the occupants of one and the same throne. This wronged One hath, ever since the early days of His life, cherished none other desire but this, and will continue to entertain no wish except this wish. There can be no doubt whatever that the peoples of the world, of whatever race or religion, derive their inspiration from one heavenly Source, and are the subjects of one God. The difference between the ordinances under which they abide should be attributed to the varying requirements and exigencies of the age in which they were revealed. All of them, except a few which are the outcome of human perversity, were ordained of God, and are a reflection of His Will and Purpose. Arise and, armed with the power of faith, shatter to pieces the gods of your vain imaginings, the sowers of dissension amongst you. Cleave unto that which draweth you together and uniteth you. This, verily, is the most exalted Word which the Mother Book hath sent down and revealed unto you. To this beareth witness the Tongue of Grandeur from His habitation of glory.

The Great Being, wishing to reveal the prerequisites of the peace and tranquillity of the world and the advancement of its peoples, hath written: The time must come when the imperative necessity for the holding of a vast, an all-embracing assemblage of men will be universally realized. The rulers and kings of the earth must needs attend it, and, participating in its deliberations, must consider such ways and means as will lay the foundations of the world's Great Peace amongst men. Such a peace demandeth that the Great Powers should resolve, for the sake of the tranquillity of the peoples of the earth, to be fully reconciled among themselves. Should any king take up arms against another, all should unitedly arise and prevent him. If this be done, the nations of the world will no longer require any armaments, except for the purpose of preserving the security of their realms and of maintaining internal order within their territories. This will ensure the peace and composure of every people, government and nation. We fain would hope that the kings and rulers of the earth, the mirrors of the gracious and almighty name of God, may attain unto this station, and shield mankind from the onslaught of tyranny. . . . The day is approaching when all the peoples of the world will have adopted one universal language and one common script. When this is achieved, to whatsoever city a man may journey, it shall be as if he were entering his own home. These things are obligatory and absolutely essential. It is incumbent upon every man of insight and understanding to strive to translate that which hath been written into reality and action. . . . That one indeed is a man who, today, dedicateth himself to the service of the entire human race. The Great Being saith: Blessed and happy is he that ariseth to promote the best interests of the peoples and kindreds of the earth. In another passage He hath proclaimed: It is not for him to pride himself who loveth his own country, but rather for him who loveth the whole world. The earth is but one country, and mankind its citizens.

The All-Knowing Physician hath His finger on the pulse of mankind. He perceiveth the disease, and prescribeth, in His unerring wisdom, the remedy. Every age hath its own problem, and every soul its particular aspiration. The remedy the world needeth in its present-day afflictions can never be the same as that which a subsequent age may require. Be anxiously concerned with the needs of the age ye live in, and centre your deliberations on its exigencies and requirements.

We can well perceive how the whole human race is encompassed with great, with incalculable afflictions. We see it languishing on its bed of sickness, sore-tried and disillusioned. They that are intoxicated by self-conceit have interposed themselves between it and the Divine and infallible Physician. Witness how they have entangled all men, themselves included, in the mesh of their devices. They can neither discover the cause of the disease, nor have they any knowledge of the remedy. They have conceived the straight to be crooked, and have imagined their friend an enemy.

Incline your ears to the sweet melody of this Prisoner. Arise, and lift up your voices, that haply they that are fast asleep may be awakened. Say: O ye who are as dead! The Hand of Divine bounty proffereth unto you the Water of Life. Hasten and drink your fill. Whoso hath been reborn in this Day, shall never die; whoso remaineth dead, shall never live.

O peoples of the earth! God, the Eternal Truth, is My witness that streams of fresh and soft-flowing waters have gushed from the rocks, through the sweetness of the words uttered by your Lord, the Unconstrained; and still ye slumber. Cast away that which ye possess, and, on the wings of detachment, soar beyond all created things. Thus biddeth you the Lord of creation, the movement of Whose Pen hath revolutionized the soul of mankind.

Know ye from what heights your Lord, the All-Glorious is calling? Think ye that ye have recognized the Pen wherewith your Lord, the Lord of all names, commandeth you? Nay, by My life! Did ye but know it, ye would renounce the world, and would hasten with your whole hearts to the presence of the Well-Beloved. Your spirits would be so transported by His Word as to throw into commotion the Greater World—how much more this small and petty one! Thus have the showers of My bounty been poured down from the heaven of My loving-kindness, as a token of My grace; that ye may be of the thankful. . . .

Beware lest the desires of the flesh and of a corrupt inclination provoke divisions among you. Be ye as the fingers of one hand, the members of one body. Thus counselleth you the Pen of Revelation, if ye be of them that believe.

Consider the mercy of God and His gifts. He enjoineth upon you that which shall profit you, though He Himself can well dispense with all creatures. Your evil doings can never harm Us, neither can your good works profit Us. We summon you wholly for the sake of God. To this every man of understanding and insight will testify.

The world's equilibrium hath been upset through the vibrating influence of this most great, this new World Order. Mankind's ordered life hath been revolutionized through the agency of this unique, this wondrous System—the like of which mortal eyes have never witnessed.

Immerse yourselves in the ocean of My words, that ye may unravel its secrets, and discover all the pearls of wisdom that lie hid in its depths. Take heed that ye do not vacillate in your determination to embrace the truth of this Cause—a Cause through which the potentialities of the might of God have been revealed, and His sovereignty established. With faces beaming with joy, hasten ye unto Him. This is the changeless Faith of God, eternal in the past, eternal in the future. Let him that seeketh, attain it; and as to him that hath refused to seek it—verily, God is Self-Sufficient, above any need of His creatures.

Say: This is the infallible Balance which the Hand of God is holding, in which all who are in the heavens and all who are on the earth are weighed, and their fate determined, if ye be of them that believe and recognize this truth. Say: Through it the poor have been enriched, the learned enlightened, and the seekers enabled to ascend unto the presence of God. Beware, lest ye make it a cause of dissension amongst you. Be ye as firmly settled as the immovable mountain in the Cause of your Lord, the Mighty, the Loving.

O ye peoples of the world! Know assuredly that My commandments are the lamps of My loving providence among My servants, and the keys of My mercy for My creatures. Thus hath it been sent down from the heaven of the Will of your Lord, the Lord of Revelation. Were any man to taste the sweetness of the words which the lips of the All-Merciful have willed to utter, he would, though the treasures of the earth be in his possession, renounce them one and all, that he might vindicate the truth of even one of His commandments, shining above the Dayspring of His bountiful care and loving-kindness.

From My laws the sweet smelling savour of My garment can be smelled, and by their aid the standards of victory will be planted upon the highest peaks. The Tongue of My power hath, from the heaven of My omnipotent glory, addressed to My creation these words: "Observe My commandments, for the love of My beauty." Happy is the lover that hath inhaled the divine fragrance of his Best-Beloved from these words, laden with the perfume of a grace which no tongue can describe. By My life! He who hath drunk the choice wine of fairness from the hands of My bountiful favour, will circle around My commandments that shine above the Dayspring of My creation.

Think not that We have revealed unto you a mere code of laws. Nay, rather, We have unsealed the choice Wine with the fingers of might and power. To this beareth witness that which the Pen of Revelation hath revealed. Meditate upon this, O men of insight! . . .

Whenever My laws appear like the sun in the heaven of Mine utterance, they must be faithfully obeyed by all, though My decree be such as to cause the heaven of every religion to be cleft asunder. He doth what He pleaseth. He chooseth; and none may question His choice. Whatsoever He, the Well-Beloved, ordaineth, the same is, verily, beloved. To this He Who is the Lord of all creation beareth Me witness. Whoso hath inhaled the sweet fragrance of the All-Merciful, and recognized the Source of this utterance, will welcome with his own eyes the shafts of the enemy, that he may establish the truth of the laws of God amongst men. Well is it with him that hath turned thereunto, and apprehended the meaning of His decisive decree.

This is the Day in which God's most excellent favours have been poured out upon men, the Day in which His most mighty grace hath been infused into all created things. It is incumbent upon all the peoples of the world to reconcile their differences, and, with perfect unity and peace, abide beneath the shadow of the Tree of His care and loving-kindness. It behoveth them to cleave to whatsoever will, in this Day, be conducive to the exaltation of their stations, and to the promotion of their best interests. Happy are those whom the all-glorious Pen was moved to remember, and blessed are those men whose names, by virtue of Our inscrutable decree, We have preferred to conceal.

Beseech ye the one true God to grant that all men may be graciously assisted to fulfil that which is acceptable in Our sight. Soon will the present-day order be rolled up, and a new one spread out in its stead. Verily, thy Lord speaketh the truth, and is the Knower of things unseen.

The Powers of the Bison and the Elk   6.2

BLACK ELK

Black Elk (1863–1950), a Lakota holy man, was born on the Little Powder River. His father, also known as Black Elk, fought against the U.S. forces that successfully usurped native land after gold was discovered on it in the 1860s. Later his family joined Crazy Horse in his attempt to avoid reservation life, but they were eventually forced to move to the reservation. However, after Crazy Horse's murder by government soldiers, Black Elk's family and many others fled to Canada where they joined Sitting Bull, Gall, and their followers who had earlier avoided reservation life by fleeing to Canada. Eventually, harsh winters and near starvation drove them back to the reservation in the United States.

Having experienced a series of visions beginning at age five, Black Elk gained a wide reputation as a healer. These visions, which he interpreted as the source of his healing power, allowed him not only to discover the remedies for illnesses, but also to predict certain aspects of the future. While in Paris recovering from an illness that he developed while traveling with Buffalo Bill's Wild West Show, Black Elk had a powerful vision of the suffering of his people. In 1890, not long after he had returned to his people, between 200 and 300 of them were massacred by government troops at Chankpe Opi Wakpala (Wounded Knee Creek) in South Dakota.

After having witnessed the frozen bodies of the people massacred, Black Elk settled on the Pine Ridge Reservation, where he died in 1950 at the age of 87. Eighteen years earlier, he had recounted the story of his life and the life of his people to John G. Neihardt. The resulting book, *Black Elk Speaks,* is a classic work of Native American spiritualism.

In "The Powers of the Bison and the Elk," which is taken from *Black Elk Speaks*, Black Elk describes two of the ceremonies that were performed to activate the healing powers of his great vision. Black Elk points out that these ceremonies were symbolic and that they were necessary to understand the meaning of his vision. As he says in two places, "the power in the ceremony was in understanding what it meant; for nothing can live well except in a manner that is suited to the way the sacred Power of the World lives and moves." Black Elk also insists that it is the power of the "outer world," that is, spiritual power, that cures people, and that he is only a medium through which this power passes.

Like the earlier selections from Benally and Ed McGaa (Eagle Man), this selection also gives us a glimpse into other spiritual aspects of Native American belief. While the ceremonies recognize the sacredness of the bison and the elk, other statements imply a belief in the sacredness of all life. The ceremonies also affirm the significance of the four directions, of the circle (especially as represented by the nation's hoop), and of the spiritual powers of both women and men.

Questions for Thought

1. What was the significance of Black Elk's vision for his life and beliefs? Why was it important that he performed the bison and elk ceremonies?
2. Have you ever had what you considered to be a spiritual vision or dream? If so, what significance did it have for you?
3. How do the religious ceremonies of Black Elk compare with and differ from other religious ceremonies with which you are familiar?
4. What do you think Black Elk means by the "power of the outer world"? Do you think that it is possible for people to be cured by this power? Why or why not?
5. What does the term *heyoka* mean? (Hint: You can find a definition in the glossary.) Can you think of heyoka-like figures in other religions?

I THINK I HAVE TOLD YOU, BUT IF I HAVE NOT, you must have understood, that a man who has a vision is not able to use the power of it until after he has performed the vision on earth for the people to see. You remember that my great vision came to me when I was only nine years old, and you have seen that I was not much good for anything until after I had performed the horse dance near the mouth of the Tongue River during my eighteenth summer. And if the great fear had not come upon me, as it did, and forced me to do my duty, I might have been less good to the people than some man who had never dreamed at all, even with the memory of so great a vision in me. But the fear came, and if I had not obeyed it, I am sure it would have killed me in a little while.

It was even then only after the heyoka ceremony, in which I performed my dog vision, that I had the power to practice as a medicine man, curing sick people; and many I cured with the power that came through me. Of course it was not I who cured. It was the power from the outer world, and the visions and ceremonies had only made me like a hole through which the power could come to the two-leggeds. If I thought that I was doing it myself, the hole would close up and no power could come through. Then everything I could do would be foolish. There were other parts of my great vision that I still had to perform before I could use the power that was in those parts. If you think about my great vision again, you will remember how the red man turned into a bison and rolled, and that the people found the good red road after that. If you will read again what is written, you will see how it was.

To use the power of the bison, I had to perform that part of my vision for the people to see. It was during the summer of my first cure that this was done. I carried the pipe to Fox Belly, a wise and good old medicine man, and asked him to help me do this duty. He was glad to help me, but first I had to tell him how it was in that part of my vision. I did not tell him all my vision, only that part. I had never told any one all of it, and even until now nobody ever heard it all. Even my old friend, Standing Bear, and my son here have heard it now for the first time when I have told it to you. Of course there was very much in the vision that even I can not tell when I try hard, because very much of it was not for words. But I have told what can be told.

It has made me very sad to do this at last, and I have lain awake at night worrying and wondering if I was doing right; for I know I have given away my power when I have given away my vision, and maybe I cannot live very long now. But I think I have done right to save the vision in this way, even though I may die sooner because I did it; for I know the meaning of the vision is wise and beautiful and good; and you can see that I am only a pitiful old man after all.

Well, I told Fox Belly all that he needed to know that he might help me. And when he had heard even so little, he said: "My boy, you had a great vision, and I can see that it is your duty to help the people walk the red road in a manner pleasing to the Powers."

This ceremony was not a long one, but it had great meaning, because it made a picture of the relation between the people and the bison, and the power was in the meaning.

First we made a sacred place like a bison wallow at the center of the nation's hoop, and there we set up the sacred tepee. Inside this we made the circle of the four quarters. Across the circle from south to north we painted a red road, and Fox Belly made little bison tracks all along on both sides of it, meaning that the people should walk there with the power and endurance of the bison, facing the great white cleansing wind of the world. Also, he placed at the north end of the road the cup of water, which is the gift of the west, so that the people, while leaning against the great wind with the endurance of bison, would be going toward the water of life.

I was painted red all over like the man of my vision before he turned into a bison. I wore bison horns, and on the left horn hung a piece of the daybreak-star herb, which bears the four-rayed flower of understanding. On the left side of my body I wore a single eagle feather, which was for my people, hanging on the side of the bison and feeding there.

One Side had come over to help me in this ceremony too. He was painted red all over, and he carried the drum and the pipe, and wherever I went, he followed, as the people follow the bison.

We stood inside the tepee at the south end of the good red road, and Fox Belly sang like this:

Revealing this, they walk.
A sacred herb—revealing it, they walk.
Revealing this, they walk.
The sacred life of bison—revealing it, they
    walk.
Revealing this, they walk.
A sacred eagle feather—revealing it, they walk.
Revealing them, they walk.
The eagle and the bison—like relatives they
    walk.

Then, after we had walked the red road, One Side and I went out of the tepee and the people flocked around us, and the sick came with scarlet offerings to be cured. We went all around among the people, acting like bison and making the sounds they make. Then we returned to the tepee, and there the people brought their little children to us, and to each I gave a little of the water of life from the wooden cup, that their feet might know the good red road that leads to health and happiness.

It is from understanding that power comes; and the power in the ceremony was in understanding what it meant; for nothing can live well except in a manner that is suited to the way the sacred Power of the World lives and moves.

After this, I went on curing sick people, and I was busy doing this. I was in doubt no longer. I felt like a man, and I could feel the power with me all the time.

It was during the next summer, when I was in my twentieth year (1883), that I performed the elk ceremony, as a duty to that part of my great vision. You will remember how the pipe and the bison were in the east and the elk in the south.

This ceremony of the elk was to represent the source of life and the mystery of growing.

I sent a pipe to Running Elk, who was Standing Bear's uncle and a good and wise old man. He came and was willing to help me. We set up a sacred tepee at the center as before. I had to use six elks and four virgins. The elks are of the south, but the power that they represented in my vision is nourished by the four quarters and from the sky and the earth; so there were six of them. The four virgins represented the life of the nation's hoop, which has four quarters; so there were four virgins. Running Elk chose two of the elks, and I, who stood between the Power of the World and the nation's hoop, chose the four others, for my duty was to the life of the hoop on earth. The six elk men wore complete elk hides on their backs and over their heads. Their limbs were painted black from the knee and elbow down, and yellow from there up; for

the growing power is rooted in mystery like the night, and reaches lightward. Seeds sprout in the darkness of the ground before they know the summer and the day. In the night of the womb the spirit quickens into flesh. The four virgins wore scarlet dresses, and each had a single eagle feather in her braided hair; for out of the woman the people grows, and the eagle feather again was for the people as in the bison ceremony. The faces of the virgins were painted yellow, the color of the south, the source of life. One had a daybreak star in red upon her forehead. One had a crescent moon in blue, for the power of woman grows with the moon and comes and goes with it. One had the sun upon her forehead; and around the mouth and eyebrows of the fourth a big blue circle was painted to mean the nation's hoop. On the back of each of the elk men was painted the nation's hoop, for upon the backs of men the nation is carried, and in the center of each hoop hung a single eagle feather for the people. They had yellow masks upon their faces, for behind the woman's power of life is hidden the power of man. They all carried flowering sticks cut from the sacred rustling tree (the cottonwood) with leaves left at the top, and the sticks were painted red. The woman is the life of the flowering tree, but the man must feed and care for it. One of the virgins also carried the flowering stick, another carried the pipe which gives peace, a third bore the herb of healing and the fourth held the sacred hoop; for all these powers together are woman's power.

Of course, before any of this was done, those who were to take part were purified in the sweat lodge as always.

We were all inside the sacred tepee, and Running Elk sang this song:

Advancing to the quarters,
Advancing to the quarters,
They are coming to behold you.
Advancing to the quarters,
Advancing to the quarters,
They are coming to behold you.

Then the elk men all made the elk sound, *unh, unh, unh*. Running Elk then sang again:

Singing, I send a voice as I walk.
Singing, I send a voice as I walk.
A sacred hoop I wear as I walk.

It was time now to come out of the sacred tepee: first came the virgin with the pipe; next she who bore the flowering stick, then the one who held the herb; and last, the bearer of the nation's hoop. The four virgins stood abreast, facing the west. Then we six elk men came out, snorting and stamping our feet. We stopped abreast, behind the virgins, who now held up the sacred things they carried, offering them to the thunder beings. When they had done this, they walked abreast to the north, while we elk men danced around them in a circle, and there they offered their sacred objects to the great white cleansing wind. In the same way we went to the east and to the south, the virgins making the offering at each place, and we elk men dancing around them in a circle all the while.

From the south, the four virgins turned straight north, following the good red road to the center of the village where the sacred tepee stood, and we elk men followed, dancing around them, for the power of the man encircles and protects the power of the woman.

The four maidens entered the tepee: first, she with the sacred hoop; then she who bore the flowering stick; next, the one who held the cleansing herb; and after her, the bearer of the pipe.

When they had all entered, we elk men followed into the tepee.

This was the ceremony, and as I said before, the power of it was in the understanding of its meaning; for nothing can live well except in a manner suited to the way the Power of the World lives and moves to do its work.

Letter from Birmingham Jail   6.3

MARTIN LUTHER KING, JR.

Martin Luther King, Jr. (1929–1968) was a leader in the American civil rights movement from 1955 until his assassination in Memphis, Tennessee, in 1968. King, who was born in Atlanta, Georgia, received his Ph.D. from Boston University in 1955. While serving as pastor of the Dexter Avenue Baptist Church in Montgomery, Alabama, King became an outspoken critic of the segregation that existed throughout the South. Starting with the bus boycott in Montgomery in the mid-1950s, King urged the use of nonviolent protest as a means of bringing about social change. After his initial focus on segregation in transportation and public facilities, King turned his attention to voting rights, economic justice, and military conflict. He strongly criticized the Vietnam War and the economic inequality that existed in the United States. By the end of his life, King had realized that the triple evils of racism, economic exploitation, and militarism could be overcome only by a radical transformation of the social and economic order. Having been the target of racial slurs and racist attacks many times during his life, he was killed by an assassin's bullet on April 4, 1968.

In addition to being a powerful force behind the enactment of civil rights and voting rights legislation, King became an internationally known advocate of social and economic justice. He was chosen as *Time* magazine's "Man of the Year" in 1963, and he was awarded the Nobel Peace Prize in 1964. King was also known as a forceful orator. His "I Have a Dream" speech, which was delivered at the March on Washington in 1963, is considered a classic. While King's activities did not allow him much time for purely theoretical analysis, his writings demonstrate a wide knowledge of philosophical and theological theories and issues. His principal works are *Stride Toward Freedom* (1958), *Strength to Love* (1963), *Why We Can't Wait* (1964), and *Where Do We Go From Here: Chaos or Community?* (1967).

"The Letter from Birmingham Jail" was written on April 16, 1963, in response to a letter from white clergymen criticizing King's presence and civil rights activities in Birmingham, Alabama. In this powerful letter, King not only defends his presence and activities in Birmingham, but he also provides a powerful philosophical defense of nonviolent direct action as a method of confronting injustice, and an impassioned critique of the silence and apathy of white moderates and the white church.

Noting that "injustice anywhere is a threat to justice everywhere," King argues that we must be prepared to confront racism and injustice wherever it arises. Noting that oppressors never voluntarily stop oppressing others, King argues that we must take direct action to create tension that brings oppression and injustice to the surface so that it can be dealt with. He also draws a clear-cut distinction between just and unjust laws, and argues that we have a duty to disobey laws that are unjust. Finally, he critiques the view that time itself will eventually conquer evil by noting that time is neutral, and that injustice can be overcome only when people act decisively to end it. Like Gandhi, King argues that this decisive activity must be nonviolent and guided by love.

Toward the end of his letter, King expresses his great disappointment with white moderates and with the white church and its leadership. King argues that in calling for patience and moderation, white moderates fail to realize the extent of racial injustice and the urgency of the movement to overcome it. While only a few of the white churches lined up with the racist opponents of the struggle for equality, most of the others "remained silent behind the anesthetizing security of the stained-glass windows." In opposition to such apathy, King calls on modern Christians to follow the example of those very early Christians who, in living according to the true meaning of the gospel, resisted oppression and injustice even to the point of death.

Questions for Thought

1. How does King describe the racial climate of Birmingham, Alabama, in 1963? How would you describe the racial climate of the city in which you live today?
2. What, according to King, are the essential differences between a just law and an unjust law? Do you agree with him that we have the right to disobey unjust laws? Why or why not?
3. Can you think of any present-day laws that would be unjust according to King's criteria?
4. How does King respond to the accusation that he is an extremist? Do you agree with his response?

5. What are King's basic criticisms of white moderates and the white church? Do you think that his criticisms are still relevant today? Why or why not?
6. Identify some of King's uses of analogy or metaphor. Do you think that he uses analogy and metaphor effectively?

April 16, 1963

My Dear Fellow Clergymen:

While confined here in the Birmingham city jail, I came across your recent statement calling my present activities "unwise and untimely." Seldom do I pause to answer criticism of my work and ideas. If I sought to answer all the criticisms that cross my desk, my secretaries would have little time for anything other than such correspondence in the course of the day, and I would have no time for constructive work. But since I feel that you are men of genuine good will and that your criticisms are sincerely set forth, I want to try to answer your statement in what I hope will be patient and reasonable terms.

I think I should indicate why I am here in Birmingham, since you have been influenced by the view which argues against "outsiders coming in." I have the honor of serving as president of the Southern Christian Leadership Conference, an organization operating in every southern state, with headquarters in Atlanta, Georgia. We have some eighty-five affiliated organizations across the South, and one of them is the Alabama Christian Movement for Human Rights. Frequently we share staff, educational and financial resources with our affiliates. Several months ago the affiliate here in Birmingham asked us to be on call to engage in a nonviolent direct-action program if such were deemed necessary. We readily consented, and when the hour came we lived up to our promise. So I, along with several members of my staff, am here because I was invited here. I am here because I have organizational ties here.

But more basically, I am in Birmingham because injustice is here. Just as the prophets of the eighth century B.C. left their villages and carried their "thus saith the Lord" far beyond the boundaries of their home towns, and just as the Apostle Paul left his village of Tarsus and carried the gospel of Jesus Christ to the far corners of the Greco-Roman world, so am I compelled to carry the gospel of freedom beyond my own home town. Like Paul, I must constantly respond to the Macedonian call for aid.

Moreover, I am cognizant of the interrelatedness of all communities and states. I cannot sit idly by in Atlanta and not be concerned about what happens in Birmingham. Injustice anywhere is a threat to justice everywhere. We are caught in an inescapable network of mutuality, tied in a single garment of destiny. Whatever affects one directly, affects all indirectly. Never again can we afford to live with the narrow, provincial "outside agitator" idea. Anyone who lives inside the United States can never be considered an outsider anywhere within its bounds.

You deplore the demonstrations taking place in Birmingham. But your statement, I am sorry to say, fails to express a similar concern for the conditions that brought about the demonstrations. I am sure that none of you would want to rest content with the superficial kind of social analysis that deals merely with effects and does not grapple with underlying causes. It is unfortunate that demonstrations are taking place in

Birmingham, but it is even more unfortunate that the city's white power structure left the Negro community with no alternative.

In any nonviolent campaign there are four basic steps: collection of the facts to determine whether injustices exist; negotiation; self-purification; and direct action. We have gone through all these steps in Birmingham. There can be no gainsaying the fact that racial injustice engulfs this community. Birmingham is probably the most thoroughly segregated city in the United States. Its ugly record of brutality is widely known. Negroes have experienced grossly unjust treatment in the courts. There have been more unsolved bombings of Negro homes and churches in Birmingham than in any other city in the nation. These are the hard, brutal facts of the case. On the basis of these conditions, Negro leaders sought to negotiate with the city fathers. But the latter consistently refused to engage in good-faith negotiation.

Then, last September, came the opportunity to talk with leaders of Birmingham's economic community. In the course of the negotiations, certain promises were made by the merchants— for example, to remove the stores' humiliating racial signs. On the basis of these promises, the Reverend Fred Shuttlesworth and the leaders of the Alabama Christian Movement for Human Rights agreed to a moratorium on all demonstrations. As the weeks and months went by, we realized that we were the victims of a broken promise. A few signs, briefly removed, returned; the others remained.

As in so many past experiences, our hopes had been blasted, and the shadow of deep disappointment settled upon us. We had no alternative except to prepare for direct action, whereby we would present our very bodies as a means of laying our case before the conscience of the local and the national community. Mindful of the difficulties involved, we decided to undertake a process of self-purification. We began a series of workshops on nonviolence, and we repeatedly asked ourselves: "Are you able to accept blows without retaliating?" "Are you able to endure the ordeal of jail?" We decided to schedule our direct-action program for the Easter season, realizing that except for Christmas, this is the main shopping period of the year. Knowing that a strong economic-withdrawal program would be the by-product of direct action, we felt that this would be the best time to bring pressure to bear on the merchants for the needed change.

Then it occurred to us that Birmingham's mayoral election was coming up in March, and we speedily decided to postpone action until after election day. When we discovered that the Commissioner of Public Safety, Eugene "Bull" Connor, had piled up enough votes to be in the run-off, we decided again to postpone action until the day after the run-off so that the demonstrations could not be used to cloud the issues. Like many others, we waited to see Mr. Connor defeated, and to this end we endured postponement after postponement. Having aided in this community need, we felt that our direct-action program could be delayed no longer.

You may well ask: "Why direct action? Why sit-ins, marches and so forth? Isn't negotiation a better path?" You are quite right in calling for negotiation. Indeed, this is the very purpose of direct action. Nonviolent direct action seeks to create such a crisis and foster such a tension that a community which has constantly refused to negotiate is forced to confront the issue. It seeks so to dramatize the issue that it can no longer be ignored. My citing the creation of tension as part of the work of the nonviolent-resister may sound rather shocking. But I must confess that I am not afraid of the word "tension." I have earnestly opposed violent tension, but there is a type of constructive, nonviolent tension which is necessary for growth. Just as Socrates felt that it was necessary to create a tension in the mind so that individuals could rise from the bondage of myths and half-truths to the unfettered realm of creative analysis and objective appraisal, so must we see the need for nonviolent gadflies to create the kind of tension in society that will help men rise from the dark depths of prejudice and racism to the majestic heights of understanding and brotherhood.

The purpose of our direct-action program is to create a situation so crisis-packed that it will inevitably open the door to negotiation. I therefore concur with you in your call for negotiation. Too long has our beloved Southland been bogged down in a tragic effort to live in monologue rather than dialogue.

One of the basic points in your statement is that the action that I and my associates have taken in Birmingham is untimely. Some have asked: "Why didn't you give the new city administration time to act?" The only answer that I can give to this query is that the new Birmingham administration must be prodded about as much as the outgoing one, before it will act. We are sadly mistaken if we feel that the election of Albert Boutwell as mayor will bring the millennium to Birmingham. While Mr. Boutwell is a much more gentle person than Mr. Connor, they are both segregationists, dedicated to maintenance of the status quo. I have hope that Mr. Boutwell will be reasonable enough to see the futility of massive resistance to desegregation. But he will not see this without pressure from devotees of civil rights. My friends, I must say to you that we have not made a single gain in civil rights without determined legal and nonviolent pressure. Lamentably, it is an historical fact that privileged groups seldom give up their privileges voluntarily. Individuals may see the moral light and voluntarily give up their unjust posture; but, as Reinhold Niebuhr has reminded us, groups tend to be more immoral than individuals.

We know through painful experience that freedom is never voluntarily given by the oppressor; it must be demanded by the oppressed. Frankly, I have yet to engage in a direct-action campaign that was "well timed" in the view of those who have not suffered unduly from the disease of segregation. For years now I have heard the word "Wait!" It rings in the ear of every Negro with piercing familiarity. This "Wait" has almost always meant "Never." We must come to see, with one of our distinguished jurists, that "justice too long delayed is justice denied."

We have waited for more than 340 years for our constitutional and God-given rights. The nations of Asia and Africa are moving with jet-like speed toward gaining political independence, but we still creep at horse-and-buggy pace toward gaining a cup of coffee at a lunch counter. Perhaps it is easy for those who have never felt the stinging darts of segregation to say, "Wait." But when you have seen vicious mobs lynch your mothers and fathers at will and drown your sisters and brothers at whim; when you have seen hate-filled policemen curse, kick and even kill your black brothers and sisters; when you see the vast majority of your twenty million Negro brothers smothering in an airtight cage of poverty in the midst of an affluent society; when you suddenly find your tongue twisted and your speech stammering as you seek to explain to your six-year-old daughter why she can't go to the public amusement park that has just been advertised on television, and see tears welling up in her eyes when she is told that Funtown is closed to colored children, and see ominous clouds of inferiority beginning to form in her little mental sky, and see her beginning to distort her personality by developing an unconscious bitterness toward white people; when you have to concoct an answer for a five-year-old son who is asking: "Daddy, why do white people treat colored people so mean?"; when you take a cross-country drive and find it necessary to sleep night after night in the uncomfortable corners of your automobile because no motel will accept you; when you are humiliated day in and day out by nagging signs reading "white" and "colored"; when your first name becomes "nigger," your middle name becomes "boy" (however old you are) and your last name becomes

"John," and your wife and mother are never given the respected title "Mrs."; when you are harried by day and haunted by night by the fact that you are a Negro, living constantly at tiptoe stance, never quite knowing what to expect next, and are plagued with inner fears and outer resentments; when you are forever fighting a degenerating sense of "nobodiness"—then you will understand why we find it difficult to wait. There comes a time when the cup of endurance runs over, and men are no longer willing to be plunged into the abyss of despair. I hope, sirs, you can understand our legitimate and unavoidable impatience.

You express a great deal of anxiety over our willingness to break laws. This is certainly a legitimate concern. Since we so diligently urge people to obey the Supreme Court's decision of 1954 outlawing segregation in the public schools, at first glance it may seem rather paradoxical for us consciously to break laws. One may well ask: "How can you advocate breaking some laws and obeying others?" The answer lies in the fact that there are two types of laws: just and unjust. I would be the first to advocate obeying just laws. One has not only a legal but a moral responsibility to obey just laws. Conversely, one has a moral responsibility to disobey unjust laws. I would agree with St. Augustine that "an unjust law is no law at all."

Now, what is the difference between the two? How does one determine whether a law is just or unjust? A just law is a man-made code that squares with the moral law or the law of God. An unjust law is a code that is out of harmony with the moral law. To put it in the terms of St. Thomas Aquinas: An unjust law is a human law that is not rooted in eternal law and natural law. Any law that uplifts human personality is just. Any law that degrades human personality is unjust. All segregation statutes are unjust because segregation distorts the soul and damages the personality. It gives the segregator a false sense of superiority and the segregated a false sense of inferiority. Segregation, to use the terminology of the Jewish philosopher Martin Buber, substitutes an "I–it" relationship for an "I–thou" relationship and ends up relegating persons to the status of things. Hence segregation is not only politically, economically and sociologically unsound, it is morally wrong and sinful. Paul Tillich has said that sin is separation. Is not segregation an existential expression of man's tragic separation, his awful estrangement, his terrible sinfulness? Thus it is that I can urge men to obey the 1954 decision of the Supreme Court, for it is morally right; and I can urge them to disobey segregation ordinances, for they are morally wrong.

Let us consider a more concrete example of just and unjust laws. An unjust law is a code that a numerical or power majority group compels a minority group to obey but does not make binding on itself. This is *difference* made legal. By the same token, a just law is a code that a majority compels a minority to follow and that it is willing to follow itself. This is *sameness* made legal.

Let me give another explanation. A law is unjust if it is inflicted on a minority that, as a result of being denied the right to vote, had no part in enacting or devising the law. Who can say that the legislature of Alabama which set up that state's segregation laws was democratically elected? Throughout Alabama all sorts of devious methods are used to prevent Negroes from becoming registered voters, and there are some counties in which, even though Negroes constitute a majority of the population, not a single Negro is registered. Can any law enacted under such circumstances be considered democratically structured?

Sometimes a law is just on its face and unjust in its application. For instance, I have been arrested on a charge of parading without a permit. Now, there is nothing wrong in having an ordinance which requires a permit for a parade. But such an ordinance becomes unjust when it is used to maintain segregation and to deny citizens the First-Amendment privilege of peaceful assembly and protest.

I hope you are able to see the distinction I am trying to point out. In no sense do I advocate evading or defying the law, as would the rabid segregationist. That would lead to anarchy. One who breaks an unjust law must do so openly, lovingly, and with a willingness to accept the penalty. I submit that an individual who breaks a law that conscience tells him is unjust, and who willingly accepts the penalty of imprisonment in order to arouse the conscience of the community over its injustice, is in reality expressing the highest respect for law.

Of course, there is nothing new about this kind of civil disobedience. It was evidenced sublimely in the refusal of Shadrach, Meshach and Abednego to obey the laws of Nebuchadnezzar, on the ground that a higher moral law was at stake. It was practiced superbly by the early Christians, who were willing to face hungry lions and the excruciating pain of chopping blocks rather than submit to certain unjust laws of the Roman Empire. To a degree, academic freedom is a reality today because Socrates practiced civil disobedience. In our own nation, the Boston Tea Party represented a massive act of civil disobedience.

We should never forget that everything Adolf Hitler did in Germany was "legal" and everything the Hungarian freedom fighters did in Hungary was "illegal." It was "illegal" to aid and comfort a Jew in Hitler's Germany. Even so, I am sure that, had I lived in Germany at the time, I would have aided and comforted my Jewish brothers. If today I lived in a Communist country where certain principles dear to the Christian faith are suppressed, I would openly advocate disobeying that country's antireligious laws.

I must make two honest confessions to you, my Christian and Jewish brothers. First, I must confess that over the past few years I have been gravely disappointed with the white moderate. I have almost reached the regrettable conclusion that the Negro's great stumbling block in his stride toward freedom is not the White Citizen's Counciler or the Ku Klux Klanner, but the white moderate, who is more devoted to "order" than to justice; who prefers a negative peace which is the absence of tension to a positive peace which is the presence of justice; who constantly says: "I agree with you in the goal you seek, but I cannot agree with your methods of direct action"; who paternalistically believes he can set the timetable for another man's freedom; who lives by a mythical concept of time and who constantly advises the Negro to wait for a "more convenient season." Shallow understanding from people of good will is more frustrating than absolute misunderstanding from people of ill will. Lukewarm acceptance is much more bewildering than outright rejection.

I had hoped that the white moderate would understand that law and order exist for the purpose of establishing justice and that when they fail in this purpose they become the dangerously structured dams that block the flow of social progress. I had hoped that the white moderate would understand that the present tension in the South is a necessary phase of the transition from an obnoxious negative peace, in which the Negro passively accepted his unjust plight, to a substantive and positive peace, in which all men will respect the dignity and worth of human personality. Actually, we who engage in nonviolent direct action are not the creators of tension. We merely bring to the surface the hidden tension that is already alive. We bring it out in the open, where it can be seen and dealt with. Like a boil that can never be cured so long as it is covered up but must be opened with all its ugliness to the natural medicines of air and light, injustice must be exposed, with all the tension its exposure creates, to the light of human conscience and the air of national opinion before it can be cured.

In your statement you assert that our actions, even though peaceful, must be condemned because they precipitate violence. But is this a logical assertion? Isn't this like condemning a robbed man because his possession of money precipitated the evil act of robbery? Isn't this like condemning Socrates because his unswerving commitment to truth and his philosophical inquiries precipitated the act by the misguided populace in which they made him drink hemlock? Isn't this like condemning Jesus because his unique God-consciousness and never-ceasing devotion to God's will precipitated the evil act of crucifixion? We must come to see that, as the federal courts have consistently affirmed, it is wrong to urge an individual to cease his efforts to gain his basic constitutional rights because the quest may precipitate violence. Society must protect the robbed and punish the robber.

I had also hoped that the white moderate would reject the myth concerning time in relation to the struggle for freedom. I have just received a letter from a white brother in Texas. He writes: "All Christians know that the colored people will receive equal rights eventually, but it is possible that you are in too great a religious hurry. It has taken Christianity almost two thousand years to accomplish what it has. The teachings of Christ take time to come to earth." Such an attitude stems from a tragic misconception of time, from the strangely irrational notion that there is something in the very flow of time that will inevitably cure all ills. Actually, time itself is neutral; it can be used either destructively or constructively. More and more I feel that the people of ill will have used time much more effectively than have the people of good will. We will have to repent in this generation not merely for the hateful words and actions of the bad people but for the appalling silence of the good people. Human progress never rolls in on wheels of inevitability; it comes through the tireless efforts of men willing to be co-workers with God, and without this hard work, time itself becomes an ally of the forces of social stagnation. We must use time creatively, in the knowledge that the time is always ripe to do right. Now is the time to make real the promise of democracy and transform our pending national elegy into a creative psalm of brotherhood. Now is the time to lift our national policy from the quicksand of racial injustice to the solid rock of human dignity.

You speak of our activity in Birmingham as extreme. At first I was rather disappointed that fellow clergymen would see my nonviolent efforts as those of an extremist. I began thinking about the fact that I stand in the middle of two opposing forces in the Negro community. One is a force of complacency, made up in part of Negroes who, as a result of long years of oppression, are so drained of self-respect and a sense of "somebodiness" that they have adjusted to segregation; and in part of a few middle-class Negroes who, because of a degree of academic and economic security and because in some ways they profit by segregation, have become insensitive to the problems of the masses. The other force is one of bitterness and hatred, and it comes perilously close to advocating violence. It is expressed in the various black nationalist groups that are springing up across the nation, the largest and best-known being Elijah Muhammad's Muslim movement. Nourished by the Negro's frustration over the continued existence of racial discrimination, this movement is made up of people who have lost faith in America, who have absolutely repudiated Christianity, and who have concluded that the white man is an incorrigible "devil."

I have tried to stand between these two forces, saying that we need emulate neither the "do-nothingism" of the complacent nor the hatred and despair of the black nationalist. For there is the more excellent way of love and nonviolent protest. I am grateful to God that, through the influence of the Negro church, the way of nonviolence became an integral part of our struggle.

If this philosophy had not emerged, by now many streets of the South would, I am convinced, be flowing with blood. And I am further convinced that if our white brothers dismiss as "rabble-rousers" and "outside agitators" those of us who employ nonviolent direct action, and if they refuse to support our nonviolent efforts, millions of Negroes will, out of frustration and despair, seek solace and security in black-nationalist ideologies—a development that would inevitably lead to a frightening racial nightmare.

Oppressed people cannot remain oppressed forever. The yearning for freedom eventually manifests itself, and that is what has happened to the American Negro. Something within has reminded him of his birthright of freedom, and something without has reminded him that it can be gained. Consciously or unconsciously, he has been caught up by the *Zeitgeist*, and with his black brothers of Africa and his brown and yellow brothers of Asia, South America and the Caribbean, the United States Negro is moving with a sense of great urgency toward the promised land of racial justice. If one recognizes this vital urge that has engulfed the Negro community, one should readily understand why public demonstrations are taking place. The Negro has many pent-up resentments and latent frustrations, and he must release them. So let him march; let him make prayer pilgrimages to the city hall; let him go on freedom rides—and try to understand why he must do so. If his repressed emotions are not released in nonviolent ways, they will seek expression through violence; this is not a threat but a fact of history. So I have not said to my people: "Get rid of your discontent." Rather, I have tried to say that this normal and healthy discontent can be channeled into the creative outlet of nonviolent direct action. And now this approach is being termed extremist.

But though I was initially disappointed at being categorized as an extremist, as I continued to think about the matter I gradually gained a measure of satisfaction from the label. Was not Jesus an extremist for love: "Love your enemies, bless them that curse you, do good to them that hate you, and pray for them which despitefully use you, and persecute you." Was not Amos an extremist for justice: "Let justice roll down like waters and righteousness like an ever-flowing stream." Was not Paul an extremist for the Christian gospel: "I bear in my body the marks of the Lord Jesus." Was not Martin Luther an extremist: "Here I stand; I cannot do otherwise, so help me God." And John Bunyan: "I will stay in jail to the end of my days before I make a butchery of my conscience." And Abraham Lincoln: "This nation cannot survive half slave and half free." And Thomas Jefferson: "We hold these truths to be self-evident, that all men are created equal . . . " So the question is not whether we will be extremists, but what kind of extremists we will be. Will we be extremists for hate or for love? Will we be extremists for the preservation of injustice or for the extension of justice? In that dramatic scene on Calvary's hill three men were crucified. We must never forget that all three were crucified for the same crime—the crime of extremism. Two were extremists for immorality, and thus fell below their environment. The other, Jesus Christ, was an extremist for love, truth and goodness, and thereby rose above his environment. Perhaps the South, the nation and the world are in dire need of creative extremists.

I had hoped that the white moderate would see this need. Perhaps I was too optimistic; perhaps I expected too much. I suppose I should have realized that few members of the oppressor race can understand the deep groans and passionate yearnings of the oppressed race, and still fewer have the vision to see that injustice must be rooted out by strong, persistent and determined action. I am thankful, however, that some of our white brothers in the South have grasped the meaning of this social revolution and committed themselves to it. They are still all too few in quantity, but they are big in quality. Some—such as Ralph McGill, Lillian Smith, Harry Golden, James McBride Dabbs, Ann Braden and Sarah Patton Boyle—have written about our struggle in eloquent and prophetic terms. Others have marched with us down nameless streets of the South. They have languished in filthy, roach-infested jails, suffering the abuse and brutality of policemen who view them as "dirty nigger-lovers." Unlike so many of their moderate brothers and sisters, they have recognized the urgency of the moment and sensed the need for powerful "action" antidotes to combat the disease of segregation.

Let me take note of my other major disappointment. I have been so greatly disappointed with the white church and its leadership. Of course, there are some notable exceptions. I am not unmindful of the fact that each of you has taken some significant stands on this issue. I commend you, Reverend Stallings, for your Christian stand on this past Sunday, in welcoming Negroes to your worship service on a nonsegregated basis. I commend the Catholic leaders of this state for integrating Spring Hill College several years ago.

But despite these notable exceptions, I must honestly reiterate that I have been disappointed with the church. I do not say this as one of those negative critics who can always find something wrong with the church. I say this as a minister of the gospel, who loves the church; who was nurtured in its bosom; who has been sustained by its spiritual blessings and who will remain true to it as long as the cord of life shall lengthen.

When I was suddenly catapulted into the leadership of the bus protest in Montgomery, Alabama, a few years ago, I felt we would be supported by the white church. I felt that the white ministers, priests and rabbis of the South would be among our strongest allies. Instead, some have been outright opponents, refusing to understand the freedom movement and misrepresenting its leaders; all too many others have been more cautious than courageous and have remained silent behind the anesthetizing security of stained-glass windows.

In spite of my shattered dreams, I came to Birmingham with the hope that the white religious leadership of this community would see the justice of our cause and, with deep moral concern, would serve as the channel through which our just grievances could reach the power structure. I had hoped that each of you would understand. But again I have been disappointed.

I have heard numerous southern religious leaders admonish their worshipers to comply with a desegregation decision because it is the law, but I have longed to hear white ministers declare: "Follow this decree because integration is morally right and because the Negro is your brother." In the midst of blatant injustices inflicted upon the Negro, I have watched white churchmen stand on the sideline and mouth pious irrelevancies and sanctimonious trivialities. In the midst of a mighty struggle to rid our nation of racial and economic injustice, I have heard many ministers say: "Those are social issues, with which the gospel has no real concern." And I have watched many churches commit themselves to a completely otherworldly religion which makes a strange, un-Biblical distinction between body and soul, between the sacred and the secular.

I have traveled the length and breadth of Alabama, Mississippi and all the other southern states. On sweltering summer days and crisp autumn mornings I have looked at the South's beautiful churches with their lofty spires pointing heavenward. I have beheld the impressive outlines of her massive religious-education buildings. Over and over I have found myself asking: "What kind of people worship here? Who is their God? Where were their voices when the lips of Governor Barnett dripped with words of interposition and nullification? Where were they when Governor Wallace gave a clarion call for defiance and hatred? Where were their voices of support when bruised and weary Negro men and women decided to rise from the dark dungeons of complacency to the bright hills of creative protest?"

Yes, these questions are still in my mind. In deep disappointment I have wept over the laxity of the church. But be assured that my tears have been tears of love. There can be no deep disappointment where there is not deep love. Yes, I love the church. How could I do otherwise? I am in the rather unique position of being the son, the grandson and the great-grandson of preachers. Yes, I see the church as the body of Christ. But, oh! How we have blemished and scarred that body through social neglect and through fear of being nonconformists.

There was a time when the church was very powerful—in the time when the early Christians rejoiced at being deemed worthy to suffer for what they believed. In those days the church was not merely a thermometer that recorded the ideas and principles of popular opinion; it was a thermostat that transformed the mores of society. Whenever the early Christians entered a town, the people in power became disturbed and immediately sought to convict the Christians for being "disturbers of the peace" and "outside agitators." But the Christians pressed on, in the conviction that they were "a colony of heaven," called to obey God rather than man. Small in number, they were big in commitment. They were too God-intoxicated to be "astronomically intimidated." By their effort and example they brought an end to such ancient evils as infanticide and gladiatorial contests.

Things are different now. So often the contemporary church is a weak, ineffectual voice with an uncertain sound. So often it is an archdefender of the status quo. Far from being disturbed by the presence of the church, the power structure of the average community is consoled by the church's silent—and often even vocal—sanction of things as they are.

But the judgment of God is upon the church as never before. If today's church does not recapture the sacrificial spirit of the early church, it will lose its authenticity, forfeit the loyalty of millions, and be dismissed as an irrelevant social club with no meaning for the twentieth century. Every day I meet young people whose disappointment with the church has turned into outright disgust.

Perhaps I have once again been too optimistic. Is organized religion too inextricably bound to the status quo to save our nation and the world? Perhaps I must turn my faith to the inner spiritual church, the church within the church, as the true *ekklesia* and the hope of the world. But again I am thankful to God that some noble souls from the ranks of organized religion have broken loose from the paralyzing chains of conformity and joined us as active partners in the struggle for freedom. They have left their secure congregations and walked the streets of Albany, Georgia, with us. They have gone down the highways of the South on tortuous rides for freedom. Yes, they have gone to jail with us. Some have been dismissed from their churches, have lost the support of their bishops and fellow ministers. But they have acted in the faith that right defeated is stronger than evil triumphant. Their witness has been the spiritual salt that has preserved the true meaning of the gospel in these troubled times. They have carved a tunnel of hope through the dark mountain of disappointment.

I hope the church as a whole will meet the challenge of this decisive hour. But even if the church does not come to the aid of justice, I have no despair about the future. I have no fear about the outcome of our struggle in Birmingham, even if our motives are at present misunderstood. We will reach the goal of freedom in Birmingham and all over the nation, because the goal of America is freedom. Abused and scorned though we may be, our destiny is tied up with America's destiny. Before the pilgrims landed at Plymouth, we were here. Before the pen of Jefferson etched the majestic words of the Declaration of Independence across the pages of history, we were here. For more than two centuries our forebears labored in this country without wages; they made cotton king; they built the homes of their masters while suffering gross injustice and shameful humiliation—and yet out of a bottomless vitality they continued to thrive and develop. If the inexpressible cruelties of slavery could not stop us, the opposition we now face will surely fail. We will win our freedom because the sacred heritage of our nation and the eternal will of God are embodied in our echoing demands.

Before closing I feel impelled to mention one other point in your statement that has troubled me profoundly. You warmly commended the Birmingham police force for keeping "order" and "preventing violence." I doubt that you would have so warmly commended the police force if you had seen its dogs sinking their teeth into unarmed, nonviolent Negroes. I doubt that you would so quickly commend the policemen if you were to observe their ugly and inhumane treatment of Negroes here in the city jail; if you were to watch them push and curse old Negro women and young Negro girls; if you were to see them slap and kick old Negro men and young boys; if you were to observe them, as they did on two occasions, refuse to give us food because we wanted to sing our grace together. I cannot join you in your praise of the Birmingham police department.

It is true that the police have exercised a degree of discipline in handling the demonstrators. In this sense they have conducted themselves rather "nonviolently" in public. But for what purpose? To preserve the evil system of segregation. Over the past few years I have consistently preached that nonviolence demands that the means we use must be as pure as the ends we seek. I have tried to make clear that it is wrong to use immoral means to attain moral ends. But now I must affirm that it is just as wrong, or perhaps even more so, to use moral means to preserve immoral ends. Perhaps Mr. Connor and his policemen have been rather nonviolent in public, as was Chief Pritchett in Albany, Georgia, but they have used the moral means of nonviolence to maintain the immoral end of racial injustice. As T. S. Eliot has said: "The last temptation is the greatest treason: To do the right deed for the wrong reason."

I wish you had commended the Negro sit-inners and demonstrators of Birmingham for their sublime courage, their willingness to suffer and their amazing discipline in the midst of great provocation. One day the South will recognize its real heroes. They will be the James Merediths, with the noble sense of purpose that enables them to face jeering and hostile mobs, and with the agonizing loneliness that characterizes the life of the pioneer. They will be old, oppressed, battered Negro women, symbolized in a seventy-two-year-old woman in Montgomery, Alabama, who rose up with a sense of dignity and with her people decided not to ride segregated buses, and who responded with ungrammatical profundity to one who inquired about her weariness: "My feets is tired, but my soul is at rest." They will be the young high school and college students, the young ministers of the gospel and a host of their elders, courageously and nonviolently sitting in at lunch counters and willingly going to jail for conscience' sake. One day the South will know that when these disinherited children of God sat down at lunch counters, they were in reality standing up for what is best in the American dream and for the most sacred values in our Judeo-Christian heritage, thereby bringing our nation back to those great wells of democracy which were dug deep by the founding fathers in their formulation of the Constitution and the Declaration of Independence.

Never before have I written so long a letter. I'm afraid it is much too long to take your precious time. I can assure you that it would have been much shorter if I had been writing from a comfortable desk, but what else can one do when he is alone in a narrow jail cell, other than write long letters, think long thoughts and pray long prayers?

If I have said anything in this letter that overstates the truth and indicates an unreasonable impatience, I beg you to forgive me. If I have said anything that understates the truth and indicates my having a patience that allows me to settle for anything less than brotherhood, I beg God to forgive me.

I hope this letter finds you strong in the faith. I also hope that circumstances will soon make it possible for me to meet each of you, not as an integrationist or a civil-rights leader but as a fellow clergyman and a Christian brother. Let us all hope that the dark clouds of racial prejudice will soon pass away and the deep fog of misunderstanding will be lifted from our fear-drenched communities, and in some not too

distant tomorrow the radiant stars of love and brotherhood will shine over our great nation with all their scintillating beauty.

Yours for the cause of Peace and Brotherhood,

MARTIN LUTHER KING, JR.

Involvement in the Liberation Process   6.4

GUSTAVO GUTIERREZ

Gustavo Gutierrez (b. 1928), a priest and theologian who was born in Lima, Peru, is one of the leading proponents of Liberation Theology. After receiving his M.A. from the University of Louvain and his M.Th. from the Institut Catholique de Lyon, Gutierrez became a professor of theology at the Universidad Catolica de Lima and the director of the Instituto Bartolome de la Casas. He also became parish priest in one of the poorest areas of Lima. His experiences while ministering to the needs of the people in Rimac, a slum area of Lima where he still lives and works, led him to re-examine many of the presuppositions of his formal theological education.

Beginning with his *La pastoral de la iglesia de America Latina*, which was published in 1969, Gutierrez has written prolifically in his attempt to reawaken and defend the Catholic church's role in serving the poor and in resisting political and economic oppression. Some of his more important writings include *Teologia de la liberacion prospectivos* (1971) [translated as *A Theology of Liberation: History, Politics, and Salvation* (1973)]; *Religion, instrumento de liberacion?* (1973); *Praxis of Liberation and Christian Faith* (1974); *Teologia desde el reverso de la historia* (1977); *La fuerza historica de los pobres* (1983) [translated as *The Power of the Poor in History*]; and *Hablar de Dios desde el sufrimiento del inocente: Una reflexion sobre el libro de Job* (1986) [translated as *On Job: God-Talk and the Suffering of the Innocent* (1987)].

In the following essay, which is taken from *The Power of the Poor in History*, Gutierrez raises some of the same concerns about the contemporary church that King does toward the end of the "Letter from Birmingham Jail." Like King, Gutierrez also notes that the church has traditionally been a force that upheld the status quo and obstructed the path of those who worked to eliminate injustice. However, whereas King only holds out hope that the revolutionary and liberating power of the gospel might find expression in the lives of some Christians, Gutierrez argues that the Latin American church itself is on the verge of affirming and living this revolutionary and liberating power.

In defending this new movement within the Latin American church, Gutierrez points to two important biblical themes as justification: the recurring claim that creation and salvation go hand in hand, and the promises of messianic peace that are found throughout the Bible. Gutierrez argues that both of these themes are incompatible with the commonly held belief that the church should minister only to spiritual needs and not to social and political needs. Rather, as he forcefully says, Christ's "salvific work embraces all dimensions of human existence." Thus, Gutierrez believes that in order to fulfill its true mission, the church must align itself with the oppressed peoples who are suffering from "institutionalized violence," and actively work to create a world from which injustice and oppression have been eliminated.

Questions for Thought

1. In what ways is Gutierrez's vision of the true meaning of the gospel the same as King's? In what ways does it differ?
2. Do you agree with Gutierrez's claim that the Christian church has traditionally been a force that obstructed the path of those who struggled against social and political injustice? Why or why not?
3. What does Gutierrez mean by "institutionalized violence"? What is his attitude toward violence in general?
4. Why does Gutierrez believe that spiritual/personal change or salvation is insufficient? Do you agree with his analysis?
5. What suggestions does Gutierrez make for transforming the church? Do you think that these changes are necessary?
6. How would you describe the proper role of the church (or religion) in modern society?

Introduction

THE LATIN AMERICAN CHURCH IS IN CRISIS. Some may try to tone down this fact or offer various interpretations of it, but that does not change the essential fact. The reality is clear enough and it cannot be hidden away or talked out of existence. We must face up to it boldly if we do not want to live in an imaginary world.

The scope and seriousness of the situation is of enormous proportions. Long gone is the era when the church could handle questions and problems by appealing to its doctrines and distinctions. Today it is the church itself that is being called into question. It is being called into question by many Christians who experience in their daily lives the terrible distance that separates the church from its roots in the gospel and its lack of harmony with the real world of Latin America. It is also being called into question by many who are far away from it—many more than our traditional pastoral outlook is willing to admit—who see it as an obstructive force in the effort to construct a more just society. And now it is even being called into question by those who are associated with the existing "order," and who look with discomfort on the initiatives being undertaken by some dynamic segments in the church.[1]

So let us grant that the church is living through a time of crisis and a moment of judgment (which is what crisis means). The ecclesial community is confronted with "happenings" and with Christ, the Lord of history, through them. And we might well raise Cardinal Suhard's old question: Does all this represent *growth* or *decline* for the church in Latin America? To pose this question aright, we must adjust our theological perspective and spell out what we really mean by "growth" and "decline" when it comes to the church. But even if we do that, there is a danger that our anxiety-ridden question will drive us to focus on the dry bones of numerical statistics or to dull our disquiet in some new form of triumphalism.

There is every indication that the coming years will provide us with very different ways of viewing the church, that we shall view its presence in ways that are quite different from those that we have been accustomed to in the past or that we might formulate today. But for the present we are faced with a more modest task: to recognize and acknowledge the emergence of a new situation that is full of promise and uncertainty, and that is leading us to a new ecclesial awareness under the impulse of the Spirit.

At the opening of the second session of Vatican II, when the shadow of John XXIII still cast a bright glow over the church, Pope Paul VI spoke of the church's desire and duty of coming at last to a full understanding of its true nature.[2] And a year later he spoke once again of the need for the church to deepen its awareness of the mission it must carry out in the world. The council faced up to this task; and the church has continued to do this, often in unexpected ways, in the years following the end of the council. Going beyond the strict letter of its documents, the council opened up perspectives that have not ceased to provoke wondrous surprise, fear, or alarm—depending on one's point of view.

In line with this spirit, the church of Latin America has sought to find its place. Accustomed to being a docile link in the chain of Christianity, the Christian community of Latin America has nevertheless begun to show an awareness of itself, to examine its presence on this continent, and to raise its voice above a whisper. There has been no lack of opposition and misunderstanding from those who regard this as insubordination pure and simple.

The documents issuing from Medellín and groups of involved bishops, priests, religious, and lay persons bear witness to this new development. Even clearer witness is provided by the gestures, initiatives, crises, experiences, and ferment of ideas that lie behind these same documents, as well as by the specific commitments they have prompted.

The church in Latin America is particularly rich in problems. But that is not a wholly negative state of affairs. If it shows the required courage, the very gravity of the problems it faces may enable it to get quickly to the heart of the matter. It can slough off the atavistic encumbrances that have plagued its gospel message and its ecclesial structures. It can frankly ask itself the most essential questions: What does being Christian mean? How can the church truly be the church in the new circumstances that surround it?

In coming to this new ecclesial awareness, we can distinguish two vital aspects. Inseparable in practice, they may be studied separately for the sake of greater clarity. These two aspects are (1) our new understanding of the Latin American situation, and (2) the quest for new ways in which the people of God might exert its presence therein.

Confronting the Real Situation of Latin America

The self-awareness of the Christian community is conditioned historically by the world of which it is a part, and by its way of viewing this world.

MOVING OUT OF THE GHETTO

We need not begin from scratch to work up our own private vision of reality. In the case of Latin America, which is what concerns us here, we must rather become really involved in the way that the people of Latin America see themselves and their course in history. Thus we must start by opening our ears and listening to them—

which presupposes that we are willing to move out of our own narrow world.

From the past right up to today, the Christian community in Latin America has lived largely in its own ghetto world. Born at a time when the Catholic Church was leading a Counter-Reformation movement, the Latin American church has always been marked by an attitude of defense. This defensive posture has led it to engage in silent retreat on numerous occasions, to act as a quiet refuge for all those who felt fearful and in need of protection as they tried to follow God's lead. This posture was reinforced by the occasional attacks from liberal and anticlerical factions during the period that followed political independence in the last century. It was further reinforced by the harsh criticism of more recent social movements, which have sought to introduce radical social change and which have regarded the church as an obstacle to such change.

All this led the church to solidify its ties with established authority, thus enjoying the latter's support and forming a common front against their presumed enemies. It also led it to create and maintain costly educational institutions, social services, and charitable works that were practically duplicates of those in the world around it. It was a futile, perhaps last-ditch effort to prolong an outdated brand of Christianity in a society that no longer evinced religious oneness and that had clearly and openly entered a period of ideological pluralism. The church thus became an easy and compliant prey for those who used it to protect their own selfish interests and the established order, in the name of the "Christian West."

PROBING THE REAL CAUSES

Moving out of the ghetto is one aspect of a broader attitude: opening up to the world. It involves sharing, in a more positive and unreserved way, the vision that Latin Americans have of their situation. It also involves contributing in an effective way to the elaboration and development of this vision, and committing ourselves wholeheartedly to the activities it entails.

Recent years have been critical ones in this respect. We have come out of a long period when ignorance about the real Latin American situation prevailed, and we have also left behind the brief period when false optimism was promoted by vested interests. We are abandoning the sketchy and hazy views of the past for an overall, integrated understanding of our real situation.

The true face of Latin America is emerging in all its naked ugliness. It is not simply or primarily a question of low educational standards, a limited economy, an unsatisfactory legal system, or inadequate legal institutions. What we are faced with is a situation that takes no account of the dignity of human beings, or their most elemental needs, that does not provide for their biological survival, or their basic right to be free and autonomous. Poverty, injustice, alienation, and the exploitation of human beings by other human beings combine to form a situation that the Medellín conference did not hesitate to condemn as "institutionalized violence."[3]

This phrase might well seem strange in a pronouncement by the hierarchy.[4] But it should be emphasized that it is not something thrown in as an aside, for the whole Medellín document on peace is focused on this concept.[5] It is a commonplace for all experts on Latin America, and a reality that is known and experienced daily by most of those who live in Latin America. It is only within this real context that one can honestly raise the complex question of the moral rightness or wrongness of putting down violence. No double standard will do. We cannot say that violence is all right when the oppressor uses it to maintain or preserve "order," but wrong when the oppressed use it to overthrow this same "order."[6]

The most important change in our understanding of the Latin American situation, however, has to do with its deeper, underlying causes. These are now seen in the context of a broader historical process. It is becoming ever more clear that underdevelopment, in a total sense, is primarily due to economic, political, and cultural dependence on power centers that lie outside Latin America. The functioning of the capitalist economy leads simultaneously to the creation of greater wealth for the few and greater poverty for the many. Acting in complicity with these outside power centers, the oligarchies of each nation in Latin America operate through various mechanisms to maintain their dominion over the internal affairs of their own countries.

This new awareness of the Latin American situation shines through various documents in varying degrees of clarity. It finds authoritative and clear-cut expression in the Medellín document on peace, which forthrightly speaks of "internal colonialism" and "external neocolonialism."[7] In Latin America these are the ultimate causes of the violence that is committed against the most basic human rights.

Our new vision, attentive to structural factors, will help Christians to avoid the fallacy of proposing a personal change detached from concrete conditions, as a necessary prerequisite to any social transformation. If any of us remain wedded to this fallacy, in the name of some hazy humanism or disembodied spiritualism, we shall only prove to be accomplices in the continuing postponement of the radical changes that are necessary. Such changes call for simultaneous work on both persons and structures, for they condition each other mutually.

INVOLVEMENT IN THE LIBERATION PROCESS

When we characterize the Latin American situation as one of dependence and unfair domination, we are naturally led to talk about liberation, and to participate in the process that will lead to it. We are in fact dealing with a term that expresses the new stance adopted by Latin Americans, a stance that is gradually taking concrete shape in official documents. It is recapitulated forcefully in the Medellín conference and in the Thirty-Sixth Episcopal Assembly of Peru. Expressions such as "development" and "integration," with their attendant retinue of international alliances, agencies, and experts, are relegated to the shadows; for they involve a different vision of the Latin American situation.

But to stress the need for liberation presupposes far more than simply differences in our analyses of the situation. At a deeper level, it means that we see the ongoing development of humanity in a particular perspective, and in terms of a specific philosophy and theology of history. It means that we see it as a process of human emancipation, aiming toward a society where men and women are truly free from servitude, and where they are the active shapers of their own destiny. Such a process does not lead us simply to a radical transformation of structures—to a revolution. It goes much further, implying the perduring creation of a wholly new way for men and women to be human.

There is an urgent need for Christians to involve themselves in the work of liberating this oppressed continent, by establishing real solidarity with the oppressed persons who are the chief victims. The first step is for the church as a whole to break its many ties with the present order, ties that it has maintained overtly or covertly, wittingly or unwittingly, up to now. This will not be an easy task, for it will mean abandoning outworn traditions, suspicions, viewpoints, advantages, and privileges, as well as the forces of inertia. It will also mean accepting the fact that the future cast of the church will be radically different from the one we know today. It will mean incurring the wrath of the groups in power—with all the risks that entails. Above all, it will mean believing in the revolutionary and liberating power of the gospel—believing in the Lord—and authentic faith, a faith that goes beyond the mere recitation and acceptance of codified truths. This will not be easy. We know it, of course, and we have said it countless times. But perhaps we have not been sufficiently aware of the fears and vacillations of the vast majority of the Christian community in Latin America. Perhaps we have not realized how much they bore ironic witness to this truth.

One manifestation of our break with injustice and exploitation, which the present economic and social structures foist upon the vast majority of our people under the guise of law, should come from the bishops. They must turn to the oppressed, declaring their solidarity with them and their desire to join with them in their struggle. This is what they must do instead of what they have done in the past, when they turned to those in power and called for necessary reforms while implying that their own position need not be affected by such change.[8]

Creating a New Ecclesial Presence

At Vatican II the church affirmed a desire to render service. The concrete forms that this pledge takes must necessarily be based on the world in which the Christian community is present.

PRESENT INADEQUACIES

A better awareness of the harsh realities in Latin America goes hand in hand with a clearer realization that the church's structures are inadequate for the world in which it lives. They show up as outdated and lacking in vitality when confronted with new questions, and in one way or another seem to be tied up with the unjust order we wish to eradicate. This fact is the chief source of the misunderstandings, frictions, crises, and desertions that we witness.

Those who want to shape their lives to the demands of the gospel find it increasingly difficult to accept vague, romantic appeals to "fellowship" and "Christian unity" that do not take account of the causes underlying the present state of affairs, or of the concrete conditions required for the construction of a just society. Such vague appeals forget that the catholicity, the universality, of the church is not something attained once for all time, or something to be maintained at any price. It must be won continuously, by courageous effort and open-eyed struggle. Wittingly or unwittingly, these appeals seem designed to palliate the real tensions that do and should exist, and ultimately to maintain the status quo. The frank and decisive stands taken by the hierarchy and other sectors of the church in the last few years have been welcome breaths of fresh air. They will undoubtedly help to separate the wheat from the chaff. They will identify the real Christian among all those who call themselves Christians.

Vatican II proclaims that the church, like Christ, must carry out its work of redemption "in poverty and under oppression." But this is not the image presented by the Latin American church as a whole. Quite the contrary. Once upon a time we may not have been clearly aware of this, but that time is past. Today the church feels the sharp pangs of its tragic inconsistency; it is aware of its disloyalty to the gospel, its failure to confront the real situation in Latin America.

This has given rise to letters, declarations, new forms of commitment, and even "protest movements" in the church. All these things can easily become grist for the sensation-seeking media. But altogether apart from their transitory news value, their sometimes ambiguous doctrinal roots, and the misleading commentaries they provoke, they have a much deeper significance, and we must try to probe it. They betoken the concern many Christians have with the form that the church's presence in Latin America now takes. They reveal a hidden vitality, a spirit that refuses to be bound to the cold letter of the law. If we do not pay heed to the message they contain, we may one day find ourselves in an atmosphere of general indifference, longing wistfully for those "hotheads" who had used unconventional means to express their desire for change in the church and for fidelity to the gospel.

The most vital sectors of the people of God in Latin America are thus committed to a search for two things: (1) the theological bases that will ground their activity on a continent caught up in a process of liberation; and (2) new ecclesial structures that will allow them to live a true life of faith in accordance with Latin Americans' growing awareness of their own specific historical destiny.

A THEOLOGY OF HUMAN LIBERATION

We have suggested that an authentic presence in Latin America presupposes a concern on the part of the church for the specifically political dimensions of that presence. Would such a concern mean the church were falling prey to some sort of aberrant temporalism, and abandoning its spiritual mission? After all, this is what frightens many persons of good will (and ill will).

The gospel, these persons say, is first and foremost a message of eternal salvation; building the earth is a task for human beings on this earth. The first task belongs to the church, the second task belongs to temporal society. The most they will admit is that the church may lay down certain ethical dictates for the work of building civil society—so long as they do not openly question the interests of those who hold the reins of economic and political power.

But a closer look at reality, such as I have outlined above, has wrought a profound change in the life and outlook of the whole church. Although I cannot discuss the process in detail here, I can point out that the church has restored its ties with the Christian tradition of antiquity and has rediscovered that salvation embraces all humanity, and each individual. It will be worth our while to spell out briefly the theological notions that form the basis for this new outlook on the part of the church.

Concrete reflection on human existence has carried contemporary theology far beyond the scholastic and essentialist outlook that was based on distinguishing various orders and levels. At the same time that it was renewing its contact with its roots in the Bible, theology was moving toward the notion that humankind had but one vocation; or, to put it more exactly, that all

human beings shared the same single vocation. Thus we do not have two juxtaposed histories, one sacred and the other profane. There is only one single process of human development, definitively and irreversibly assumed by Christ, the Lord of history. His salvific work embraces all the dimensions of human existence. Two major biblical themes clearly illustrate this viewpoint: the relationship between creation and salvation, and the messianic promises.

In the rather simplistic catechetics of the past, creation was presented as the explanation for the existing world. This is not incorrect, but it is incomplete. In the Bible, creation is not a stage prior to the work of salvation; it is the first salvific activity. "Before the world was made, he chose us in Christ" (Eph. 1:4). Creation is inserted in the salvation process, in God's self-communication. The religious experience of Israel is primarily history, but this history is simply the prolongation of God's creative activity. That is why the Psalms praise Yahweh simultaneously as Creator and Savior (see Ps. 136). The God who transformed chaos into cosmos is the same as the one who acts in salvation history. The redemptive work of Christ, in turn, is presented in the context of creation (see John 1). Creation and salvation have a christological import; in Christ all have been created and all have been saved (see Col. 1:15–20).

Thus when we say that men and women fulfill themselves by carrying on the work of creation through their own labors, we are asserting that they are operating within the framework of God's salvific work from the very first. Subduing the earth, as Genesis bids them do, is a salvific work. To work in the world and transform it is to save it. Inasmuch as it is a humanizing factor that transforms nature, work tends to build a society that is more just and more worthy of humankind—as Marx clearly saw. The Bible helps us to appreciate the deeper reaches of this effort. Building the earthly city is not simply a humanizing phase prior to evangelization, as theology used to put it. Building the earthly city actually immerses human beings in the salvation process that touches all humanity. Every obstacle that degrades or alienates the work of men and women in building a humane society is an obstacle to the work of salvation.

A second major theme of the Bible echoes this same thinking. The messianic promises, the events that announce and accompany the coming of the Messiah, are not isolated happenings. Like the first theme, the thread of messianism runs through the whole Bible. It is actively present in the history of Israel, and thus has its proper place in the historical development of God's people.

The prophets proclaim a reign of peace. But peace presupposes the establishment of justice, the defense of the rights of the poor, the punishment of oppressors, and a life free from the fear of enslavement. A benighted spiritualization has often caused us to forget the human power imbedded in the messianic promises and the transforming effect they might have on unjust social structures. The conquest of poverty and the abolition of exploitation are signs of the Messiah's arrival and presence. According to the book of Isaiah, the kingdom will become a reality when "they shall not build for others to live in, or plant for others to eat" (Isa. 65:22)—when everyone profits from their own labor. To work for a just world where there is no servitude, oppression, or alienation is to work for the advent of the Messiah. The messianic promises establish a close tie between the kingdom of God and living conditions that are worthy of human beings. God's kingdom and social injustice are incompatible.

The message to be gleaned from these two biblical themes is clear. Salvation embraces all, as *Populorum Progressio* (21) reminds us. Preaching the gospel message is not preaching escape from the world. On the contrary, the word of God deepens and fortifies our involvement in history. Concretely, this involvement means solidarity with the oppressed of Latin America and participation in their struggle for emancipation. And this solidarity and participation involve the realization that salvation history is a continuing process of liberation. It is through encounters with the poor and the exploited that we shall encounter the Lord (see Matt. 25:31ff). To be a Christian in our day is to involve ourselves creatively in the different phases of humanity's liberation process. Faith opens up infinite horizons to our human effort, giving dynamic vitality to our active presence in history.

These are some of the theological notions that implicitly or explicitly underlie the new Christian statements coming from Latin America. Only against this backdrop can we properly understand the efforts of certain Christian groups to be authentically present in the world of Latin America. Theirs is not a suspect temporalism; theirs is a desire, though undoubtedly flawed and imperfect, to be wholly loyal to the word of the Lord.

NEW ECCLESIAL STRUCTURES

There was a time when the vitality or decrepitude of the Latin American church was measured by the number of its priests. You simply calculated the number of faithful per priest and made your analysis on that basis. If you were at all in touch with the actual situation, you made mention of the disturbing geographical distance between the priests and most of their faithful. The scarcity of vocations seemed to be the major obstacle to be overcome if the underdeveloped church were to grow. Today, few still view the matter that way. The problem of priests has other, more delicate, facets. Everything seems to indicate that the lifestyle of the priest, which had remained static for centuries, is about to undergo a profound transformation in the near future. But even more important is the fact that it is merely one symptom of the broader and graver crisis afflicting the Christian community.

The older approach to this whole problem had a markedly clerical cast, which tended to minimize the problematical nature of the situation. Its gravest error was undoubtedly the type of solution it suggested for the church's problems. It was felt we could move out of the past by making efforts to modernize certain ecclesiastical structures or to inaugurate certain pastoral adaptations. Basically it is that whole approach that is today being called into question.

From now on we shall have to attack this issue with greater boldness, with the fortitude that Scripture enjoins on Christ's disciples (see Acts 4:31). That fortitude must induce us to carry out not halfway reforms that gloss over our fears and trepidations, but a transformation far more radical than anything we know today. The times demand of us a creative spark that will allow us to work up and create new ecclesial structures and new ways for the Christian community to be present to the world. The alarmed reaction of certain factions in the church that rise up in protest against those who would explore the signs of the times is no solution.

One solid line of endeavor for the Latin American church in this quest will be for it to assert its own distinctive personality. We have lived in a state of dependence that has not allowed us to fully develop our own qualities up to now. As a church, we have been a mirror image rather than a fountainhead, in the terms of Father de Lima Vas. We have been mirroring the European church—uncritically borrowing our theology, institutions, canon law, spirituality, and lifestyle. We have not been a creative fountainhead for new activities that would fit in with a world in revolution, for ecclesial structures that would be appropriate for a Third World church, or for ideas that would allow us to strike deep roots in our own reality. Working free of the colonial mentality is undoubtedly one of the major tasks confronting the Christian community of Latin America. It will also be one way in which we can make a genuine contribution to the universal church.

Another solid line of endeavor will be our commitment to genuine poverty. This is an area where Christians offer ample witness to the con-

trary. We often confuse making a vow of poverty with living a life of poverty. We often confuse possession of absolute essentials with comfortable ensconcement in the world. We often confuse instruments for service with power leverage. We need an honest, clear-headed reform that will put an end to the discrepancy between our preaching and our practice. We must live in a church that is not only open to the poor but poor itself. Only in this way can we radically change the present face of the Christian community.

In this context, the episcopal conference at Medellín may represent for the Latin American church what Vatican II was for the whole church. It was not an end point but a point of departure. It was not only a forum for documents that sum up the ecclesial community's present awareness of this moment in history, but also a stimulus to push on further and to put life into our words. All this will not be done without difficulty. We shall always feel light-headed impulses that will prompt us to sensation-seeking postures rather than deep commitments. But the greatest threat will be the temptation to immobility and a preference for changes that do not really change the existing situation. We are more bound to the old structures than we realize.

Vatican II, and, one hopes, the Medellín conference, opened up the floodgates and allowed long-dammed waters to flow freely. When the flood is over, we shall realize that it has done more cleansing than destroying. Right now, however, our task is not to anxiously protect the texts of Vatican II and Medellín from erroneous interpretations, or to provide erudite commentaries. The important thing for us is to expound them in our deeds—to verify their truth in our daily Christian life.

The church is experiencing the effects of living in a world that is undergoing profound and decisive changes. The church itself must set out on uncharted roads, turn down new byways, without knowing what risks and obstacles will be encountered. It is not easy to believe that the Spirit will lead us to the whole truth (see John

16:13). It is not easy to set out without consulting a road map in advance. But today that is what the Christian community in Latin America must do.

Some may well complain that the positions expressed in these documents do not offer any responses or solutions. That may be true. But we must not forget that those who change the course of history are usually those who pose a new set of questions, rather than those who offer solutions.

NOTES

1. This alarm is clearly reflected in an article by Alberto Lleras Camargo that was published in the North American magazine *Vision* (September 29, 1968). In line with a similar article on the Medellín conference that was published in a Peruvian periodical, Lleras Camargo pejoratively labels one group of participating bishops "progressivists" and "radicals."

2. Address at the opening of the second session of Vatican Council II (September 29, 1965).

3. See the Medellín Document on Peace, in *Between Honesty and Hope* (Maryknoll, N.Y.: Maryknoll, 1970).

4. The expression was not retracted, as some uninformed commentators had hoped. Nor is it derived from Marxist sociology, as these same persons opined. The basic notion and the term itself can be found before Medellín in various statements issued by lay apostolic groups.

5. The idea is present at the very beginning of the Document on Peace and is developed throughout (see nos. 1 and 14, for example).

6. See the interesting article by Gonzalo Arroyo, "Violencia institucionalizada en América Latina," *Mensaje*, November 1968. The author concludes on a forceful note: "Have we Christians, who profess belief in the rewards of peace, done more than talk about global structural changes? Have we devoted all our energy to eliminating institutionalized injustice? If we are not doing that today, we have no right to cast the first stone!" (p. 544).

7. See the Document on Peace.

8. In this connection it is interesting to note the section directed to "our fellow peasants and laborers" in a statement of the Peruvian Episcopal Assembly, January 1969. Citing the Medellín document on peace, they state that they "will do everything in our power to foster and promote your grassroots organizations, so that you may reclaim your rights and obtain authentic justice" (Justice and Peace Commission, 2.4.2). In another section they stress that their forthright denunciation of abuses and injustices will be accompanied by "concrete action in solidarity with the poor and the oppressed" (ibid., 2.4.6).

6.5   Why Women Need the Goddess: Phenomenological, Psychological and Political Reflections

CAROL P. CHRIST

Carol P. Christ (b. 1945), who received advanced degrees from Stanford University and Yale University, has been very active in feminist, peace, and Goddess movements. She is former co-chair of the Women and Religion Section of the American Academy of Religion, and former professor of Women's Studies and Religious Studies at San Jose State University. She currently spends a lot of her time writing and making rituals on the island of Lesbos, where she has also taught classes at the Aegean Women's Studies Institute.

Co-editor of the influential anthology *Womanspirit Rising: A Feminist Reader in Religion* (first published in 1979 and revised in 1991), Christ is also the author of

Diving Deep and Surfacing: Women Writers on Spiritual Quest (1986) and *Laughter of Aphrodite* (1988). The following essay, which was the keynote address at the University of California at Santa Cruz Extension conference on "The Great Goddess Re-Emerging," was originally published in *Heresies* (Spring 1978).

In this essay, Christ describes several aspects of the emerging Goddess movement, and explains the significance of this movement for women's psychological and spiritual development. In doing so, she contrasts the beliefs and practices of the Goddess movement with certain beliefs and practices of patriarchal religion as represented by the Judeo-Christian tradition. Unlike King and Gutierrez, Christ believes that this tradition is beyond redemption, that it symbolizes oppression and not liberation, especially in the case of women.

In contrast to the paternalistic symbolism of God the Father, Christ argues that the Goddess symbolizes "the newfound beauty, strength, and power of women." Specifically, she claims that the symbolism of the Goddess has four important implications for the lives of women. First, unlike the Judeo-Christian tradition, it validates female power as both beneficent and effective. Second, it affirms the body, especially the female body, as well as the cycles of life and nature. Third, it provides a positive valuation of the will, while at the same time offering a model of the will that differs from the egocentric model associated with patriarchal thinking. Finally, the symbolism of the Goddess revalues women's bonds and heritage, especially the bond between mother and daughter. In short, Christ claims that the symbol of the Goddess is a powerful psychological and political tool in the struggle for liberation and self-affirmation.

Questions for Thought

1. What does Christ mean by the Goddess? Does she think that the Goddess physically exists?
2. What are Christ's main criticisms of the Judeo-Christian tradition? How do you think King and Gutierrez would respond to these criticisms? What is your response to them?
3. Why does Christ believe that symbols are so important? Do you agree with her claims about the value of symbols?
4. What do you think is the most adequate symbol of divinity?
5. Why does Christ believe that it is important for people, especially women, to affirm the value of the body and the will? Do you agree with her on this point?
6. What are the nature and purpose of the rituals described in Christ's essay? Have you participated in religious rituals? If so, what were the nature and purpose of the rituals in which you participated?

AT THE CLOSE OF NTOSAKE SHANGE'S STUPEN-dously successful Broadway play "For Colored Girls Who Have Considered Suicide When the Rainbow Is Enuf," a tall beautiful black woman rises from despair to cry out, "I found God in myself and I loved her fiercely."[1] Her discovery is echoed by women around the country who meet spontaneously in small groups on full moons, solstices, and equinoxes to celebrate the Goddess as symbol of life and death powers and

First appeared in *Heresies* No. 5, "The Great Goddess."

waxing and waning energies in the universe and in themselves.[2]

> It is the night of the full moon. Nine women stand in a circle, on a rocky hill above the city. The western sky is rosy with the setting sun; in the east the moon's face begins to peer above the horizon. . . . The woman pours out a cup of wine onto the earth, refills it and raises it high. "Hail, Tana, Mother of mothers!" she cries. "Awaken from your long sleep, and return to your children again!"[3]

What are the political and psychological effects of this fierce new love of the divine in themselves for women whose spiritual experience has been focused by the male God of Judaism and Christianity? Is the spiritual dimension of feminism a passing diversion, an escape from difficult but necessary political work? Or does the emergence of the symbol of Goddess among women have significant political and psychological ramifications for the feminist movement?

To answer this question, we must first understand the importance of religious symbols and rituals in human life and consider the effect of male symbolism of God on women. According to anthropologist Clifford Geertz, religious symbols shape a cultural ethos, defining the deepest values of a society and the persons in it. "Religion," Geertz writes "is a system of symbols which act to produce powerful, pervasive, and long-lasting moods and motivations"[4] in the people of a given culture. A "mood" for Geertz is a psychological attitude such as awe, trust, and respect, while a "motivation" is the *social* and *political* trajectory created by a mood that transforms mythos into ethos, symbol system into social and political reality. Symbols have both psychological and political effects, because they create the inner conditions (deep-seated attitudes and feelings) that lead people to feel comfortable with or to accept social and political arrangements that correspond to the symbol system.

Because religion has such a compelling hold on the deep psyches of so many people, feminists cannot afford to leave it in the hands of the fathers. Even people who no longer "believe in God" or participate in the institutional structure of patriarchal religion still may not be free of the power of the symbolism of God the Father. A symbol's effect does not depend on rational assent, for a symbol also functions on levels of the psyche other than the rational. Religion fulfills deep psychic needs by providing symbols and rituals that enable people to cope with limit situations[5] in human life (death, evil, suffering) and to pass through life's important transitions (birth, sexuality, death). Even people who consider themselves completely secularized will often find themselves sitting in a church or synagogue when a friend or relative gets married, or when a parent or friend has died. The symbols associated with these important rituals cannot fail to affect the deep or unconscious structures of the mind of even a person who has rejected these symbolisms on a conscious level—especially if the person is under stress. The reason for the continuing effect of religious symbols is that the mind abhors a vacuum. Symbol systems cannot simply be rejected, they must be replaced. Where there is not any replacement, the mind will revert to familiar structures at times of crisis, bafflement, or defeat.

Religions centered on the worship of a male God create "moods" and "motivations" that keep women in a state of psychological dependence on men and male authority, while at the same time legitimating the *political* and *social* authority of fathers and sons in the institutions of society.

Religious symbol systems focused around exclusively male images of divinity create the impression that female power can never be fully legitimate or wholly beneficent. This message need never be explicitly stated (as, for example, it is in the story of Eve) for its effect to be felt. A woman completely ignorant of the myths of female evil in biblical religion nonetheless acknowledges the anomaly of female power when she prays exclusively to a male God. She may see herself as like God (created in the image of God) only by denying her own sexual identity and affirming God's transcendence of sexual identity. But she can never have the experience that is freely available to every man and boy in her culture, of having her full sexual identity affirmed as being in the image and likeness of God. In Geertz' terms, her "mood" is one of trust in male power as salvific and distrust of female power in herself and other women as inferior or dangerous. Such a powerful, pervasive, and longlasting "mood" cannot fail to become a "motivation" that translates into social and political reality.

In *Beyond God the Father*, feminist theologian Mary Daly detailed the psychological and political ramifications of father religion for women. "If God in 'his' heaven is a father ruling his people," she wrote, "then it is the 'nature' of things and according to divine plan and the order of the universe that society be male dominated. Within this context, a *mystification of roles* takes place: The husband dominating his wife represents God 'himself.' The images and values of a given society have been projected into the realm of dogmas and 'Articles of Faith,' and these in turn justify the social structures which have given rise to them and which sustain their plausibility."[6]

Philosopher Simone de Beauvoir was well aware of the function of patriarchal religion as legitimater of male power. As she wrote, "Man enjoys the great advantage of having a god endorse the code he writes; and since man exercises a sovereign authority over women it is especially fortunate that this authority has been vested in him by the Supreme Being. For the Jew, Mohammedans, and Christians, among others, man is Master by divine right; the fear of God will therefore repress any impulse to revolt in the downtrodden female."[7]

This brief discussion of the psychological and political effects of God religion puts us in an excellent position to begin to understand the significance of the symbol of Goddess for women. In discussing the meaning of the Goddess, my method will first be phenomenological. I will isolate a meaning of the symbol of the Goddess as it has emerged in the lives of contemporary women. I will then discuss its psychological and political significance by contrasting the "moods" and "motivations" engendered by Goddess symbols with those engendered by Christian symbolism. I will also correlate Goddess symbolism with themes that have emerged in the women's movement, in order to show how Goddess symbolism undergirds and legitimates the concerns of the women's movement, much as God symbolism in Christianity undergirded the interests of men in patriarchy. I will discuss four aspects of Goddess symbolism here: the Goddess as affirmation of female power, the female body, the female will, and women's bonds and heritage. There are, of course, many other meanings of the Goddess that I will not discuss here.

The sources for the symbol of the Goddess in contemporary spirituality are traditions of Goddess worship and modern women's experience. The ancient Mediterranean, pre-Christian European, native American, Mesoamerican, Hindu, African, and other traditions are rich sources for Goddess symbolism. But these traditions are filtered through modern women's experiences. Traditions of Goddesses' subordination to Gods, for example, are ignored. Ancient traditions are tapped selectively and eclecticly, but they are not considered authoritative for modern consciousness. The Goddess symbol has emerged spontaneously in the dreams, fantasies, and thoughts of many women around the country in the past several years. Kirsten Grimstad and Susan Rennie reported that they were surprised to discover widespread interest in spirituality, including the Goddess, among feminists around the country in the summer of 1974.[8] *WomanSpirit* magazine, which published its first issue in 1974 and has contributors from across the United States, has expressed the grass roots nature of the women's spirituality movement. In 1976, a journal, *Lady*

Unique, devoted to the Goddess emerged. In 1975, the first women's spirituality conference was held in Boston and attended by 1,800 women. In 1978, a University of Santa Cruz course on the Goddess drew over 500 people. Sources for this essay are these manifestations of the Goddess in modern women's experiences as reported in *WomanSpirit*, *Lady Unique*, and elsewhere, and as expressed in conversations I have had with women who have been thinking about the Goddess and women's spirituality.

The simplest and most basic meaning of the symbol of Goddess is the acknowledgement of the legitimacy of female power as a beneficent and independent power. A woman who echoes Ntosake Shange's dramatic statement, "I found God in myself and I loved her fiercely," is saying "Female power is strong and creative." She is saying that the divine principle, the saving and sustaining power, is in herself, that she will no longer look to men or male figures as saviors. The strength and independence of female power can be intuited by contemplating ancient and modern images of the Goddess. This meaning of the symbol of Goddess is simple and obvious, and yet it is difficult for many to comprehend. It stands in sharp contrast to the paradigms of female dependence on males that have been predominant in Western religion and culture. The internationally acclaimed novelist Monique Wittig captured the novelty and flavor of the affirmation of female power when she wrote, in her mythic work *Les Guerilleres*,

> There was a time when you were not a slave, remember that. You walked alone, full of laughter, you bathed bare-bellied. You say you have lost all recollection of it, remember . . . you say there are no words to describe it, you say it does not exist. But remember. Make an effort to remember. Or, failing that, invent.[9]

While Wittig does not speak directly of the Goddess here, she captures the "mood" of joyous celebration of female freedom and independence that is created in women who define their identities through the symbol of Goddess. Artist Mary Beth Edelson expressed the political "motivations" inspired by the Goddess when she wrote,

> The ascending archetypal symbols of the feminine unfold today in the psyche of modern Every woman. They encompass the multiple forms of the Great Goddess. Reaching across the centuries we take the hands of our Ancient Sisters. The Great Goddess alive and well is rising to announce to the patriarchs that their 5,000 years are up—Hallelujah! Here we come.[10]

The affirmation of female power contained in the Goddess symbol has both psychological and political consequences. Psychologically, it means the defeat of the view engendered by patriarchy that women's power is inferior and dangerous. This new "mood" of affirmation of female power also leads to new "motivations"; it supports and undergirds women's trust in their own power and the power of other women in family and society.

If the simplest meaning of the Goddess symbol is an affirmation of the legitimacy and beneficence of female power, then a question immediately arises, "Is the Goddess simply female power writ large, and if so, why bother with the symbol of Goddess at all? Or does the symbol refer to a Goddess 'out there' who is not reducible to a human potential?" The many women who have rediscovered the power of Goddess would give three answers to this question: (1) The Goddess is divine female, a personification who can be invoked in prayer and ritual; (2) the Goddess is symbol of the life, death, and rebirth energy in nature and culture, in personal and communal life; and (3) the Goddess is symbol of the affirmation of the legitimacy and beauty of female power (made possible by the new becoming of women in the women's liberation movement). If one were to ask these women which answer is the "correct" one, different responses would be given. Some would assert that the Goddess definitely is *not* "out there," that the symbol of a divinity "out there" is part of the legacy of patriarchal oppression, which brings with it the authoritarianism, hierarchicalism, and dogmatic rigidity associated with biblical monotheistic religions. They might assert that the Goddess symbol reflects the sacred power within women and nature, suggesting the connectedness between women's cycles of menstruation, birth, and menopause, and the life and death cycles of the universe. Others seem quite comfortable with the notion of Goddess as a divine female protector and creator and would find their experience of Goddess limited by the assertion that she is not *also* out there as well as within themselves and in all natural processes. When asked what the symbol of Goddess means, feminist priestess Starhawk replied, "It all depends on how I feel. When I feel weak, she is someone who can help and protect me. When I feel strong, she is the symbol of my own power. At other times I feel her as the natural energy in my body and the world."[11] How are we to evaluate such a statement? Theologians might call these the words of a sloppy thinker. But my deepest intuition tells me they contain a wisdom that Western theological thought has lost.

To theologians, these differing views of the "meaning" of the symbol of Goddess might seem to threaten a replay of the trinitarian controversies. Is there, perhaps, a way of doing theology, which would not lead immediately into dogmatic controversy, which would not require theologians to say definitively that one understanding is true and the others are false? Could people's relation to a common symbol be made primary and varying interpretations be acknowledged? The diversity of explications of the meaning of the Goddess symbol suggests that symbols have a richer significance than any explications of their meaning can express, a point literary critics have long insisted on. This phenomenological fact suggests that theologians may need to give more than lip service to a theory of symbol in which the symbol is viewed as the primary fact

and the meanings are viewed as secondary. It also suggests that a *thea*logy[12] of the Goddess would be very different from the *theo*logy we have known in the West. But to spell out this notion of the primacy of *symbol* in thealogy in contrast to the primacy of the *explanation* in theology would be the topic of another paper. Let me simply state that women, who have been deprived of a female religious symbol system for centuries, are therefore in an excellent position to recognize the power and primacy of symbols. I believe women must develop a theory of symbol and thealogy congruent with their experience at the same time as they "remember and invent" new symbol systems.

A second important implication of the Goddess symbol for women is the affirmation of the female body and the life cycle expressed in it. Because of women's unique position as menstruants, birthgivers, and those who have traditionally cared for the young and the dying, women's connection to the body, nature, and this world has been obvious. Women were denigrated because they seemed more carnal, fleshy, and earthy than the culture-creating males.[13] The misogynist anti*body* tradition in Western thought is symbolized in the myth of Eve who is traditionally viewed as a sexual temptress, the epitome of women's carnal nature. This tradition reaches its nadir in the *Malleus Maleficarum (The Hammer of Evil-Doing Women)*, which states, "All witchcraft stems from carnal lust, which in women is insatiable."[14] The Virgin Mary, the positive female image in Christianity, does not contradict Christian denigration of the female body and its powers. The Virgin Mary is revered because she, in her perpetual virginity, transcends the carnal sexuality attributed to most women.

The denigration of the female body is expressed in cultural and religious taboos surrounding menstruation, childbirth, and menopause in women. While menstruation taboos may have originated in a perception of the awesome powers of the female body,[15] they degenerated into a simple perception that there is something "wrong" with female bodily functions. Menstruating women were forbidden to enter the sanctuary in ancient Hebrew and premodern Christian communities. Although only Orthodox Jews still enforce religious taboos against menstruant women, few women in our culture grow up affirming their menstruation as a connection to sacred power. Most women learn that menstruation is a curse and grow up believing that the bloody facts of menstruation are best hidden away. Feminists challenge this attitude to the female body. Judy Chicago's art piece "Menstruation Bathroom" broke these menstrual taboos. In a sterile white bathroom, she exhibited boxes of Tampax and Kotex on an open shelf, and the wastepaper basket was overflowing with bloody tampons and sanitary napkins.[16] Many women who viewed the piece felt relieved to have their "dirty secret" out in the open.

The denigration of the female body and its powers is further expressed in Western culture's attitudes toward childbirth.[17] Religious iconography does not celebrate the birthgiver, and there is no theology or ritual that enables a woman to celebrate the process of birth as a spiritual experience. Indeed, Jewish and Christian traditions also had blood taboos concerning the woman who had recently given birth. While these religious taboos are rarely enforced today (again, only by Orthodox Jews), they have secular equivalents. Giving birth is treated as a disease requiring hospitalization, and the woman is viewed as a passive object, anesthetized to ensure her acquiescence to the will of the doctor. The women's liberation movement has challenged these cultural attitudes, and many feminists have joined with advocates of natural childbirth and home birth in emphasizing the need for women to control and take pride in their bodies, including the birth process.

Western culture also gives little dignity to the postmenopausal or aging woman. It is no secret that our culture is based on a denial of aging and death, and that women suffer more severely from this denial than men. Women are placed on a pedestal and considered powerful when they are young and beautiful, but they are said to lose this power as they age. As feminists have pointed out, the "power" of the young woman is illusory, since beauty standards are defined by men, and since few women are considered (or consider themselves) beautiful for more than a few years of their lives. Some men are viewed as wise and authoritative in age, but old women are pitied and shunned. Religious iconography supports this cultural attitude towards aging women. The purity and virginity of Mary and the female saints is often expressed in the iconographic convention of perpetual youth. Moreover, religious mythology associates aging women with evil in the symbol of the wicked old witch. Feminists have challenged cultural myths of aging women and have urged women to reject patriarchal beauty standards and to celebrate the distinctive beauty of women of all ages.

The symbol of Goddess aids the process of naming and reclaiming the female body and its cycles and processes. In the ancient world and among modern women, the Goddess symbol represents the birth, death, and rebirth processes of the natural and human worlds. The female body is viewed as the direct incarnation of waxing and waning, life and death, cycles in the universe. This is sometimes expressed through the symbolic connection between the twenty-eight-day cycles of menstruation and the twenty-eight-day cycles of the moon. Moreover, the Goddess is celebrated in the triple aspect of youth, maturity, and age, or maiden, mother, and crone. The potentiality of the young girl is celebrated in the nymph or maiden aspect of the Goddess. The Goddess as mother is sometimes depicted giving birth, and giving birth is viewed as a symbol for all the creative, life-giving powers of the universe.[18] The life-giving powers of the Goddess in her creative aspect are not limited to physical birth, for the Goddess is also seen as the creator of all the arts of civilization, including healing, writing, and the giving of just law. Women in the middle of life who are not physical mothers may give birth to poems, songs, and books, or nurture other women, men, and children. They too are incarnations of the Goddess in her creative, life-giving aspect. At the end of life, women incarnate the crone aspect of the Goddess. The wise old woman, the woman who knows from experience what life is about, the woman whose closeness to her own death gives her a distance and perspective on the problems of life, is celebrated as the third aspect of the Goddess. Thus, women learn to value youth, creativity, and wisdom in themselves and other women.

The possibilities of reclaiming the female body and its cycles have been expressed in a number of Goddess-centered rituals. Hallie Mountainwing and Barbry My Own created a summer solstice ritual to celebrate menstruation and birth. The women simulated a birth canal and birthed each other into their circle. They raised power by placing their hands on each other's bellies and chanting together. Finally they marked each other's faces with rich, dark menstrual blood saying, "This is the blood that promises renewal. This is the blood that promises sustenance. This is the blood that promises life."[19] From hidden dirty secret to symbol of the life power of the Goddess, women's blood has come full circle. Other women have created rituals that celebrate the crone aspect of the Goddess. Z. Budapest believes that the crone aspect of the Goddess is predominant in the fall, especially at Halloween, an ancient holiday. On this day, the wisdom of the old woman is celebrated, and it is also recognized that the old must die so that the new can be born.

The "mood" created by the symbol of the Goddess in triple aspect is one of positive, joyful affirmation of the female body and its cycles and acceptance of aging and death as well as life. The "motivations" are to overcome menstrual taboos, to return the birth process to the hands of women, and to change cultural attitudes about age and death. Changing cultural attitudes toward the female body could go a long way toward overcoming the spirit–flesh, mind–body dualisms of Western culture, since, as Ruether has pointed out, the denigration of the female body is at the heart of these dualisms. The Goddess as symbol of the revaluation of the body and nature thus also undergirds the human potential and ecology movements. The "mood" is one of affirmation, awe, and respect for the body and nature, and the "motivation" is to respect the teachings of the body and the rights of all living beings.

A third important implication of the Goddess symbol for women is the positive valuation of will in a Goddess-centered ritual, especially in Goddess-centered ritual magic and spellcasting in womanspirit and feminist witchcraft circles. The basic notion behind ritual magic and spellcasting is energy as power. Here the Goddess is a center or focus of power and energy; she is the personification of the energy that flows between beings in the natural and human worlds. In Goddess circles, energy is raised by chanting or dancing. According to Starhawk, "Witches conceive of psychic energy as having form and substance that can be perceived and directed by those with a trained awareness. The power generated within the circle is built into a cone form, and at its peak is released—to the Goddess, to reenergize the members of the coven, or to do a specific work such as healing."[20] In ritual magic, the energy raised is directed by willpower. Women who celebrate in Goddess circles believe they can achieve their wills in the world.

The emphasis on the will is important for women, because women traditionally have been taught to devalue their wills, to believe that they cannot achieve their will through their own power, and even to suspect that the assertion of will is evil. Faith Wildung's poem "Waiting," from which I will quote only a short segment, sums up women's sense that their lives are defined not by their own will, but by waiting for others to take the initiative.

Waiting for my breasts to develop
Waiting to wear a bra
Waiting to menstruate
. . .

Waiting for life to begin, Waiting—
Waiting to be somebody
. . .

Waiting to get married
Waiting for my wedding day
Waiting for my wedding night
. . .

Waiting for the end of the day
Waiting for sleep. Waiting . . . [21]

Patriarchal religion has enforced the view that female initiative and will are evil through the juxtaposition of Eve and Mary. Eve caused the fall by asserting her will against the command of God, while Mary began the new age with her response to God's initiative, "Let it be done to me according to thy word" (Luke 1:38). Even for men, patriarchal religion values the passive will subordinate to divine initiative. The classical doctrines of sin and grace view sin as the prideful assertion of will and grace as the obedient subordination of the human will to the divine initiative or order. While this view of will might be questioned from a human perspective, Valerie Saiving has argued that it has particularly deleterious consequences for women in Western culture. According to Saiving, Western culture encourages males in the assertion of will, and thus it may make some sense to view the male form of sin as an excess of will. But since culture discourages females in the assertion of will, the traditional doctrines of sin and grace encourage women to remain in their form of sin, which is self-negation or insufficient assertion of will.[22] One possible reason the will is denigrated in a patriarchal religious framework is that both human and divine will are often pictured as arbitrary, self-initiated, and exercised without regard for other wills.

In a Goddess-centered context, in contrast, the will is valued. *A woman is encouraged to know her will, to believe that her will is valid, and to believe that her will can be achieved in the world*, three powers traditionally denied to her in patriarchy. In a Goddess-centered framework, a woman's will is not subordinated to the Lord God as king and ruler, nor to men as his representatives. Thus a woman is not reduced to waiting and acquiescing in the wills of others as she is in patriarchy. But neither does she adopt the egocentric form of will that pursues self-interest without regard for the interests of others.

The Goddess-centered context provides a different understanding of the will than that available in the traditional patriarchal religious framework. In the Goddess framework, will can be achieved only when it is exercised in harmony with the energies and wills of other beings. Wise women, for example, raise a cone of healing energy at the full moon or solstice when the lunar or solar energies are at their high points with respect to the earth. This discipline encourages them to recognize that not all times are propitious for the achieving of every will. Similarly, they know that spring is a time for new beginnings in work and love, summer a time for producing external manifestations of inner potentialities, and fall or winter times for stripping down to the inner core and extending roots. Such awareness of waxing and waning processes in the universe discourages arbitrary ego-centered assertion of will, while at the same time encouraging the assertion of individual will in cooperation with natural energies and the energies created by the wills of others. Wise women also have a tradition that whatever is sent out will be returned and this reminds them to assert their wills in cooperative and healing rather than egocentric and destructive ways. This view of will allows women to begin to recognize, claim, and assert their wills without adopting the worst characteristics of the patriarchal understanding and use of will. In the Goddess-centered framework, the "mood" is one of positive affirmation of personal will in the context of the energies of other wills or beings. The "motivation" is for women to know and assert their wills in cooperation with other wills and energies. This of course does not mean that women always assert their wills in positive and life-affirming ways. Women's capacity for evil is, of course, as great as men's. My purpose is simply to contrast the differing attitudes toward the exercise of will *per se*, and the female will in particular, in Goddess-centered religion and in the Christian God-centered religion.

The fourth and final aspect of Goddess symbolism that I will discuss here is the significance of the Goddess for a revaluation of woman's bonds and heritage. As Virginia Woolf has said, "Chloe liked Olivia," a statement about a woman's relation to another woman, is a sentence that rarely occurs in fiction. Men have written the stories, and they have written about women almost exclusively in their relations to men.[23] The celebrations of women's bonds to each other, as mothers and daughters, as colleagues and coworkers, as sisters, friends, and lovers, is beginning to occur in the new literature and culture created by women in the women's movement. While I believe that the revaluing of each of these bonds is important, I will focus on the mother–daughter bond, in part because I believe it may be the key to the others.

Adrienne Rich has pointed out that the mother–daughter bond, perhaps the most important of woman's bonds, "resonant with charges . . . the flow of energy between two biologically alike bodies, one of which has lain in amniotic bliss inside the other, one of which has labored to give birth to the other,"[24] is rarely celebrated in patriarchal religion and culture. Christianity celebrates the father's relation to the son and the mother's relation to the son, but the story of mother and daughter is missing. So, too, in patriarchal literature and psychology the mothers and the daughters rarely exist. Volumes have been written about the oedipal complex, but little has been written about the girl's relation to her mother. Moreover, as de Beauvoir has noted, the mother–daughter relation is distorted in patriarchy because the mother must give her daughter over to men in a male-defined culture in which women are viewed as inferior. The mother must socialize her daughter to become subordinate to men, and if her daughter challenges patriarchal norms, the mother is likely to defend the patriarchal structures against her own daughter.[25]

These patterns are changing in the new culture created by women in which the bonds of women to women are beginning to be celebrated. Holly Near has written several songs that celebrate women's bonds and women's heritage. In one of her finest songs she writes of an "old-time woman" who is "waiting to die." A young woman feels for the life that has passed the old woman by and begins to cry, but the old woman looks her in the eye and says, "If I had not suffered, you wouldn't be wearing those jeans/ Being an old-time woman ain't as bad as it seems."[26] This song, which Near has said was inspired by her grandmother, expresses and celebrates a bond and a heritage passed down from one woman to another. In another of Near's songs, she sings of a "a hiking-boot mother who's seeing the world/For the first time with her own little girl." In this song, the mother tells the drifter who has been traveling with her to pack up and travel alone if he thinks "traveling three is a drag" because "I've got a little one who loves me as much as you need me/And darling, that's loving enough."[27] This song is significant because the mother places her relationship to her daughter above her relationship to a man, something women rarely do in patriarchy.[28]

Almost the only story of mothers and daughters that has been transmitted in Western culture is the myth of Demeter and Persephone that was the basis of religious rites celebrated by women only, the Thesmophoria, and later formed the basis of the Eleusian mysteries, which were open to all who spoke Greek. In this story, the daughter, Persephone, is raped away from her mother, Demeter, by the God of the underworld. Unwilling to accept this state of affairs, Demeter rages and withholds fertility from the earth until her daughter is returned to her. What is important for women in this story is that a mother fights for her daughter and for her relation to her daughter. This is completely different from the mother's relation to her daughter in patriarchy. The "mood" created by the story of Demeter and Persephone is one of celebration of the mother–daughter bond, and the "motivation" is for mothers and daughters to affirm the heritage passed on from mother to daughter and to reject the patriarchal pattern where the primary loyalties of mother and daughter must be to men.

The symbol of Goddess has much to offer women who are struggling to be rid of the "powerful, pervasive, and long-lasting moods and motivations" of devaluation of female power, denigration of the female body, distrust of female will, and denial of the women's bonds and heritage that have been engendered by patriarchal religion. As women struggle to create a new culture in which women's power, bodies, will, and bonds are celebrated, it seems natural that the Goddess would reemerge as symbol of the newfound beauty, strength, and power of women.

NOTES

1. From the original cast album, Buddah Records, 1976.

2. See Susan Rennie and Kristen Grimstad, "Spiritual Explorations Cross-Country," *Quest*, I(4), 1975, 49–51; and *WomanSpirit* magazine.

3. See Starhawk, "Witchcraft and Women's Culture," in this volume.

4. "Religion as a Cultural System," in William L. Lessa and Evon V. Vogt, eds., *Reader in Comparative Religion*, 2nd ed. (New York: Harper and Row, 1972), p. 206.

5. Geertz, p. 210.

6. Boston: Beacon Press, 1974, p. 13, italics added.

7. *The Second Sex*, trans. H. M. Parshley (New York: Alfred A. Knopf, 1953).

8. See Grimstad and Rennie.

9. *Les Guerilleres*, trans. David LeVay (New York: Avon Books, 1971), p. 89. Also quoted in Morgan MacFarland, "Witchcraft: The Art of Remembering," *Quest*, I(4), 1975, 41.

10. "Speaking for Myself," *Lady Unique*, I, 1976, 56.

11. Personal communication.

12. A term coined by Naomi Goldenberg to refer to reflection on the meaning of the symbol of Goddess.

13. This theory of the origins of the Western dualism is stated by Rosemary Ruether in *New Woman: New Earth* (New York: Seabury Press, 1975), and elsewhere.

14. Heinrich Kramer and Jacob Sprenger (New York: Dover, 1971), p. 47.

15. See Rita M. Gross, "Menstruation and Childbirth as Ritual and Religious Experience in the Religion of the Australian Aborigines," in *The Journal of the American Academy of Religion*, 45(4), 1977, Supplement 1147–1181.

16. *Through the Flower* (New York: Doubleday and Company, 1975), plate 4, pp. 106–107.

17. See Adrienne Rich, *Of Woman Born* (New York: Bantam Books, 1977), Chapters 6 and 7.

18. See James Mellaart, *Earliest Civilizations of the Near East* (New York: McGraw-Hill, 1965), p. 92.

19. Barbry My Own, "Ursa Maior: Menstrual Moon Celebration," in Anne Kent Rush, ed., *Moon, Moon* (Berkeley, Calif., and New York: Moon Books and Random House, 1976), pp. 374–387.

20. Starhawk, "Witchcraft and Women's Culture."

21. In Judy Chicago, pp. 213–217.

22. "The Human Situation: A Feminine View," in *Journal of Religion*, 40, 1960, 100–112.

23. *A Room of One's Own* (New York: Harcourt Brace Jovanovich, 1928), p. 86.

24. Rich, p. 226.

25. De Beauvior, pp. 448–449.

26. "Old Time Woman," lyrics by Jeffrey Langley and Holly Near, from *Holly Near: A Live Album*, Redwood Records, 1974.

27. "Started Out Fine," by Holly Near from *Holly Near: A Live Album*.

28. Rich, p. 223.

6.6 Witchcraft and Women's Culture

STARHAWK

Starhawk (b. 1951) is an American witch, feminist, and peace activist who teaches at several colleges in the San Francisco Bay area. Having been taught witchcraft as a college student, she practiced as a solitary for several years before forming her first coven, Compost. She later formed another coven, Honeysuckle (which was composed solely of women), and became the first national president of the Covenant of the Goddess (a church in the Bay area). Starhawk also founded Reclaiming, a feminist collective in San Francisco that offers classes, workshops, and public rituals in witchcraft, and that participates in peace activities and demonstrations.

Starhawk's first book, *The Spiral Dance: A Rebirth of the Ancient Religion of the Great Goddess*, was based on the faery tradition of witchcraft. Her other books include *Dreaming the Dark* (1982) and *Truth or Dare: Encounters of Power, Authority and Mystery* (1987). She is also a freelance screenwriter and novelist.

In the following essay, which was first discussed at the 1977 meetings of the American Academy of Religion, Starhawk discusses the history and philosophy of witchcraft. Focusing on the history of Northern Europe, she notes that traces of the ancient practice of witchcraft can be found in many places. She also observes that the old tradition of witchcraft initially coexisted with the newer religion of Christianity. But this peaceful coexistence ended in the Middle Ages, when the persecution of witches and the distortion of the meaning of witchcraft became widespread. Because of this persecution, and the later emphasis on science during the Age of Reason, much of the traditional wisdom was lost. Starhawk believes, however, that the present era is marked by a reawakening of awareness of the Great Goddess, and a renewed interest in the "craft of the wise."

Like Christ in the preceding selection, Starhawk contrasts the philosophy and rituals of witchcraft with those of the Judeo-Christian tradition. In opposition to a transcendent Father God, witchcraft recognizes the existence of an immanent Earth Mother. In opposition to dualisms between God and nature and between spirit and flesh, witchcraft recognizes the interconnectedness and sacredness of all life. In opposition to dogma and dependence, witchcraft contains no set of doctrines and recognizes the autonomy of each practitioner. Finally, in opposition to "the formless, abstracted *agape* of the early Christians," witchcraft emphasizes the passionate, personal, uniting love that individual humans feel for other individuals.

Questions for Thought

1. Why, according to Starhawk, were witches persecuted during the Middle Ages? Why do you think they were persecuted?
2. What are the essential philosophical or religious differences between witchcraft and Christianity? Which set of beliefs is closer to your own views?

3. What does the Goddess symbolize within the tradition of witchcraft? How do Starhawk's views on the Goddess compare with and differ from the views of Carol Christ?
4. Which psychological or spiritual qualities are most valued by witchcraft? Do you agree that these qualities ought to be valued? Why or why not?
5. What, according to Starhawk, is the structure and purpose of a coven? What are the principal benefits of belonging to a coven?
6. Why do craft rituals take place in a circle? How does Starhawk's explanation compare with what Black Elk says about the function of the circle in Native American religion?
7. If you were to create a religious ritual, what form would it take?

THE UNHEWN STONES ARE NEWLY RISEN. WITHIN their circle, an old woman raises a flint knife and points it toward the bright full moon. She cries out, a wail echoed by her clan folk as they begin the dance. They circle wildly around the central fire, feeling the power rise within them until they unite in ecstatic frenzy. The priestess cries again, and all drop to the earth, exhausted but filled with a deep sense of peace. A cup of ale is poured into the fire, and the flames leap up high. "Blessed be the mother of all life," the priestess says, "May She be generous to Her children."

The birth is a difficult one, but the midwife has brought many women through worse. Still, she is worried. She has herbs to open the womb and stop the blood, herbs to bring sleep, and others to bring forgetfulness of pain. But now her baskets are almost empty. This year she could not go gathering at the proper times of the moon and sun. The new priest and his spies are everywhere—if she were to be caught digging simples in the moonlight it would be sure proof of witchcraft, not just against herself but against her daughters and sisters and her daughter's daughters. As she pours out the last of her broth for the laboring woman, the midwife sighs. "Blessed Tana, Mother of mothers," she breathes softly, "When will the old ways return?"

The child is in a state of shock. Her memories of the last three days are veiled in a haze of smoke and noise that seem to swirl toward this climax of acrid smells and hoarse shouting. The priest's grip is clawlike as he forces her to watch the cruel drama in the center of the square. The girl's eyes are open, but her mind has flown far away, and what she sees is not the scene before her: her mother, the stake, the flames. She is running through the open field behind their cottage, smelling only clean wind, seeing only clear sky. The priest looks down at her blank face and crosses himself in fear. "Devil's spawn!" he spits on the ground. "If I had my way, we'd hold to custom and burn you too!"

It is the night of the full moon. Nine women stand in a circle, on a rocky hill above the city. The western sky is rosy with the setting sun; in the east the moon's face begins to peer above the horizon. Below, electric lights wink on the ground like fallen stars. A young woman raises a steel knife and cries out, a wail echoed by the others as they begin the dance. They circle wildly around a cauldron of smoldering herbs, feeling the power rise within them until they unite in ecstasy. The priestess cries again, and all drop to the earth, exhausted, but filled with an overwhelming sense of peace. The woman pours out a cup of wine onto the earth, refills it and raises it high. "Hail, Tana, Mother of mothers!"

"Witchcraft and Women's Culture" by Starhawk from *Womanspirit Rising* by Carol P. Christ and Judith Plaskow. © 1979 by Carol P. Christ and Judith Plaskow. Reprinted by permission of HarperCollins Publishers, Inc. and the author.

she cries. "Awaken from your long sleep, and return to your children again!"

From earliest times,[1] women have been witches, *wicce*, "wise ones"—priestesses, diviners, midwives, poets, healers, and singers of songs of power. Woman-centered culture, based on the worship of the Great Goddess, underlies the beginnings of all civilization. Mother Goddess was carved on the walls of paleolithic caves, and painted in the shrines of the earliest cities, those of the Anatolian plateau. For her were raised the giant stone circles, the henges of the British Isles, the dolmens and cromlechs of the later Celtic countries, and for her the great passage graves of Ireland were dug. In her honor, sacred dancers leaped the bulls in Crete and composed lyric hymns within the colleges of the holy isles of the Mediterranean. Her mysteries were celebrated in secret rites at Eleusis, and her initiates included some of the finest minds of Greece. Her priestesses discovered and tested the healing herbs and learned the secrets of the human mind and body that allowed them to ease the pain of childbirth, to heal wounds and cure diseases, and to explore the realm of dreams and the unconscious. Their knowledge of nature enabled them to tame sheep and cattle, to breed wheat and corn from grasses and weeds, to forge ceramics from mud and metal from rock, and to track the movements of moon, stars, and sun.

Witchcraft, "the craft of the wise," is the last remnant in the west of the time of women's strength and power. Through the dark ages of persecution, the covens of Europe preserved what is left of the mythology, rituals, and knowledge of the ancient matricentric (mother-centered) times. The great centers of worship in Anatolia, Malta, Iberia, Brittany, and Sumeria are now only silent stones and works of art we can but dimly understand. Of the mysteries of Eleusis, we have literary hints; the poems of Sappho survive only in fragments. The great collections of early literature and science were destroyed by patriarchal forces—the library of Alexandria burnt by Caesar, Charlemagne's collection of lore burnt by his son Louis "the Pious," who was offended at its "paganism." But the craft remains, in spite of all efforts to stamp it out, as a living tradition of Goddess-centered worship that traces its roots back to the time before the triumph of patriarchy.

The old religion of witchcraft before the advent of Christianity was an earth-centered, nature-oriented worship that venerated the Goddess, the source of life, as well as her son–lover–consort, who was seen as the Horned God of the hunt and animal life. Earth, air, water, fire, streams, seas, wells, beasts, trees, grain, the planets, sun, and most of all, the moon, were seen as aspects of deity. On the great seasonal festivals—the solstices and equinoxes, and the eves of May, August, November, and February,—all the countryside would gather to light huge bonfires, feast, dance, sing, and perform the rituals that assured abundance throughout the year.

When Christianity first began to spread, the country people held to the old ways, and for hundreds of years the two faiths coexisted quite peacefully. Many people followed both religions, and country priests in the twelfth and thirteenth centuries were frequently upbraided by church authorities for dressing in skins and leading the dance at the pagan festivals.

But in the thirteenth and fourteenth centuries, the church began persecution of witches, as well as Jews and "heretical" thinkers. Pope Innocent the VIII, with his Bull of 1484, intensified a campaign of torture and death that would take the lives of an estimated 9 million people, perhaps 80 percent of whom were women.

The vast majority of victims were not coven members or even necessarily witches. They were old widows whose property was coveted by someone else, young children with "witch blood," midwives who furnished the major competition to the male-dominated medical profession, free-thinkers who asked the wrong questions.

An enormous campaign of propaganda accompanied the witch trials as well. Witches were said to have sold their souls to the devil, to practice obscene and disgusting rites, to blight crops and murder children. In many areas, the witches did worship a Horned God as the spirit of the hunt, of animal life and vitality, a concept far from the power of evil that was the Christian devil. Witches were free and open about sexuality—but their rites were "obscene" only to those who viewed the human body itself as filthy and evil. Questioning or disbelieving any of the slander was itself considered proof of witchcraft or heresy, and the falsehoods that for hundreds of years could not be openly challenged had their effect. Even today, the word *witch* is often automatically associated with "evil."

With the age of reason in the eighteenth century, belief in witches, as in all things psychic and supernatural, began to fade. The craft as a religion was forgotten; all that remained were the wild stories of broomstick flights, magic potions, and the summoning of spectral beings.

Memory of the true craft faded everywhere except within the hidden covens. With it, went the memory of women's heritage and history, of our ancient roles as leaders, teachers, healers, seers. Lost, also, was the conception of the Great Spirit, as manifest in nature, in life, in woman. Mother Goddess slept, leaving the world to the less than gentle rule of the God-Father.

The Goddess has at last stirred from sleep, and women are reawakening to our ancient power. The feminist movement, which began as a political, economic, and social struggle, is opening to a spiritual dimension. In the process, many women are discovering the old religion, reclaiming the word *witch* and, with it, some of our lost culture.

Witchcraft, today, is a kaleidoscope of diverse traditions, rituals, theologies, and structures. But underneath the varying forms is a basic orientation common to all the craft. The outer forms of religion—the particular words said, the signs made, the names used—are less important to us than the inner forms, which cannot be defined or described but must be felt and intuited.

The craft is earth religion, and our basic orientation is to the earth, to life, to nature. There is no dichotomy between spirit and flesh, no split between Godhead and the world. The Goddess is manifest in the world; she brings life into being, *is* nature, *is* flesh. Union is not sought outside the world in some heavenly sphere or through dissolution of the self into the void beyond the senses. Spiritual union is found in life, within nature, passion, sensuality—through being fully human, fully one's self.

Our great symbol for the Goddess is the moon, whose three aspects reflect the three stages in women's lives and whose cycles of waxing and waning coincide with women's menstrual cycles. As the new moon or crescent, she is the Maiden, the Virgin—not chaste, but belonging to herself alone, not bound to any man. She is the wild child, lady of the woods, the huntress, free and untamed—Artemis, Kore, Aradia, Nimue. White is her color. As the full moon, she is the mature woman, the sexual being, the mother and nurturer, giver of life, fertility, grain, offspring, potency, joy—Tana, Demeter, Diana, Ceres, Mari. Her colors are the red of blood and the green of growth. As waning or dark moon, she is the old woman, past menopause, the hag or crone that is ripe with wisdom, patroness of secrets, prophecy, divination, inspiration, power—Hecate, Ceridwen, Kali, Anna. Her color is the black of night.

The Goddess is also earth—Mother Earth, who sustains all growing things, who is the body, our bones and cells. She is air—the winds that move in the trees and over the waves, breath. She is the fire of the hearth, of the blazing bonfire and the fuming volcano; the power of transformation and change. And she is water—the sea, original source of life; the rivers, streams, lakes and wells; the blood that flows in the rivers of our veins. She is mare, cow, cat, owl, crane, flower, tree, apple, seed, lion, sow, stone, woman. She is found in the world around us, in the cycles and seasons of nature, and in mind, body, spirit, and emotions within each of us. Thou art Goddess. I am Goddess. All that lives (and all that is, lives), all that serves life, is Goddess.

Because witches are oriented to earth and to life, we value spiritual qualities that I feel are especially important to women, who have for so long been conditioned to be passive, submissive and weak. The craft values independence, personal strength, *self*—not petty selfishness but that deep core of strength within that makes us each a unique child of the Goddess. The craft has no dogma to stifle thought, no set of doctrines that have to be believed. Where authority exists, within covens, it is always coupled with the freedom every covener has, to leave at any time. When self is valued—in ourselves—we can see that self is everywhere.

Passion and emotion—that give depth and color and meaning to human life—are also valued. Witches strive to be in touch with feelings, even if they are sometimes painful, because the joy and pleasure and ecstasy available to a fully alive person make it worth occasional suffering. So-called negative emotion—anger—is valued as well, as a sign that something is wrong and that action needs to be taken. Witches prefer to handle anger by taking action and making changes rather than by detaching ourselves from our feelings in order to reach some nebulous, "higher" state.

Most of all, the craft values love. The Goddess' only law is "Love unto all beings." But the love we value is not the airy flower power of the hippies or the formless, abstracted *agape* of the early Christians. It is passionate, sensual, personal love, *eros*, falling in love, mother–child love, the love of one unique human being for other individuals, with all their personal traits and idiosyncrasies. Love is not something that can be radiated out in solitary meditation—it manifests itself in relationships and interactions with other people. It is often said "You cannot be a witch alone"—because to be a witch is to be a lover, a lover of the Goddess, and a lover of other human beings.

The coven is still the basic structure of the craft, and generally covens meet at the times of full moons and the major festivals, although some meet also on new moons and a few meet once a week. A coven is a small group, at most of thirteen members—for the thirteen full moons of the year. Its small size is important. Within the coven, a union, a merging of selves in a close bond of love and trust, takes place. A coven becomes an energy pool each member can draw on. But, because the group remains small, there is never the loss of identity and individuality that can happen in a mass. In a coven, each person's individuality is extremely important. Each personality colors and helps create the group identity, and each member's energy is vital to the working of the group.

Covens are separate and autonomous, and no one outside the coven has any authority over its functioning. Some covens may be linked in the same tradition—meaning they share the same rituals and symbology—but there is no hierarchy of rule. Elder witches can and do give advice, but only those within the coven may actually make decisions.

Covens are extremely diverse. There are covens of hereditary witches who have practiced rites unchanged for hundreds of years, and covens who prefer to make up their own rituals and may never do the same thing twice. There are covens of "perfect couples"—an even number of women and men permanently paired, and covens of lesbian feminists or of women who simply prefer to explore women's spirituality in a space removed from men. There are covens of gay men and covens that just don't worry about sexual polarities. A few covens are authoritarian—with a high priestess or high priest who makes most of the decisions. (Coveners, of course, always have the option of leaving.) Most are democratic, if not anarchic, but usually older or more experienced members—"elders"—assume leadership and responsibility. Actual roles in rituals are often rotated among qualified coveners.

Rituals also vary widely. A craft ritual might involve wild shouting and frenzied dancing, or silent meditation, or both. A carefully rehearsed drama might be enacted, or a spontaneous poetic chant carried on for an hour. Everyone may enter a deep trance and scry in a crystal ball—or they may pass around a bottle of wine and laugh uproariously at awful puns. The best rituals combine moments of intense ecstasy and spiritual union, with moments of raucous humor and occasional silliness. The craft is serious without being dry or solemn.

Whether formal or informal, every craft ritual takes place within a circle—a space considered to be "between the worlds," the human world and the realm of the Goddess. A circle can be cast, or created, in any physical space, from a moonlit hillside to the living room of a modern apartment. It may be outlined in stones, drawn in chalk or paint, or drawn invisibly with the point of a sword or ceremonial wand. It may be consecrated with incense, salt water, and a formal invocation to each of the four quarters of the universe, or created simply by having everyone join hands. The casting of the circle begins the ritual and serves as a transition into an expanded state of consciousness. The power raised by the ritual is contained within the circle so that it can reach a higher peak instead of dissipating.

The Goddess, and if desired, the Horned God (not all traditions of the craft relate to the male force) can be invoked once the circle is cast. An invocation may be set beforehand, written out and memorized, but in our coven we find the most effective invocations are those that come to us spontaneously, out of the inspiration of the season, the phase of the moon, and the particular mood and energy of the moment. Often we invoke the Goddess by chanting together a line or phrase repeated over and over: "Moon mother bright light of all earth sky, we call you" is an example. As we chant, we find

rhythms, notes, melodies, and words seem to flow through us and burst out in complex and beautiful patterns.

Chanting, dancing, breathing, and concentrated will, all contribute to the raising of power, which is the essential part of a craft ritual. Witches conceive of psychic energy as having form and substance that can be perceived and directed by those with a trained awareness. The power generated within the circle is built into a cone form, and at its peak is released—to the Goddess, to reenergize the members of the coven, or to do a specific work such as a healing.

When the cone is released, any scattered energy that is left is grounded, put back into the earth, by falling to the ground, breathing deeply, and relaxing. High-energy states cannot be maintained indefinitely without becoming a physical and emotional drain—any more than you could stay high on methedrine forever without destroying your body. After the peak of the cone, it is vital to let go of the power and return to a calm, relaxed state. Silent meditation, trance, or psychic work are often done in this part of the ritual.

Energy is also shared in tangible form—wine, cakes, fruit, cheesecake, brownies, or whatever people enjoy eating. The Goddess is invited to share with everyone, and a libation is poured to her first. This part of the ritual is relaxed and informally social, devoted to laughing, talking, sharing of news and any business that must be done.

At the end, the Goddess is thanked and bid farewell, and the circle is formally opened. Ending serves as a transition back into ordinary space and time. Rituals finish with a kiss and a greeting of "Merry meet, merry part, and merry meet again."

The underlying forms of craft rituals evolved out of thousands of years of experience and understanding of human needs and the potentials of human consciousness. That understanding, which is part of women's lost heritage, is invaluable, not just in the context of rituals and spiritual growth, but also for those working toward political and social change, because human needs and human energies behave the same in any context.

Witches understand that energy, whether it is psychic, emotional, or physical, always flows in cycles. It rises and falls, peaks and drops, and neither end of the cycle can be sustained indefinitely, any more than you could run forever without stopping. Intense levels of energy must be released and then brought down and grounded; otherwise the energy dissipates or even turns destructive. If, in a ritual, you tried to maintain a peak of frenzy for hours and hours, you would find that after a while the energy loses its joyful quality, and instead of feeling union and ecstasy, you begin to feel irritated and exhausted. Political groups that try to maintain an unremitting level of anger—a high-energy state—also run out of steam in precisely the same way. Releasing the energy and grounding out allows the power itself to work freely. It clears channels and allows you to rest and recharge and become ready for the next swing into an up cycle. Releasing energy does not mean losing momentum; rather, real movement, real change, happens in a rhythmic pattern of many beats, not in one unbroken blast of static.

Craft rituals also add an element of drama and fantasy to one's life. They allow us to act out myths and directly experience archetypes of symbolic transformation. They allow us, as adults, to recapture the joy of childhood make-believe, of dressing up, of pretending, of play. Magic, by Dion Fortune's definition, "the art of changing consciousness at will," is not so far removed from the creative fantasy states we enter so easily as children, when our dolls become alive, our bicycles become wild horses, ourselves arctic explorers or queens. Allowing ourselves, as adults, to play and fantasize with others, puts us in touch with the creative child within, with a deep and rich source of inspiration.

The craft also helps us open our intuitive and psychic abilities. Although witchcraft is commonly associated with magic and the use of extrasensory powers, not all covens put a great deal of stress on psychic training. Worship is more often the main focus of activity. However, any craft ritual involves some level of psychic awareness just in sensing the energy that is raised.

Ordinarily, the way into the craft is through initiation into an already established coven. However, because covens are limited in size and depend on some degree of harmony between personalities, it is often difficult to find one that is open to new members and that fits your preferences. In San Francisco, Los Angeles, and New York, covens often run open study groups and can be found through publications and open universities. In other areas of the country, it may be difficult to locate a practicing coven at all.

However, there is nothing to stop you from starting a coven or a *circle*—a term I use for a group whose members meet for rituals but are not formally initiated—on your own. Women, especially, are more and more joining together to explore a Goddess-oriented spirituality and to create rituals and symbols that are meaningful to us today. Starting your own circle requires imagination, creativity, and experimentation, but it is a tremendously exciting process. You will miss formal psychic training—but you may discover on your own more than anyone else could teach you. Much of what is written on the craft is biased in one way or another, so weed out what is useful to you and ignore the rest.

I see the next few years as being crucial in the transformation of our culture away from the patriarchal death cults and toward the love of life, of nature, of the female principle. The craft is only one path among the many opening up for women, and many of us will blaze new trails as we explore the uncharted country of our own interiors. The heritage, the culture, the knowledge of the ancient priestesses, healers, poets, singers, and seers were nearly lost, but a seed survived the flames that will blossom in a new age into thousands of flowers. The long sleep of

Mother Goddess is ended. May She awaken in each of our hearts—Merry meet, merry part, and blessed be.

NOTE

1. This article is limited to the history of traditions that come from northern Europe. Southern and eastern Europe, Asia, India, Africa, and the Americas all have rich traditions of Goddess religions and matricentric cultures, but to even touch on them all would be impossible in a short essay. The history presented here is the "inner" or "mythic" history that provides a touchstone for modern witches. Like the histories of all peoples, its truth is intuited in the meaning it gives to life, even though it may be recognized that scholars might dispute some facets of the story.

6.7   Why I Am a Pagan

LIN YUTANG

Lin Yutang (1895–1976) was born in Changchow, China. After attending St. John's College, Harvard University, and the University of Leipzig (from which he received his Ph.D. in 1923), Lin returned to China where he became a professor of English philology at Peking National University. He later taught at National Amoy University and served as chancellor of Nanyang University in Singapore. Lin also briefly worked in the Ministry of Foreign Affairs of the Chinese government and headed the arts and letters division of UNESCO in Paris. Lin, who resided in the United States for thirty years and was a critic of the Chinese Communist Revolution, died in Hong Kong.

Throughout his career, Lin was a prolific editor, translator, essayist, and novelist. He edited and translated many anthologies of Chinese literature and philosophy, and compiled a Chinese–English modern-usage dictionary, which was one of his proudest achievements. His other writings include *My Country and My People* (1935); *A History of the Press and Public Opinion in China* (1936); *Confucius Saw Nancy, and Essays About Nothing* (1937); *The Importance of Living* (1937); *Moment in Peking: A Novel of Contemporary Chinese Life* (1939); *On the Wisdom of America* (1950); *The Secret Name* (1958); *The Importance of Understanding* (1960); and *The Pleasures of a Nonconformist* (1962).

In the following selection, which is excerpted from *The Importance of Living*, Lin describes the personal journey that leads him from Christianity to paganism. He also contrasts pagan belief with Christian belief, and provides several reasons for preferring the former. In one of his most powerful contrasts, Lin says that Christians have the security of having a wise father watch over them, but that such belief promotes immaturity and dependence. Pagans, on the other hand, are like orphans—less secure than Christians, but much more independent.

Lin also argues that the pagan world is simpler than the Christian world, and in many ways less arrogant. Whereas Christianity is characterized by a complex theology of sin and redemption, paganism rejects theology as irrelevant to human existence. Whereas Christianity believes that morality requires the threat of eternal reward or punishment, paganism believes that virtue is its own reward. And whereas Christianity expresses its arrogance by believing in human immortality and God's concern for humankind, paganism accepts the natural cycles of life and death. However, Lin stresses that while being pagan means being non-Christian, it does not mean being atheistic or godless. While pagans would find any claim to know the true nature of God as another example of Christian arrogance, they do recognize the existence of divine mystery. Indeed, in a provocative statement near the end of the selection, Lin suggests that the path of the pagan is closer to the path of primitive Christianity than is the path of later Christian revelation and theology.

Questions for Thought

1. What, according to Lin, is a pagan? Would you classify yourself as a pagan? Why or why not?
2. What events in Lin's life lead him to become a pagan?
3. How, according to Lin, does pagan belief differ from Christian belief? Can you think of other differences?
4. In what ways, if any, are Lin's criticisms of Christianity similar to the criticisms made by Starhawk and Christ?
5. Lin claims that he has no feeling of sin. What do you think that he means by sin? Do you feel sinful? If so, why do you think that you feel this way?
6. Why does Lin reject the concept of revelation? Do you think that revelation is an important religious concept? Why or why not?

RELIGION IS ALWAYS AN INDIVIDUAL, PERSONAL thing. Every person must work out his own views of religion, and if he is sincere, God will not blame him, however it turns out. Every man's religious experience is valid for himself, for . . . it is not something that can be argued about. But the story of an honest soul struggling with religious problems, told in a sincere manner, will always be of benefit to other people. That is why, in speaking about religion, I must get away from generalities and tell my personal story.

I am a pagan. The statement may be taken to imply a revolt against Christianity; and yet "revolt" seems a harsh word and does not correctly describe the state of mind of a man who has passed through a very gradual evolution, step by step, away from Christianity, during which he clung desperately, with love and piety, to a series of tenets which, against his will, were slipping away from him. Because there was never any hatred, therefore it is impossible to speak of a rebellion.

As I was born in a pastor's family and at one time prepared for the Christian ministry, my natural emotions were on the side of religion during the entire struggle rather than against it. In this conflict of emotions and understanding, I gradually arrived at a position where I had, for instance, definitely renounced the doctrine of redemption, a position which could most simply

Reprinted by permission of Taiyi Lin Lai and Hsiang Ju Lin.

be described as that of a pagan. It was, and still is, a condition of belief concerning life and the universe in which I feel natural and at ease, without having to be at war with myself. The process came as naturally as the weaning of a child or the dropping of a ripe apple on the ground; and when the time came for the apple to drop, I would not interfere with its dropping. In Taoistic phraseology, this is but to live in the Tao, and in Western phraseology it is but being sincere with oneself and with the universe, according to one's lights. I believe no one can be natural and happy unless he is intellectually sincere with himself, and to be natural is to be in heaven. To me, being a pagan is just being natural.

"To be a pagan" is no more than a phrase, like "to be a Christian." It is no more than a negative statement, for, to the average reader, to be a pagan means only that one is not a Christian; and, since "being a Christian" is a very broad and ambiguous term, the meaning of "not being a Christian" is equally ill-defined. It is all the worse when one defines a pagan as one who does not believe in religion or in God, for we have yet to define what is meant by "God" or by the "religious attitude toward life." Great pagans have always had a deeply reverent attitude toward nature. We shall therefore have to take the word in its conventional sense and mean by it simply a man who does not go to church (except for an æsthetic inspiration, of which I am still capable), does not belong to the Christian fold, and does not accept its usual, orthodox tenets.

On the positive side, a Chinese pagan, the only kind of which I can speak with any feeling of intimacy, is one who starts out with this earthly life as all we can or need to bother about, wishes to live intently and happily as long as his life lasts, often has a sense of the poignant sadness of this life and faces it cheerily, has a keen appreciation of the beautiful and the good in human life wherever he finds them, and regards doing good as its own satisfactory reward. I admit, however, he feels a slight pity or contempt for the "religious" man, who does good in order to get to heaven and who, by implication, would not do good if he were not lured by heaven or threatened with hell. If this statement is correct, I believe there are a great many more pagans in this country than are themselves aware of it. The modern liberal Christian and the pagan are really close, differing only when they start out to *talk* about God.

I think I know the depths of religious experience, for I believe one can have this experience without being a great theologian like Cardinal Newman—otherwise Christianity would not be worth having or must already have been horribly misinterpreted. As I look at it at present, the difference in spiritual life between a Christian believer and a pagan is simply this: the Christian believer lives in a world governed and watched over by God, to whom he has a constant personal relationship, and therefore in a world presided over by a kindly father; his conduct is also often uplifted to a level consonant with this consciousness of being a child of God, no doubt a level which is difficult for a human mortal to maintain consistently at all periods of his life or of the week or even of the day; his actual life varies between living on the human and the truly religious levels.

On the other hand, the pagan lives in this world like an orphan, without the benefit of that consoling feeling that there is always someone in heaven who cares and who will, when that spiritual relationship called prayer is established, attend to his private personal welfare. It is no doubt a less cheery world; but there is the benefit and dignity of being an orphan who by necessity has learned to be independent, to take care of himself, and to be more mature, as all orphans are. It was this feeling rather than any intellectual belief—this feeling of dropping into a world without the love of God—that really scared me till the very last moment of my conversion to paganism; I felt, like many born Christians, that if a personal God did not exist the bottom would be knocked out of this universe.

And yet a pagan can come to the point where he looks on that perhaps warmer and cheerier world as at the same time a more childish, I am tempted to say a more adolescent, world; useful and workable, if one keep the illusion unspoiled, but no more and no less justifiable than a truly Buddhist way of life; also a more beautifully coloured world but consequently less solidly true and therefore of less worth. For me personally, the suspicion that anything is coloured or not solidly true is fatal. There is a price one must be willing to pay for truth; whatever the consequences, let us have it. This position is comparable to and psychologically the same as that of a murderer: if one has committed a murder, the best thing he can do next is to confess it. That is why I say it takes a little courage to become a pagan. But, after one has accepted the worst, one is also without fear. Peace of mind is that mental condition in which you have accepted the worst. (Here I see for myself the influence of Buddhist or Taoist thought.)

Or I might put the difference between a Christian and a pagan world like this: the pagan in me renounced Christianity out of both pride and humility, emotional pride and intellectual humility, but perhaps on the whole less out of pride than of humility. Out of emotional pride because I hated the idea that there should be any other reason for our behaving as nice, decent men and women than the simple fact that we are human beings; theoretically and if you want to go in for classifications, classify this as a typically humanist thought. But more out of humility, of intellectual humility, simply because I can no longer, with our astronomical knowledge, believe that an individual human being is so terribly important in the eyes of that Great Creator, living as the individual does, an infinitesimal speck on this earth, which is an infinitesimal speck of the solar system, which is again an infinitesimal speck of the universe of solar systems. The audacity of man and his presumptuous arrogance are what stagger me. What right have we to conceive of the character of a Supreme Being, of whose work we can see only a millionth part, and to postulate about His attributes?

The importance of the human individual is undoubtedly one of the basic tenets of Christianity. But let us see what ridiculous arrogance that leads to in the usual practice of Christian daily life.

Four days before my mother's funeral there was a pouring rain, and if it continued, as was usual in July in Changchow, the city would be flooded, and there could be no funeral. As most of us came from Shanghai, the delay would have meant some inconvenience. One of my relatives—a rather extreme but not an unusual example of a Christian believer in China—told me that she had faith in God, Who would always provide for His children. She prayed, and the rain stopped, apparently in order that a tiny family of Christians might have their funeral without delay. But the implied idea that, but for us, God would willingly subject the tens of thousands of Changchow inhabitants to a devastating flood, as was often the case, or that He did not stop the rain because of them but because of us who wanted to have a conveniently dry funeral, struck me as an unbelievable type of selfishness. I cannot imagine God providing for such selfish children.

There was also a Christian pastor who wrote the story of his life, attesting to many evidences of the hand of God in his life, for the purpose of glorifying God. One of the evidences adduced was that, when he had got together 600 silver dollars to buy his passage to America, God lowered the rate of exchange on the day this so very important individual was to buy his passage. The difference in the rate of exchange for 600 silver dollars could have been at most ten or twenty dollars, and God was willing to rock the bourses in Paris, London, and New York in order that this curious child of His might save ten or twenty dollars. Let us remind ourselves that this way of glorifying God is not at all unusual in any part of Christendom.

Oh, the impudence and conceit of man, whose span of life is but three-score and ten! Mankind as an aggregate may have a significant history, but man as an individual, in the words of Su Tungp'o, is no more than a grain of millet in an ocean or an insect *fuyu* born in the morning and dying at eve, as compared with the universe. The Christian will not be humble. He will not be satisfied with the aggregate immortality of his great stream of life, of which he is already a part, flowing on to eternity, like a mighty stream which empties into the great sea and changes and yet does not change. The clay vessel will ask of the potter, "Why hast thou cast me into this shape and why hast thou made me so brittle?" The clay vessel is not satisfied that it can leave little vessels of its own kind when it cracks up. Man is not satisfied that he has received this marvellous body, this almost divine body. He wants to live for ever! And he will not let God alone. He must say his prayers and he must pray daily for small personal gifts from the Source of All Things. Why can't he let God alone?

There was once a Chinese scholar who did not believe in Buddhism, and his mother who did. She was devout and would acquire merit for herself by mumbling, *"Namu omitabha!"* a thousand times day and night. But every time she started to call Buddha's name, her son would call, "Mamma!" The mother became annoyed. "Well," said the son, "don't you think Buddha would be equally annoyed, if he could hear you?"

My father and mother were devout Christians. To hear my father conduct the evening family prayers was enough. And I was a sensitively religious child. As a pastor's son I received the facilities of missionary education, profited from its benefits, and suffered from its weaknesses. For its benefits I was always grateful and its weaknesses I turned into my strength. For according to Chinese philosophy there are no such things in life as good and bad luck.

I was forbidden to attend Chinese theatres, never allowed to listen to Chinese minstrel singers, and entirely cut apart from the great Chinese folk tradition and mythology. When I entered a missionary college, the little foundation in classical Chinese given me by my father was completely neglected. Perhaps it was just as well—so that later, after a completely Westernized education, I could go back to it with the freshness and vigorous delight of a child of the West in an Eastern wonderland. The complete substitution of the fountain pen for the writing brush during my college and adolescent period was the greatest luck I ever had and preserved for me the freshness of the Oriental mental world unspoiled, until I should become ready for it. If Vesuvius had not covered up Pompeii, Pompeii would not be so well preserved, and the imprints of carriage-wheels on her stone pavements would not be so clearly marked to-day. The missionary college education was my Vesuvius.

Thinking was always dangerous. More than that, thinking was always allied with the devil. The conflict during the collegiate–adolescent period, which, as usual, was my most religious period, between a heart which felt the beauty of the Christian life and a head which had a tendency to reason everything away, was taking place. Curiously enough, I can remember no moments of torment or despair, of the kind that drove Tolstoy almost to suicide. At every stage I felt myself a unified Christian, harmonious in my belief, only a little more liberal than the last, and accepting some fewer Christian doctrines. Anyway, I could always go back to the Sermon on the Mount. The poetry of a saying like "Consider the lilies of the field" was too good to be untrue. It was that and the consciousness of the inner Christian life that gave me strength.

But the doctrines were slipping away terribly. Superficial things first began to annoy me. The "resurrection of the flesh," long disproved when the expected second coming of Christ in the first century did not come off and the Apostles did not rise bodily from their graves, was still there in the Apostles' Creed. This was one of those things.

Then, enrolling in a theological class and initiated into the holy of holies, I learned that another article in the creed, the virgin birth, was open to question, different deans in American theological seminaries holding different views. It enraged me that Chinese believers should be required to believe categorically in this article before they could be baptized, while the theologians of the same church regarded it as an open question. It did not seem sincere and somehow it did not seem right.

Further schooling in meaningless commentary scholarship as to the whereabouts of the "water gate" and such minutiæ completely relieved me of responsibility to take such theological studies seriously, and I made a poor showing in my grades. My professors considered that I was not cut out for the Christian ministry, and the bishop thought I might as well leave. They would not waste their instruction on me. Again this seems to me now a blessing in disguise. I doubt, if I had gone on with it and put on the clerical garb, whether it would have been so easy for me to be honest with myself later on. But this feeling of rebellion against the discrepancy of the beliefs required of the theologian and of the average convert was the nearest kind of feeling to what I may call a "revolt."

By this time I had already arrived at the position that the Christian theologians were the greatest enemies of the Christian religion. I could never get over two great contradictions. The first was that the theologians had made the entire structure of the Christian belief hang upon the existence of an apple. If Adam had not eaten an apple, there would be no original sin, and if there were no original sin, there would be no need of redemption. That was plain to me, whatever the symbolic value of the apple might be. This seemed to me preposterously unfair to the teachings of Christ, who never said a word about the original sin or the redemption. Anyway, from pursuing literary studies, I feel, like all modern Americans, no consciousness of sin and simply do not believe in it. All I know is that

if God loves me only half as much as my mother does, He will not send me to Hell. That is a final fact of my inner consciousness, and for no religion could I deny its truth.

Still more preposterous another proposition seemed to me. This was the argument that, when Adam and Eve ate an apple during their honeymoon, God was so angry that He condemned their posterity to suffer from generation to generation for that little offence but that, when the same posterity murdered the same God's only Son, God was so delighted that He forgave them all. No matter how people explain and argue, I cannot get over this simple untruth. This was the last of the things that troubled me.

Still, even after my graduation, I was a zealous Christian and voluntarily conducted a Sunday school at Tsing Hua, a non-Christian college at Peking, to the dismay of many faculty members. The Christmas meeting of the Sunday school was a torture to me, for here I was passing on to the Chinese children the tale of herald angels singing upon a midnight clear when I did not believe it myself. Everything had been reasoned away, and only love and fear remained: a kind of clinging love for an all-wise God which made me feel happy and peaceful and suspect that I should not have been so happy and peaceful without that reassuring love—and fear of entering into a world of orphans.

Finally my salvation came. "Why," I reasoned with a colleague, "if there were no God, people would not do good and the world would go topsy-turvy."

"Why?" replied my Confucian colleague. "We should lead a decent human life simply because we are decent human beings," he said.

This appeal to the dignity of human life cut off my last tie to Christianity, and from then on I was a pagan.

It is all so clear to me now. The world of pagan belief is a simpler belief. It postulates nothing, and is obliged to postulate nothing. It seems to make the good life more immediately appealing by appealing to the good life alone. It better justifies doing good by making it unnecessary for doing good to justify itself. It does not encourage men to do, for instance, a simple act of charity by dragging in a series of hypothetical postulates—sin, redemption, the cross, laying up treasure in heaven, mutual obligation among men on account of a third-party relationship in heaven—all so unnecessarily complicated and roundabout, and none capable of direct proof. If one accepts the statement that doing good is its own justification, one cannot help regarding all theological baits to right living as redundant and tending to cloud the lustre of a moral truth. Love among men should be a final, absolute fact. We should be able just to look at each other and love each other without being reminded of a third party in heaven. Christianity seems to me to make morality appear unnecessarily difficult and complicated and sin appear tempting, natural, and desirable. Paganism, on the other hand, seems alone to be able to rescue religion from theology and restore it to its beautiful simplicity of belief and dignity of feeling.

In fact, I seem to be able to see how many theological complications arose in the first, second, and third centuries and turned the simple truths of the Sermon on the Mount into a rigid, self-contained structure to support a priestcraft as an endowed institution. The reason was contained in the word *revelation*—the revelation of a special mystery or divine scheme given to a prophet and kept by all apostolic succession, which was found necessary in all religions, from Mohammedanism and Mormonism to the Living Buddha's Lamaism and Mrs. Eddy's Christian Science, in order for each of them to handle exclusively a special, patented monopoly of salvation. All priestcraft lives on the common staple food of revelation. The simple truths of Christ's teaching on the Mount must be adorned, and the lily He so marvelled at must be gilded. Hence we have the "first Adam" and the "second Adam," and so on and so forth.

But Pauline logic, which seemed so convincing and unanswerable in the early days of the Christian era, seems weak and unconvincing to the more subtle modern critical consciousness; and in this discrepancy between the rigorous Asiatic deductive logic and the more pliable, more subtle appreciation of truth of the modern man, lies the weakness of the appeal to the Christian revelation or any revelation for the modern man. Therefore, only by a return to paganism and renouncing the revelation can one return to primitive (and for me more satisfying) Christianity.

It is wrong, therefore, to speak of a pagan as an irreligious man: irreligious he is only as one who refuses to believe in any special variety of revelation. A pagan always believes in God but would not like to say so, for fear of being misunderstood. All Chinese pagans believe in God, the most commonly met with designation in Chinese literature being the term *chaowu*, or the Creator of Things. The only difference is that the Chinese pagan is honest enough to leave the Creator of Things in a halo of mystery, toward whom he feels a kind of awed piety and reverence. What is more, that feeling suffices for him. Of the beauty of this universe, the clever artistry of the myriad things of this creation, the mystery of the stars, the grandeur of heaven, and the dignity of the human soul he is equally aware. But that again suffices for him. He accepts death as he accepts pain and suffering and weighs them against the gift of life and the fresh country breeze and the clear mountain moon and he does not complain. He regards bending to the will of Heaven as the truly religious and pious attitude and calls it "living in the Tao." If the Creator of Things wants him to die at seventy, he gladly dies at seventy. He also believes that "heaven's way always goes round" and that there is no permanent injustice in this world. He does not ask for more.

Writing Philosophically

The general introduction, the chapter introductions, and the summaries and questions for thought found in this text are intended to help you get more out of your reading and to aid in class discussion. They should also prove useful in studying for the exams that you will probably be required to take. Since most philosophy classes require writing in addition to exams, the following appendix offers some suggestions about how to write philosophically.

Choosing a Topic

Just as it was difficult for me to decide how to begin this book, it may be difficult for you to decide how to begin a philosophy paper. Of course, your first decision will be choosing a topic. Sometimes professors will provide a list of topics from which you must choose, and this will make it somewhat easier to decide. However, other professors will allow you to create your own topic. Whether the topics are provided or self-chosen, it is important that you come up with a topic that you can "relate to," that is, a topic that you find interesting and personally significant. If you can't relate to your topic, then you will most likely find the writing process to be boring. This boredom may be reflected in your finished product.

Another consideration in choosing a topic is making sure that the topic is narrow enough to be covered in the assigned length. For example, if you are required to write a short five- to ten-page paper, you don't want to choose the philosophical foundations of Hinduism or the philosophy of Simone de Beauvoir as your topic. These topics are much too broad to be covered in a short paper. However, you might decide to choose some aspect of one of these topics. For instance, rather than choosing the philosophical foundations of Hinduism, you might decide to write on the concept of self-identity found in one of the Upanishads. Or in the Simone de Beauvoir example, you might examine her claim that men have traditionally attempted to deny women their transcendence or freedom in light of your own experience.

Choosing a Literary Form

Once you have decided on an interesting and manageable topic, the next step in beginning a philosophy paper is choosing a literary form. While some professors may limit your choice to the essay form, others will allow you to choose other forms. These may include the dialogue form, the parable form, or the journal form. However, even if you are limited to the essay form, there are still choices to be made about the best way to proceed.

On the one hand, you may decide to use the straightforward essay strategy that you learned in English class. In its simplest formulation, the straightforward essay requires that you write an opening paragraph that introduces your topic and that contains a statement of your thesis or main point. You then write several other paragraphs in which you present evidence for your thesis in a clearly stated and coherent manner. After presenting your evidence, you conclude the paper with a paragraph that restates your thesis and summarizes your principal pieces of evidence.

On the other hand, you may decide to try something a bit less formulaic. One possibility, which is somewhat more difficult (but often more interesting), is to begin with a question or a small piece of evidence and then work toward your thesis or main point. In this type of essay, as in a detective story, the revelation comes at the end. Of course, abandoning the straightforward essay strategy involves a certain element of risk. In writing a straightforward essay, the thesis is clearly stated at the beginning, and this shows the reader where you are heading. Since this more complex type does not provide a road map for the reader, it is crucial that your essay be constructed in a well-conceived, coherent manner. In other words, you must lead your reader from point one to point two, from point two to point three, and so on, until he or she discovers your thesis or main point. If you do not provide clear connections between your main points, you may lose your reader along the way.

As mentioned above, some professors may allow you to use literary forms other than the essay form. One fairly common form found scattered throughout the history of philosophy is the dialogue form. Most of the writings of Plato, the ancient Greek philosopher, were composed in this form, as were many of the ancient philosophical writings of India and China. Modern philosophers such as David Hume, George Berkeley, Arthur Schopenhauer, and Robert Solomon have occasionally employed this form as well. The first two selections in Chapter 1 of this text represent good examples of the dialogue form.

If you are allowed to use this literary form and choose to do so, the best way to begin is to provide an introductory paragraph that provides the setting. I tell my own students to be as imaginative as possible. For example, after a long night of reading your philosophy text, you decide to go down to the local pub for a brew. When you arrive you notice two people shooting pool, and you decide to put down the next quarter. It turns out that the winner of the game in progress is Simone de Beauvoir. During your own game with her, you discuss some of her philosophical views. (Of course if you wish to discuss the views of more than one philosopher, you can play partners.)

The body of your dialogue should be constructed so that the reader can easily tell who said what. The easiest way of accomplishing this is to use the technique that was used in "A Dialogue with Death," the first selection in this text. You simply put the person's name in capital letters, followed by a colon, at the beginning of each part of the dialogue spoken by that person. The body of your dialogue should also show clearly the characters' positions on whatever issue they are discussing. By introducing yourself as a character in the dialogue, you can provide the evaluation or critical analysis required in most philosophy papers. Finally, the body of your dialogue should be written in a lively, conversational manner. There should be give and take, agreements and disagreements, questions and answers. By all means make sure that your dialogue is really a dialogue, and not two or three long monologues. For example, if you were writing the dialogue with Simone de Beauvoir mentioned above, you would not want to have de Beauvoir speak for a couple of pages giving her views, and then have yourself speak for a couple of pages giving your evaluation of what she said. Rather, the dialogue should frequently alternate between speakers, and there should be an animated exchange of ideas.

Another literary form that you may be allowed to use is the parable form. A parable is a short fictional story that is used to illustrate a point. A good example of a philosophical parable, the Buddhist parable of the poisoned arrow, is found in Chapter 3 of this text. The selection from Borges in Chapter 1 contains two parables as well.

What these selections have in common is that they tell an imaginative story as a way of supporting a philosophical point. For example, in the Buddhist parable of the poisoned arrow, the writer gives you the story of a man who has been shot with a poisoned arrow. Whereas many people would remove the arrow as quickly as possible, this man (a stereotypical philosopher no doubt) asks many questions about the arrow before removing it. While awaiting answers to these numerous questions, the man dies from the poison. The point of this parable is that many people clutter their lives with insignificant problems and questions, and thus forget about the really important thing in life—the removal of the poisoned arrow (in Buddhist philosophy, to remove the poisoned arrow means to eliminate *tanha*, or desire, from your life).

If you are allowed to use the parable form and choose to do so, the difficult thing is to come up with an engaging story that is clearly relevant to the point that you wish to make. If the story is not engaging, then you will not keep the reader's interest. And even if the story is engaging, the reader may not be able to see how it illustrates the point that you are trying to make. However, if you like to write creatively, then the parable form will provide you with an excellent opportunity to display your talents.

The final literary form that I will discuss is the journal form. While this form is not used in all philosophy classes, some professors require the writing of philosophical journals in lieu of papers. Others require a journal as well as papers, and still others give you the choice of writing papers or keeping a journal. While there are no examples of journal writing contained in this text, several well-known philosophers have written in this form. A good example of the journal form is found in the *Journals* of the Danish philosopher Søren Kierkegaard.

A philosophical journal consists of a collection of dated entries in which you discuss your ideas on a variety of topics. If the journal is a class assignment, you will probably be expected to devote at least some of the entries to the discussion of class materials. One of the nice things about philosophical journals is that they usually leave more room for personal expression than do philosophical essays, dialogues, or parables.

The following is an example of how a journal may be used as a class assignment. In my Comparative Religions class, I require that students keep a philosophical journal throughout the semester, and that they write in the journal at least two times per week. Although there is no set length to entries, I have found that entries of less than one page are usually not well developed. I tell my students that the journal should contain three types of entries, and that the ideal journal contains roughly one-third of each type. The first type of entry describes and reacts to class materials (the textbook, films shown in class, and class discussions). The second type of entry describes and reacts to nonclass materials related to the class content (textbooks from other classes, television programs, newspaper articles, conversations with friends outside of class, and so on, which deal with religious issues). Finally, the third type of entry is what I call personal reflection or meditation. In these entries, students are expected to write about their own spiritual beliefs and experiences. Many students are very creative with their journals. They include newspaper articles, poems and drawings. Most of my students find journal writing to be a refreshing alternative to class essays.

Doing Research

Once you have picked a topic and chosen a literary form, you may have to do research. While some writing assignments do not require outside research, longer essays generally do. Since most of you have written a research paper at some point in your educational career, I assume that you basically know how to proceed. I also assume that most of you know your way around a library. (However, if you are a new college student, you may find university libraries large and somewhat frightening. If this is the case, I suggest that you schedule a library tour, or at least make friends with the reference librarian.) Given these assumptions, I am limiting my discussion in this section to specific suggestions about how to do research in philosophy.

Because of the wealth of material available in most university and college libraries, you may wonder where to start. One good place to begin is with *The Encyclopedia of Philosophy*, which can be found in the reference section of most campus libraries. *The*

Encyclopedia of Philosophy contains entries on many important philosophers and philosophical concepts. The entries are informative, and they are usually written in a style that you can understand. Entries also include brief bibliographies, which can guide you to additional sources of information. However, because the *Encyclopedia* was published in 1967, it does not contain entries on very recent subjects. Also, the *Encyclopedia* is oriented toward traditional philosophers and philosophical concerns, and some of the authors and concepts covered in this text do not receive coverage in the *Encyclopedia*.

Another place to begin is with the *Philosopher's Index*, which is also found in the reference section of many campus libraries. The *Philosopher's Index* is basically the philosophical equivalent of *The Reader's Guide to Periodical Literature*. It contains listings of the articles published in philosophical journals during a given period of time. The articles are listed according to author and subject matter. There are two problems with using the *Philosopher's Index*, however. Libraries, especially small ones, do not carry many of the journals indexed in it, and many of the articles written in philosophical journals cannot be understood by beginning students in philosophy. (I still have problems understanding some of them myself.)

A third place to begin is with the trusty old card catalog (or the more modern electronic version of it). The card catalog, which is arranged by author, title, and subject, will usually provide you with the titles of several books that may be useful sources of information. By scanning the table of contents and indexes of each book, you should be able to locate this information without having to read large portions of the text. However, I should provide some words of warning about philosophy books. Some of the primary texts are extremely difficult to understand without using secondary sources, and many of the secondary sources are just as difficult to understand as the primary texts (an example of a primary text is one of the Upanishads; an example of a secondary text is a commentary on that Upanishad). Also, secondary sources that discuss the same primary text often disagree on the exact meaning of the text under discussion. So one of the key skills required in doing philosophical research is knowing what to use and what to ignore. If you come across a text that is extremely difficult to understand, try to find another source that is written in a more accessible manner. Or if you must use that text, try to find someone that can help you comprehend the text. It would be a good idea to consult with your professor before relying heavily on any secondary text.

Organizing Your Thoughts

Once you have chosen a topic and literary form, and done any necessary research, the next step is to organize your notes and thoughts. By this time you should have some idea of what you want to say about your topic, and the main problem is making sure that you say it in a coherent manner. Many of you will be using a word processor to prepare your writing project, and this wonderful advance in technology allows you to easily rearrange what you have written. Still, it is a good idea to think about the order of your paper before you begin writing. Doing an outline, even if you are not required to turn it in, should make organizing much easier.

The way in which you organize your paper will depend in part on the literary form that you choose. Of the forms mentioned above, the journal form is the easiest to organize. In a philosophical journal, entries are arranged according to the dates on which they were written. While a succeeding entry may continue a line of thinking that was begun in the preceding one, often it will be devoted to an entirely different question or issue. For this reason, there is rarely a problem of coherence between entries.

The dialogue form, like the journal form, may also be loosely structured. In writing a dialogue, you must make sure that the conversation covers the philosophical points under consideration, and that your reader is able to follow the movement from one speaker to the next. However, a good philosophical dialogue, like a real-life conversation, allows for interesting digressions. The point is to make sure that you do not allow your digressions to go on so long that the reader loses sight of your main points (as sometimes happens in real-life conversations). Interesting digressions can spice up your dialogue, but they can also make it difficult for your reader to follow your line of thinking.

In contrast to the journal and dialogue forms, the parable form must be tightly structured. However, since the parable form consists of telling a story to illustrate a philosophical point, the structuring will often be sequential in nature. In other words, the story will describe a series of events, and these events will be organized according to the passage of time. For example, the Borges parable found in Chapter 1, "Everything and Nothing," uses the life of Shakespeare to illustrate the point that the notion of a fixed and abiding self-identity is illusory. He first describes some events in Shakespeare's early life, then moves to his days as an actor and theater manager, and concludes with some remarks about his retirement to his native village. The other two parables in the text, "Borges and I" and "The Parable of the Poisoned Arrow," are also arranged sequentially according to the passage of time. If you use this typical way of organizing your parable, then the important thing is to make sure that your reader can follow the temporal progression of the events that take place.

Let us now turn to the essay form, the form that is perhaps the most difficult to organize. One of the reasons for this difficulty is that there are several different ways to organize material in essay form. As mentioned earlier, you may choose the straightforward strategy or the strategy in which you work toward your thesis or main point. It should be obvious that each of these general strategies will require a different organization of materials. In fact, at least as far as the thesis is concerned, the order of the second type of essay is the reverse of the first. In the straightforward essay, the thesis is stated at the beginning, whereas in the other type it first appears near the end.

Another reason for the difficulty is that a good essay requires tighter cohesion than does a good journal or dialogue. In a well-written essay there is little room for digression—your reader must be able to easily follow your line of thinking from one paragraph to the next. While some of this cohesion can be provided by linguistic elements, which will be discussed later, these linguistic elements will not hold the essay together if you have not organized your materials and thoughts carefully.

As a good example of how to organize a straightforward essay, let us look at one of the selections in Chapter 3. In "Navajo Ways of Knowing," Herbert John Benally discusses the four types of knowledge that make up traditional Navajo wisdom. He arranges his essay around the four types, with a separate section for each one. Within each section he highlights the essential features and applications of the type of knowledge that is being discussed. If you were writing this essay, you might decide to begin with the type of knowledge that you considered least important (or somehow lowest) and end with the type that you considered most important (or somehow highest). Or you might decide to use the opposite strategy, devoting the first part of your essay to the most important (highest) type of knowledge and the last part to the least important (lowest) type. Such hierarchical orderings are common to Western European thinking and writing. However, they are not common to Native American thinking, and Benally does not organize his essay according to this principle. Rather, he notes that each type of knowledge is traditionally associated with a part of the day, and he uses this traditional ordering to organize the parts of his essay. Thus he begins by discussing the type of knowledge that is associated with the dawn, and ends by discussing the type of knowledge that is associated with darkness or night.

Of course you may not be so lucky as to be writing on a topic that contains such a ready-made principle of organization. However, if you think about your notes and other materials carefully, you will usually find that one particular arrangement of the material makes more sense to you than other arrangements. Perhaps you will discover a temporal order as Benally did. Or you might find that the material can be better organized according to some sort of hierarchical principle, with some points being more or less important than others. Another possibility is that you might discover a logical progression, that is, a series of necessary steps leading to your main point or thesis. For example, you might discover that you must get to point B in order to get to point C. But you realize that you can't get to point B without first arriving at point A. The obvious place to begin, then, is with point A.

Whatever method or principle of organization you employ, it is crucial that your reader be able to follow your line of thinking. You should continually ask yourself, "How did I get from this idea or paragraph to the next idea or paragraph?" "Have I made this connection clear to my reader?" If you spend some time organizing your material before beginning, the writing process will be much easier. It is also much more likely that your reader will be able to follow your line of thinking.

Making Your Ideas Clear

A good topic, an acceptable literary form, and careful organization—with these accomplished, you are well on the way toward constructing an excellent piece of philosophical writing. However, you still have the difficult task of making your ideas clear, that is, of making sure that your reader can understand what you have to say. Making your ideas clear depends on two very important things: (1) your choice of terms or words, and (2) the way in which you structure your sentences. Unfortunately many philosophers, even some very famous ones, provide less than ideal models of clear writing.

As far as the choice of terms is concerned, you should attempt to use everyday words whenever possible. Although many philosophers have adopted a specialized vocabulary (a less flattering term for specialized vocabulary is *jargon*), the use of this vocabulary often causes problems for readers. The reader may not be familiar with the meaning of some of the terms used, and technical philosophical terms are frequently not found in standard dictionaries. Thus, as the late Professor Robert Whittemore used to tell us in his graduate seminars at Tulane, the ideal is to use words that your seven-year-old sister can understand.

Of course, this ideal may not always be realizable, and you may be forced to use specialized terminology in some instances. Whenever this is necessary, you need to define these terms clearly, either in the body of your paper or in footnotes. If you find it essential to use a large number of technical or foreign words, a glossary, similar to the one found in this text, will be helpful for your readers.

Another thing to look for in your choice of terms is consistency of meaning. If you use a key term in a certain sense in one part of your paper, it will confuse your reader if you use the same term in a different sense elsewhere. For instance, the term *justice* can be used in a legal sense (as when we talk about the administration of justice in society), in an economic sense (as when we talk about the justice of equal pay for equal work), or in a religious sense (as when we speak of divine justice). It would be extremely confusing to a reader if you alternated between the senses of this term in your paper, without making it evident in what sense the term was being used in each case.

Closely connected with consistency of meaning is the goal of precision. What this goal requires is that you choose words that are best suited to say what you mean, and that you avoid wordiness and ambiguity. Wordiness refers to using many more words than are necessary to say something. For example, it is better to use the word *dam* than the phrase "a concrete structure built across a river for the purpose of blocking the passage of water." Ambiguity refers to using a term that has more than one meaning, without making clear which of the meanings you intend. If you say that "all men are created equal," do you mean that all males or all humans are created equal? (Note: To avoid sexism in language, modern usage requires that sexually biased terms not be used, such as using the word *man* to represent both males and females.) Or if you say that something is wrong, what exactly do you mean? Do you mean morally wrong? Or legally wrong? Or religiously wrong? Or wrong according to what your parents told you? Since most words in the English language have more than one meaning, it is important that you use your words carefully so that your reader will know which sense is intended in each case.

Moving to the subject of sentence structure, a good rule of thumb is that the simpler the sentence structure the better. This does not mean that your entire paper has to be written in simple declarative sentences. It does mean, however, that if you use compound sentence structures, you should provide needed punctuation: commas, semicolons, colons, hyphens, periods, and so on. When I was a teaching assistant at McGill University, I once received a three-page paper that had only one punctuation mark—a period at the end. Although this was a rare occurrence, I often find that students do not know how to use certain punctuation marks, especially semicolons and colons. If you are not sure how these are used in a compound sentence, a brief review of your English text or a quick trip to the writing lab is probably a good idea.

Moreover, it is important to recognize that proper punctuation does not always guarantee clarity. Sometimes a sentence that is properly punctuated is just too complex to be easily understood. Consider the following example in which the British philosopher John Locke discusses his idea of substance:

> The mind being, as I have declared, furnished with a great number of the simple ideas conveyed in by the senses, as they are found in exterior things, or by reflection on its own operations, takes notice, also, that a certain number of these simple ideas go constantly together; which being presumed to belong to one thing, and words being suited to common apprehensions, and made use of for quick dispatch, are called, so united in one subject, by one name; which, by inadvertency, we are apt afterward to talk of and consider as one simple idea, which indeed is a complication of many ideas together: because, as I have said, not imagining how these simple ideas can subsist by themselves, we accustom ourselves to suppose some substratum wherein they do subsist, and from which they do result; which therefore we call "substance." (from *Essay Concerning Human Understanding*, ed. by A. C. Fraser, Oxford: Clarendon Press, 1894)

After reading this sentence several times, you still may not be sure what Locke means. The reason for this is not that what Locke is saying is extremely difficult to understand. The problem is that Locke says it in such a convoluted manner. Of course, if you spend several minutes on this sentence, you should be able to unravel it. But a reader should not have to unravel a writer's sentences in order to understand what the writer is trying to say. By breaking this complex sentence into several shorter sentences, Locke would have been able to say the same thing in a much more accessible manner.

Making Your Writing Cohesive

By organizing your thoughts and structuring your sentences correctly, you are already well on the way to making your writing cohesive. Cohesiveness requires that your reader be able to follow your thinking from one sentence to the next, and from one paragraph to the next. As long as your sentences are clearly written and you remain focused on your subject, cohesion between sentences should pose no problem. By using appropriate transition words and phrases ("in addition," "after all," "moreover," "furthermore," "nevertheless," "on the contrary," "on the one hand," "on the other hand," "however," "yet," and so on), you can strengthen the cohesion between sentences even more.

Cohesion between paragraphs is a bit more difficult to attain. The main thing to remember is that each paragraph should have a topic sentence, that is, a sentence that lets the reader know what the paragraph is about. Cohesiveness between paragraphs is achieved when the reader is able to see the connection between the topic sentences in successive paragraphs. Your job as a writer is to make sure that this connection is discernible. As in the case with sentences, transition words and phrases are often helpful. For example, if a succeeding paragraph continues the line of thinking of the previous paragraph, you may want to use "in addition," "moreover," or "furthermore" to begin the succeeding paragraph. However, if the succeeding paragraph contains information that denies or qualifies what was contained in the previous paragraph, you could use "on the contrary" or "on the other hand" to link the two together. Whether or not you choose to use transition words or phrases between paragraphs, it is a good idea to isolate the topic sentences in your paragraphs, and to ask yourself whether one topic sentence "flows into" the other. In less metaphorical terms, when the topic sentences are isolated, are you able to easily see how one topic sentence leads to the next? If you are unable to see the connections between your topic sentences, it is likely that your reader will be unable to see them as well.

Using Argumentation

Most philosophy writing assignments require the use of argumentation. Argumentation, in its most general sense, means the attempt to persuade someone of the truth or acceptability of something you believe. If the argumentation is effective, then the person you are addressing will be convinced to accept your views on that particular matter.

Examples of argumentation abound in everyday life. Television commercials attempt to persuade you to buy various products or to vote for certain candidates. Letters on the editorial pages of newspapers try to get you to believe that certain actions or events are good or bad. People come to your door and try to convince you to accept certain religious claims. Your parents try to persuade you to stay in college or to stay off drugs. In all of these cases, someone is trying to get you to believe something that you may not now believe. In writing a philosophy paper requiring argumentation, your goal is to do likewise. You should provide the strongest evidence that you can muster in support of your position or thesis.

But how do you go about doing this? In the everyday examples of argumentation that you have encountered, you may have noticed two things: (1) Many different strategies are used to try to get you to agree with or buy something, and (2) you find some of these examples of argumentation totally convincing, others only slightly convincing, and some of them not convincing at all. To describe successful argumentation, both of these observations need to be discussed.

Turning first to differences in strategy, it should be obvious that some examples of argumentation rely heavily on powerful images. A television commercial that is trying to get you to purchase a particular model of car may show the car cruising down a scenic highway, or perched on top of a mountain, or swerving around the curves of a test course. If you were making a philosophy video instead of writing a philosophy paper, part of your argumentation would likely consist of such powerful images as well. Since you are not making a philosophy video, however, you may decide that powerful images are not appropriate to your project. But this decision is not necessarily warranted. Words, like televised pictures and sounds, can be used to create powerful images, images that may convince readers of the point you are trying to make. For example, if you were trying to convince someone of the unacceptability of capital punishment, you might offer a powerful description of the way that executions are carried out. Or if you were trying to convince someone not to join the military, you might offer a graphic description of what the person would be subjected to in boot camp.

In addition to powerful images and descriptions, examples can also be used as argumentation. If you are claiming that not all televangelists practice what they preach, you might point to the example of Jim Bakker to support your claim. Or if you claimed that it is sometimes acceptable to kill a human being, you might point to killing in wartime and killing in self-defense as examples of justified killing. Of course, not all examples are used as argumentation. Sometimes the purpose of an example is merely to clarify something that has been said. For example, I have used numerous examples in this appendix to clarify statements that I have made about philosophical writing. (Indeed the preceding sentence is an example of how examples are often used for clarification rather than argumentation.) Whether examples are used to support a position or to clarify a claim, they are extremely useful in philosophical writing.

Powerful images and examples, however, will not suffice to convince many of your readers, and other types of argumentation may be necessary. Unfortunately, once we get beyond persuasion by images and examples, then we enter the domain of logical argumentation, a domain that could only be adequately covered in a separate text. Still, since logical argumentation is a crucial component of most philosophical writing, I will provide a brief introduction to logical argumentation in the remainder of this section.

The first step in discussing logical argumentation is to define exactly what it means for something to be an argument. An argument is a group of two or more statements, in which one statement is claimed to be true on the basis of one or more of the others. In other words, in an argument, certain statements that are assumed to be true are used as evidence or support for another statement that is not known to be true. The statements that provide evidence or support are called *premises*, and the statement that is being supported or argued for is called the *conclusion*. In a good argument, the truth of the premises strongly supports the truth of the conclusion.

While some cases of argumentation found in everyday life consist solely of powerful images or examples, many others contain logical arguments. Consider, for example, one of the instances of argumentation mentioned above. When someone comes to your door and tries to convince you of certain religious claims, you may close the door in her face, or you may politely accept the literature that is offered to you. You may even decide to ask the person to explain exactly what she believes, without questioning or disagreeing with anything said. On the other hand, you may decide to ask the person why she believes what she does. By asking the question "Why?" you are asking for evidence or support. If the person provides this evidence or support, then she has given you premises for her original claims. In other words, the person has provided a logical argument for her religious beliefs. Other examples of logical arguments can be found on editorial pages of newspapers, in conversations with your parents or friends, even in brief commercials found on television. Indeed, if the car commercial mentioned above combined claims about how good or how safe the car was with the powerful images of the car in action, then the commercial would contain a logical argument.

Now that I have briefly explained the concept of an argument, the next task is to discuss the different types of arguments. For the purposes of this text, we can limit our discussion to the two principal types: deductive arguments and inductive arguments.

A deductive argument is an argument that claims to offer indisputable support for a conclusion. In other words, in a deductive argument, the truth of the initial statements or premises is claimed to guarantee the truth of the thesis or conclusion. An example of a simple deductive argument would be the following:

All dogs are mammals.
Lassie is a dog.
Therefore, Lassie is a mammal.

As you should be able to see, if it is true that all dogs are mammals and that Lassie is a dog, then it follows necessarily that Lassie is a mammal. The truth of the premises in this argument guarantees the truth of the conclusion. This guarantee or certainty is an important virtue of good deductive arguments. But what might also be apparent to you is that the conclusion of this argument does not give you any information beyond the information already contained in the premises. This is a principal shortcoming of deductive arguments. A good deductive argument with true premises gives you certainty, but only because the conclusion does not give you any truth not already contained in the premises. For this reason, unless you are writing a paper on logic or mathematics, it is highly unlikely that you will be able to use deduction to support your position or thesis. Instead, you will probably have to rely to a large extent on inductive arguments.

Inductive arguments, unlike deductive ones, do allow you to go beyond the truth contained in your premises. But they do so only by sacrificing the virtue of certainty. Even if you have a very good inductive argument with true premises, you cannot know for certain that the conclusion is true. What you will know, however, is that the truth of the conclusion is highly probable. On most issues, this is all that we can humanly hope to achieve.

While there are many types or categories of inductive argumentation, I will limit my discussion to the four types that you will most likely encounter in your research or use in your own writing. These four types are generalization, statistical induction, causal argument, and argument by analogy.

One of the most common types of inductive argument is the generalization. In a generalization, the arguer collects bits of related data and uses them to support a general claim. For instance, you might observe that your mother loves you and that your friends' mothers love them. From these observations, you could go on to make the general claim that all mothers love their children. Notice that this last claim, the conclusion of your argument, goes far beyond the premises. The premises are statements about a few mothers that you know, and the conclusion is a statement about every mother who has ever existed. For this reason, the truth of your conclusion (unlike the truth of the above conclusion about Lassie being a dog) is not guaranteed by the premises. In fact, the truth of these premises does not even make the truth of your conclusion very probable, since you clearly would not have sufficient data to support such a general claim. In logic talk, we would say that you committed the fallacy of hasty generalization, that is, that you made the mistake of arguing for a general claim with too little relevant data. The falsity of your conclusion could be clearly demonstrated by providing one example (called a *counterexample*) of a mother who did not love her children.

Unfortunately, while it is often easy to show when a generalization goes wrong, it is much harder to say exactly when it goes right. We can say that a generalization is good when sufficient data are provided to support the general claim, but the term *sufficient data* cannot be precisely defined. The amount of data that is needed depends on the nature of the conclusion that you wish to support. The point is that when you use this type of inductive argument, you should gather as much relevant data as possible. You should also be on the lookout for potential counterexamples, since one genuine counterexample will undermine your conclusion.

A second type of inductive argument that you may find useful in your writing is statistical induction. Like generalization, statistical induction begins with the gathering of relevant data. In gathering your data, however, you might find that the data are not uniformly consistent, and thus that they do not support a general claim. For instance if you were gathering data about mothers loving their children, you might find that in the group of mothers observed or surveyed, 70 percent loved their children, 20 percent seemed indifferent, and 10 percent did not love their children. Given these data, you obviously could not make a statement about all mothers loving or not loving their children. But what you could do, using a statistical induction, is to claim that these same percentages hold for a larger group of mothers that were not observed or surveyed. Since 70 percent of the mothers in your sample group (that is, the group that you observed or surveyed) loved their children, you might claim that 70 percent of mothers in the United States love their children. Of course your conclusion might be the smaller claim that 70 percent of the mothers in California love their children or the larger claim that 70 percent of the mothers in the world love their children.

Even if your paper does not call for you to do a statistical induction of your own, you may find it useful to use statistical inductions made by others (for instance, you may decide to use data from public opinion polls, which rely on statistical inductions). Whether you do your own statistical induction or rely on statistical inductions done by others, there are a few things of which you should be aware. First, you have to make sure that the statistical induction is not biased. A biased statistical induction results from a lack of correspondence between the group of people surveyed and the larger group of people referred to in the conclusion. In other words, the group of people surveyed differs in some significant respect from many of the members of the larger group. For example, in the imaginary survey of mothers above, the sample could be biased if you surveyed only mothers who lived in Oregon, or if you surveyed only mothers who belonged to the upper socioeconomic class. For a statistical induction to be good, the group surveyed must be representative of the larger group referred to in the conclusion.

The second thing to be aware of is that statistical inductions can be flawed in several other ways. Often the question or questions asked can be slanted. For instance, if you are interested in genuinely determining how people feel about the acceptability of abortion, you should not ask them whether they believe that a woman has the right to murder her unborn child. Even the person asking the questions and the context in which the questions are asked can flaw statistical inductions. If you are a priest interested in finding out how many people approve of premarital sex, then you need to leave your priestly robes at home.

The final thing to be aware of when using statistical inductions is the danger of relying on numbers alone to support your position. Given that you live in a democracy and that you are frequently presented with polls telling you what the majority of people believe, you may come to think that majority opinion determines truth or acceptability. However, it shouldn't take much reflection to recognize the inadequacy of such thinking. If 75 percent of all people think that abortion is acceptable, does that make it acceptable? Or to take an even clearer example, if 75 percent of people living in the twelfth century thought the earth was flat, did that make the earth flat?

A third type of inductive argument that you may discover in your research or use in your writing is the causal argument. A causal argument is a type of induction that is used to support a claim about the existence of a causal connection (or the lack of a causal connection) between two events. This type of induction is an important component in learning from experience, and it is used by children at a very early age. For example, when my children were small, I installed those "child-proof" gadgets designed to keep children from opening cabinet doors. But around age two, each of my children used causal thinking to defeat the gadget. They probably first observed that their mother and I were able to open the cabinets with ease. Next, they tried various means of opening the cabinet door, before finally discovering that by pushing down the top of the gadget and pulling on the door at the same time they could open the door. After trying this combination a few more times, they knew how to open the door. Put into logic talk, we would say that they had discovered a causal connection between one event (pushing down the top of the gadget while pulling on the door) and another event (the opening of the door).

More sophisticated causal arguments rely on statistical analyses rather than hands-on experimentation. For example, medical researchers may note a statistical correlation between a certain physical state or activity and the occurrence of a certain disease or medical problem. If this statistical correlation constantly recurs in various studies, the researchers will assert that there is a causal connection between the physical state or activity and the occurrence of the disease or medical problem (unless there is some overriding reason for believing that the two things cannot possibly be causally connected). This type of reasoning is the basis of such causal claims as "Cigarette smoking causes lung cancer"; "Being overweight increases the risk of having a heart attack"; "Brushing your teeth with fluoride toothpaste reduces cavities."

As with other types of inductive arguments, you must be careful when using causal arguments. The main problem with this type of argument results from the fact that the word *cause* has more than one meaning. In one sense, to say that event A causes event B means that whenever A occurs, B will follow. In logic talk, we would say that in this case A is the sufficient cause of B. For example, heating water to a certain temperature is sufficient to cause the water to boil (at least under normal earthly conditions). But not all causal statements assert sufficient causality between events. Another type of causality, what logicians call *necessary causality*, makes the weaker claim that event A is required for the occurrence of event B, but that A alone is not sufficient to bring about B. This can be illustrated if you think about your car or any other sophisticated machine. Many things are necessary for your engine to run (such as having gasoline in the tank), but none of these things by itself suffices to make your engine run. We would thus say that each of these things is a necessary cause of your running engine, but that none of them, taken singly, is a sufficient cause.

A third sense of the word *cause* can be discerned if we look at the statement "Cigarette smoking causes lung cancer." In saying this, medical scientists are not saying that everyone who smokes will get lung cancer (sufficient causality). Nor are they saying that only people who smoke will get lung cancer (necessary causality). Rather, they are saying that smoking increases the likelihood of getting lung cancer. In logic talk, this means scientists are claiming that smoking cigarettes is a contributing cause of lung cancer.

In employing causal argumentation, you must not confuse these senses of causality. When making a causal claim, you must make sure that your reader knows clearly which type of causality you are claiming. Not knowing which type of causality is being claimed can lead people to dismiss your conclusion on irrelevant grounds. For instance, you are probably familiar with some of the rationalizations about smoking that rely on misinterpretations of the meaning of the statement "Cigarette smoking causes lung cancer." Someone might point to his Uncle Ned who was a chain smoker all his life, lived to the ripe old age of eighty, and never developed lung cancer. But this example would be relevant only if scientists were claiming that smoking was a *sufficient* cause of lung cancer. Someone else might point to her Aunt Sally who died of lung cancer at age thirty-five, and who never smoked a cigarette in her life. But this other example would be relevant only if scientists were claiming that smoking was a *necessary* cause of lung cancer. Once it is made clear that scientists are only claiming that cigarette smoking is a contributing cause of lung cancer, then it is evident that such examples are not adequate grounds for rejecting the claim that cigarette smoking causes lung cancer.

The final type of inductive argumentation that I will discuss is argument by analogy. In an argument by analogy, you use known similarities between two things, plus some additional fact about one of the two, to draw some conclusion about the other one. This rather abstract definition will become more concrete if I provide an example. Suppose you share many common characteristics with your best friend. You are both the same age, and you both went to the same high school and synagogue when you were growing up. In addition, you both like the Grateful Dead and Japanese food. Suppose also that you just read the Upanishads and loved them, but you know that your friend has never heard of the Upanishads. Nevertheless, you might buy your friend a copy of the Upanishads for his or her birthday, reasoning as follows: "Since my friend and I have so much in common and since I loved reading the Upanishads, it is probable that my friend will love reading them too." If you reasoned in this manner, you would have used an argument by analogy to justify your choice of gift.

As its name indicates, the crucial thing in formulating an argument by analogy is coming up with a good analogy or comparison. If the things compared have just as many differences as similarities, then there is no good reason to think that because one of them has a particular characteristic, the other one will have it as well. However, if the two things compared have many more similarities than differences, then it is often reasonable to use an argument by analogy to conclude that something you know to be true about one of them is also true about the other.

Avoiding Fallacies

Now that I have briefly discussed some of the types of argumentation that you may find useful in your philosophical writing, I will describe a few of the fallacies (that is, mistakes in reasoning) that are often found in student papers. Committing several fallacies in your paper will almost always result in an unsatisfactory grade.

In most cases, it is considered fallacious to base your position solely on an appeal to authority. An appeal to authority is using what some person or some text says as the reason for accepting a claim. For example, you might claim that you know ghosts exist because Plato (a famous Greek philosopher) said they did. Or you might claim that God exists because the Quran or the Bible or the *Bhagavad Gita* says so. While it is acceptable to discuss the views of other people or texts that agree with your position, you should not rely on these views alone. One of the goals of doing philosophy is to develop the ability to do your own thinking, and you can't do your own thinking if you are constantly relying on the beliefs of others. By basing your conclusion solely on the beliefs of others, you will also probably be accused of committing the fallacy of appeal to authority.

Another logical mistake or fallacy often found in student writing is inconsistency. Inconsistency occurs when two of the statements made in your paper contradict each other, that is, when the truth of one of the statements implies the falsity of the other. The simplest case of inconsistency is saying something and then immediately denying it. For instance, you might say "The earth is round," and then immediately say "The earth is not round." Since one of these statements contradicts or says the opposite of the other, one of them must be false. Of course, it is unlikely that you would commit this simplest sort of inconsistency in your paper, but you must be careful to avoid more sophisticated types as well. If, for example, you claim that no human being has the right to take the life of another human being, then you should not claim that capital punishment is an acceptable form of punishment (since capital punishment is clearly a case of one human being taking the life of another). When writing and editing your paper, be on the lookout for inconsistencies.

A third fallacy that often occurs in philosophical writing is the fallacy of begging the question. While this fallacy takes several different forms, the form most frequently found in student writing results from assuming the truth of a more general claim in order to prove a less general claim. If you know that a general claim is true, then by using deductive argumentation you can show that particular instances of that general claim are true as well. For example, if you know that stealing is always wrong, then you know that shoplifting (which is one type of stealing) is also wrong. Begging the question occurs when you simply assume the truth of the more general claim in order to deduce the truth of a particular instance of it. Continuing the example above, if you wanted to prove that shoplifting is wrong, you might begin by assuming that stealing is always wrong. Once you have made this assumption, of course, your conclusion follows deductively from it. The reason that this move commits the fallacy of begging the question is that the general claim you assumed is just as uncertain as what you are trying to prove (if not more so). Is stealing always wrong? Perhaps it is, but it is begging the question to accept this more general claim without some support.

A fourth fallacy found in student writing, the fallacy of vicious circle, is sometimes classified as a version of begging the question. As the name indicates, the fallacy of vicious circle consists of arguing in a circle. In other words, it consists of using your conclusion to argue for one or more of your premises. A short and rather clear-cut example of vicious circle is illustrated in the following conversation: Person A: "Allah (God) exists, because the Quran says that He does." Person B: "But how do you know that what the Quran says is true?" Person A: "Because it is the eternal word of Allah." Notice that in this short conversation, person A uses the Quran to prove the existence of Allah, but then uses the fact that the Quran is the eternal word of Allah to prove its validity. This way of arguing is obviously circular.

Still another fallacy that you need to be concerned about is the fallacy of bifurcation (also known as the *either–or fallacy*). Bifurcation results from the human tendency to oversimplify the world by dividing it into pairs of opposites. People often see things as either good or evil, desirable or not desirable, correct or incorrect. Or when applied to problem solving, bifurcation refers to the tendency to oversimplify an issue by limiting the potential solutions to two. Once this is done, it is often easy to use a type of deductive argument to eliminate one of the positions and to choose the other. "There are only two solutions, and solution 1 is obviously not the answer. So the answer must be solution 2." Unfortunately, the world cannot usually be neatly divided into pairs of opposites, and most problems admit of more than two solutions. Put into testing terms, the world and most problems must be formulated into multiple-choice questions rather than true/false questions, and the fallacy of bifurcation is committed when a person sees the world and problem solving in terms of true/false questions rather than multiple-choice questions.

Whereas bifurcation results from the tendency to oversimplify, another fallacy, the fallacy of appeal to ignorance, results from the human tendency to draw conclusions even when there is no evidence for doing so. If you have no good reasons for believing one way or another on some issue, then the wise thing is to admit that you don't know. Or if you are really interested in the issue, then you should do research before stating your opinion.

Sometimes, however, you may be tempted to use a lack of information to draw a definite conclusion. For example, you read about someone who claims to have had an out-of-body experience. If you merely accept the person's claim as proof that such experiences are possible, then you would probably be committing the fallacy of appeal to authority. You might argue, however, that since no one has been able to prove that such experiences don't exist, then it is obvious that they do. In this case, you would be guilty of committing the fallacy of appeal to ignorance. Rather than coming to a quick conclusion by either of these means, the way to proceed would be to do more research on out-of-body experiences.

Speaking of research, the final fallacy that will be discussed, the fallacy of straw man, often results from inadequately researching your topic. To say that a person commits the straw man fallacy means that he or she has, either intentionally or unintentionally, distorted the position that he or she is arguing against. Straw man fallacies are common during election times. In trying to make themselves look better than their opponents, candidates often distort the records of their opponents. They then argue against the straw man candidate rather than the real candidate. The same thing is true when there is debate over controversial, highly emotional issues such as abortion. For example, a person opposed to abortion might criticize the *Roe v. Wade* Supreme Court decision because it allows abortion on demand. However, since *Roe v. Wade* puts several restrictions on abortion in the third trimester of pregnancy (and thus does not allow abortion on demand), the person opposed to abortion would be committing the straw man fallacy.

When writing philosophically, it is very important that you take the time to carefully read and to fully comprehend the positions that you are discussing in your paper. And when you are describing a position, especially a position to which you are opposed, it is crucial that you portray the position accurately and fairly. If you misrepresent the position, whether or not such misrepresentation is intentional, the fallacy of straw man will result.

Avoiding Plagiarism

While not technically a fallacy, plagiarism is considered to be a serious mistake in writing. Plagiarism refers to the unacknowledged borrowing of material from an outside source. Of course, the worst case of plagiarism is copying your entire paper from an outside source, or having someone else do the paper for you. If such plagiarism is discovered, then you will no doubt receive a failing grade.

Assuming that you avoid this worst case type of plagiarism, you still must be careful about unacknowledged borrowing. Direct quotations should be placed within quotation marks, and the source should be acknowledged in parentheses or in a footnote. (Check with your professor to see if he or she has a preferred format for acknowledging quoted material.) The use of another person's ideas, even if not directly quoted, should also be acknowledged. One way of doing this is to provide a footnote stating your indebtedness to the person or text from which the ideas are taken. For example, you might state that you are "indebted to Professor D. T. Suzuki for the ideas contained in the following three paragraphs." Or you might acknowledge that "a similar position is found in the *Bhagavad Gita.*"

While plagiarism is never acceptable, most professors will allow you to paraphrase. Paraphrasing refers to the practice of rewording or restating someone else's position. In most cases, paraphrasing is used to summarize and/or to clarify the original wording. For this reason, successful paraphrasing requires that you fully understand the original position and that you choose words that are indeed clearer than those originally used.

However, students sometimes use close paraphrasing as a way to avoid effort. By simply changing a few words here and there in the original, a student avoids the necessity of fully comprehending and clearly restating the position. This sort of paraphrasing is problematic for two reasons. First, it borders on plagiarism and may be construed as plagiarism by your professor. Second, even if not construed as plagiarism, it does not show whether you genuinely understand the position about which you are writing. Because of these problems, you should avoid close paraphrasing.

Some Additional Remarks on Style

While much of what I have written in this appendix deals mainly with the content of your paper, some of my remarks touch on the style of your paper as well. In contrast to the content or subject matter of your writing, style refers to the way in which you express what you have to say. In reading your paper for content, your professor checks the accuracy of your claims, whether these claims are organized in a coherent manner, and whether you have provided the needed argumentation for your claims. In reading your paper for style, your professor looks at whether what you have said is written in an engaging fashion. You might say that the content of your paper is like a mannequin and the style is like the garments in which the mannequin is clothed. Just as a well-dressed mannequin is pleasant to view, a well-written paper is pleasant to read.

But what exactly is required for a paper to be well written? Two of the essential requirements for a well-written paper, organization and clarity, have already been discussed. However, in addition to being well organized and clearly expressed, a well-written paper must be rhetorically appealing to your readers. Of course, different readers find different styles appealing, and it is sometimes difficult to know exactly what rhetorical techniques to employ. This problem is especially acute if you are writing for a general audience with which you are unfamiliar. But there are stylistic features that most audiences will find unattractive and others that will appeal to most audiences.

One stylistic feature that will turn off most readers is making your style too academic. A few people may find professional journals and encyclopedias to be interesting reading, but most people will not. On the other hand, most audiences appreciate personal anecdotes and experiences. By personalizing the paper, such anecdotes and experiences allow the reader to identify with you as a human being. And getting the audience to identify with you as a human being is one of the most effective rhetorical strategies you can employ.

Another way of personalizing your paper is to write in the first person (that is, to begin sentences stating your own position with the word *I*). Several years ago, it was considered improper to use the first person in essay writing. When stating their own position, writers were taught to use the third-person form (that is, *we* instead of *I*). Today, however, it is not generally considered improper usage to write in the first person.

While it is usually acceptable to write in the first person if you are comfortable doing so, you should avoid phrasings that make your paper seem mechanical or contrived. For example, if you are writing a straightforward essay, you should let your reader know early on what your thesis is. But you should probably not preface your thesis statement with the words "My thesis is" (or "In this paper I will"). These two expressions, and others like them, are purely mechanical ways of introducing your thesis. Likewise, near the end of a straightforward essay, it is a good idea to restate your thesis and to summarize your main reasons. However, using the words "In this paper I have" (or any similar phrase) to begin your summary will seem contrived to most readers.

Another stylistic feature that most readers appreciate is fluidity. In one sense, fluidity is closely connected with organization, coherence, and clarity. Papers that are poorly organized, that are incoherent, or that use unclear language will not flow. However, in addition to the requirements of good organization, coherence, and clarity, fluidity also depends on varied sentence structure and the avoidance of unnecessary repetition. One good way of testing for fluidity is to read your paper out loud to yourself. Do you get tongue-tied trying to read what you have written? Do you run out of breath before you finish reading one of your sentences? If you do get tongue-tied or run out of breath, then chances are you need to work to make your paper more fluid.

Revising and Proofreading

Unless you are an extremely gifted and experienced writer, successful writing will require more than one draft of your paper. Revising will allow you to work out the kinks that will almost certainly exist in your first draft. It will give you a chance to make sure that your thoughts are organized and that your paper is written in a coherent manner. It will also provide you with the opportunity to fine-tune your style. If time allows, it is a good idea to complete the first draft and let it sit for a day or two before attempting revisions. This will allow you to distance yourself from your first draft. Such distancing will usually make it more likely that you will spot any problems with organization or coherence. Also, if you are not an experienced writer, it might be a good idea to have someone else read your paper before revising it. An outside reader will often discover problems that you have overlooked.

Proofreading should also occur at the revision stage. The main purpose of proofreading is to detect grammatical and spelling mistakes. While grammatical errors are usually considered more serious than spelling errors, numerous spelling mistakes are often annoying to your reader. It is especially annoying if you repeatedly misspell a key word in your paper, such as the name of one of the philosophers about whom you are writing.

Once you have completed your revised paper, the final step is to proofread it quickly one last time before handing it in. The main purpose of this final proofreading is to make sure that you are indeed handing in a completed paper. Although it is not likely, the possibility exists that you may have lost part of your paper during the revision process. You would be surprised how many students hand in papers with paragraphs or entire pages missing. This last quick proofreading will also serve as a closure to the writing process—at least until your next paper assignment.

Glossary

Abhidhamma The third section of the *Tripitaka* or *Three Baskets*, the sacred writings of Theravada Buddhism.

Advaita A Sanskrit word that translates as "nonduality." It refers to any school of Hindu thought that accepts the sameness or identity of the Atman and Brahman.

Agape Nonerotic love. This term, which is used by New Testament writers to refer to the kind of love that Jesus urges, is criticized by Starhawk for being too abstract and impersonal.

Agemo In Yoruba religion, the chameleon who serves as messenger of Olorun.

Aha'áná'oo'níí ł One of the four categories of knowledge in Navajo philosophy. Translated as "the gathering of family," this type of knowledge focuses on family ties and emotional connections. It is associated with the yellow evening twilight.

Ahimsa The Sanskrit word that literally means "nonkilling." It is the most important moral term in the religion or philosophy of Jainism, and underlies the Jain commandment to respect and preserve life in all its forms.

Anatman Literally, without an Atman; the Buddhist doctrine of "no self" or "no soul," which implies that living beings lack a spiritual essence.

Arahatship The state of attaining sainthood in Buddhism; the ideal state of Theravada Buddhism.

Atman In Hinduism, one's spiritual essence or soul. Given Hindu beliefs about reincarnation, this essence or soul is not restricted to human beings.

Aufhebung A German term that literally means "raising" or "annulment"; it was used by the nineteenth-century German philosopher G. W. F. Hegel to describe the process that accounted for the movement of history, a process in which the present moment in history results from the *Aufhebung* of earlier dialectically opposed moments or positions.

Autonomy Another word for freedom of thought or action. An autonomous thought is one that is not determined by external factors.

Avidya In Hinduism, the state of ignorance or not-knowing that prevents one from achieving *moksha*.

Babalawo The Yoruba term for diviner.

Bik'ehgo da'iináanii One of the four categories of knowledge in Navajo philosophy. Translated as "that which gives direction to life," this type of knowledge emphasizes character development and moral deliberation. It is associated with the dawn.

Bildungsroman A mixed German and French term for an educational novel. More specifically, it refers to a novel that focuses on the early development or spiritual education of the main character.

Boshongo One of the groups of Bantu peoples living in central and south Africa.

Brahma The Hindu god who is viewed as creator of this world and countless others. In the lengthy epic poem, the *Mahabharata*, Brahma is one member of a triumvirate of gods: Brahma (the creator), Vishnu (the preserver), and Shiva (the destroyer).

Brahman In the Upanishads, the all-pervading divine essence that constitutes all reality. One achieves spiritual salvation or liberation when one realizes the basic identity between one's spiritual essence (one's Atman) and Brahman.

Brahmin A member of the highest level of the varna or caste system in Hinduism. The traditional role of a brahmin is to serve as holy man and teacher.

Bumba The creator god of the Boshongo people.

Campesino A native of a Latin American rural area, especially a farmer or farm laborer.

Chaowu A term found in Chinese literature that means the "Creator of Things."

Chih In the philosophy of Mencius, a term that means wisdom or right decision.

Confucians The philosophical followers of Kung Fu-tzu (Kung the master) who lived in China from 551 to 479 B.C.E. Kung Fu-tzu's name was Latinized to Confucius.

Deracination Literally, "to be plucked up by the roots"; the conscious rejection of racial identification or classification.

Drylongso An African American term that refers to the ordinary, everyday aspects of life.

En-soi Literally, "in itself"; this term is used by existentialist writers, such as Simone de Beauvoir, to refer to the nonhuman aspect of being, an aspect that is devoid of conscious choice and freedom.

Epistemology The branch of philosophy that examines the nature of knowledge and tries to determine its origin and limits.

Eros From the ancient Greek god of carnal love, this term refers to physical or sexual love. Eros is one of the types of love that, according to Starhawk, is promoted by the religion of Witchcraft.

Forms Plato's term for the perfect entities that occupy the world of Being. According to Plato, things existing in the everyday world of sense experience, a world that he designates as the world of Becoming, are imperfect copies of the Forms.

Genealogy A term that is used philosophically to refer to the method of tracing the cultural origin and development of a concept or practice in order to evaluate it; this method, which was first used by the German philosopher Friedrich Nietzsche in the nineteenth century, has become popular within certain contemporary philosophical movements.

Griot The oral historian or storyteller in traditional African societies.

Guajiros The Cuban term for peasants.

Háá'ayííh, sihasin dóó hodílzin One of the four categories of knowledge in Navajo philosophy. Translated as "rest, contentment, and respect for creation," this type of knowledge focuses on the interconnectedness of all life and reverence for nature. It is associated with darkness.

Hermeneutics The art or practice of interpretation; used especially in connection with biblical interpretation.

Heteronomy The opposite of autonomy; the belief that one's actions are caused by external factors over which one has no control.

Heyoka The sacred clown or contrary in Lakota culture whose powers came from the thunder beings (*Wakinyan*) in the west. The heyoka acted in opposite or unexpected ways (e.g., speaking backward). His antics, which were considered holy, were intended to make people laugh, to lighten their burdens.

Homophobia Literally, fear of persons having the same sex as oneself. It is often claimed that hatred or prejudice directed against homosexuals results from homophobia.

Hózhǫ The Navajo term for harmony or the "Beauty Way of Life." According to Navajo philosophy, this is the ultimate goal of knowing and living.

Hsin-hsin The Chinese term *hsin* is often translated as mind; hsin-hsin refers to the ability to find joy, delight, or happiness in the present moment.

Immanence The opposite of transcendence; the lack of ability or opportunity to make conscious choices or decisions.

Jainism An ancient Indian religion that was probably founded by Nataputta Vardhamana (later known as Mahavira, the "great hero") in the sixth or fifth century B.C.E. According to Jain tradition, however, the Jain religion has always existed, and Mahavira was just the latest of a long line of founders, or Tirthankaras.

Jen In Chinese philosophy, a term that refers to inner goodness or perfection. It is sometimes translated as "love," "benevolence," or "universal kindness." Whereas Confucius suggested that jen was extremely hard to attain and thus that only a few human beings were capable of realizing it, Mencius took the more "democratic" view that jen, as humane conduct, was within the grasp of most human beings.

Karma The fruits or consequences of one's actions that determine one's lot in future lives; that which binds us to the endless cycle of birth, life, and rebirth. This concept is found in Hinduism, Buddhism, and Jainism, although it is explained somewhat differently in each religion.

K'é The Navajo word for love or reverence. It implies the recognition of the inherent value of others, a recognition that is the basis of caring, love, and esteem.

Lakota One of the groups of Native Americans that formerly occupied most of the Great Plains; the language spoken by this group.

Li In Chinese thought, a term that refers to the observance of rites. However, in Confucian philosophy li, which is often translated as "propriety," also refers to the outward, behavioral expression of jen or inner goodness. Occasionally the term is translated as "etiquette."

Mahayana One of the two main branches of Buddhism. Mahayana, which literally means "greater vehicle," originated around the first century B.C.E. It is the version of Buddhism most frequently found in Japan, China, Vietnam, Tibet, and Korea.

Mahdi In Shi'ite Islam, a messiah figure who will one day appear on earth and lead the world into an era of peace and justice. In 1853, Bahá'u'lláh, the founder of Baha'i, proclaimed that he was such a figure.

Mana A term that refers to an impersonal, invisible force or power that is thought to pervade nature. In the nineteenth century, R. H. Codrington discovered this term during missionary work in Melanesia, and he argued that the experience of *mana*, of an impersonal, invisible natural force, was the experience that served as the origin of religious belief.

Mantras The first and oldest parts of the Vedas; more generally, the term may refer to any chant or sacred verse.

Manumission Emancipation; freedom from slavery or bondage.

Materialism The philosophical doctrine that only physical matter and the properties of physical matter exist.

Maya A Sanskrit term that means unreality or false knowledge. In the Upanishads, *maya* is that which stands between us and salvation, that is, that which keeps us from realizing the sameness of Atman and Brahman.

Mestiza A woman of mixed Native American and European ancestry.

Metaphysics The branch of philosophy that deals with questions concerning the ultimate nature of reality. Metaphysics is often divided into ontology, the study of being, and cosmology, the study of the cosmos or universe. Typical metaphysical questions include What is real? What is the origin of what is real? How does change occur?

Misogyny The extreme dislike or hatred of women. Often misogyny is claimed to be the foundation of sexism.

Mitakuye Oyasin Literally, "we are all related." In the philosophy of the Lakota, this term, which is used as a greeting and in ceremonies, points to the interconnectedness of all life forms.

Mohists The philosophical followers of Mo-tzu, a Chinese thinker who lived during the fifth century B.C.E. Mo-tzu was originally a Confucian, but he later broke with Confucian doctrines. Mo-tzu's own philosophy emphasized universal benevolence and love.

Moksha In Hindu thought, a term that means liberation or release, usually liberation from the cycle of reincarnation. According to Hinduism, *moksha* is the goal of one's religious or spiritual journey.

Nihigáál One of the four categories of knowledge in Navajo philosophy. Translated as "sustenance," this type of knowledge focuses on self-reliance and on becoming a contributing member of one's community. It is associated with the blue twilight.

Nirvana The spiritual goal in Buddhism; literally, the word means "extinguished," and refers to the cessation of *tanha* or desire.

Nous The Greek word for mind or reason.

Obatala In Yoruba religion, the orisha or god who creates land and fashions human beings from clay.

Oglala One of the groups of Native Americans that formerly occupied most of the Great Plains; Black Elk was an Oglala holy man.

Olokun A female orisha or goddess in Yoruba religion. Olokun is identified as the orisha of the sea and as a rival of the sky deities.

Olorun The highest orisha or god in Yoruba religion. Olorun has many other honorific titles, including Olodumare, and he is identified as the Sky God.

OM First found in the Upanishads, this became the most sacred word or sound in Hinduism. Often used in meditational chants, the word also serves to introduce or conclude important papers and books.

Orisha The general term for a divine or spiritual being in traditional Yoruba religion.

Orunmila The son of Olorun and the diviner of the orisha. Orunmila is also known as Ifa.

Oshun A female orisha; the goddess of love and rivers in Yoruba mythology.

Philosophes A group of popular eighteenth-century French intellectuals or philosophers; Rousseau and Voltaire are the best-known members of the group.

Praxis A term that refers to practical application as opposed to mere theory.

Psychic activism Jane Caputi's term for the attempt, made by several feminists, to reconceptualize reality, that is, to reconfigure the world by reinterpreting myths and symbols.

Purusha In the Vedas, this term referred to a deity or cosmic giant; however, in the Upanishads, it is used as another word for Atman, that is, for one's spiritual essence or soul.

Quran Often transcribed as "Koran," this is the basic sacred literature of Islam. It is traditionally believed to be the literal word of God (Allah), which was revealed to Mohammed in the seventh century C.E.

Raja A ruler or "king" in India.

Reincarnation The belief that one has been, or can be, reborn into another body. The Hindu doctrine of *samsara* is one example of a philosophical belief in reincarnation.

Samsara In Indian thought, the cycle of birth, life, and death that one is bound to until one achieves liberation or salvation.

Sangha The order or society of Buddhist monks.

Satyagraha Gandhi's term for the active practice of nonviolence in a political situation. Gandhi is careful to distinguish this term, which is sometimes translated as "soul force" or "love force," from passive resistance.

Shi'ite Islam The branch of Islam found in Iran, and parts of Iraq, India, and Yemen, which comprises approximately 14 percent of all Muslims. Shi'ites disagree with the more numerous Sunnis over the legitimate successor of Mohammed. Unlike the Sunnis, they also believe that revelation did not end with the Quran and that a messiah figure will one day appear on earth.

Shudra The lowest class of the classical Hindu *varna* system. *Shudras* are servants, whose sole duty in life is to take care of the needs of others.

Skandhas In Buddhism, the five constituent elements or processes that constitute being. These five elements or processes, some physical and some mental, are believed to cease to exist at death.

Skepticism Fear or doubt about the possibility of knowledge.

Soma One of the deities of the Vedas who was the lord of medicinal plants. The term *soma* is also used for the moon and for a sacred plant in ancient India that was a favorite drink of the gods.

Somatophobia Literally, fear of the body. According to Elizabeth Spelman, somatophobia characterizes much of Western philosophy.

Sutra A Sanskrit word meaning "row." It refers to any collection of sayings that are devoted to the same topic. One of the best-known of the *sutras* is the *Kama Sutra*, whose topic is sexual positions and relationships.

Tanha The Buddha's term for the cause of suffering and pain; often translated as "desire," tanha must be overcome or eliminated if one is to achieve Nirvana or enlightenment.

Tao One of the most important concepts of Chinese philosophy, the term is often translated as "the Way." In Taoism, the term refers to the ultimate principle or nature of the universe, a principle or nature that cannot be encompassed by logical or rational categories.

Taoism An ancient Chinese religion whose founder was traditionally claimed to be Lao-tzu, a legendary figure from the sixth century B.C.E. According to Taoism, the ultimate goal in life was to harmonize oneself with the Tao, the ultimate "Way" or nature of the universe.

Tathāgata An early, honorary title of the Buddha. The meaning is not universally agreed on, but one possible meaning is "one who has fully realized the ultimate."

Theravada One of the two principal branches of Buddhism. Literally, the "Way of the Elders," many scholars believe that the practices and beliefs of Theravada most closely resemble the practices and beliefs of the Buddha and his earliest followers. Today Theravada is mainly found in Sri Lanka and the countries of Southeast Asia (Laos, Thailand, Myanmar, and Cambodia).

Tirthankara Literally, bridge or crossing builder. According to traditional Jain belief, in this age twenty-four of these builders were necessary to build a bridge between this life and Nirvana or salvation. Mahavira, the probable historical founder of Jainism, is the last of the twenty-four.

Transcendence Those aspects of one's existence that are consciously chosen. This term may also refer to the ability and opportunity to make conscious choices in one's life. As such, it is contrasted with the term *immanence*, which refers to the lack of ability or opportunity to make such choices.

Transcendental A term used by Vasconcelos to refer to the categories or basic rules of human knowledge; it is the element of the knowing process that is contributed by the human intellect.

Ts'its'tsi'nako The creator deity in the mythology of the Keres people (pueblo peoples of New Mexico). Represented as Thought-Woman or Spider Grandmother, Ts'its'tsi'-nako creates by thinking and speaking.

Upanishads The most philosophical parts of the sacred literature of Hinduism. The probable literal meaning of the term is "near sitting," which indicates that these writings originated from philosophical discussions about the Vedas between students and their gurus (teachers).

Varna A term that literally means "color," and that refers to the fourfold hierarchical ordering in Hindu society. In this ordering, the four classes are holy men (Brahmin), warriors (Kshatriya), merchants (Vaishya), and servants (Shudra). This term is often confused with the term *caste*, but the caste system in India is much more extensive than the four classes represented by the term *varna*.

Vedagu Another term for one's Atman, that is, for one's spiritual essence or soul.

Vedas The most sacred texts of Hinduism.

Vijñānavāda Mentalism; an Indian philosophical doctrine that only the mind has reality.

Wakan Tanka Literally, father or grandfather. This is one of the words used to address the Lakota great spirit or supreme deity.

Weltanschauung A German term meaning worldview or the way the world appears. In philosophy, the term often carries the sense of a comprehensive worldview in comparison or contrast with another comprehensive worldview.

Wu Wei A Taoist concept that is often translated as "actionless activity." It refers to the Taoist belief that the ideal life is a life that follows the movement of the Tao, without struggling against it.

Yahweh The god who revealed himself to Moses in the form of a burning bush that was not consumed and who became the god of the Israelites. In the Hebrew text, the term is written without vowels as YHWH.

Yang Literally, the bright or sunny side of a hill; in Chinese thought, yang is the positive force in nature that is associated with Heaven and the male, among other things. All life requires a combination of yang and yin (negative force).

Yi In Chinese thinking, a word that refers to economic and social justice. For Mencius, the term *yi*, or justice, refers to an internal state or virtue, which is the source or foundation of justice in society.

Yin Literally, the dark side of a hill; in Chinese thought, yin is the negative force in nature that is associated with the earth and the female, among other things. This force should not be viewed as bad or evil, for in Chinese thought yin is just as essential as yang (positive force). Indeed, a harmonious existence requires a balance of both.

Yoga One of the philosophical systems of Hinduism; more generally, a Hindu discipline or system of physical and mental exercises designed to lead to heightened awareness and ultimately to *moksha*.

Yoruba A West African group who today live principally in southwestern Nigeria.

Yu One of the three ancient legendary heroes of China (along with Yao and Shun). In fourth century B.C.E. Chinese history, it was believed that the world began with a great flood and was made inhabitable by the work of these three heroes. To prevent further flooding, Yu supposedly built dams and mountains.

Yüeh In its modern sense, the word refers to the Chinese dialect spoken in the Kwangtung Province in southern China; as used by Mencius, it seems to refer to a geographical area in southern China.